The Virtual University?

The Virtual University?

Knowledge, Markets, and Management

Edited by
KEVIN ROBINS AND FRANK WEBSTER

OXFORD
UNIVERSITY PRESS

OXFORD

UNIVERSITY PRESS

Great Clarendon Street, Oxford OX2 6DP

Oxford University Press is a department of the University of Oxford.
It furthers the University's objective of excellence in research, scholarship,
and education by publishing worldwide in

Oxford New York

Auckland Bangkok Buenos Aires Cape Town Chennai
Dar es Salaam Delhi Hong Kong Istanbul Karachi Kolkata
Kuala Lumpur Madrid Melbourne Mexico City Mumbai Nairobi
São Paulo Shanghai Taipei Tokyo Toronto

Oxford is a registered trade mark of Oxford University Press
in the UK and in certain other countries

Published in the United States
by Oxford University Press Inc., New York

© the several contributors, 2002

The moral rights of the author have been asserted

Database right Oxford University Press (maker)

First published 2002

A catalogue record for this title is available from the British Library

Library of Congress Cataloging in Publication Data
(Data available)

ISBN 0-19-924557-6 (hbk.)
ISBN 0-19-925793-0 (pbk.)

10 9 8 7 6 5 4 3 2 1

Typeset by Newgen Imaging Systems (P) Ltd., Chennai, India
Printed in Great Britain
on acid-free paper by
Biddles Ltd., Guildford and King's Lynn

CONTENTS

NOTES ON CONTRIBUTORS

Philip E. Agre is an associate professor of information studies at UCLA. He received his PhD in computer science from MIT in 1989, having conducted dissertation research in the Artificial Intelligence Laboratory. He is the author of *Computation and Human Experience*, and the co-editor of *Technology and Privacy: The New Landscape, Reinventing Technology, Rediscovering Community: Critical Studies in Computing as a Social Practice*, and *Computational Theories of Interaction and Agency*. He edits an Internet mailing list called the Red Rock Eater News Service that distributes useful information on the social and political aspects of networking and computing to 5,000 people in 60 countries.

Lee Benson was educated at Brooklyn College, Columbia University, and Cornell University. He is Professor Emeritus of History and a Distinguished Fellow of the Center for Community Partnerships at the University of Pennsylvania. He collaborates with Ira Harkavy on action-oriented research and teaching designed to exemplify their conviction that the primary mission of the American universities is to practically help realize an optimally democratic society and world. Lee Benson is co-executive Editor of *Universities and Community Schools*, and he is author of seven books. His most recent book is: *Progressing Beyond John Dewey: Developing and Implementing Practical Means to Realize Dewey's Utopian Ends* (with Ira Harkavy and John L. Puckett) (forthcoming).

James Cornford is a Senior Lecturer in the Business School, based at the University of Newcastle's Centre for Urban and Regional Development Studies (CURDS). James joined CURDS in 1998 having studied politics and political economy at the University of Sheffield. Recent publications include 'The Virtual University is . . . the university made concrete?', in *Information, Communication and Society*, (Vol. 3 No. 4, 2000). He is currently writing a book, with Neil Pollock, on the process of putting the university online for the Open University Press, *Putting the University Online: Information, Technology and Organisational Change* (2002).

Charles Crook studied at the universities of Wales and Cambridge. He is currently Reader in Psychology at Loughborough University. He has published widely in developmental psychology and education. Current research interests revolve around establishing the importance of a cultural approach to psychological themes.

Rosemary Deem is currently Professor of Education at the University of Bristol and Director of the Learning and Teaching Support Network Education Subject Centre ESCalate. Until December 2000 she was Professor of Educational Research at Lancaster University and Director of its University Graduate School and was also Dean of Social Sciences there from 1994–97. Her research interests include higher education, organizational cultures, gender and education, women's leisure, and educational governance and management. She is on the governing council of the Society for Research in Higher Education and a member of the Economic and Social Research Council's Grants Board.

Gerard Delanty is Professor of Sociology in the University of Liverpool, UK. He was Visiting Professor York University, Toronto in 1998, in 2000 at Doshisha University, Kyoto, Japan and has taught at universities in Ireland, Germany, and Italy. He is the Chief Editor of the *European Journal of Social Theory* and author of eight books including *Inventing Europe: Idea, Identity, Reality* (Macmillan, 1995), *Social Theory in a Changing World* (Polity Press, 1999), *Modernity and Postmodernity: Knowledge, Power, the Self* (Sage, 2000), *Citizenship in a Global Age* (Open University Press, 2000); *Challenging Knowledge: The University in the Knowledge Society* (Open University Press, 2001); and (with Patrick O'Mahony) *Nationalism and Social Theory* (Sage, forthcoming 2002).

Yiannis Gabriel is Professor of Organization Theory at Imperial College, London. He studied engineering and industrial sociology, before obtaining a PhD in Sociology at the University of California, Berkeley. He has taught at Preston Polytechnic, Thames Polytechnic, and Bath University. Recent publications include *Organizations in Depth* (Sage, 1999), *Storytelling in Organizations* (OUP, 2000) and *Organizing and Organizations*, co-authored with Sims and Fineman (Sage, 2000). He has also written numerous books and articles which bring together his research interests in labour process theory, consumer studies, psychoanalytic theory, and organizational studies. He was editor of *Management Learning* and is currently Associate Editor of *Human Relations*.

Ira Harkavy received his BA and PhD from the University of Pennsylvania. He is Associate Vice President and Director of the Center for Community Partnerships, University of Pennsylvania. He teaches in the departments of history, urban studies, and city and regional planning. He is co-executive editor of *Universities and Community Schools* and an editorial board member of *Non-Profit Voluntary Sector Quarterly* and *Michigan Journal of Community Service Learning*. His most recent publications are: *Connecting Past and Present: Concepts and Models for Service-Learning in History* (with Bill M. Donovan) 2000 (American Association for Higher Education) and *Progressing Beyond John Dewey: Developing and Implementing Practical Means to Realize Dewey's Utopian Ends* (with Lee Benson and John L. Puckett) (forthcoming).

Les Levidow is a researcher and writer on the politics of technoscience. He has been Managing Editor of *Science as Culture* since its inception in 1987, and of its predecessor, the *Radical Science Journal*. He is co-editor of several books, including *Science, Technology and the Labour Process; Anti-Racist Science Teaching;* and *Cyborg Worlds: The Military Information Society* (Free Association Books, 1983, 1987, 1989). He has been active in the Campaign Against Casualization within the UK's Association of University Teachers (AUT). Contact: email: Les.Levidow@btinternet.com, tel.: +44-20-7482 0266.

Timothy W. Luke was educated at the University of Arizona and Washington University, St Louis. He is University Distinguished Professor of Political Science at Virginia Polytechnic Institute and State University in Blacksburg, Virginia. Recent publications include *Museum Politics* (University Of Minnesota Press, 2002), *Capitalism, Democracy, and Ecology* (University of Illinois Press, 1999), *The Politics of Cyberspace*, (edited with Chris Toulouse) (Routledge, 1998), and *Ecocritique* (University of Minnesota Press, 1997).

Masao Miyoshi Hajime Mori Professor of Literature at the University of California, San Diego, which he joined in 1987 after teaching in the English Department at the University of California, Berkeley, for 24 years. Among his recent publications are: *Off Center* (Harvard, 1991), and *The Cultures of Globalization*, co-edited with Fredrick Jameson, (Duke, 1998). *The University in Globalization: Culture, Economy, and Ecology* is forthcoming in 2003 (Harvard).

David Noble was educated at the Universities of Florida and Rochester. He has worked at M.I.T., the Smithsonian Institution, and Drexel University, and is currently a Professor at York University, Ontario. He is author of several major works, including *America by Design: Science, Technology and the Rise of Corporate Capitalism* (1977), *Forces of Production: A Social History of Industrial Automation* (1984), *A World Without Women: the Christian Clerical Culture of Western Science* (1992), *and The Religion of Technology: The Divinity of Man and the Spirit of Invention* (1997).

Neil Pollock is a Lecturer in the Management School at the University of Edinburgh. He has conducted research on virtual universities under the auspices of the Economic & Social Research Council's (UK) Virtual Society? Programme, and more recently he has been researching the implementation of Enterprise Resource Planning systems within universities. Together with James Cornford he is writing *Putting the University Online: Information, Technology and Organisational Change*, which will be published in 2002 by the Open University Press.

Mike Reed was educated at the Universities of Swansea and Cardiff, University of Wales. He is Professor of Organization Theory, Department of Behaviour in Organizations, Lancaster University Management School. He has published in major international journals and is an editor of *Organization: The*

Interdisciplinary Journal of Organization, Theory and Society. Recent publications include *The Sociology of Organisations* (Harvester, 1992), *Rethinking Organization* (with Mike Hughes) (Sage, 1992), and *Organizing Modernity* (with Larry Ray) (Routledge, 1994).

Kevin Robins studied at the Universities of Sussex, York, and Kent. He is Professor of Communications, Goldsmiths College, University of London. His books include *The Technical Fix: Education, Computers and Industry* (1989, with Frank Webster), *Into the Image* (1996), *Times of the Technoculture* (1999, with Frank Webster), and *Spaces of Identity* (1995, with David Morley).

Andrew Sturdy is Reader in Organisational Studies in the School of Management at Imperial College, University of London. With a PhD from the Manchester School of Management, UMIST, he has held teaching and research posts at Bristol, Cardiff, Melbourne and, most recently, Bath. His research interests are focused on the global and local diffusion (or otherwise) of management ideas and practices, particularly those of customer service and within the context of personal financial services. He has published widely and his most recent work includes: *Beyond Organisational Change—Structure, Discourse and Power in UK Financial Services* (with G. Morgan) and *Customer Service—Empowerment and Entrapment* (with I. Grugulis and H. Willmott). He is currently researching the role of management consultancy in organizational transformations.

Martin Trow was born in New York City in 1926. He took a degree in Mechanical Engineering at Stevens Institute of Technology in New Jersey. After working briefly as an engineer he completed his doctoral degree in Sociology at Columbia in 1957. In 1957 he joined the Sociology Department at the University of California, Berkeley. In 1969 he moved to the Graduate School of Public Policy at Berkeley, where he has held a professorship ever since. From 1976 to 1988 he also served as Director of the Center for Studies in Higher Education at Berkeley. He has written or edited many books and articles, among these are *Union Democracy* (with S.M. Lipset and James Coleman, 1956); *The British Academics*, (with A.H. Halsey, 1971); 'Problems in the Transition from Elite to Mass Higher Education' (1974); *The New Production of Knowledge* (with Michael Gibbons *et al.*, 1994).

John Urry is Professor of Sociology at Lancaster University. Author/joint author of various books including *The Tourist Gaze* (1990/2001), *Economies of Signs and Space* (1994), *Consuming Places* (1995), *Contested Natures* (1998), *Sociology Beyond Societies* (2000), *Global Complexity* (2002). Chair Sociology RAE Panel 1996, 2001.

Frank Webster was educated at the University of Durham and LSE. He was Professor of Sociology in the Department of Cultural Studies and Sociology, University of Birmingham from 1999 to 2002, and is currently Professor of Sociology at City University, London. Recent publications are *Times of the Technoculture* (with Kevin Robins) (Routledge, 1999), *Theories of the Information Society*, 2nd edn (Routledge, 2002), and *Culture and Politics in the Information Age* (Routledge, 2001).

THE NEW GLOBAL CONTEXT

1

The Virtual University?

Kevin Robins and Frank Webster

The 'virtual university' is becoming a commonplace idea or trope. In this book, we aim to explore both the concept and the practice of the 'virtual university'. Our exploration will be a critical one, hence the insertion of the question mark into our title—the 'virtual university?'. Here, at the outset of our discussion, it will be useful to signal two particularly significant issues that must be addressed. The first concerns the importance of distinguishing between futurological predictions about the 'virtual university', on the one hand, and the more complex situation of what is actually happening in higher education, on the other. We need, that is to say, to separate the myths and ideologies that are proliferating about the 'university of the future' from changing realities and practices in actual universities now, in the present. The second issue concerns the problem of the narrow and restrictive technological bias that distinguishes most accounts of the 'virtual university'. The basic assumption is that the 'virtual university' is the outcome and consequence of a new technological revolution, and that we may start and end our discussion of contemporary transformations in higher education with the question of new digital or virtual technologies. A principal aim of this volume is to counter the futurological and technological biases in the debate on the meaning and significance of the 'virtual university'.

The contributors to this collection are all concerned with the contemporary realities of change in universities in different parts of the world. And they all go beyond technological reductionism, in order to address the broader economic, social, and political dynamics that have been bringing about change in

This book stems from a study of Virtual Universities funded by the Economic and Social Research Council's (ESRC's) Virtual Society? Programme, grant no. R000223276. We would like to thank Steve Woolgar who directed the Programme for his unqualified support, and John Goddard, David Charles, Neil Pollock, and James Cornford whose ideas we have found of immeasurable value.

the higher education sector. What will be apparent in the chapters that follow this introduction is the range and the complexity of issues raised by the 'virtual university' agenda. There are, of course, immediate issues to do with the day-to-day activities of higher education institutions, where new information and communications technology (ICTs) may play a significant role (distance education, virtual learning, information resources, new management, and administration systems) (*Information, Communication and Society* 2000). Then there are issues to do with the emergence of a new political economy of higher education (Robertson 1998), the development of what has been called 'academic capitalism' (Slaughter and Leslie 1997), associated with new (transnational) educational markets and new corporate forms of academic management. And, at the most fundamental level, there are the more philosophical and theoretical issues, associated with a shift in the paradigm of knowledge (Gibbons *et al.* 1994; Delanty 2001), which manifest in the emergence of a new ideology, or even mythology, of information and the information society (Garnham 2000; Webster 2002). The contributors to this book range across all these different dimensions of academic and intellectual change.

The issues that are being raised in discussions of the virtual university are of the utmost importance. Ronald Barnett puts it dramatically in his announcement that 'the Western university is dead'. 'We have lost any clear sense as to what a university is for in the modern age', he continues. 'We need a new vocabulary and a new sense of purpose. We have to reconstruct the university if it is to match the challenges before it' (Barnett 1997: 1). It might seem as if these challenges, and the invention of a new vocabulary and sense of purpose, are matters for educational theorists and policy-makers—for specialists in higher education. We believe that the challenges are of much greater significance, and that they must be of concern to a much broader intellectual constituency, across the sciences, social sciences, and humanities. For what is at issue is the future of intellectual life and culture, no less.

THE UNIVERSITY, THE NATION-STATE, AND CULTURE

We should be more specific about what it is that is being challenged by contemporary developments. What is in crisis is, in fact, the university as a national institution. A key point of reference here is the work of Bill Readings (1996), which somewhat echoes Ronald Barnett's sense of an ending, but which makes apparent that, if the university is now a 'ruined institution', it is the national model of the university that is in ruins. What Readings demonstrates is how the modern university developed as an adjunct of the modern state, and was instrumental especially in that state's project of national cultural integration. And what he argues is that, in the context of contemporary developments associated with globalization, the relation between nation-state, national culture, and higher education is breaking down.

The nation-state and the modern notion of culture arose together, and they are, I argue, ceasing to be essential to an increasingly transnational global economy. This shift has major implications for the University, which has historically been the primary institution of national culture in the modern nation-state (Readings 1996: 12).

Like a number of other public institutions, the university has ceased to be '[a] privileged site of investment of popular will' (Readings 1996: 14)—by which is meant national will. Its status has shifted from that of ideological apparatus of the nation-state to being a relatively independent bureaucratic system. The era of the 'university of culture' is thus giving way to that of what Readings calls the 'university of excellence', alias the 'technological university' or the 'corporate university'.

The modern university was, then, a historically specific agency, concerned with the reproduction of national knowledge and national culture. And it developed into a particular kind of national agency, shaped through the transmutation of classical and medieval scholarly principles into the codes and practices of nineteenth-century professionalism. This liberal model of the university was an elite or expert institution—in its commitment to the nationalization of culture and knowledge, it was pre-eminently concerned with high or official culture. Whatever its national pretensions, it could also regard itself as a defender of higher, civilizational values—in Newman's resonant phrase, it was 'a place of teaching universal knowledge'. As with other nineteenth-century professions, academic institutions were self-regulating—the principle of academic freedom was one of professional autonomy. The integrity of the profession was under-pinned by a particular ethic of academic responsibility, and by the 'gentlemanly' ideal of collegiality. And this ethic was further sustained by the principle of co-location—Newman's idea of the university was to do with a *place* for teaching universal knowledge. As Krishan Kumar (1997: 29) puts it, 'universities bring people together'. They have been about 'attendance and participation in a certain sort of social and cultural life'. In summary, we may say that the modern university was organized around a particular culture and ethos of academic community.

It is this particular culture and ethos of what we might call the national-liberal university that is now in crisis. And we may say that there have been two prevailing kinds of response to this perceived crisis, each of them, we think, problematical. The first—it is the minority perspective—is that of cultural critics—amongst whom we would include the neo-conservative Allan Bloom (1987), but also Bill Readings himself—who are primarily concerned with what has gone wrong with the 'university of culture' (to use Readings' term). We can agree with much of what Readings says about the crisis of the national university, but we think that Dominick LaCapra identifies an important weakness in his narrative. Readings is, he argues,

close to the neo-conservatives in relying on an abstract intellectual history to elaborate his big picture based on a contrast between past and present. Indeed Readings's very understanding of institutions is largely conceptual rather than oriented to institutions as historically variable sets of practices relating groups of people . . . Readings's big picture fits into conventional oppositions between a past-we-have-lost (for good or ill) and a present-we-find problematic—a picture that may be too simplistic to do the critical work Readings wants it to do   (LaCapra 1998: 38–9).

Readings' conceptual—and as such unsociological—historiography produces a conventional history of decline and fall. The second response to the crisis of the national-liberal university—which has by now become the hegemonic response—is associated with the idea of educational technological revolution and the virtual university project. It is an approach that has little concern for historical reality or nuance—if Readings' thinking tends to be abstract and conceptual, then we may say that this approach presents us with a crude mythology of the liberal university. What is painted is generally a caricature of the academy as a solipsistic, unworldly, and irrelevant institution. Thus, when Majid Tehranian (1996: 443) tells us that 'universities can no longer pretend to be the ivory towers of yesterday', he is mobilizing a familiar and potent stereotype—one that is familiar to us all—to discredit everything that universities have stood for until now. Here, too, the big picture is based on a contrast between past and present—but this time it is a contrast between a past-we-must-lose and a present/future-we-find-'progressive'. Desecration of the image of the bad ivory tower of the past is rhetorically translated into affirmation and vindication of the corporate, technological, or virtual university of the future.

What we are offered, then, in each of these responses to the crisis of the university, is a contrast between two successive epochs in the history of higher education (in one case good turns into bad, and, in the other, bad into good). The point, in each case, is to bring out the differences between the liberal-national model and the virtual-global model of the university. As is always the case with such epochal schemes of historical development, the internal coherence of each epoch is overstated, and the contrast between epochs consequently overdrawn. In order to more adequately address what is actually happening in higher education now, it seems to us that we need to find an alternative way to think about the nature of historical change. And what we suggest, in place of the metaphor of passage between epochs or eras, is a geological style of metaphor, in which we can think of change in terms of the accumulation or accretion of new layers of complexity over what already exists from the past. The virtual-global university might then be seen in terms of new (transnational) ideas and initiatives layered over (rather than displacing) already existing strata of (national) educational discourses, practices, and institutions. This shift of frame works against the false polarization of past and present, making it easier, we think, to develop a more sociologically grounded narrative of change in higher education—one that is aware of continuities, as well as transformations, and that acknowledges the complexities, conflicts, and contradictions that must necessarily exist in any real-world institution.

The first imperative is to be aware that the liberal-national university has not been what it seems to be in its 'ivory tower' caricature. This image—which combines sentiments of both nostalgia and resentment—should not be confused with the experience and reality of most higher education institutions. Nor have actual universities corresponded with Readings' ideal historical image of 'the university of culture' (as Desmond Morton (1997) puts it, 'the university, is theory, whilst universities are facts'). Let us consider some important areas in which university culture has been a great deal more complex than contemporary discussions of the virtual university would lead us to believe:

1. The liberal university is characterized as elitist, in terms of both access and the construction of the curriculum. This has, of course, clearly been a powerful dynamic in the idea of the university, and we must recognize that elitist agendas and interests are still deeply entrenched (in Britain, for example, Oxbridge continues to be a preserve largely of the rich and privileged (Adonis and Pollard 1997)). But at the same time, we should acknowledge that— partly as a consequence of economic forces, and partly as a response to campaign after campaign for equality in higher education—there has been constant pressure for democratization. The push for mass education has forced universities to expand (Scott 1995)—though to different degrees in different countries—helping bring about significant decline in what A.H. Halsey (1992) has called 'donnish dominion', as a consequence. The same pressures have been progressively exerted on the curriculum—culture wars on the national intellectual patrimony—opening up new fields of study and new perspectives (women's studies, cultural studies, postmodernism, post-colonialism, etc. (Nussbaum 1997)).

2. Another issue concerns the collegial model as the basis for ordering university life and culture—it is a model that seems to epitomize the university's lack of connection to, and relevance for, the 'real world'. Two points should be made here. The first is that this principle of self-regulation was held in common with other professional domains that came into existence in the nineteenth century, and was intended to ensure internal probity and prevent external interference or corruption. As David Pan (1998: 70) puts it, with regard to the particular context of universities: 'Because the knowledge produced at universities is held to be objective and universal, academics claim to provide for society a moral centre protected from the prejudices of sectarian religious and political interests as well as from instrumentalization by a technocratic government and a capitalist economy.' If this principle has now become much more difficult to maintain, this does not mean that it has ceased to be an important issue. The second point is that many universities have also acknowledged the need to adopt a more managerial

approach—this is a move that has appeared necessary in the face of the growing scale and complexity of higher education institutions. As Ronald Barnett (1997: 7) observes, 'the fundamental clash in the modern university is that between instrumental reason and reason guided by a collaborative search for the better argument; crudely, we might say, between managerialism and collegiality'—let us note that this clash is only possible because managerialism has been allowed into the university system.

3. We have already referred to Bill Readings' argument that the university of culture was fundamentally a servant of the nation-state and the national culture. This, it seems to us, is a crucial point. But we should also recognize that academics and intellectuals (at their best) have always aspired to produce knowledge that transcended local and particular interests. For those with more progressive aspirations, that has been a crucial aspect of their personal and professional self-image. We should recall that, according to Newman's (Catholic) principles, universities deal in universal knowledge. Bryan Turner (1998: 73) refers to a historical 'tension between national and cosmopolitan standards', arguing that 'the University has been, since its medieval foundations, fractured around a contradiction between nationalistic particularity and a commitment to more universalistic standards'. We need to be cautious in our claims for what these universal aspirations have achieved. David Pan (1998: 87) reminds us that there have, in fact, been connections between the idea of universal knowledge and the interests of Western nations ('the very idea of knowledge as secular and value-free brings with it a colonizing perspective which seeks to eradicate all other cultures by claiming that they are sectarian and prejudicial rather than neutral and objective'). We should not underestimate the gravity field of the nation-state and the national imaginary. But, at the same time, we have to take account of counter-national imaginations—forms of cosmopolitan culture and thinking that, in the context of globalization, have seemed to be gathering further momentum.

4. Through its 'ivory tower' image, the university is associated with the idea of liberal knowledge—knowledge as an end in itself. What we also have to take into account is the extent to which universities also made accommodation for applied or instrumental knowledge. In Britain, where universities have had a particular reputation for being shy of the 'real world', the late nineteenth and early twentieth centuries saw a significant expansion in scientific and technological education and research. The establishment of universities in industrial regions of Britain—Birmingham, Leeds, Manchester—was in large part a resistance to the Oxbridge model, as well as an endeavour to service the growing industrial need for engineers, chemists, physicists, and so on (Sanderson 1972). What we have to recognize, then, is that there has been a long history of compromise between liberal and utilitarian models of knowledge (Rothblatt and Wittrock 1993). And, as Gerard Delanty (1998) makes clear, the nature of this compromise has varied in different national

contexts. In France, there is a long tradition of technocratic education, asso-ciated particularly with the *grandes écoles*, whilst in Germany there has been a stronger emphasis on culture (*Bildung*). The point, again, is that the culture of universities has in reality been far more complex than the stereo-type of the 'ivory tower' would have us believe. The development of applied knowledge and research in the service of corporate interests has long been an integral aspect of higher education. As an essentially national institution, the university has been able to respond to both the 'spiritual' needs of the *Kulturnation* and the more pragmatic and competitive aspirations of the nation-state (Delanty 1998: 7–11).

What we are drawing attention to here is the actual complexity and diversity of universities as institutions. Universities have been remarkably adaptable, demonstrating the capacity to continuously re-invent themselves, whilst appar-ently continuing to pursue their fundamental mission and sustaining their core values. Reflecting on the *raison d'être* of the university in 1980, Lord Robbins looked comfortably back to Newman's *The Idea of the University*. 'I am not out of sympathy with the value which Newman attaches to knowledge as such,' he noted, '—quite the contrary so far as I am personally concerned. But I find entirely unworldly and unhistorical the idea of a university devoted entirely to such ends, regardless of training for subsequent careers or the utility which comes from knowledge' (Robbins 1980: 7). He was quite at ease with the world of 'utility', the world of 'the practical knowledge which has raised the standard of living of the majority of the western world from the state of nature, where life is poor, precari-ous and short' (Robbins 1980: 8). Universities are institutions where 'cultivation of scholarships and of scientific speculation (should be) carried on side by side' (Robbins 1980: 11). The idea of the university here is, in fact, compatible with both liberal ideals and instrumental reason. And the key point that we want to make here is that this accommodation was made possible by the national con-text in which the issues were framed. Liberal and instrumental models both made sense in terms of an agenda determined by the economic and cultural object-ives of nation-states—within a national project and agenda for higher education. The function of national universities was to hold these two models together, in productive tension.

But now, just two decades on from Robbins' musings, this compromise formation seems a far more difficult thing to sustain . . .

A DIFFERENT KIND OF INSTITUTION: GLOBAL–CORPORATE–VIRTUAL

So we return to Bill Readings and his idea of the university as a ruined national institution. As Readings (1996: 3) says, the university now seems to be becom-ing 'a different kind of institution, one that is no longer linked to the destiny of the nation-state by virtue of its role as producer, protector, and inculcator of an idea of national culture'. Universities have been changing significantly as a consequence of developments associated with globalization, and the complex implications of these developments for nation-states and national cultures. They are developments that are increasingly taking universities (like other public services) into the marketplace, and into a marketplace that is becoming increasingly transnational or global. At the same time, the marketplace has been entering into universities, compelling them to adopt a more corporate ethos and a new managerial approach to their business (like other corporate actors, they are now expected to cultivate new kinds of competitive 'flexibility'). Along with these changes, we are seeing new kinds of 'product' (i.e. changing curricula), new styles of 'delivery' (with new ICTs expected to play a key role), and a new kind of relation to what have now become 'consumers' of higher education. Back in 1970—a decade before Lord Robbins' satisfied reflections—there were early intimations of these developments from a thinker who was very dissatisfied with what was happening, even then, in higher education. E.P. Thompson was then attacking Warwick University as the 'business university', arguing that it had established a 'symbiotic relationship with the aims and ethos of industrial capitalism, but built within a shell of public money and public legitimation' (Thompson 1970*a*: 301, 307; see also Thompson 1970*b*). Even Thompson could surely never have anticipated the rate at which the corporate takeover of higher education would progress over the next thirty years (see Monbiot 2000; Press and Washburn 2000).

In recent years, the term 'virtual university'—which seems especially able to evoke both the global and technological aspects of change—has been used with increased frequency to characterize the 'new' higher education. It is a term that, in fact, covers a variety of developments. There are new showcase distance-learning institutions like the University of Phoenix and Jones International University. The latter self-consciously regards itself as operationalizing 'a new model for higher education':

JIU learned that adult learners desired the following: flexibility and convenience to overcome time and distance challenges, high quality, relevant education, and value for their money. The research resulted in the development of a virtual campus, using the asynchronous attributes of the internet and the WWW. 'Anytime and anywhere' aspects of online learning provide a venue for a flexible and convenient learning environment   (Pease 2000: 627).

(For those who invest in JIU, the ultimate reward is a web-cast Cybergraduation.) At the other end of the spectrum, the concept of the 'virtual university' is invoked to refer to the complex range of changes affecting already established universities. In this context, the concern is with how new practices can be reconciled with an already existing institutional structure and ethos (for the 'old' model of the university cannot simply be abolished by fiat). Our point, then, is that the idea of the 'virtual university' encompasses a diverse range of initiatives and developments in higher education. And (as with the liberal university) we must consider it, not in terms of its ideal type (or self-mythologization), but sociologically—addressing the realities, that is to say, of 'actually existing' universities in transition.

If conceptions of the virtual university prioritize two key dynamics— globalization and technological innovation—then we would highlight developments in three closely connected domains which signal important changes taking place in higher education. These, from which we take the subtitle of this book, are *knowledge, markets,* and *management.*

Knowledge In recent years, there has been a growing awareness of transformations in the domain of knowledge—an awareness that the quantity of knowledge has grown explosively, and that new dynamics have come to regulate the production of knowledge. There are two prevailing logics at work, we would suggest. First, there is the growing significance of the logic of performativity, which has increasingly come to undermine the Enlightenment justification of knowledge in terms of the pursuit of 'truth' (Lyotard 1984). In the sciences, it is clearly the case that discovery-led or 'pure' research has been increasingly rivalled by applied research, which has been more concerned with the pursuit of patents and profitable solutions to problems. But it is more generally the case that the imperative of performativity has now become primary definer of knowledge. New subjects— Business and Management Studies, Marketing and Information Science (Bolton 2001)—have come to gain a hold inside the institutions of higher education on the basis of satisfying productive and utilitarian needs. These developments have also been associated with challenges to the university from without (Bauman 1987). It is now impossible to ignore the contribution to knowledge production from private corporations, media organizations, and dedicated think tanks (*Economist*, 1997). A significant consequence of it is that the university has been increasingly losing its position as the privileged locus of authoritative knowledge.

The second logic at work in the transformation of knowledge has been that of globalization. Globalization has been associated with what Bill Readings (1996) identifies as the 'dereferentialization' of knowledge. What he is referring to is knowledge that is de-linked from specific and particular contexts, that is to say from the contexts of the national culture. In the context of new academic knowledge, what are valued are knowledge and curricula that will 'travel'—ones that will be bought and consumed in as many places in the world as possible. What also become particularly significant in a 'globalizing' world are what Robert Reich calls 'symbolic analysts', knowledge workers whose prime skills are the capacity for abstraction, system thinking, experimentation and collaboration, all marshalled to 'solve, identify, and broker problems' (Reich 1991: 178). In this context, it is not surprising that universities have come to put an increasing emphasis on the promotion of 'transferable skills' (skills without content). The concern with 'competencies'—such as 'analytical abilities', 'problem solving', and 'communication skills'—is also clearly about generalized forms of knowledge and expertise—knowledge that is disentangled from local (i.e. national) contexts.

Markets These changes in the domain of knowledge are closely connected with a heightened concern for markets, involving the commodification or 'marketization' of teaching and research activities in universities (Brown and Lauder 2001). This has been apparent in a variety of developments, for example, the shift towards the idea of the student as consumer, the adoption of corporate accounting and management systems, or the trend towards individuated salaries and contracts for faculty. One key issue clearly concerns the increased corporate presence on the campus (in sponsored buildings, in support for dedicated research, and so on). The spread of what has been called the 'corporate classroom', which has been estimated now to account for over 50 per cent of spending on higher education (*Economist*, 28 October 1995), has clearly had a marked influence on the form and content of university activities. But what has been just as significant as these connections with industry—and in fact a result of them—has been adoption by universities themselves of a corporate-style mentality and approach to their 'business'. The logic of the market is evident in the new discourses of higher education, where talk of 'customers', 'products', 'growth', 'investment', and 'human capital' is now quite routine. What we are also seeing as a consequence of this increasingly entrepreneurial orientation is the take off of higher educational consortia and alliances, intended to ensure a competitive position in what are regarded (by the leading institutions, at least) as a global educational market. Here the 'business of borderless education' (CVCP/HEFCE 2000) is increasingly germane to the university's future, as both opportunity and threat. In this context, it is scarcely surprising that universities are also paying close attention to their 'brand' image, which is vigorously promoted and protected to maximize advantage in competition in relation to other institutions. Universities have entered the marketplace, and as a consequence, the marketplace has entered the soul of the university.

Management New styles of management and a new 'business-like' ethos have accompanied these changing economic arrangements. In the context of their new market orientation, universities have tended to distance themselves from the older style of collegial ethos, and have adopted a new, corporate-style managerial approach. The old-style Principal has now given way to the CEO, working with a 'central management team', according to a 'business plan', and with clearly established 'targets' and 'performance criteria'. Legitimation of these shifts has come from the emergence of what Michael Power (1997) has termed the 'audit society', a term which captures a tendency towards making universities (along with other institutions) into more 'transparent' and 'accountable' organizations (Strathern 2000). This new managerial and audit culture has been facilitated by the way in which the logic of globalization has been undermining the national university frame (Newby 1999). Globalization has disrupted the relative stability of the old order, and introduced a new unpredictability into the environment and activities of higher education institutions. The accelerated mobilities of knowledge, the relative ease of movement of academics and students, the heightened competitive circumstances of universities in competition, have all had destabilizing consequences. And it is precisely this uncertainty that has served to boost the new managerial culture. The remit of the new managers in higher education is to plan for uncertainty (Thorne 1999)—to make the university 'flexible', adaptable, and capable of responding quickly to the shifting circumstances of global competition.

These, then, are the key contexts of change—change with respect to knowledge, markets, and management strategies—that are of significance in the contemporary transformations of higher education. Out of, and in response to, these diverse contexts there have been various efforts to address both philosophical and policy issues relating to new developments in higher education. These have ranged from pleas for the defence of liberal educational values, via advocacy of virtual technologies and distance learning, to eager endorsement of the business of borderless education. For the most part, however, we would say that the debate on the future of the university has taken place within relatively narrow educational circles. The present volume has been produced from a conviction that the discussion now needs to be opened up to a much more wide-ranging constituency, for it poses important and urgent questions for the future of intellectual and cultural life more generally.

STRUCTURE OF THE BOOK

We have organized the present volume into three parts. Part 1 introduces the broader dynamics that are now challenging the coherence of the national university. Without an appreciation of these contemporary features and historical trends (Chs 2 and 3), as well as alertness to the conditioning effects of political economic processes (Ch. 4), it is impossible to adequately comprehend current changes in higher education. In Part 2, our contributors take up case studies and policy issues, and make clear the actual complexities and unevenness of changes that are taking place in higher education now. Each of the chapters takes up a different issue, and all are concerned to resist simplistic presumptions. Whether it is in assessing the introduction of management information systems (Ch. 5), looking at students' experiences of virtual education (Ch. 6), examining new management formations (Ch. 7), exploring the recent history of MBA degrees (Ch. 8), or gauging conflicts between commodification tendencies and more communal values (Chs 9–10), these chapters each warn of the perils of assuming that ICTs, or distance-learning developments more generally, automatically announce progress, or even change. What is conveyed is the sense that on-the-ground developments are complex and shifting. In Part 3, we return to more general concerns, with our contributors exploring broader prospects and possibilities for higher education. Chapters 11–14, as well as our Afterword, explore possible future scenarios, considering the new economic and technological forces now shaping the strategies of higher education institutions, as well as the question of how to adequately respond to these dynamics.

Part I: The New Global Context

John Urry (Ch. 2) highlights the need to situate developments in higher education within wider contexts of change, drawing attention to the importance of
emerging transnational 'scapes' and 'flows' for the culture of higher education.
At the outset of the book, he reminds us that developments associated with the
'virtual university' have to be situated in this context of processes of globalization,
that is to say, that the virtual university is about a great deal more than the impact
of new technologies on higher education. Gerard Delanty (Ch. 3) complements
Urry's contemporary analysis, providing a historical overview of the development
of higher education to the present—from the Enlightenment-oriented university,
via the civic-liberal university of the nineteenth century and the mass university
of the late twentieth century. This development should not be seen in terms of
a straightforward succession of stages. What is clear is that elements of earlier
formations continue to persist, and to be fought over, in the university. What
we have, then, as we shift into the new circumstances and challenges of what
Delanty acknowledges as the virtual university, is the co-presence of both residual and innovative elements, with all the attendant tensions and contradictions
that follow from this.

Masao Miyoshi (Ch. 4) then provides a review of the growing corporate and
global character of higher education, addressing an issue to which all considerations of higher education must surely pay heed now. This is a development in
which the Humanities (a traditional home of critical and imaginative thought)
become marginalized, as they lack potential for profit. In Miyoshi's view,
higher education is becoming increasingly subordinated to corporate goals and
values—dependent on commercial sponsorship, concerned with the protection
of intellectual property, and willing to adapt teaching and research agendas in
line with the dictates of market forces.

Part II: Practices and Policies

The chapters in Part II are substantive and empirically informed accounts of
recent changes in higher education, each in this own way underlining the need
for caution and nuance when it comes to analysing complex developments on the
ground. James Cornford and Neil Pollock (Ch. 5) warn of the dangers of assuming
that it is ICTs alone that will take the university into a virtual era. Their contribution insists that such linear thinking is a misrepresentation of what is actually
taking place in higher education institutions. In the context of the introduction
of a university management information system, they note that the condition for
effective operation of this new system of accountancy and management is that
established university practices—which have been diverse, *ad hoc*, and often only
implicit—must be brought into the domain of the new system's rules and procedures. This requires that the administrative and management practices across

the university become formalized and standardized, and thereby synchronized and coordinated. As such, virtuality may not so much introduce new procedures as standardize and formalize what went on before.

When we conceive of the development of virtuality in the university, we also need to appreciate that applications of ICT are introduced across a variegated terrain where there is much diversity of response and much to play for. Here Charles Crook's (Ch. 6) criticisms of orthodox (and narrow) models of learning that inform the approaches of virtual university enthusiasts is especially apposite. Crook draws on the perspectives of 'cultural psychology', drawing attention to the significance of student participation and location in a broad learning environment—one that includes such matters as time-tabling arrangements, the architecture of buildings, and friendship networks among students. This offers a far more complex and subtle understanding of virtual education than one which assumes that a combination of technology and software are the sum of web-based teaching and learning.

Rosemary Deem and Mike Reed (Ch. 7) address the 'new managerialism' in higher education, a phenomenon that we have suggested is a key feature of the changing university. The picture that Deem and Reed draw is one in which there is considerable confusion and tension between collegial pressures and new demands placed on heads of department who are required to operationalize changed protocols. Developments are thus paradoxical, noticeably with regard to new technologies. On the one hand, ICTs encourage audit and accountability, and are thereby powerful tools in the service of more hierarchically oriented managers. On the other hand, new technologies make management practices more transparent than before, a development that may encourage openness and participation. Again then, while the trend is towards more corporate, hierarchical, and directive management in higher education, on-the-ground implementation is more complex and contradictory—with possibilities for the negotiation of alternative practices.

Yiannis Gabriel and Andrew Sturdy (Ch. 8) then offer a sceptical interpretation of the global expansion of Master in Business Administration (MBA) programmes. It is often argued that MBA programmes through distance learning can serve to benefit less privileged parts of the world. Gabriel and Sturdy reject such idealism, arguing that MBA programmes offered by universities in metropolitan centres are in fact about commercial advantage and opportunity—in their view, what is happening is something comparable to the marketing of motor cars. Here we have a vivid illustration of the priority of market principles over educational ideals (whatever is said in the sales pitch, the priority is selling).

In their reflection on policy directions in higher education, Lee Benson and Ira Harkavy (Ch. 9) recognize the scale and significance of market pressures. However, they also believe that the present time also presents opportunities for democratization and for opening up the university to hitherto excluded groups, as well as for reforming curriculum. New technologies can be harnessed, they suggest, for a radical and reforming agenda in higher education. They challenge readers to consider what interventions may be made in higher education, and what goals and values are most desirable.

Philip Agre (Ch. 10) addresses associated conflicts revolving round the forces of community and commodification, those of the collegium and the market. Agre is at once less enthusiastic about community (it can easily be exclusive and exclusionary) and less scathing as regards commodification (an emphasis on economic return can encourage efficiency in higher education). In his view, the university must change with the spread of digitization, and it will need to find ways to manage the inevitable tensions that surround the community and commodity constituents of higher education. In line with the argument of Benson and Harkavy, the argument is again made that developments in higher education are open to direction by human decisions. There is no preordained path to the virtual university.

Part III: Prospects and Possibilities

Part III returns to broader issues. Throughout this book, the importance of considering virtual education within wider contexts leads our contributors to reject the popular discourse that suggests that the virtual university will be introduced by ICTs alone. Les Levidow (Ch. 11) also argues in these terms. To be sure, he is sensitive to technological innovation, but Levidow keeps his eye on the major political economic factors shaping the higher education environment. Let no one be deceived: it is to the growing forces of commercialism, competition, and corporate organization to which those concerned with higher education will have to attend.

Tim Luke (Ch. 12), while acutely aware of the commercial agenda that now drives higher education, sees possibilities in the new technology for improved pedagogy and more effective learning. Luke refuses to take an excessively hard-line anti-commercial position, since that, he believes, means defending the indefensible—the old-fashioned 'sovereignty of professors', minority access, and demonstrably inadequate systems of teaching and learning. What Luke underscores is that there is no way forward for higher education in trying to defend uncritically what has gone before. Nostalgia may have a place in resisting unpalatable developments, but it cannot provide an alternative.

David Noble (Ch. 13) compares recent developments in distance learning with the experience of the growth of correspondence courses in the inter-War years, discovering that much the same rhetoric we hear with respect to the virtual university was current in the 1930s. This is a salutary message to those who announce the new and insist that we must adapt to its imperatives. Historical analysis enables us to contextualize today's realities, and to resist the seductions of a discourse of virtual technological revolution.

Martin Trow (Ch. 14) contends that we need to acknowledge that the introduction of ICTs is inflected by substantive decisions and relationships. However, this does not mean that their effects may be straightforwardly foreseen from established patterns. As Trow argues, one of the most important features of the take-up of ICTs is that their consequences are difficult to predict and sure to be mixed, precisely because so many variables are in play. This is not to suggest that we shrug our shoulders and mutter that we do not know what is happening around us. It is, rather, to say that we must engage in the exercise of serious research and thought.

These, then, are the various contributions to *The Virtual University*? Certain themes run throughout—the refusal of a narrow focus on higher education alone; a rejection of the kind of approaches that put an excessive emphasis on ICTs; caution about the logic of the corporate agenda and the 'business of borderless education'; and an insistence that there must be possibilities for intervention and re-direction of the higher education agenda. It is in this spirit that the editors offer an Afterword that sets out our own hopes and fears for the virtual university. Insisting that nostalgia for national-liberal university is misplaced, and even disabling, we want to put high on the agenda the issue of globalization—the cultural threats and possibilities in higher education institutions that are now permeated by global and transnational knowledges and cultures. Our concern, at the end of this volume, is with the possibilities for the global-cosmopolitan university.

REFERENCES

Adonis, A. and Pollard, S. (1997) *A Class Act: The Myth of Britain's Classless Society.* London: Hamish Hamilton.

Barnett, R. (1997) *Realizing the University.* London: Institute of Education.

Bauman, Z. (1987) *Legislators and Interpreters: Modernity, Postmodernity and the Intellectuals.* Cambridge: Polity.

Bloom, A. (1987) *The Closing of the American Mind: How Higher Education has Failed Democracy and Impoverished the Souls of Today's Students.* New York: Simon & Schuster.

Bolton, A. (2001) 'The cuckoo in the nest? The business school in a university', in D. Warner and D. Palfreyman (eds) *The State in UK Higher Education: Managing Change and Diversity.* Buckingham: SRHE and Open University Press, pp. 127–37.

Brown, P. and Lauder, H. (2001) *Capitalism and Social Progress: The Future of Society in a Global Economy.* Basingstoke: Palgrave.

CVCP/HEFCE (2000) *The Business of Borderless Education: UK Perspectives.* London: CVCP/HEFCE.

Delanty, G. (1998) 'The idea of the university in the global era: from knowledge as an end to the end of knowledge?', *Social Epistemology,* **12**(1): 3–25.

—— (2001) *Challenging Knowledge: The University in the Knowledge Society.* Buckingham: SRHE and Open University Press.

Economist (1997) 'Survey: Universities', 4 October.

Garnham, N. (2000) ' "Information society" as theory or ideology: a critical perspective on technology, education and employment in the information age', *Information, Communication and Society*, **3**(2): 139–52.

Gibbons, M., Limoges, C., Nowotny, H., Schwartzmann, S., Scott, P., Trow, M. (1994) *The New Production of Knowledge*. London: Sage.

Halsey, A. H. (1992) *Decline of Donnish Dominion*. Oxford: Clarendon Press.

Information, Communication and Society (2000) 'New Media in Higher Education and Learning', Special Issue, **3**(4).

Kumar, K. (1997) 'The need for place', in A. Smith and F. Webster (eds), *The Postmodern University? Contested Visions of Higher Education in Society*. Buckingham: SRHE and Open University Press, pp. 27–35.

LaCapra, D. (1998) 'The university in ruins?', *Critical Inquiry*, **25**(1): 32–55.

Lyotard, J.-F. (1984) *The Postmodern Condition: A Report on Knowledge*. Manchester: Manchester University Press.

Monbiot, G. (2000) *The Captive State: The Corporate Takeover of Britain*. London: Macmillan.

Morton, D. (1997) ' "The university" is theory: universities are facts', *University of Toronto Quarterly*, **66**(4): 593–600.

Newby, H. (1999) *Higher Education in the 21st century: Some Possible Futures*. London: Committee of Vice-Chancellors and Principals of the Universities of the United Kingdom.

Nussbaum, M. (1997) *Cultivating Humanity: A Classical Defence of Reform in Liberal Education*. Cambridge, MA: Harvard University Press.

Pan, D. (1998) 'The crisis of the humanities and the end of the university', *Telos*, **111**: 69–106.

Pease, P. (2000) 'The virtual university: Jones International University, Ltd.', *Information, Communication and Society*, **4**(3): 627–8.

Power, M. (1997) *The Audit Society: The Rituals of Verification*. Oxford University Press.

Press, E. and Washburn, J. (2000) 'The kept university', *Atlantic Monthly*, in four parts, available from www.theatlantic.com/egi-bin/o/issues/2000/03/press/htm

Readings, B. (1996) *The University in Ruins*. Cambridge, MA: Harvard University Press.

Reich, R. (1991) *The Work of Nations: Preparing Ourselves for 21st century Capitalism*. New York: Vintage.

Robbins, L. (Lord) (1980) *Higher Education Revisited*. London: Macmillan.

Robertson, D. (1998) 'The emerging political economy of education', *Studies in Higher Education*, **23**(2): 221–8.

Rothblatt, S. and Wittrock, B. (eds) (1993) *The European and American University since 1800*. Cambridge: Cambridge University Press.

Sanderson, M. (1972) *The Universities and British Industry, 1850–1970*. London: Routledge.

Scott, P. (1995) *The Meanings of Mass Higher Education*. Buckingham: SRHE and Open University Press.

Slaughter, S. and Leslie, L.L. (1997) *Academic Capitalism: Politics, Policies and the Entrepreneurial University*. Baltimore, MD: Johns Hopkins University Press.

Strathern, M. (ed.) (2000) *Audit Cultures—Anthropological Studies in Accountability, Ethics and the Academy*. London: Routledge.

Tehranian, M. (1996) 'The end of university?', *The Information Society*, **12**: 441–7.

Thompson, E. P. (1970*a*) 'The business university', *New Society*, 19 February: 301–7.

Thompson, E. P. (1970*b*) *Warwick University Ltd*. Harmondsworth: Penguin.

Thorne, M. (ed.) (1999) *Universities in the Future.* London: Office of Science and Technology.

Turner, B. S. (1998) 'Universities, élites and the nation-state: a reply to Delanty', *Social Epistemology,* **12**(1): 73–7.

Webster, F. (2002) *Theories of the Information Society,* 2nd edn. London: Routledge.

2

Globalizing the Academy

John Urry

THE GLOBAL LANDSCAPE

We appear to be living through some extraordinary times, times involving exceptional changes to the very fabric of social life. This sense of transformation has been described by academics, journalists, management specialists, educationalists, politicians, media commentators, computer experts, and others. One way to characterize these transformations is through the claim that economic, social, and political life is being globalized (see Held *et al.* 1999, for wide-ranging detail).

Analogies have been drawn with the end of the nineteenth and beginning of the twentieth centuries when a somewhat similar restructuring of the dimensions of time and space took place. New technological and organizational innovations 'compressed' the time taken to travel across, and to communicate over, large distances. Some innovations that changed these dimensions of time–space included the telegram, the telephone, steamship travel, the bicycle, cars and lorries, skyscrapers, aircraft, the mass production factory, X-ray machines and the development of Greenwich Mean Time (Kern 1983). Today something similar seems to be occurring. New technologies are producing 'global times' in which distances between places and peoples again seem to be dramatically reducing, redrawing the very categories of time and space. Some commentators have suggested that time and space are 'de-materialising' (Urry 1998).

However, the term used here, 'globalization', is somewhat confusing since it refers both to certain global processes (from the verb, to globalize) and to certain global outcomes (from the noun, the globe). In this chapter I mainly use

I am grateful for hearing material presented at the International Symposium on the Future of Universities, held at the University of Newcastle, September 2000. In the following I use 'universities' and 'higher education' interchangeably although I am well aware that much higher education provision is not strictly speaking delivered within universities as such.

globalization in the first sense since most of the processes discussed are incomplete and there is nothing approaching a single global society. 'Globalization' does not exist as a finished and complete world order. However, there are many different kinds of globalization-argument as summarized in the box below (and see Urry 2000: chapters 1 and 2).

MAIN FORMS OF GLOBALIZATION-ARGUMENT

Strategy	Used by transnational corporations which operate on a world-wide basis and involves a lack of commitment to particular places, labour forces or governments
Image	Images of the 'earth' or 'globe' used in the advertising of products (airlines for example) and for recruiting people to join groups protesting about the environment
Ideology	Those with economic interests in promoting capitalism throughout the world argue that globalization is inevitable and national governments should not seek to regulate the global marketplace
Basis of political mobilization	Characterizing an issue as 'global' makes it likely that a wide range of individuals and organizations will mobilize for or against the phenomenon in question
Scapes and flows	People, information, ideas and images 'flow' along various 'scapes' organized through networks within and across different societies

I concentrate mainly upon the last of these, namely 'scapes and flows' (Brunn and Leinbach 1991; Lash and Urry 1994; Castells 1996; Urry 2000). Scapes are the networks connecting together machines, technologies, organizations and documents. Together such networks produce sets of nodes that are inter-connected in sustained and enduring ways. The following are the main global scapes:

(1) the system of transportation of people by air, sea, rail, motorway roads, other roads;
(2) the transportation of objects via postal and other systems;
(3) the wire, co-axial and fibre-optic cables that carry telephone messages, television pictures and computer information and images;
(4) the micro-wave channels used by cellular phones;
(5) the satellites used for transmitting and receiving radio and television signals.

And once such scapes have been established, then individuals, places and especially companies will try to become connected to them, to become nodes within a particular scape. Examples include the way that towns try to get connected to the motorway network, or have flights organized to major 'hub' airports, or get their local schools plugged into the internet.

Various flows occur along these scapes:

(1) *people* travelling along transportation scapes for work, education, and holidays;
(2) *objects* being sent and received by companies and individuals which move along postal and other freight systems;
(3) *information, messages, and images* flowing along various cables and between satellites;
(4) *messages* travelling along micro-wave channels from one mobile phone to another.

These scapes and flows create new social inequalities, of access. Some groups are well 'plugged-in' to these scapes (such as those universities with good internet access), while others can be excluded. What has become significant is the 'relative', as opposed to the 'absolute', location of a particular social group or town or university in relation to these scapes. These telecommunication and transportation structures reshape the very nature of time and space. Scapes pass by some areas while connecting others along information and transportation rich 'tunnels', which in effect compress the distances of time and space between those places (such as the so-called 'Golden Triangle' of universities, London–Oxford–Cambridge, within the UK).

The metaphor appropriate to capture these scapes and flows is not that of a structure, which implies a centre, a concentration of power, vertical hierarchy and a formal or informal constitution. Castells argues rather that we should employ the metaphor of network:

Networks constitute the new social morphology of our societies, and the diffusion of networking logic substantially modifies the operation and outcomes in processes of production, experience, power, and culture...the network society, characterized by the preeminence of social morphology over social action   (Castells 1996: 469).

A network is a set of interconnected nodes, the distance between social positions being shorter where such positions constitute nodes within a network as opposed to those outside the particular network. Networks are dynamic open structures so long as they can continue to effect communication with new nodes (Castells 1996: 470–1). Networks thus produce complex and enduring connections across space and through time between peoples and things (see Murdoch 1995: 745). They spread across time and space. Otherwise, according to Law: 'left to their own devices *human actions and words do not spread very far at all*' (Law 1994: 24). Different networks thus possess different reaches or abilities to bring home distant events, places or people, so overcoming the friction of space within appropriate periods of time.

So far I have outlined some general developments in the global landscape, resulting from various scapes, flows, and networks. In the next section, I consider four developments directly related to higher education, information, branding, desires, and states (for more detail, see Smith and Webster 1997; Scott 1998; Gibbons 1998; Newby 2000; other chapters in this collection).

TRANSFORMING THE HIGHER EDUCATION LANDSCAPE

Most obviously, the new global landscape is being transformed by what Castells (1996) terms, the 'informational society' that especially developed within North America in the 1970s and 1980s. Some of its features include:

(1) bits of electronically transmitted information as the building blocks;
(2) such technologies are pervasive as information has become integral to almost all forms of human practice;
(3) there are complex and temporally unpredictable patterns of informational development occurring in a distributed fashion within very specific localities;
(4) technologies are organized through loosely organized and flexibly changing networks;
(5) different technologies gradually converge into integrated informational systems (especially the once-separate biological and microelectronic technologies);
(6) these systems permit organizations to work in real time 'on a planetary scale';
(7) such instantaneous electronic impulses, or 'timeless time', provide material support for the development of new scapes.

Contemporary technologies and social practices are based upon time-frames that lie beyond conscious human experience. Tom Peters talks of the 'nano-second nineties' (Peters 1992). Such technologies also change at astonishing speed with a 100 times increase in computing power every ten years (see Brand 1999). The new 'computime' represents the abstraction of time and its separation from human experience and the rhythms of nature. This instantaneous time stems from the shift from the atom to the bit, that the information-based digital age 'is about the global movement of weightless bits at the speed of light' (Negroponte 1995: 12). The information can become instantaneously and simultaneously available more or less anywhere, although not everywhere. Knowledge has become dramatically 'de-territorialized' and turned into bits of information resulting in what Keane calls 'information blizzards' (Keane 1991; Delanty 1998). Once information was physically and uniquely stored in libraries or archives, which could of course be burnt down (see Brand 1999, chapter 12; Featherstone 2000). Now through its digitalization, information adopts patterns and modes of mobility almost wholly separate from any material form or presence (Hayles 1999: 18–20). Information is everywhere (and nowhere) travelling instantaneously along the fluid network of global communications. It cannot be burnt down although particular computers can, as everyone knows, have their memories wiped out.

Information blizzards leave universities with their relatively slow-moving curricula and traditions of scholarly work badly placed to compete with new faster-moving competitors in information-producing and handling. Higher Education (HE) is organized in terms of a daily cycle of unchangeable time-tabled classes, a seasonal cycle of weeks, terms and years, a lengthy cycle of degrees, and traditions and ritual that hark back to Medieval Europe. Compared with these relatively fixed and medium term times, some contemporary organizations are more able to mimic the instantaneous time of the informational revolution. Universities will have to develop new ways of organizing themselves in these global times, and especially in what Newby refers to as 'just-for-you' (and 'right now') modes of higher education (Newby 2000).

Second, branding. Many global commodities are produced in predictable, calculable, routinized and standardized environments by globally organized companies. Such branding presupposes enormously effective networks stretching across the globe. These networks depend upon allocating a very large proportion of resources to branding, advertizing, quality control, staff training and the internalization of the corporate image in each country. These aspects of the brand cross societies in standardized patterns so sustaining the global image, even where there is franchizing and not single ownership. McDonalds is the paradigm case of such branding, as Ritzer describes (Ritzer 1998). It has resulted in new ways of organizing companies on a global scale with a minimum of central control. It has produced new kinds of low skilled standardized jobs for, especially, students (McJobs), generated new products (Chicken McNuggets) and encouraged the eating of standardized fast food bought from take-out restaurants (hence students' 'grazing'), and of course established its own 'university' (Hamburger University).

No university worldwide has established a brand with such widespread recognition—they are mostly poor at establishing and sustaining their networks that ensure that the same product is delivered in the same way at the same standard (OU is a partial counter-example). This is so even within a region, let alone across the globe. But this stems from the complex character of the academic product and the degree to which that product presumes face-to-face social interaction of students with particular scholars, and students with students. Can those scholars be replaced by cheaper replacements or by their visual images? Do those core scholars ever have to be present within the distant parts of the institution in question? There are apparently 140,000 students now doing UK degrees without actually being at a UK institution; what we can ask is the product that they are consuming (see Macleod 1998)?

This makes one further consider what is the core characteristic of a university in a world of intense global brand competition. How much is face-to-faceness, of corporeal co-presence, part of that core and what is the relationship between those face-to-face 'moments of truth' (as the former managing director of the airline SAS put it) and the overall experience of that institution? What is the significance of talk, interaction, and the enforced proximity that a university campus typically provides (4 per cent of the UK adult population study or work in university 'campuses')? And this in turn relates to what I call desires since much of what is involved in university is 'social', the complex, messy, unpredictable, and risky social interactions that a university campus/quarter facilitates and which forms the experience of students and staff (see Boden 2000, on the importance even for financial businesses of mundane face-to-face talk).

Third, then, globalization allows people new opportunities and desires to develop. For young people these desires include:

(1) to travel away from the family home, to meet and engage with other young people in a novel and liminal environment (whatever the virtual development of universities);
(2) to travel overseas so permitting something of a global market for students (so far though fairly undeveloped) and to facilitate 'academic tourism' especially using the global academic language of English;
(3) to buy consumer goods and life-styles from across the world (Mexican food, Harvard T-shirts, Nike shoes, world music and so on);
(4) to communicate with people in many countries via the internet and to form 'new social groups' often opposed, or providing alternatives, to aspects of globalization (as in the Seattle WTO protest);
(5) to participate in global cultural events such as the World Cup, 'world music', and so on.

Global enthusiasts see these processes as producing a new world order, a cosmopolitan 'borderlessness' (Ohmae 1990). This offers new opportunities, especially to overcome the limitations and restrictions that societies and states have exercised on the freedom of corporations and individuals to treat the world as 'their oyster'. Students, in particular, from diverse continents increasingly desire to 'see the world' (and corresponding scapes have developed to facilitate their treating the world as their oyster!). Universities are much more rooted in place and are less able to roam globally. Students and staff have much greater mobility and will be motivated by various desires, for learning and qualifications but also for travel, friendship, leisure activities, learning English, and so on. HE institutions have to respond to this mobility and to the way that such institutions are part of a system of global tourism, for academic staff and for prospective students seeking to acquire 'overseas experience' (what in New Zealand is known as their 'OE'). This will almost certainly involve the capacity of universities to act 'glocally'—to connect global processes to appropriate aspects of local economy, culture, and identity, including the place within which a university is located and the specific campus or quarter.

Fourth, states. Territories are less obviously subject to governance by national states while many traditional domains of state action cannot be fulfilled without international collaboration. These flows across societal borders make it hard for states to mobilize clearly separate and coherent *nations* in pursuit of societal goals. The breaking down of the coherence of 'national economies' has been combined with an increased political unwillingness of states to increase taxation and spending (and of taxpayers to pay). States are shifting to a regulative rather than a direct production/employment function, such a shift being facilitated by new forms of information gathering, storage and retrieval (as with data on student dropouts, for example). As has been said of Japan: 'network-type systems emphasize a type of human control that involves *inducement or persuasion by manipulating information* rather than a method of control that depends upon power-based or contractual political action' (cited Dale 1997: 33).

Both within countries and especially across the EU there has been a massive increase in the 'regulation' of how goods and services are produced and of certain environmental and other consequences (Majone 1996; Urry 2000: chapter 8). Less emphasis is placed upon ensuring that a particular service remains in public ownership and more is placed upon establishing effective regulation by supposedly independent agencies. The EU is the regulatory state par excellence; there are now more rules introduced each year by the EU than are initiated by the typical European state (Majone 1996: 57). Other global regulators include UNESCO, World Bank, IMF, the World Intellectual Property Organisation, the International Air Transport Association, the Olympic movement, the Rio Earth Summit held in 1992, WHO, the Association of Commonwealth Universities, many international academic associations and so on. There are two main implications for HE. First, attempts to defend their position as 'publicly' owned and funded bodies will mostly fall on deaf ears and one can expect further uneven privatization as the global marketplace becomes ever-more omnipotent. Second, there will be an increased regulation of universities, somewhat comparable to that experienced by many other industries and occupations. Such regulation is greatly enhanced by new modes of information gathering that enable individuals, departments, and institutions to be compared with each other, often across national borders. The production of information and knowledge *and* the regulation of those conditions of production will be increasingly separated from each other.

More generally, global processes problematize the notion of a society that is, in and of itself, able to mobilize for action. These configurations weaken the power of the society as a system of governance to draw together its citizens as one, to govern in its unique name, to endow all with national identity and to speak with a single voice (Rose 1996). Global processes weaken the notion of a shared national culture that is produced exclusively through HE that has exhaustive rights to determine that national culture. Indeed societies were once organized through public debate occurring within a relatively delimited public sphere. The information and knowledge produced by its few institutions of HE centrally formed those debates and delimited possible outcomes. The academy was particularly implicated in contributing knowledge to such a public sphere, and indeed in constituting that sphere. But there are now many other providers as information becomes much more widely produced, circulated and of course traded. The outputs of the academy compete with the outputs of many other entities, including, especially, the media, private research establishments, companies and so on.

In particular, such a public sphere has become globalized through mediatization. It is not that the mass media reflects what goes on elsewhere, so much as what happens in and through the media *is* what happens elsewhere. HE is part of that mediated and partially globalized public sphere that is no longer confined and reproduced within national boundaries. The sphere of public life that has historically provided the context for knowledge that is produced within the academy is now increasingly mediatized. Consider how oppositional environmental groups have very effectively employed media images. The media are an integral part of the process by which environmental information and debate is created, circulated, and consumed. Ross summarizes:

In recent years we have become accustomed to seeing images of a dying planet, variously exhibited in grisly poses of ecological depletion and circulated by all sectors of genocidal atrocities. The clichés of the standard environmental movement are well known to us all: on the one hand, belching smokestacks, seabirds mired in petrochemical sludge, fish floating belly-up, traffic jams in Los Angeles and Mexico City, and clearcut forests; on the other hand, the redeeming repertoire of pastoral imagery, pristine, green, and unspoiled by human habitation, crowned by the ultimate global spectacle, the fragile, vulnerable ball of spaceship earth   (Ross 1994: 171).

In such a public staging of environmental issues globally circulated media images play a major role in the forming of public debate. The findings of science and the philosophical branch of aesthetics are not irrelevant to this public sphere but they are only part of what it is that helps to develop debate. And such a debate is concerned as much with image, meaning, and emotion, as it is with written texts, cognition, and science (Macnaghten and Urry 1998). The global economy of signs is transforming the public sphere into an increasingly visual and emotional public stage; and in a world in which 'seeing is believing', such media images may be far more persuasive than the abstract ideas and information historically associated with the academy (see Szerszynski *et al.* 2000).

Some commentators have described these developments in highly dystopic terms—that globalization has many of the characteristics of the pre-Enlightenment *medieval* world (Cerny 1997). Such a neo-Medievalism can be seen in a number of features:

(1) powerful *empires* such as Microsoft, CNN, New International, and so on roam the globe and are major competitors in the development of new kinds of information and meaning;

(2) competing *cities*, such as Newcastle, New Orleans, Sydney, develop and use HE as part of their global branding and place-marketing;

(3) individual societies are often unable to *reform* themselves on their own to improve the conditions of their home population—and hence are dependent upon imperial patronage;

(4) there is an increasing dependence also of HE upon *imperial patronage* (Bill Gates as the most powerful of contemporary emperors, as in the case of the University of Cambridge);

(5) large numbers of *wandering intellectuals* (academic mercenaries?) with relatively few links to particular national projects and willing to go where resources happen to be best located (something which contradicts the emphasis of the UK research assessment of localized research cultures).

IVORY TOWERS?

How to conclude? First, there is no unified global society but there are exceptional levels of global interdependence. Huge flows of information, images, peoples, objects, and dangerous wastes circulate around the globe along various networked scapes. The scapes of information flow include universities, but by no means exclusively, while HE is also cross-cut by these other global scapes and flows. Thus, any university is dependent upon the systems of global communications and transportation since its contribution to the global stock of information is tiny. HE institutions are massively dependent upon each other and many other knowledge providers. No ivory tower remains. So, just as the world is being organized through the generalization of global competition so HEIs are forced into global cooperation both with other HEIs and with numerous other information and image-producers. There is also a shift away from a culture of individual authors working within separate disciplines located within a given nation-state, to a culture of multi-author, multi-disciplinary, multinational and multi-institutional 'research' (Delanty 1998; Gibbons 1998).

The new global landscape is hugely heterogeneous. No single social group controls the globe—there is intense competition between global capitals, various global organizations, national and regional states, organizations of professional experts, work and leisure-based global networks, NGOs often opposed to aspects of globalization, various powerful institutions including universities, and so on (Castells 1996, 1997). The resulting global order involves unpredictable shock waves. These can spill out chaotically from one element to the system as a whole, displaying what elsewhere I call 'global complexity' where small changes in one site can generate massive changes distant in time and space (Urry 2002; Mann 1993).

The internet provides a powerful metaphor for such a world (Castells 1996; Urry 2000). It is the best example of how a technology invented for one purpose in one place, military communication within the US in the event of a nuclear attack, chaotically evolved across the globe into meeting desires wholly unintended by original 'inventors'. The internet has developed into a system enabling hugely extensive horizontal communication that cannot be controlled or effectively censored by national societies. It is also a metaphor for social life as networked and fluid. It involves thousands of networks, of people, machines, programmes, texts and images in which quasi-subjects and quasi-objects are mixed together in new hybrid forms. Ever-new computer networks and links proliferate in unplanned and mixed forms. In such a fluid space it is not possible to determine identities and cultures once and for all, since a fluid world is a world of *mixtures*. Messages 'find their way'. Such networks are not solid or stable and are hugely contingent; and yet states and international organizations seek to regulate the internet while global corporations seek to tailor it to their commercial interests.

Conceiving of the system of universities in this chaotic, mobile global landscape as analogous to the internet, as unstable, contingent, and fluid-like is a challenging set of metaphors and conceptions for 'thinking the academy' as we flow into the twenty-first century.

REFERENCES

Boden, D. (2000) 'Worlds in action: information, instantaneity and global futures trading', in B. Adam, U. Beck, and J. van Loon (eds) *The Risk Society and Beyond*. London: Sage.

Brand, S. (1999) *The Clock of the Long Now*. London: Phoenix.

Brunn, S. and Leinbach, R. (eds) (1991) *Collapsing Space and Time: Geographic Aspects of Communications and Information*. London: Harper Collins.

Castells, M. (1996) *The Rise of the Network Society*. Oxford: Blackwell.

—— (1997) *The Power of Identity*. Oxford: Blackwell.

Cerny, P. (1997) 'Globalization, fragmentation and the governance gap: towards a new mediaevalism in world politics', *Globalization Workshop*, University of Birmingham Politics Dept, March.

Dale, P. (1997) 'Ideology and atmosphere in the informational society', *Theory, Culture and Society*, 13: 27–52.

Delanty, G. (1998) 'The idea of the university in the global era: from knowledge as an end to an end of knowledge', *Social Epistemology*, 12: 3–25.

Featherstone, M. (2000) 'Archiving cultures', *British Journal of Sociology*, 51: 161–84.

Gibbons, M. (1998) *Higher Education Relevance in the 21st Century*. The World Bank: UNESCO.

Hayles, N. K. (1999) *How We Became Posthuman*. Chicago: University of Chicago Press.

Held, D., McGrew, A., Goldblatt, D., and Perraton, J. (1999) *Global Transformations*. Cambridge: Polity.

Keane, J. (1991) *The Media and Democracy*. Cambridge: Polity.

Kern, S. (1983) *The Culture of Time and Space, 1880–1914*. London: Wiedenfeld and Nicolson.

Lash, S. and Urry, J. (1994) *Economies of Signs and Space*. London: Sage.

Law, J. (1994) *Organizing Modernity*. Oxford: Basil Blackwell.

Macleod, D. (1998) 'Academic war to end all wars', *Guardian Higher*, Nov. 17th.

Macnaghten, P. and Urry, J. (1998) *Contested Natures*. London: Sage.

Majone, G. (ed) (1996) *Regulating Europe*. London: Routledge.

Mann, M. (1993) *The Sources of Social Power: The Rise of Classes and Nation-states. Vol. 2.* Cambridge: Cambridge University Press.

Murdoch, J. (1995) 'Actor-networks and the evolution of economic forms: combining description and explanation in theories of regulation, flexible specialisation, and networks', *Environment and Planning A*, 27: 731–57.

Negroponte, N. (1995) *Being Digital*. New York: Alfred A. Knopf.

Newby, H. (2000) 'Higher Education futures', *Royal Society of Arts Education Futures*. London: RSA: 41–5.

Ohmae, K. (1990) *The Borderless World*. London: Collins.

Peters, T. (1992) *Liberation Management*. London: Macmillan.

Ritzer, G. (1998) *The McDonaldization Thesis*. London: Sage.

Rose, N. (1996) 'Refiguring the territory of government', *Economy and Society*, 25: 327–56.

Ross, A. (1994) *The Chicago Gangster Theory of Life: Nature's Debt to Society*. London: Verso.

Scott, P. (ed.) (1998) *Globalization of Higher Education*. London: SRHE/ Open University Press.

Smith, A. and Webster, F. (eds) (1997) *The Post-modern University?* London: SRHE/Open University Press.

Szerszynski, B., Urry, J., and Myers, G. (2000) 'Mediating Global Citizenship', in J. Smith (ed.) *The Daily Globe*. London: Earthscan.

Urry, J. (1998) 'Contemporary transformations of time and space', in P. Scott (ed.) *Globalization of Higher Education*. London: SRHE/ Open University Press.

—— (2000) *Sociology Beyond Societies*. London: Routledge.

—— (2002) *Global Complexity*. Cambridge: Polity.

3

The University and Modernity:
A History of the Present

Gerard Delanty

INTRODUCTION

In this chapter, I offer an interpretation of the current situation of the university by means of a sketch of a historical sociology of the university (Delanty 1998, 2001). Such a 'history of the present' will allow us to see the university as a reflection of the major social transformations of modernity with regard to the institutional organization of the sciences, cultural production, the polity, and the mode of production. From this perspective, there is not one dominant model of modernity but rather there are several, for modernity is a site of tensions and contradictions (Arnason 1991). This leads to a view of the university as a site where many of these contradictions are expressed, for instance, the conflicts between cosmopolitanism and national culture, universalism and particularism, secularism and religion, modernity and tradition, power and culture, intellectuals and experts, democracy and knowledge.

I argue that the university is a paradigmatic expression of what Habermas (1981) has called the 'project of modernity': the professionalization of knowledge and of cultural reproduction in the autonomous spheres of science, art, and morality. The project of modernity, of course, was always incomplete and, as Habermas argued, could be complete only by entering the life-world where it would have an emancipatory function. In this view of modernity, the Enlightenment project underwent major ruptures, each of which are vividly reflected in the university. Today, its historical project has entered a new phase and in order to assess it, we need to see it in the longer perspective of history. By placing the current situation of the university in such a historical framework, I hope to demonstrate that the university is a resilient institution, capable of adapting to the external environment.

In this chapter, I describe four major revolutions that have shaped the present institution, revolutions which have mirrored the major ruptures in modernity. Though the current revolution is far from over, it is sufficiently advanced to assess its significance. These revolutions are:

1. The German academic revolution of the idealist philosophers, which inaugurated the liberal, humanistic university of the nineteenth century, was the first revolution that shaped the modern university, the so-called Humboldtian university. In this period of high or liberal modernity, the Enlightenment project brings about the rationalization of culture in the name of universalistic science (Wagner 1994).

2. The American academic revolution followed, leading to the birth of the twentieth-century university—the 'civic university'—based on disciplinary organized knowledge and the accreditation of professionals. In this period of 'organized modernity', or industrial modernity, the university, though still an elite institution, became linked with the industrial mode of production, societal modernization, and became a key institution of the democratic national state. In its most distinctive form, it was an American-led revolution and reflected the social project of modernity.

3. The democratic revolution of the second half of the twentieth century led to the mass university. In this period of 'late modernity', the university becomes linked to the transformative project of democratic politics and enters the life-world.

4. The coming global revolution of the twenty-first century—the postmodern era—marks the current situation, when the university dissolves disciplinarity, institutionalizes market values and enters the post-industrial information age. It is in this revolution that the first intimations of the virtual university can be found. These revolutions in the modern university roughly correspond to the innovations of the later eighteenth century, the late nineteenth century, the mid-twentieth century, and the late twentieth century. These four conceptions of the university along with their cognitive models and their relationship to modernity are summarized in Table 3.1.

Such a historical and sociological framework allows us to assess the current situation in a more nuanced way than simply announcing the end of the university. My contention is that the university must be seen in the wider context of modernity and its cultural, social, material, political, and technological projects. It is important to see that these projects do not unfold simultaneously, but according to different, and frequently contradictory, paces. In this sense, then, history is always part of the present. Thus, the cultural project preceded the social project, which in turn preceded the political project, and today the technological project is coming into focus, and as it does so there is an exacerbated tension between the different projects. In the university this is particularly apparent and, far from being the expression of a crisis, it is a source of strength for the university,

Table 3.1. The university and modernity

Four academic revolutions	Model of modernity	Cognitive model	Social transformations of modernity
The Humboldtian university (late eighteenth and nineteenth century)	The Enlightenment and the cultural project of modernity	Universal knowledge and the unity of teaching and research, autonomy of knowledge/academic freedom	Cultural rationalization, secularization, cultural nationalism
The civic university (late nineteenth century to 1960s)	Industrial modernity and the social project of modernity	Disciplinary specialization, separation of basic and applied research	Societal differentiation/ modernization, rise of the national 'governmental' state
The mass university (late twentieth century)	Late/advanced modernity and the political project of modernity	Knowledge as transformative, entry of the cognitive structures of the life-world	Democratization, radical politics, multiculturalism, post-industrial society
The virtual university (twenty-first century)	Postmodernity and the technological and economic projects	Multidisciplinarity, reflexivity, uncertainty, diversity, market values	Globalization, decline of the national state, post-Fordism, neoliberalism

which is one of the few sites in society where some kind of interconnectivity is possible between different projects and discourses.

THE GERMAN ACADEMIC REVOLUTION

The Enlightenment in Germany played a major role in shaping the modern university. It was eventually the German Enlightenment university that was imported into the United States and which also played a major role in shaping British and many other European universities. What can be called the academic revolution of the German idealist philosophers established the idea of the research-based university. In Germany, unlike in France, the Enlightenment was rooted in the universities, and in the absence of a mature national state, the universities found themselves in a fortuitous position. The concept of a research-based university and the overall unity of teaching and research emerged in Germany in the late eighteenth and early nineteenth century in the context of a gradual movement towards the formation of a national state (Anrich 1956; Müller 1990).

The universities in Germany served two functions, which ultimately led to the cause for academic freedom being linked to the sovereignty of the national state. On the one side, they represented the attempt of the Enlightenment to bring about the rationalization of culture, through secularization, intellectualization, the advancement and professionalization of science, the reproduction of universalistic values and, on the other side, the leaders of the universities saw their task to be the reproduction of cultural traditions which might provide the nascent national state with a cultural identity. This tension between cosmopolitanism and nationalism existed in the German university from the beginning. The Kantian model (Kant 1979), for instance, emphasized the autonomy and the critical function of the university in the pursuit of knowledge, while the von Humboldtian ideal of the university (von Humboldt 1970), which led to the formation of the University of Berlin in 1810, postulated culture as *Bildung* as the foundation of the university. This neo-humanist understanding of culture as self-formation or cultivation expressed the fascination of German Enlightenment with a deeper notion of culture than mere science. In Fichte, there is a yet more pronounced sense of the university as the protector of the culture of the nation, a conception that would eventually lead to Heidegger's (1985) demand for the university to assert national destiny. Arising from these strands with the German Enlightenment, the university that was to emerge in Germany from the early nineteenth century gave a special position to teaching and research as fundamentally connected. Teaching was the communication of research, not merely the reproduction of a received body of knowledge. A university education was a matter of *Bildung* which would be served by the pursuit of knowledge. This was an important step in shaping the modern university because the medieval university separated teaching and research. The attempt to unify teaching and research was the concrete achievement of the German Enlightenment university and it made the German university the most advanced in the world.

This tradition was quite different from the French and English models. From 1793, Napoleon subordinated the university to the state and privileged the écoles as leaders in research and professional training, in effect separating teaching and research. One of the consequences of this was that the French university never generated the same level of debate that was the case in Germany (Boudon 1981). In England, Cambridge and Oxford were rooted in a more pastoral tradition of the university and the traditional disciplines. Unlike in Scotland, the English university tradition was not a modernizing one and the dominant ethos was anti-Enlightenment and resistant to the modern experimental sciences.[1] It was designed to produce gentlemen and clerics, rather than industrialists and scholars as was the case in Germany where, as I have argued, the universities were crucial agents of modernization and nation-state formation. Moreover, the English university model was based on colleges, while the German tradition was a professorial one based on the faculty. As Durkheim (1977) argued, the residential college tended to 'domesticate' the university and stood for a less differentiated concept of knowledge than was suggested by the European faculty model, where the differentiation of modern cognitive structures was born (Bertillson 2000). In the German tradition, the lecture which served the function of the tutorial and graduate studies, with the creation of the PhD, became differentiated from undergraduate education. Despite the role it played in shaping German nationhood, the German university was above all an agent of modernity and of cultural rationalization. Thus, philosophy epitomized the German academic revolution, in stark contrast to the dominant position of the classics in the English system. The English model was the basis of the famous vision of Cardinal Newman (1996), whose *Idea of the University* in 1852, while embodying the liberal humanist ethos of the age, did not champion the unity of teaching and research that Wilhelm von Humboldt stood for. His vision, in contrast, was one of the university as the transmission of universal knowledge that did not require basic research to further knowledge.[2]

The research university based on the modern faculty structure grew in importance in Germany, where the university also cultivated the cultural identity of the German nation. The autonomy of the professorate was enhanced after the unification of Germany in 1870 when the professorate became an important part of the civil service. Undoubtedly, the importance the university played in Germany in defining the national culture has greatly contributed to the prestige of the university in the modern age. It was the German Humboldtian model of

---

[1] An exception was the foundation of University College in London. Influenced by German ideas, the utilitarians who supported it attempted to create a modern alternative to the traditional world of Oxbridge.

[2] A further important difference was that Newman was more concerned about justifying the existence of a faculty of theology under the conditions of modernity.

the research-based university, not the English pastoral one, that inspired the American tradition and was the reference point for some of the major debates of the twentieth century on the university (e.g. Jaspers 1960). Randall Collins (1998) argues that it was one of the crucial innovations in the West for the rise of modern science: 'The differentiation of disciplines, and the routinization of the impetus to innovate, have shaped the reflexively modern world we have inhabited ever since' (p. 383). It was an elite institution and one isolated from the life-world, but in it some of the core values of modernity were nurtured. The very notion that the university, while being internally differentiated in the disciplinary organization of the sciences, rests on an underlying idea: the unity of teaching and research.

In sum, the first academic revolution was a cultural one and expressed the project of modernity as defined by the Enlightenment: the rationalization of culture. Once this project advanced and shaped the nineteenth century, a second revolution got underway: the revolution of modernization. In this revolution, which was American-led and would shape the twentieth century, the university was drawn into the great changes that were taking place in material life.

THE AMERICAN ACADEMIC REVOLUTION OF MODERNIZATION: THE CIVIC UNIVERSITY

The modern university was primarily a creation of the late nineteenth century. While bearing the imprint of the German Enlightenment and the earlier medieval university, some of the most important developments took place in the period of organized or industrial modernity, from 1870s to the 1950s. This was the academic revolution of modernization, and above all else of industrialization (Reisman and Jencks 1968). In this primarily American revolution, the earlier German revolution in cultural rationalization was continued in the evolving relationship of the university to the industrial mode of production. From the last quarter of the nineteenth century onwards, an additional function is added to the functions of teaching and research: vocational training. This was the first major period of university expansion. The function of the university is no longer merely cultural but social: it becomes a core institution in the worldwide revolution of modernization. The American university was in no need of a legitimating idea, as was the case with the German Enlightenment university where the fate of the university became inextricably linked to the destiny of the state.

The first major reforms of the Enlightenment university were in the United States, where the German academic model was imported and, one might say, was reinvented around a more civic understanding of education. The university thus served a different function there, one less tied to the state. What marked the American academic revolution was the social, or civic, role the university was to play. This was in contrast to the decline of the German university profession into the sterile and elitist culture of the mandarins in the period 1890–1930

(Ringer 1969). Influenced by the philosophical movement of pragmatism, associated with the work of Dewey, Peirce, and James, the American university sought to make the university serve the civic community rather than the state. Thus was born the tradition of the land-grant university, which provided an important alternative to the liberal arts college. The primary function of this kind of state university was to provide training for the new agricultural and industrial professions that were emerging as a result of modernization. In Britain, this was the era of the civic universities, such as Birmingham, Liverpool, Nottingham, Manchester, which were also responses to the emergence of professional society outside the metropolitan centres. At this juncture in the history of the university, identity with the state was by no means taken for granted, and many universities had a stronger identity with their regions and cities (Bender 1988).

We can now speak of the 'modern' university, as opposed to the 'Enlightenment' university. This does not mean that the process of cultural rationalization was complete. On the contrary, in many ways it had only begun as was evident in the battles that were fought in many American universities over science and religion (Reuben 1996). It took a long time before religion and morality would be separated from science and the Enlightenment's demand for the divorce of facts and values finally accepted. The intellectual battles over science and religion continued to be fought out in the university, which was an important vehicle of secularization, but equally important in shaping the modern university was the pragmatic role of the university in an increasingly knowledge-dependent society.[3]

In recent times it has become fashionable to refer to the older university model as one of disinterested inquiry, irrelevant to the practice of life and a contrast to the applied nature of science in today. The reality, however, was that the modern university was linked very closely to instrumental pursuits. Even in Germany, from the second half of the nineteenth century, the university was central to basic and applied science, although there the applied dimension of science was generally relegated to the technical colleges and technical institutes. However, in the United States, especially since the foundation of the land grant universities, this separation was not so apparent. During the middle of the twentieth century, the university was central to national defence systems.

We are now in the age of 'organized modernity', that is, the advanced stage of modernization when the societal subsystems of modern society become functionally differentiated to a point that cultural rationalization is now complemented by a more general rationalization of societal functions. Nowhere is this more evident than in the university, where specialization is now fully institutionalized in disciplinarity and, accordingly the older faculties become less significant. The new administrative and academic unit is the department, the home of the discipline. New academic and professional associations emerged

---

[3] It must also be pointed out, as Veblen (1962) did in his famous book on the American university, that the American innovations privileged research over teaching.

along with disciplinarity. Just as the political landscape was mapped out in a world of sovereign nation-states, so too was the academic world divided into separate domains. Like Kuhn's paradigms, they cannot be criticized since they are the basis of criticism (Fuller 2000). This has meant a decline in the critical function of the university.

The specialization of science calls into question an overall sense of an overarching idea. Teaching and research become rationalized and fragmented, along with the wider differentiation in society. However, the unity of the university is not called into question since the institution was enjoying remarkable prestige. The university was now a national institution, though research would always be truly cosmopolitan. Despite the specialization of functions with the university, as Parsons and Platt (1973) argued in their remarkable study of the university, there was still an 'interpenetration' of functions and an overall complementarity of functions. In their vision of the American university, the parts all added up to an overall unity of functions. As Parsons (1974) puts it, the university is a 'bundling' institution, for there is an overall integration. Parsons and Platt believed the centre of gravity lay in the research function of university and is located in the graduate schools, rather than in vocational training. A slightly different argument was put forward by Clark Kerr (1963), who announced the end of the traditional university based on the quest for university knowledge on the grounds that specialization has led to the arrival of 'multiversity', which is based on its usefulness to society. He detected a growing flexibility in the university in its relation to society. Teaching also becomes more flexible, with a shift from courses to credit systems and electives, a development that would ultimately undermine the disciplinary organization of teaching since new courses could more easily be created (Rothblatt 1997; Rothblatt and Wittrock 1973).

The American academic revolution occurred within the confines of what was still an elite institution but one that was opening its doors to the nascent middle-class society. The implications of this for the university were enormous. It meant that the university would become more closely bound up in the project of modernization and the centralizing bureaucratic state. The present section can be summed up by saying that by the late nineteenth century, the university did not rest content with remaining within the mould of cultural modernity: the economic and social processes of modernization would have to be engaged with. However, the entry of material life into the university occurred in a relatively unpolitical context. But this was to change as a result of the third academic revolution, which was one of radical self-governance by students.

THE DEMOCRATIC REVOLUTION AND THE MASS UNIVERSITY

The third academic revolution began in the United States in the 1960s but was not an American revolution as such. It was a genuinely international academic revolution that while beginning in North America, quickly spread to all advanced societies and became an important part of revolutionary upheaval in the developing world. In the 1960s and 1970s, the mass university emerged along with the deepening of social citizenship in the western world. Initially this was part of the process of modernization. The social project of organized modernity created the conditions for the mass university, which followed in the wake of the welfare state and the post-industrial society. However, the mass university, while being a product of the process of modernization as it unfolded in the aftermath of the Second World War became one of the most important sites of resistance to modernization.

As organized modernity—the era of big institutions and state building—gave way to late modernity a mood of crisis set in. It became apparent that there was not one, inexorable logic of modernization but several and that they did not unfold coevally. The various projects of modernity—cultural rationalization, nation-state formation, industrialism, and democratization—frequently collided. Modernization held out the promise of an overall unity of purpose in the project of modernity, but the reality was one of crisis and contradiction. The university, once an enclave of bourgeois and Christian culture, became the site of a new political consciousness among the western secular middle class. The earlier academic revolutions did not have a significant impact on political consciousness. The university, while being drawn into the project of the national state, remained relatively unpolitical and immersed in the cultural ethos of an earlier modernity. This all changed in the late 1960s when the cultural project of the university became drawn into a new transformative political project. Until now the university was quite disengaged from all the great political movements of modernity, such as the anti-slavery movement, the civil rights movement, the workers movement, early nationalism. In it the cultural forms of modernity—the battle over secularism, the struggle for intellectual autonomy and academic freedom, universalistic rights—developed, but without a political consciousness. The university gradually ceased to be a neutral site and came to incorporate voices from the margins of society. As a result of cultural and political revolution in the western world, the university became a political actor. With the rise of the adversary culture of the 1960s, the university ceased to be a transmitter of a received cultural tradition but a transformer.

In Germany, the university was a crucial agent in de-Nazification and of democratic reform. Throughout the western world, the university played a central role in shaping feminism, multiculturalism, democratic, and anti-authoritarian values and advancing the cause of human rights. In addition to the functions of teaching, research, and training, we can now add the role of public critique. The public function of the university is not reducible to the transmission or creation of new knowledge, but also has the function of furthering public debate. The university was one of the most important institutions which made a more open and democratic society possible (Shils 1997). As Karl Popper (1945) also argued, the freedom of science and political freedom were thus to become linked, whereas previously in the Enlightenment model as espoused by Kant they were strictly separate. For Kant (1996), the price for academic critical debate was the de-politicization of the rest of society. The democratic revolution stemmed largely from the students, in contrast to the academic revolution of the Enlightenment, which stemmed from professors seeking professional autonomy.

The democratic revolution was reflected in several changes in the organization of the university, such as the emergence of the seminar. The open form of the seminar rather than the passive form of the lecture epitomized the cognitive shift that occurred in higher education to a more democratic and discursive model. The older idea of self-governance was radicalized by student participation in admissions policy and in the determination of the curriculum, bringing about, as David Riesman (1998) has argued in his famous book, the decline of the academic profession in an era of rising student consumerism. The adversary culture brought politics into the very constitution of knowledge. Knowledge thus became a matter of critical dialogue with the wider society, ceasing to be prepolitical as in the von Humboldtian ideal. As Habermas argued in his writings on the university, the unity of the culture is henceforth possible only through communication. Only in this limited sense is it possible to speak of the 'idea' of the university. Habermas's (1992) point was that the idea of the university no longer derives exclusively from the university. As he puts it, a 'new life can be breathed into the idea of the university only outside its walls' (Habermas 1969). What this means is that the university loses its cherished autonomy.

From this point onwards, views differ sharply on the implications of the crisis of academic autonomy. Major works on the university in the late 1960s to mid-1970s explored the links between the university and other social movements, and for a time the idea that the university might be the central space where revolution in the western world might occur (de Certeau 1997; Marcuse 1964, 1968; Touraine 1971; Wallerstein 1969). For Parsons there was a functional link between knowledge and citizenship. Habermas's theory of the university knowledge was rooted in socially shaped interests and the university can have an emancipatory function if it is articulated in communicative contexts. We see quite a different view in the work of Pierre Bourdieu (1996, 1998), whose writings on the university date from the same period. Bourdieu saw the university as a self-preserving institution in which different kinds of power are produced, circulated, and reproduced. The academic profession is a 'state nobility' and the university is primarily an autonomous site in which different orders of power clash as their holders struggle for self-reproduction. In sharp contrast, Parsons and Habermas while differing theoretically and politically, saw the university as connected. For Parsons, these links were primarily functional with respect to the working of society and cognitive structures, and for Habermas, they had an emancipatory potential in enhancing the self-understanding of society. In contrast, Bourdieu sees the university as relatively autonomous from society and, sharing with Foucault the view that knowledge is power, maintains that knowledge is not primarily emancipatory but is socially located in contexts of power. Thus, where others see the decline of the university as an autonomous institution based on self-governance by the academic profession, Bourdieu sees only the ascendancy of the professorate who constitute a 'state nobility' and are capable of resisting outside forces by virtue of their ability to control forms of capital crucial to the working of society. It is a picture of the university as capable of transforming the external social world into the internal logic of academic fields of power. In this interpretation, the university rests not on an idea, but on power. Bourdieu's work on the university derives from a period prior to the great upheaval in higher education that came with mass education and the transformative project of democratization. His vision of the university as a state nobility may reflect the privileged position in France of the *grandes écoles*, which have not suffered the same fate as the university. In any case, it was one of the last modernist visions of the university that was challenged by subsequent developments, anticipated by Lyotard (1984) in his famous book on the postmodern condition.

In sum, the third academic revolution brought about the politicization of the university in the context of new social movements in western societies. There are now clear signs that the assumptions that underlay this revolution, and which derived from the previous era, are now question, as is the entire project of modernity. This brings us to the fourth revolution in higher education: the global revolution in information and communications technology.

THE GLOBAL REVOLUTION AND THE COMING OF THE VIRTUAL UNIVERSITY

That the university is in the midst of a tremendous change has been apparent for some time, but only recently it is being recognized as a revolution. Unlike the three revolutions discussed above, the present revolution, in the view of many, may be a counter-revolution in that the dominant tendency is reactive, as opposed to the earlier forward looking projects with their affirmative and offensive programmes for the expansion of higher education and the enhancement of the status of the university in a world bereft of knowledge. Today in contrast, as capitalism undergoes major restructuring, the mood is one of defence and uncertainty. The political mission of the university has waned, its material basis is in question, and the earlier cultural project has resulted in the notorious 'culture wars' of recent years. Hence notions of the demise of the university, the exhaustion of the project of modernity, and the coming of the 'postmodern university' (Smith and Webster 1997).

Since the mid-1980s, a major transformation of higher education has been taking place alongside wider processes of postmodernization and globalization and is reflected in the institutional organization of the sciences, in the relation of the university to the state and market, and in cultural reproduction. The chief feature of the current revolution is the emergence of new technologies of communication, which are presenting the spectre of a 'virtual university'. The information revolution has led to the diffusion of a more connected society and which is no longer nationally defined but is, to follow Manuel Castell's (1996) characterization of it, a tendentially global society connected together by networks of communication. For the university this means that it is going to be more connected with its environment and that its hard won autonomy will become diffused in the new social relations. Thus, for instance, electronic communication has greatly altered the nature of communication, eliminating time and space as obstacles. It is inevitable that the emerging networks will be less controlled by academics.

With regard to the institutionalization of the sciences, the age of disciplinarity has given way to multi-disciplinarity. The department is no longer the primary location of science, which has considerably moved out of the university to other knowledge producers. The collapse of disciplinarity is one of the clearest signs we have of the break-up of the categories of modernity. Even the notion of the curriculum is in question, as a result of a growing influence of consumerism, cultural wars, and modularization, the result of which is the fragmentation of knowledge. These developments have been much discussed under the rubric of postmodernization (Aronowitz and Giroux 1991; Green 1997). However, one of the most far-reaching changes is the embracing of market values by the university.

According to a well-known study, there is a new mode of production which will undermine the role of the university which is becoming irrelevant to the emerging applied and user-shaped kind of knowledge that is now required (Gibbons *et al.* 1994). While it is clear that there is a shift from the producer to the user in the construction of knowledge, the reality is that in fact the university is adjusting very rapidly to the emergence of the new mode of production, as is witnessed by the growing phenomenon of what Slaughter and Leslie (1997) call 'academic capitalism' or what has been aptly termed the 'triple helix' of university, industry, and state by Etzkowitz and Leydesdorff (1997). These perspectives suggest that the university has become a major player in the market and is, therefore, far from being irrelevant to the user-dominated economy of information-based capitalism (Curie and Newson 1998).

The state is no longer the exclusive provider for the university, which instead depends on multiple resources, such as profitable research contracts with industry, student fees, and donations. Many countries have experienced the shift from grants to loans and the decrease in the state bloc grant, and have accordingly restructured higher education around a model of expansion at lower costs. In the view of many critics, these developments mark a change as great as the earlier academic revolutions. In the past, the university responded to changes in the state and the emergence of mass society; today it is changing in response to the emergence of global markets and new kinds of technology. While one interpretation is that the university is in crisis as a result of the decline of the state, whose destiny has also determined the fate of the university ever since the first academic revolution, another view is that the university is in fact quite adept at responding to the changed circumstances of the present. Thus where critics, such as Bill Readings (1996), see only the demise of the university, others, such as Manuel Castells (1996) and Howard Newby (1999) see a resilient institution becoming a major actor in the global economy. But this is clearly a revolution led by managers, not by students or by academics, as was the case in the earlier revolutions in higher education, since the commercialization of teaching and research leads to a strengthening of central administration. With less funding available to higher education and increased demands for subsidies as a result of student expansion, the state has responded by forcing universities to become competitive, with league tables, quality assurance tests, research assessments, and various performance indicators used to determine the allocation of scarce resources. Universities have internalized this external environment, which is one of regulation and privatization, in new managerial structures and in championing commercial research, such as biotechnology. Partnerships with industry are becoming more important in the area of technoscience and in the commercialization of teaching the university is able to increase its revenue. Universities reduce labour costs by resorting to more and more contract work, and information technology allows universities to expand in the area of distance learning and also to make course curricula the property of the university. Thus, it has been estimated by the University of Phoenix that the entire US higher education system could be reduced from 740,000 fully tenured staff to 250,000 course assistants, with bought-in 1,000 star performers (Newby 1999: 5). However, this is the extreme scenario and in most European countries globalization has not had the massive impact on the university as has been the case in the United States (Scott 1998).

The information revolution was in many ways spearheaded by universities. Universities have always been global in their commitment to knowledge, since research by its nature has always been global. Manuel Castells (1996) had documented that the University was one of the two sources of the Net (the other being the military science establishment). The lead was taken at UCLA in 1969 and spread worldwide from a core group of US universities. He argues the 'university origin of the Net has been, and is decisive for the development of electronic communication throughout the world .... Indeed, against the assumption of social isolation suggested by the image of the ivory tower, universities are major agents of diffusion of social innovation because generation after generation of young people go through them, becoming aware of and accustomed to new ways of thinking, managing, acting, and communicating' (p. 355–6).

Finally, the global revolution is reflected in debates on the cultural rationale of the university. No longer tied to the cultural project of the nation-state, the university evolved in the course of the twentieth century a more multicultural identity by becoming attached to the transformative project. It was an important space in society for the articulation of new cultural models and was the space in which marginal voices were incorporated. Today, while this project is still alive and one of the most important dimensions of the university, the cultural rationale of the university has suffered a major crisis and many critics complain about the fragmentation of the cultural project of the university. Thus, Readings sees the emergence of an empty culture of 'excellence' devoid of any moral or intellectual purpose, Allan Bloom (1987) bemoans the attack on the traditional curriculum in the name of diversity, and Russell Jacoby (1987) regrets the decline of the public intellectual who has disappeared from the university. Bloom and Jacoby, despite their different positions, see the culture wars as a symptom of the crisis of the university, not a sign of its strength.

Against these somewhat polemical positions, I would argue that what is occurring in the university is primarily a reflection of wider cultural change in society towards greater uncertainty. Culture no longer serves to provide a security against anarchy, as Matthew Arnold (1960) once believed. Culture has itself become anarchic, pervaded by a sense of obscurity, risk, and uncertainty. This is what can be more generally called postmodernization. Culture and with it the cognitive models of society have lost their ability to be easily defined by institutions, such as universities, and expertise is today faced with greater contestability in society. Thus, such taken for granted aspects of the identity of the university as self-governance and academic freedom have become highly questioned.

In sum, the global revolution has been brought about by managerialism responding to the new information technologies and global markets rather than by academics, although it must be pointed out that academics have been heavily involved in bringing the university closer to the market.[4] It is a revolution closely linked to the information technology and global capitalism. In this revolution, which has led to increased central administration, technoscience has driven the university from the state to the market. But this only means a change in the relation to the state, which becomes more of a regulatory order than a provider. In a way, what is happening is that in the knowledge and technologically based economy of today, the university is becoming too important to be allowed to govern itself.

CONCLUSION: THE FUTURE OF THE UNIVERSITY

In view of the preceding discussion, we can now return to the question raised at the beginning concerning the question of whether the university today is in crisis or in transition. By locating the university in the context of major shifts in modernity, we are in a better position to understand the current situation. While recent developments clearly do undermine many of the traditional functions of the university, it is important to see that the university is a resilient institution that has been formed in a continuous process of change. Even in the UK, the far-reaching Dearing Report did not recommend major restructuring of higher

---

[4] In 2000 the Japanese universities abandoned civil service status for academics in order to allow them to become players for profit.

education. Moreover, there have been many historical as well as national models of the university, which as an institution that is based on universalistic values—such as science and the world scientific community—is also, and necessarily so, very flexible and can accommodate different demands. This is so because in the modern world, as Weber and Habermas have argued, universalistic values have withdrawn from most areas of life, leaving only procedural forms of rationality in the place of substantive values. The limited universalism that is preserved in the university, and which justifies the continued use of the term 'university' despite pluralization and ever greater differentiation, is one of interconnectivity. But what does the university connect?

The university is one of the few sites in society where several societal functions coincide, albeit within the context of highly specialized domains. Despite specialization, as already noted above, multidisciplinarity and de-differentiation has become more salient in recent times. Nowotny (2000) thus argues expertise today is increasingly having to address different audiences, such as the public. The university is forced to live in a world that has been transformed by knowledge. In this context, Beck (1996) has argued that due to the scientization of the public, there is a greater consciousness of science and also a growing distrust of expert systems. This means a new role of the university will have to be found as a result of new kinds of communication between expert systems and public discourse. Burns (1999) argues that democratic governance is increasingly having to take more and more account of scientific knowledge with the result that parliaments will eventually have to create a role for experts. In the knowledge society, the university is more organically connected with society. This kind of interconnectivity is organic in the sense that there are multiple and reciprocal links, with the consequence that the university is forced to be more reflexive in its relationship to its environment. As a result of the new links between the university and society that have arisen due to the scientization of politics, the new technologies and mass education as well as new links between the sciences, the university finds itself drawn more and more into issues of governance that go beyond the traditional notion of academic self-governance.

One of the chief characteristics of knowledge in the knowledge society is the growing importance of the cognitive dimension. Knowledge is more than science or information, it also entails the deeper level of cultural models. While views differ on the nature of this relationship and its political implications, a sociologically constructivist approach to knowledge, which I am drawing upon here (Delanty 2001), sees knowledge as a socially constructed structure having a creative as well as an intellectual dimension (Strydom 1999, 2000). However, knowledge is more than a social construction, it is also an open structure that admits of internal development. I see the university as a zone of mediation between knowledge as science (or academic knowledge) and this deeper kind of cultural cognition. Viewing the university as a site of interconnectivity, communication becomes more central to it. The university cannot enlighten society as the older model of the university dictated, but it can provide the structures for public debate between expert and lay cultures. This, then, is the chance for the university to evolve a new identity in the global age.

Central to this project is the challenge of learning to live with choice in a global world of uncertainty.[5] As Bauman (1991) has argued, the current period is characterized by seemingly endless choice. Politics is unable to provide answers let alone solutions to all the problems it is presented with. Many of these problems relate to technology and to culture, perhaps the two most potent forces challenging the nation-state. On the one side, the new technologies (in communications, biotechnology, medicine, and defence) are undermining the older forms of system integration based on the state and, on the other side, the wars over cultural identity and belonging (nationalism, ethnicity and race, religion, communitarian populism) are undermining the older forms of social integration based on the autonomy of the social. The project of modernity, as it has traditionally been conceived, is poorly equipped to unite these domains and reestablish a principle of unity and purpose, for knowledge has ceased to offer the prospect of emancipation. In the global crisis of the risk society, the Enlightenment's 'republic of science' has suffered the same fate as the modern republic. Perhaps it is the role of the university to enable society to live with choice and uncertainty. Taming the new technologies and providing a cultural orientation for society is central to that challenge. It is for this reason that we can speak of the continued relevance of the university.

REFERENCES

Anrich, E. (ed.) (1956) *Die idee der deutschen Universität: Die fünf Grundschriften, Fichte, Schleiermacher, Steffens, Humboldt.* Darmstadt: Hermann Gentner Verlag.

Arnason, Johann (1991) 'Modernity as a project and as a field of tension', in A. Honneth and H. Joas (eds), *Communicative Action.* Cambridge: Polity.

Arnold, Matthew (1960) *Culture and Anarchy.* Cambridge: Cambridge University Press.

Aronowitz, Stanley and Giroux, H. (1991) *Postmodern Education: Politics, Culture and Social Criticism.* Minneapolis: University of Minnesota Press.

Barnett, Ron (2000) *Realizing the University.* Buckingham: Open University Press.

Bauman, Zygmunt (1991) *Modernity and Ambivalence.* Cambridge: Polity.

Beck, Ulrich (1996) *The Risk Society.* London: Sage.

Bender, T. (ed.) (1988) *The University and the City: From Medieval Origins to the Present.* Oxford: Oxford University Press.

Bertillson, Margareta (2000) 'From elite to mass education—what is next?', in C. Lindquist and L.-L. Wallenius (eds) *Globalization and its Impact.* Stockholm: FRN.

Bloom, Allan (1987) *The Closing of the American Mind.* New York: Simon and Schuster.

Boudon, Raymond (1981) 'The French University since 1968,' in C. Lemert (ed.) *French Sociology: Rapture and Renewal since 1968.* New York: Columbia University Press.

---

[5] Ron Barnett (2000) thus speaks of the challenge of learning to live with uncertainty as one of the tasks of the university.

Bourdieu, Pierre (1988) *Homo Academicus*. Cambridge: Polity Press.

—— (1996) *The State Nobility*. Cambridge: Polity.

Burns, Tom (1999) 'The evolution of parliaments and societies in Europe: challenges and prospects', *European Journal of Social Theory*. **2**(2): 167–94.

Castells, Manuel (1996) *The Rise of the Network Society*, Oxford: Blackwell.

Collins, Randall (1998) *The Sociology of Philosophies: A Global Theory of Intellectual Change*. Cambridge, MA: Harvard University Press.

Curie, J. and Newson, J. (eds) (1998) *Universities and Globalization: Critical Perspectives*. London: Sage.

De Certeau, Michel (1997) *Culture in the Plural*. Minneapolis: Minnesota University Press.

Delanty, Gerard (1998) 'The idea of the university in the global era: from knowledge as an end to the end of knowledge?', *Social Epistemology: A Journal of Knowledge, Culture and Policy*, **12**(1): 3–25.

—— (2001) *Challenging Knowledge: The University in the Knowledge Society*. Buckingham: Open University Press.

Durkheim, Emile (1977) *The Evolution of Educational Thought*. London: Routledge & Kegan Paul.

Etzkowitz, H. and Leydesdorff, L. (eds) (1997) *Universities in the Global Economy: A Triple Helix of University Industry Government Relations*. London: Cassell Academic.

Fuller, Steve (2000) *Thomas Kuhn: A Philosophical History for our Times*. Chicago: University of Chicago Press.

Gibbons, M., Limoges, C., Nowotny, H., Schwartzman, S., Scott, P., and Trow, M. (1994) *The New Production of Knowledge*. London: Sage.

Green, Andy (1997) *Education, Globalization and the University*. London: Macmillan.

Habermas, Jürgen (1969) *Protestbewegung und Hochschulenreform*. Frankfurt: Suhrkamp.

—— (1981) 'Modernity and postmodernism', *New German Critique* **22**: 3–14.

—— (1992) 'The idea of the university—learning processes', *The New Conservatism: Cultural Criticism and the Historians' Debate*. Cambridge: Polity.

Heidegger, Martin (1985) 'The self-assertion of a German university', *Review of Metaphysics*, **38**: 467–502.

Jacoby, Russell (1987) *The Last Intellectuals: American Culture in the Age of Academe*. New York: Basic Books.

Jaspers, Karl (1960) *The Idea of the University*. London: Peter Owen.

Kant, Immanuel (1996) 'An answer to the question: what is enlightenment?', in J. Schmidt (ed.) *What is Enlightenment? Eighteenth-Century Answers and Twentieth-Century Questions*. Berkeley: University of California Press.

—— (1979) *The Conflict of the Faculties*. New York: Abaris Books.

Kerr, Charles (1963) *The Uses of the University*. Cambridge, MA: Harvard University Press.

Lyotard, Jean-Francois (1984) *The Postmodern Condition: A Report on Knowledge*. Manchester: Manchester University Press.

Marcuse, Herbert (1964) *One-Dimension Man*. London: Routledge & Kegan Paul.

—— (1968) *Essay on Liberation*. Boston: Beacon Press.

Müller, E. (ed.) (1990) *Gelengenliche Gedanken Über Universitäten*. Leipzig: Reclam Verlag.

Newby, Howard (1999) 'Higher education in the twenty-first century', *New Reporter*, **16**(14), March.

Newman, John Henry (1996) edited by F. Turner (ed.) *The Idea of the University*. New Haven: Yale University Press.

Nowotny, Helga (2000) 'Transgressive competence: the narrative of expertise', *European Journal of Social Theory*, **3**(1): 5–21.

Parsons, Talcott (1974) 'The university "bundle": a study of the balance between differentiation and integration', in N. Smelser and G. Almond (eds) *Public Higher Education in California: Growth, Structural Change, and Conflict*. Berkeley: University of California Press.

—— and Platt, Gerald (1973) *The American University*. Cambridge, MA: Harvard University Press.

Popper, Karl (1945) *The Open Societies and its Enemies*. New York: Harper & Row.

Readings, Bill (1996) *The University in Ruins*. Cambridge, MA: Harvard University Press.

Reuben, Julie (1996) *The Making of the Modern University: Intellectual Transformation and the Marginalization of Morality*. Cambridge, MA: Harvard University Press.

Riesman, David (1998) *On Higher Education: The Academic Enterprise in an Era of Rising Student Consumerism*. New Brunswick: Transaction Publishers.

—— and Jencks, Charles (1968) *The Academic Revolution*. New York: Doubleday.

Ringer, Fritz (1969) *The Decline of the German Mandrians*. Cambridge, MA: Harvard University Press.

Rothblatt, Sheldon (1997) *The Modern University and its Discontents: The Fate of Newman's Legacies in Britain and America*. Cambridge: Cambridge University Press.

—— and Wittrock, Bjorn (eds) (1993) *The European and American University since 1800*. Cambridge: Cambridge University Press.

Scott, Peter (ed.) (1998) *The Globalization of Higher Education*. Buckingham: Open University Press.

Shils, Edward (1997) *The Calling of Higher Education: The Academic Ethic and Other Essays on Higher Education*. Chicago: Chicago University Press.

Slaughter, Shelia and Leslie, Larry (1997) *Academic Capitalism: Politics, Policies, and the Entrepreneurial University*. Baltimore: Johns Hopkins University Press.

Smith, Anthony and Webster, Frank (eds) (1997) *The Postmodern University?* Buckingham: Open University Press.

Strydom, Piet (1999) 'Triple contingency—the theoretical problem of the public in communication societies', *Philosophy and Social Criticism*, **25**(2): 1–25.

—— (2000) *Discourse and Knowledge: The Making of Enlightenment Sociology*. Liverpool: Liverpool University Press.

Touraine, Alain (1971) *The May Movement: Revolt and Reform*. New York: Random House.

Veblen, Thorstein (1962) *The Higher Learning in America*, New Haven, CT: Yale University Press.

von Humboldt, Wilhelm (1970) 'University reform in Germany: reports and documents', *Minerva*, **8**: 242–50.

Wagner, Peter (1994) *A Sociology of Modernity: Liberty and Discipline*. London: Routledge.

Wallerstein, Immanuel (1969) *University in Turmoil: The Politics of Change*. New York: Atheneum.

4

The University in the 'Global' Economy

Masao Miyoshi

INTRODUCTION

Higher education is undergoing a rapid sea change. Everyone knows and senses it, but few try to comprehend its scope or imagine its future. This two-part chapter makes some guesses by observing recent events and recalling the bygone past. Part 1 describes the quickening conversion of learning into intellectual property and of the university into the global corporation in today's research universities in the United States—and, increasingly, everywhere else. Part 2 puzzles over the failure of the humanities at this moment as a supposed agency of criticism and intervention.

I have presented this essay in various stages at the following institutions and conferences: the conference on Critical Theories: China and West, at the Chinese Academy of Social Sciences and the Humanities and the Human Normal University; the Border Studies Research Circle, the University of Wisconsin, Madison; the Inter-Asia Cultural Studies Conference, the National Tsing Hua University, Taipei; the conference on Aesthetics and Difference: Cultural Diversity, Literature, and the Arts, at UC Riverside; the Center for the Study of Race and Ethnicity and the Department of Ethnic Studies, UC San Diego; the Critical Theory Institute, UC Irvine; the Institute for Global Studies, the University of Minnesota; and the Freeman Lecture Series in Oregon. I am in debt to the organizers and audiences for their responses. Many friends and colleagues have read the manuscript also in various versions, and I am grateful for their comments and critiques: Marti Archibald, Paul Bové, Chen Kuan-Hsing, Eric Cazdyn, Noam Chomsky, Rey Chow, Arif Dirlik, H. D. Harootunian, Gerald Iguchi, Fredric Jameson, Mary Layoun, Meaghan Morris, Richard Okada, Edward Said, Rosaura Sanchez, Ulrike Schaede, Don Wayne, Wang Fengzhen, and Rob Wilson. I would like to thank especially Allen Paau, the director of the Office of Technology Transfer, UC San Diego, who spent a generous amount of time with me on this chapter.

PART I. THE CONVERSION OF LEARNING INTO INTELLECTUAL PROPERTY

Richard C. Atkinson, the president of the University of California (UC) since 1995, has repeatedly sought to identify the role of the world's largest research university. As he sees it, the goal of today's research university is to build an alliance with industries: 'The program works like this. A UC researcher joins with a scientist or engineer from a private company to develop a research proposal. A panel of experts drawn from industry and academia selects the best projects for funding' (Atkinson and Penhoet 1996). Thus, although university research encompasses 'basic research, applied research, and development,' basic research, now called 'curiosity research . . . driven by a sheer interest in the phenomena,' is justified only because 'it may reach the stage where there is potential for application and accordingly a need for applied research' (Atkinson 1997a). Development—that is, industrial utility—is the principal objective of the research university.

In another short essay titled 'Universities and the Knowledge-Based Economy,' Atkinson remarks that 'universities like Cambridge University and other European universities almost all take the view that university research should be divorced from any contact with the private sector.' In contrast to this 'culture that eschewed commercial incentives,' there has always been in the United States 'a tendency to build bridges between universities and industry' (Atkinson 1996a; cf. Gracie 1999). This is the background, as he sees it, of places such as Silicon Valley and Route 128, and he proceeds to claim that one in four American biotech companies is in the vicinity of a UC campus, and that 40 per cent of Californian biotech companies, including three of the world's largest, Amgen, Chiron, and Genetech, were started by UC scientists.

How does this marketized university protect its academic integrity? Atkinson is confident: 'Our experience over the last 15 years or so has taught us a great deal about safeguarding the freedom to publish research findings, avoiding possible conflicts of interest and in general protecting the university's academic atmosphere and the free rein that faculty and students have to pursue what is of interest to them' (Atkinson 1996b). The issue of academic freedom—as well as the conflict of interest and commitment—is in fact complex and treacherous in today's entrepreneurial university, as we will see later. However, in this essay, written soon after he took office, Atkinson dismisses academic freedom as an already resolved negotiation between 'academic atmosphere' and personal interest, and he has not touched the subject again since.

Like most university administrators today, Atkinson makes no extensive educational policy statement, not to say a full articulation of his educational views and thoughts, most announcements being scattered among truncated speeches or Op-Ed pieces (Atkinson and Tuzin 1992). The days of Robert M. Hutchins and Derek Bok, never mind Wilhelm von Humboldt and John Henry Newman, are long gone. It is thus perfectly understandable, if somewhat disquieting to a few, that he should give minimally short shrift to research in the humanities and social sciences in the university.

According to Atkinson (1997*b*), the university does have another role as 'the shaper of character, a critic of values, a guardian of culture,' but that is in 'education and scholarship,' which presumably are wholly distinct activities from serious R & D. He thus pays tributes, in his Pullias Lecture at the University of Southern California, to only one specific example each from the two divisions of human knowledge. As for the social sciences, he mentions just one book, *Habits of the Heart*, a mainstream recommendation of American core values, and asserts that the social sciences shape 'our public discussion of the values that animate our society.' The Humanities Research Institute, at UC Irvine, similarly, is 'an important voice in the dialogue about the humanities and their contributions to our culture and our daily lives.' Aside from this reference to one book and one institution, Atkinson has little else to say about the work in the humanities and in the social sciences. He then goes on to assert that the existence of research programs in the humanities and the social sciences at a university devoted to applied science is itself important. Of course, it is possible that I missed some of his pronouncements, but as far as I could discover, there is no other statement concerning the humanities and the social sciences by Atkinson (1998*a*). His listlessness to any research outside of R & D is unmistakable.

A mere generation ago, in 1963, another president of the UC system, Clark Kerr (1995), published *The Uses of the University*, originally given as one of the Godkin Lectures at Harvard University, in which he defined the university as a service station responsive to multiple social forces rather than an autonomous site of learning. These forces, in actuality, consisted mainly of national defence, agribusiness, and other corporate interests. Yet the multiversity was defined as the mediator of various and diverse expectations, however one-sided its arbitration may have been. It was still proposed to be an interventionary agent. The book was reread the following year when the UC Berkeley campus exploded with the demand for free speech by students, many of whom were fresh from the voter registration drive in the South that summer. The students and faculty who took an antimultiversity stand insisted that the university not only produced multiple skills and applications but also 'enrich[ed] and enlighten[ed] the lives of its students—informing them with the values of the intellect.' Intellectual honesty, health, and the social vision of a better future were the components of higher education for them (Wolin and Schaar 1965). Thus the movement for civil rights, racial equality, peace, feminism—together with free speech—found its place inside the university.

Kerr's multiversity was perhaps the first candid admission of the university as part of the corporate system by anyone in the administration of higher education. It is crucial, however, to realize that his recognition of its multiple functions was yet a far cry from Atkinson's unself-conscious idea of the university as a site dedicated to corporate R & D. Conversely, the antimultiversity view of the students and faculty of the 1960s matter-of-factly countered Kerr's reformulation with the long-established tradition of 'liberal education.' In the hindsight of the new millennium, this mainstream fable of liberal education as free inquiry also requires re-examination and reformulation. We need to register here, at any rate, that today's corporatized university—which would have been an unspeakable sacrilege for many less than a generation ago—is now being embraced with hardly any complaint or criticism by the faculty, students, or society at large. What is it that has transpired between the university as the mediator and the university as the corporate partner, between the protest of the 1960s and the silence of today? Why this acquiescence? We need to return to the beginning of the modern university so that we may see more clearly the institutional changes alongside the unfolding of modern history.

The modern university was built around 1800 to fill the need for knowledge production as Europe and the United States prepared themselves for expansion overseas. Scientific and technological research was its primary programme, as it was launched in the name of enlightenment and progress. Together with practical knowledge, however, what is now called the humanities and the social sciences was advanced by the emerging bourgeoisie. But the educational transformation from the ancient regime to the revolutionary bourgeois democracy was not as radical as one might suspect. On the one hand, an old-style university education was the noblesse oblige of aristocracy, and despite the self-serving devotion to the maintenance of its class position, it claimed to be anti-utilitarian or useless. Erudition, learning for the sake of learning, refinement, intellectual pleasure—such privileged and elevated play constituted the goal of aristocratic education. Bourgeois revolutionary education, on the other hand, was rational, universal, secular, and enlightened. It, too, claimed to be neutral and objective rather than partisan or utilitarian. It is under these circumstances that 'liberal' education continued to be a crucial idea of the modern university. There was, however, a more central agenda of founding the modern national state, which demanded the construction, information, and dissemination of the national identity by inculcating common language and centralizing history, culture, literature, and geography. The state promoted national knowledge closely aligned with practical knowledge. Despite its pretence, national knowledge was thus profoundly partisan, and liberal education and national education were often in conflict. They could be, at the same time, in agreement, too: After all, the nineteenth-century state was founded by the bourgeoisie, and it was willing to accommodate the surviving aristocracy, although it was adamant in excluding the interest of the emergent working class. Liberal education was tolerated, or even encouraged, since it promoted bourgeois class interests. It appropriated courtly arts, music, poetry, drama, and history, and, over the years, established the canon now designated as high and serious culture. Liberal education and national education contradicted and complemented each other, as the state was engaged in its principal task of expanding the market and colony by containing overseas barbarians, rivalling the neighbouring nations, and suppressing the aspiring underclass. The modern university as envisioned by Johann Gottlieb

Fichte, Humboldt, Newman, Charles Eliot, T. H. Huxley, Matthew Arnold, Daniel Coit Gilman, Thorstein Veblen, Hutchins, and Jacques Barzun contained such contradiction and negotiation of utilitarian nationism and anti-utilitarian inquiry.

Newman had his church, and his university—a separate site—was merely to educate the 'gentlemen,' Lord Shaftsbury's cultured men, who were aloof to the utility of expertise and profession as well as oblivious to lives and aspirations of the lower order. Newman's (1996) heart always belonged to aristocratic Oxford, even while he was writing *The Idea of a University* for a Catholic university in Dublin. Huxley's scientific research, on the other hand, was devoted to practice and utility, and, unlike the Oxbridge tradition, it was to provide expertise and profession, not Arnoldian culture and criticism. The myth of the university as a site of liberal education, that is, class-free, unrestricted, self-motivated, and unbiased learning, survives to this day. And yet academia has always been ambivalent. In the name of classless learning, it sought to mould its members in the bourgeois class identity. Emerson's 'American Scholar' deployed a strategy of defining American learning as non-American or trans-American. In short, it managed to be both American and non-American at the same time, while making American synonymous with universal. This hidden contradiction can readily be compared to Arnold's idea of 'culture,' free and spontaneous consciousness, which is supposedly free from class bias and vulgar self-interest. To safeguard this culture, however, Arnold (1932) did not hesitate to invoke the 'sacred' 'state,' which will unflinchingly squash any working-class 'anarchy and disorder,' as he advocated during the second Reform Bill agitation around the late 1860s.

In the United States, Abraham Lincoln signed the Morrill Act in 1862, setting 'the tone for the development of American universities, both public and private' (Kerr 1995, p. 35). This land-grant movement introduced schools of agriculture, engineering, home economics, and business administration; and later, the land-grant colleges and universities were required to teach a military training program, ROTC. Thus no modern university has been free from class interests, and many critical writers chose, and were often forced, to stay outside—for example, Marx, Nietzsche, Rosa Luxemburg, Bertrand Russell, Antonio Gramsci, I. F. Stone, and Frantz Fanon. But perhaps because of the as yet not completely integrated relations of money and power, the university has at times allowed some room for scholars who would transcend their immediate class interests. Such eccentrics, though not many in number, have formed an important history of their own, as we can see in our century in Jun Tosaka, Herbert Marcuse, Jean-Paul Sartre, Simone de Beauvoir, Raymond Williams, C. Wright Mills, and E. P. Thompson, all deceased now. There are others who are still active, yet the university as an institution has served Caesar and Mammon all the while manifesting its fealty to Minerva, Clio, and the Muses.

The three wars in the twentieth century—the First World War, the Second World War, and the cold war (which included the conflicts in Korea and Vietnam)—intensified the proclivity of the university to serve the interests of the state. Beginning with weapons research, such as the Manhattan Project, research extended far beyond physics and chemistry, and engineering and biology, to reach the humanities and the social sciences. Following the organization of the intelligence system (the Office of Strategic Services, or OSS), the humanities soon became far more broadly complicit with the formation of state/capitalist ideology (Winks 1987; Chomsky 1997). In literature, the fetishism of irony, paradox, and complexity helped to depoliticize, that is, to conceal capitalist contradictions, by invoking the 'open-minded' distantiation of bourgeois modernism (Moretti 1988). The canon was devised and reinforced. In arts, abstract expressionism was promoted to counter Soviet realism (Guilbaut 1983), and in history, progress and development were the goal toward which democracy inexorably marched. In the United States at least, the social sciences have always been directed towards policy and utility; and by compartmentalizing the world into areas, area studies has mapped out national interests in both the humanities and the social sciences (Cumings 1997). Such nationalization of the university was slowly challenged after the 1960s, and by the end of the cold war, around 1990, the hegemony of the state was clearly replaced by the dominant power of the global market.

What separates Atkinson from Kerr is the end of the cold war and the globalization of the economy, two events that are merely two aspects of the same capitalist development. What, then, is this event, and how does it affect the university? Globalization is certainly not new: Capitalism has always looked for new markets, cheaper labour, and greater productivity everywhere, as Marx and Engels pointed out in the *Manifesto of the Communist Party* 150 years ago. The internationalization of trade between 1880 and the First World War was proportionately as great as the current cross-border trade.[1] This time, however, expansion is thoroughly different in its intensity and magnitude as a result of the startling technological development and sheer volume of production.

Because of the phenomenal advance in communication and transportation since Second World War, capital, labour, production, products, and raw materials circulate with unprecedented ease and speed in search of maximum profit across nations and regions, radically diminishing along the way local and regional differences. The state has always been in service for the rich and mighty, and yet it did, from time to time, remember that it had regulatory and mediatory roles. The state was not always exclusively their agency. Now, however, with the rise of immense multinational and transnational corporations, the state, with its interventionary power, has visibly declined. It cannot deter the dominant downsizing and cost-cutting trends that often produce acute pain and suffering among the workers. It cannot restrain the immense flow of cash and investment in the world. If anything, the state supports the corporate interest, as can be seen in its repeated drives for the North American Free Trade Agreement (NAFTA) and

---

[1] 'One measure of the extent to which product markets are integrated is the ratio of trade to output. This has increased sharply in most countries since 1950. But by this measure Britain and France are only slightly more open to trade today than they were in 1913, while Japan is less open now than then' (*Economist*, 18 October 1997, 79–80).

the Multilateral Agreement on Investment (MAI) (Lazarus 1997). Untrammelled entrepreneurship and profiteering thus grow. And the extraordinary rejection of the public sector, totality, and communitarianism in favour of privatization, individualism, and identitarianism is pervasive. This results in a fierce intensification of competition, careerism, opportunism, and, finally, the fragmentation and atomization of society.

Environmentally, the earth has reached the point of no return for the human race. There is no longer a square inch left on earth that is not contaminated by industrial pollution. Environmental degradation is now irreversible: The only thing humans can do under the capitalist system is to try to slow down the rate of decay and to attempt a little local patchwork repair (McKibben 1998; Harvey 1996).

The most conspicuous social consequence of globalization, however, is the intensification of the gap between the rich and the poor. Globally, 80 per cent of capital circulates among two dozen countries. Wealth is concentrated in the industrialized countries, and yet it continues to flow only in one direction, toward the North. To take just one example, Uganda's income per capita is $200 a year—compared to $39,833 of the richest country, Luxembourg. The life expectancy in Uganda is forty-two years—compared to Japan's eighty years—and one in five children there dies before the age of five. Finally, 20 per cent of its population is now afflicted with HIV and yet its annual debt service is twice the government's spending on primary health. There are countries worse off than Uganda. The uneven distribution of wealth is indeed pervasive in every region. Thus 225 of the richest individuals have assets totaling $1 trillion, equal to the collective annual income of the poorest 47 per cent of the human population (2.5 billion), and these billionaires, though mostly concentrated in the North, include seventy-eight in developing countries (United Nations Development Programme 1998).

The national picture is no better. The inequity in wages and incomes in the United States was widely discussed from 1995 to 1997. Although we do not hear much about it nowadays, it does not mean the discrepancy is narrowing. Everyone knows the epic salary and stock options of Michael Eisner, CEO of Walt Disney Company, or the assets of Bill Gates. Twenty-five years ago, in 1974, CEOs of major American corporations were paid thirty-five times the wage of an average American worker. In 1994, compensation for CEOs jumped to 187 times the pay of ordinary workers. According to a special report in *Business Week* (1998), the average executive pay is now 326 times what a factory worker earns. This gap is greater than that between Luxembourg and Uganda. Wealth is far more concentrated as the income goes up—that is, between 1979 and 1995, the income of the bottom 20 per cent fell by 9 per cent, while the top 20 per cent gained by 26 per cent (Sanger 1997). From 1992 to 1995, a recent three-year period in which household net worth grew by more than $2.7 trillion, the richest 1 per cent boosted their share of the total from 30.2 per cent to 35.1 per cent. What's more, almost all of that gain accrued to the top half of that segment, a group that saw its average net worth jump from $8 to $11.3 million. On the other hand, the bottom 90 per cent of households slipped to just 31.5 per cent, down from 32.9 per cent (Koretz 1997; Madrick 1997). Although the unemployment rate has fallen dramatically recently, many jobs are on a contingency basis—that is, part-time or temporary—with no health and retirement benefits, even in the late spring of 1999, after a long period of the so-called booming economy (Reich 1999). The state does not intervene: On the contrary, the tax structure, public works programmes, defence expenditures, health and welfare policies, and business deregulation are all being reorganized on behalf of the rich and the corporate (Johnston 1997; *Economist* 1997*b*). The poor are left to the paltry trickle down or simply to their own meagre resources.

Such an economy—transnational and all absorbing—obviously has effects on the university. The most structural and decisive change is the so-called technology transfer from the university to industry, accelerated with the passage of the Bayh-Dole Act of 1980. I will discuss it fully later, but let me start here with the obvious. In the specific curricula, nation-centred disciplines have been in decline, and area studies, too, has been re-examined since the end of the cold war. The studies of national literatures and histories, the cornerstone of the humanities for several generations, are visibly losing their attraction. The middle class sends its children to land-grant public institutions that cost less, while the rich send theirs to socially elite private institutions that take pride in their rising tuition fees. The richer students might be more inclined to study the humanities—as they traditionally did before the Second World War—while the poorer students, who need to support themselves by working at least part-time while in school, are prone to choose practical and useful majors that might lead to careers after graduation. The ruling class always likes to remain useless, while expecting the workers to be useful. And such political economy of student enrollment obviously affects the curriculum. The humanities suffer. Pure science—mathematics and physics, for instance—similarly languishes from diminished support. Thus academic programmes are being discontinued, while disciplines in greater demand are being expanded—often regardless of their intellectual significance (Miyoshi 1998).

The so-called job crisis in the humanities is not a consequence of an economic downturn as it was, in fact, in the 1970s, nor is it a temporary event resulting from a demographic shift. The basis of national literatures and cultures is very much hollowed out, as the nation-state declines as the hegemonic imaginary. The humanities as they are now constituted in academia are no longer desired or warranted. There is a decisive change in the academic outlook and policy to de-emphasize the humanities and to shift resources to applied sciences. Culture—arts and literature—is being driven out of academia, just as in the old days, and has every sign of being reorganized into media, entertainment, and tourism—all consumer activities—that would be assigned a far more legitimate role in the emergent global economy. I will discuss this further in Part II.[2]

---

[2] In the fall of 1998, the Modern Language Association of America (MLA) published Profession 1998, a booklet 'covering a range of topics of professional concern.' It is, however, hopelessly out of touch with the changing conditions of the profession and the global culture around it. Its last essay, 'Bob's Job: Campus Crises and "Adjunct" Education,' by former president Sandra

Aside from such vicissitudes in specific disciplines, the impact of global corporatization is clearest in the radical change in the general outlook and policy on academic productivity. The university is re-examined in terms of cost and output. Course enrollment, degree production, and PhD placement are closely watched and policed, as if all such figures were industrial statistics (MLA 1997).[3] Scholarship is measured by quantified publication and citation record. More importantly, the development office dealing with grants and endowments is one of the most active parts of the university (Arenson 1998). University presses—which used to publish scholarly monographs for the sake of the autonomous academic enterprise, not for profit but for scholarship—are now reorganizing their inventories to make themselves commercially self-supporting. Once, every university-press title had more than one thousand orders in a vanity-press setup, where 'one group wrote, one published, and one bought the books: a comfortable circuit leading to secure and tenured jobs all around.' Library orders have since been radically cut, now averaging below three hundred copies per title and falling. Whole academic areas, such as 'literary criticism or Latin American history,' are already being eliminated from university presses (Pochoda 1997; Miller 1997). The conventional trajectory of the completion of a doctoral dissertation, followed by its publication for tenure and another monograph for full professorship, is not likely to last much longer. Stanley Fish, professor of English, who also served as the director of Duke University Press, describes/prescribes that university presses 'no longer think in terms of a 900 to 1,500 print run' but switch to those that 'sell between 5,000 and 40,000 copies.' Similarly, the director of the

M. Gilbert, personalizes the historical transformation of today's American culture into a memory of her friend Bob J. Griffin. Profoundly saddening, Bob's death, however, demands a far more clear-headed analysis of the political economy of the United States in the 1990s than the episode of a man with a PhD in English from UC Berkeley who died in his mid-sixties as a part-time composition teacher earning $15,000 without health insurance. The MLA seems committed to evading the real historical situation, thereby perhaps duplicating similar cases in the future as it keeps its operation. As another erstwhile friend of Bob's, I feel the urgency of the need to face honestly the academic–professional situation today.

[3] Placement statistics are, of course, indispensable. The question is: What to do with these figures? A recent MLA report finds that of the 7,598 PhDs in English and foreign languages earned between 1990 and 1995, 4,188—55 per cent—failed to find a tenure-track job in the year the degree was awarded. The report then compares the job crisis to earlier crises and to those in other disciplines. The report readily recognizes the 'pedagogical and professional—indeed, a cultural—crises of great magnitude.' It then points out that the current graduate programme is mainly 'aimed at the major research institution rather than a future in the community colleges, junior colleges, and small sectarian schools that now provide our profession with so large a proportion of its work.' Its subsequent recommendations—to cut the size of the graduate program, for instance—should be taken seriously. Yet the report hardly considers the changing nature of the humanities programme, or rather of the university itself, which is at the root of this change in higher education. Even if all the funding crises were solved today, the crisis in the intellectual content of learning and teaching in higher education in the United States, or perhaps any other place, would not change. Suppose all the PhDs in the humanities were able to secure tenure-track positions this year. Would this solve the crisis of the content of the humanities teaching (MLA 1997)?

University of Minnesota Press ominously predicts that 'in two years there will be hardly any monographs on the market' (Shulevitz 1995).

Academic downsizing is now accepted as inevitable (O'Brien 1997; Honan 1998; Martin 1998). Instead of regular faculty, contingency instructors—graduate students and temporary hires without benefits and tenure—are shouldering a major portion of undergraduate teaching (MLA 1997; Mydans 1995; Berger 1998).[4] Universities are making use of Internet Web sites for many undergraduate classes. The California Virtual University (CVU) has now been officially launched, offering hundreds of on-line courses through extension programs. The CVU involves both public and private institutions of higher education (the UC and California State University campuses, Stanford University, the University of Southern California, among others) to form a 'global academic village,' as one of its planners calls it. As an instructional supplement, digital programmes can, of course, be helpful. But the main objective of CVU lies elsewhere. Although distance learning has yet to replace human faculty and its popularity is indeed far from guaranteed, its money-saving potential is quite obvious. Numerous virtual universities are spreading across the nation and even the world: In addition to CVU, there are New York University's profit-seeking subsidiary; Western Governors University; Pennsylvania State University's 'World Campus;' Florida State University; as well as Britain's well-tested Open University. There is also a for-profit behemoth, the University of Phoenix, now the largest degree-granting private university in the United States, which employed, until a few years ago, just seven full-time faculty aided by thirty-four hundred part-time teachers who were paid $1,500 for teaching a course. The profit of the Apollo Group, which owns the University of Phoenix, is rising dramatically.[5] There are resistance movements among the faculty who might be replaced by the growing digital simulacra. Thus, nationally, institutions such as UCLA, the University of Maine, the University of Washington, and York University in Canada are testing the strength of faculty opposition (Weiss 1998; Noble 1999).

To remain competitive in attracting students as well as grants and endowments, however, stellar professors are fiercely fought over: A dozen universities now have at least one faculty member who makes more than $750,000 in salary and benefits—very much like corporate CEOs who tower over hugely underpaid workers (Griffiths 1998). The policy of forging alliances with industries is firmly in place on American campuses everywhere. Fearful of the disappearance of federal support, the universities not only are in search of corporate assistance

[4] 'In the PhD-granting [English] departments, graduate student instructors taught 63% of the first-year writing sections, part-timers 19%, and full-time non-tenure-track faculty members 14%, on average.' The corresponding figures in foreign-language departments are 68, 7, and 15 per cent (MLA 1997). A large number of PhDs from literature departments remain jobless, and for them even such temporary lecturerships are highly desirable.

[5] 'Because of questions raised by accreditors, the university increased the size of its full-time faculty—it now has 45 full-times on board' (Solely 1998, p. 16). The Apollo Group (nd), Phoenix's parent corporation, has increased its revenues more than three times in five years, from $124,720,000 in FY 1994 to $391,082,000 in FY 1998.

but are aggressively forming joint research centres. In southern California alone, UC Irvine is building a biomedical centre to facilitate the commercialization of university science and to aid the formation of companies. UCLA and USC each received $100 million from an entrepreneur to build a biomedical engineering centre (Flanagan 1998). Examples seem endless, as we will see below.

Such close alliance unavoidably leads to a clubby intercourse between university and industrial managers. Thus many university presidents and chancellors sit on corporate boards, including the presidents of the University of Pennsylvania (Aetna Life and Casualty Company and Electronic Data Submission Systems); Lehigh University (Parker Hannifin Corporation); Georgetown University (Walt Disney Company); UC Berkeley (Wells Fargo); Drew University (Aramark, Bell Atlantic, United HealthCare, Beneficial Corporation, Fiduciary Trust Company International, Amerada Hess Corporation); the University of Texas (Freeport McMoRan Copper and Gold Inc.); Occidental College (ARCO, IBM, Northrop Grumman Corporation); the University of California system (Consolidated Nevada Goldfields Corporation, Qualcomm Inc., and San Diego Gas and Electric/Enova Corporation); just to name a few. Many of these administrators also receive sizable compensation in addition to their academic salaries (e.g. the president of Penn received $200,000 in addition to her regular compensation of $514,878) (Lively 1998; Arenson 1998). Finally, Robert C. Dynes, who had left Bell Laboratories after twenty-two years of service as a researcher and manager to become the vice-chancellor under Atkinson at UC San Diego, produced a booklet called 'Partners in Business' after he replaced Atkinson as the chancellor. At a breakfast meeting in 1996 of the San Diego Biocommerce Association (BIOCOM), Dynes remarked that basic research is no longer being conducted by major corporations and that universities are the source of new technologies. Before this talk, he was introduced by the BIOCOM board member as the 'CEO' of UC San Diego. The MC for the occasion was a UC regent, who also served on the committee that chose Dynes for the chancellorship of UC San Diego.

Conversely, many captains of industry have for generations served on university boards of trustees and regents. Veblen (1969) complained about this intrusion of the moneyed and powerful into the academic territory years back. There are other studies of university ownership in the early twentieth century (Barrow 1990). Although there may be a few exceptions, nearly all the trustees and regents of state universities are political appointments, making certain that the corporate interest is securely represented. In more recent days, the selection of the members of the governing board seems to be more blatantly corporation oriented, although systematic studies, reflecting the general apathy of scholars, are not widely available, as far as I have been able to determine.

More importantly, the CEO has now become the only model for presidents and chancellors of universities. Harold T. Shapiro (1998), president of Princeton University, for one, asserts that 'university presidents are their institutions' CEO.' The age-old tradition of choosing a college president for his scholarship, vision, character, or even political or military fame is irretrievably gone for now. At least for the foreseeable future, the academic head is a corporate manager who is expected to expand the institutional and corporate base and alliance, build intellectual property, raise funds and endowments, increase labour productivity, finesse the public relations with external organizations, including various governmental agencies, and run the machinery with dexterity. The university–corporation identification cannot be much closer.

Let me turn at this point to the issue that is central to the structural transformation of the knowledge industry, that is, today's practice of university 'technology transfer.' Atkinson's remarks cited at the beginning of this essay are neither exceptional nor extreme, although they are rhetorically more explicit and less guarded than most in today's academic world. Similar views are being expressed by administrators of higher education—his neighbour, Gerhard Casper (1998), president of Stanford, for one—and they accurately express the policies and practices of most research universities in the United States now.

On 12 December 1980, Senators Birch Bayh and Bob Dole passed a bipartisan bill, the Bayh–Dole Act (Public Law 96-517), the Patent and Trademark Act Amendments of 1980. This law was written in response to the prospects of an intensifying global economic competition, a feared (though not actual) cutback in federal research funding, pressure toward corporate downsizing, including R & D, and the resultant greater need of academic research. During the years of the Reagan–Thatcher economy, the use of public resources for private enterprises was fast gaining respect and significance. The law, as it has been since repeatedly revised, enables universities to commercialize—that is, to own, patent, and retain title to—inventions developed from federally funded research programmes. Universities and research institutions could at first commercialize through non-profit start-ups or small national companies, but later through any businesses, regardless of size or nationality. Prior to 1980, fewer than 250 patents were granted to institutions each year, whereas in Fiscal Year 1996, over 2,000, and in Fiscal Year 1997, over 2,740 patents (up by 26 per cent) were granted. Since 1980, more than 1,500 start-up companies, including 333 in FY 1997 (up 34 per cent from 246 in FY 1996), have been formed on technologies created at universities and research institutions. The revenues, in the form of licences, equity, options, fees, and so forth, are still relatively small. Total gross licence income received from licences and options of the respondents to the Association of University Technology Managers (AUTM) in FY 1997 was only $698.5 million. (Still, it was up 18 per cent from 591.7 million in FY 1996, which in turn was up 19.6 per cent from $494.7 million in FY 1995. That is, there has been an 'exponential' increase in technology licencing activities.) Although the direct revenues constitute merely a fraction of the total university budget, or even of the university-sponsored research expenditures (from 1 to 5 per cent), these small figures belie the actual economic dynamics of university R & D (Council on Governmental Relations 1993).

University–industry relations are far more conjoined than usually understood. First, start-up companies form a satellite R & D community, providing students and graduates, for instance, with jobs and training, while the companies receive information and technology from the universities. Also, academic licencing is said to have supported 250,000 high-paying jobs and generated $30 billion in the American economy in FY 1997 (compared to 212,500 jobs and $24.8 billion in the previous year). Second, some of the university-related labs and companies grow into corporations that then form industrial research parks such as Silicon Valley, Route 128, Research Triangle (Duke, University of North Carolina, and North Carolina State University), Princeton Corridor, Silicon Hills (Texas), the Medical Mile (Penn and Temple University), Optics Valley (University of Arizona), and the Golden Triangle (UC San Diego). These are the late-twentieth-century campus landscapes that have replaced the Gothic towers of Heidelberg with their duels, songs, and romance, or Oxford and Cambridge with their chapels, pubs, and booksellers.

The competition among universities for a larger share in R & D resources is fervent in search of both project grants and licence incomes themselves and the prestige that comes with being among the top research universities. The UC system is by far the largest research university, with sponsored research expenditures surpassing $1.6 billion, followed by Johns Hopkins University at $942 million and MIT at $713 million in FY 1997 (AUTM 1998). In gross licence income, too, UC leads at $67.3 million, followed by Stanford ($51.8 million), Columbia University ($50.3 million), and MIT ($21.2 million). UC is also a major recipient of federal research dollars, attracting over 10 per cent of all federal funds spent on research in American universities ($12.3 billion in FY 1996). It must be remembered that these federal funds generate university inventions that are then licensed or contracted to commercial developers. (The corresponding figure for industrial sources in FY 1996 is $1.5 billion, a little over one-tenth of the federal funding.) In the middle of this heightened economic activity, the university faculty ('inventors') earn from 25 to 50 per cent—depending on the amount and institutions—of the licence royalties from the institutions in whose names the research is conducted and the patents are issued. According to Atkinson (1998b), UC is 'an $11.5 billion-a-year enterprise. The State of California contributes about two billion of that $11.5 billion, which means that for every dollar the State provides we generate almost five dollars in other funds.' Isn't this the source of his conviction regarding the future of the research university of the United States or the world?

Concerning the transfer of federally funded research results to industry, the conversion of nonprofit scholarship to for-profit R & D might well be deemed justifiable on the grounds that inert federal funds are being used and activated by private developers for public benefits. The private sector makes profits, thereby expanding the economic base; students receive direct training, too. Thus the university is made directly serviceable to the public. The high-tech inflow may be said to result in a sharp rise in living standards and the urbanization of an area, benefiting the entire community around the university and the research park, as mentioned above.

There are, however, a number of traps and snares that enthusiastic administrators and policymakers are all too eager to ignore. First, the emphasis on patenting, that is, the conversion of knowledge into intellectual property, means the exclusion of others from sharing the knowledge. The fear of public disclosure that would nullify the commercial possibility of a patent and licensing income hampers the free flow of information that would be facilitated by the conventional means of papers in scholarly journals. Federal sponsorship ought to offer wide-open access to all discoveries and inventions created under it. Patenting delays the dissemination of information, and the principle of free inquiry is compromised. 'Communication among researchers suffers, when "the rules of business precede the rules of science"; colleagues become unwilling to share their data.' (Shulman 1999, p. 51).

Second, the real beneficiaries of academic technological inventions are not consumers and general taxpayers but corporations and entrepreneurs who often reap enormous profits through less-than-equitable pricing. If the Bayh–Dole Act was meant to make federally funded inventions available to the public at large, such an intention is not always fulfilled. Let me cite two instances of the abuse of federal funding. One of the most notorious cases is the 1993 agreement between the Scripps Research Institute and Sandoz, an aggressive Switzerland-based biotechnology multinational corporation. In exchange for a grant of $300 million, Scripps gave Sandoz a major role in its Joint Scientific Council, access to research findings even before notifying the funding agency (the National Institutes of Health [NIH]), and licences for marketing Scripps's entire discoveries, all funded by the federal government to the tune of $1 billion. The deal was investigated by a congressional subcommittee, and Scripps and Sandoz were eventually forced to scale down the contract (Coale 1998). Scripps may not strictly be a university, but it is a degree-granting academic institution. A very similar agreement was made between Sandoz and the Dana-Farber Institute, a Harvard teaching hospital. For a $100 million grant, Dana-Farber gave Sandoz the rights to colon-gene research that had been funded by the US government (Soley 1995). Further, the agreement stipulates that anyone who accepts Sandoz money must give Sandoz licensing rights to their research findings. Corporations are saving a huge amount of money by letting universities conduct research and are reaping the profits by investing a relatively meagre amount in fees and royalties. Their funding of some aspects of the research is far from ample or sufficient. Shouldn't a portion of the corporate profit be returned to the public, that is, the taxpayers?

Just as alarming as the uses made of federally funded research is the problem of conflict of interest and/or commitment—inasmuch as it involves the question of academic integrity, free intellectual inquiry, and academic freedom. A case that is not a direct instance of technology transfer and yet is closely related to the topic suggests the risks of the university–industry alliance. In April 1998, a task force was formed by Atkinson to look into the legitimacy of the active UC faculty to pursue professional interests outside the university. The dean of the College of Natural Resources, a professor of business, a professor of economics, and a professor of law, all from the UC Berkeley campus, had together formed a legal and eco-nomic consulting firm called the Legal and Economic Consulting Group (LECG). According to the official newsletter of the UC Academic Senate, the San Francisco Chronicle discovered that the member of the firm who earned the least stood to own $14 million in LECG stock after the initial public offering, while the mem-ber who earned the most received $33 million in stock. Academics from across the country serve as consultants for the firm, and several have significant con-nections in Washington, DC. The law professor has been a senior economist on the Council of Economic Advisors, and another law professor from UC Berkeley is a major shareholder currently on leave while serving as the deputy assistant attorney general for antitrust at the Justice Department—a job the economist in the group previously held. One of the firm's principals is Laura D'Andrea Tyson, the dean of the UC Berkeley Haas School of Business. She served, one recalls, in the first Clinton administration, first as chair of the White House Council of Economic Advisers, then as national economic adviser to the president and chair of the National Economic Council. The firm has wide-ranging expertise in areas such as antitrust, environmental and natural resource economics, intellectual property, international trade and policy, and privatization, among many others. The firm's clients include not only large corporations but also the governments of such countries as Argentina, Japan, and New Zealand. The dean, Gordon Rausser, sees no conflict of interest or of commitment, while the university administration announces that 'it not only accepts, but encourages outside professional work by its faculty, as such work provides two-way benefits.' (University of California 1998). A conflict of commitment par excellence as I see it, the case divides the jury between those who believe that what one does in one's free time is no one else's business and those who dispute the presumed divisibility of one's commitment. Legally, the distribution of work in an academic employee's time schedule (com-pany time versus private time) is nearly impossible to ascertain (don't the minds wander?), while ethically, the direct and full-scale commercialization of scholarly expertise clearly challenges the idea of a university as a site of free inquiry. In fact, tension is palpable between old-fashioned 'pure' scientists and 'future-oriented' entrepreneurial faculty in many research universities nowadays.

The second conflict-of-interest case—and another example of technology transfer—also concerns the division of one's interest, time, and energy between nonprofit scholarship and for-profit R & D. Gordon Rausser, the same enterpris-ing dean of the College of Natural Resources, UC Berkeley, is involved in another case, this one concerning Sandoz, which has now merged with Ciba-Geigy and is renamed Novartis Pharmaceuticals Corporation, the world's largest biotech firm. The deal is similar to the Sandoz–Harvard partnership. A new Novartis sub-sidiary, the La Jolla based Novartis Agricultural Discovery Institute, Inc., will pay $25 million to UC for research in plant genomics, housekeeping, and graduate-student stipends at the college. In exchange, Novartis will receive first rights to negotiate licences for 30–40 per cent of the research products. Research will be guided by a committee of three Novartis scientists and three UC Berkeley faculty members. Another committee, which will determine which projects to fund, will consist of three UC Berkeley faculty and two Novartis scientists. This is the first research agreement ever made between an entire instructional department of a university and a for-profit corporation. Is this university–industry alliance what was intended by the framers of the 1980 act? Is the public the beneficiary of the released research results? Or the Swiss multinational and the UC entrepreneurs? Is the public private, and the private public? At any rate, the cumulative effects of such research preferences will have a profound and lasting effect on the nature of university learning.

It should also be noted that genetically engineered corn produced by Novartis in Germany has cross-pollinated with nearby natural corn, stirring up a storm of protests in Europe. Future problems involving academic freedom are pre-dictable. As if to pre-empt such fears of infringement, the vice-chancellor for research at UC Berkeley stated, 'This research collaboration was arrived at in an open process that was highly sensitive to the public interest and to traditional campus concerns for academic freedom.' The CEO of the La Jolla Novartis, on the other hand, expressed his view: 'This research is, in my view, the final statement in academic freedom. It's not just the freedom to wish you could do something, it's the resources that give you the freedom to actually do it.' It is quite obvious that this man doesn't know that academic freedom is a concept different from free enterprise in academia. As of this writing, a proposed $25 million lab to be provided by Novartis for UC Berkeley and the appointment of Novartis scient-ists to adjunct professorships at UC Berkeley are still being discussed. Since the negotiation was made public, there have been several protests, including those from graduate students of the College of Natural Resources. The faculty at large, including the Academic Senate, however, have not as yet been heard from.[6]

Universities—presumably nonprofit—are thus now engrossed in forming part-nerships with business. They seek greater funds and resources that will generate marketable intellectual property, which will in turn benefit academia and busi-ness. The cycle will be repeated by the corporations that repay the universities in grants and funds. Take the example of the University of Chicago. As UC, Stanford, and Columbia compete for the leadership in licencing their tech-nology, Chicago, which has no engineering school, saw its national rank in science funding sink over two decades from among the top ten universities to about the top twenty. To catch up, Chicago launched, in 1986, an in-house venture-capital operation. Called ARCH Development Corporation (nd), it is a joint venture with Argonne National Laboratory to 'cultivate an expanded com-munity' of administrators, faculty, 'potential CEOs, consultants, associates, and investors.' The director of its biomedical operation, hired from Harvard, has replaced 50 per cent of his department heads, and the place, according to him,

---

[6] The preceding two paragraphs are based on the following reports: Coale (1998), Rosset and Moore (1998), Cerny (1998), Carter (1998), Locke (1998), *San Francisco Examiner*, (1998); Burress (1998), Levine and West (1998).

is now staffed 'with entrepreneurial people responsible both for raising funds and for turning out actual products.' The head of the operation talks of 'a new ethic': 'I've told the faculty they have an additional responsibility to go beyond the discovery of new knowledge. . . . No longer is the job description to sit in your laboratory and think, and expect me to provide all the resources.' (Melcher 1998).

The University of Pittsburgh and Carnegie Mellon University together have formed Innovation Works, Inc. to provide start-up funding grants to help with R & D, marketing, and other business support services (*University Times* 1998). UC has its own BioSTAR (Biotechnology Strategic Targets for Alliances in Research), which similarly seeks to draw private investments for biological studies. It has the MICRO programme for microelectronics and the computer industry, and also has plans to establish several more system-wide programmes dedicated to engineering and communication technology. Its Office of Technology Transfer, both system-wide and campus-specific, guides the practical application of the results of university research by matching them to active licence seekers. In the words of the UC Office of Technology Transfer 'the resulting licensing income provides an incentive to University inventors and authors [i.e. faculty and researchers] to participate in the complex technology transfer process [i.e. sales], funds further University research, and supports the operation of the University technology transfer program.' Each campus has its own programmes, such as San Diego's Connect, which facilitates the contact and matchup between the campus and local industries. The California State University System, Stanford, USC, and the California Institute of Technology, just to mention Californian institutions, each has a project, and all these ventures show signs of a growing synergic relationship between industry and academia (Weiss and Jacobs 1998). The bureaucracy reproduces and expands itself, as Bourdieu (1988) and Passeron (1979) would observe, while converting scholars into corporate employees and managers. University administration is now a steady growth industry, far outpacing the conventional scholars in every discipline. 'Historically,' says the director of industrial partnerships and commercialization for Lawrence Livermore National Laboratory, Alex Gove (1995), 'we were a closed place until about five years ago. But now we are more interested in maximizing the bang for buck.' From the East Coast to the West, from America to Japan, from Australia to Europe, the transformation of academia is indisputable now in nearly all the institutions that are capable of attracting corporate interests (Slaughter and Leslie 1997).

Not a matter of technology transfer, though certainly related, direct corporate involvement in academic research threatens to intensify the conflict of interest and jeopardize the integrity of scholarly projects and judgements. Sheldon Krimsky (1991), professor of urban and environmental policy at Tufts University, surveyed 789 articles on biology and genetics published in 1992 in fourteen leading journals in the field. The articles were written by life scientists from nonprofit research institutions in the state of Massachusetts. Authors were defined as having a financial interest if they (1) were listed on a patent or patent application; (2) served on a scientific advisory committee of a biotech company developing a related product; or (3) served as an officer or shareholder of a company with commercial ties to the research. Krimsky's discovery was that 34 per cent of the articles examined had a financial interest in the described research. Consultancies and honoraria were not included because they are impossible to trace. When these factors are considered, he believes that the percentage is likely to be much higher (Kreeger 1997).

The conflict-of-interest issue is far from clear-cut. Does financial involvement in itself necessarily destroy the validity of a scientific finding? Stock ownership? Should all financial activities be disclosed? There are many scientists who believe otherwise. Kenneth J. Rothman (1993), a professor of public health at Boston University and editor of the journal *Epidemiology*, wrote in the *Journal of the American Medical Association* that 'while disclosure may label someone as having a conflict of interest, it does not reveal whether there actually is a problem with the work or whether the implicit prediction is a "false positive."' He called it the 'new McCarthyism in science.' Since 1992, several journals—the *Journal of the American Medical Association, Science,* the *Lancet,* the *New England Journal of Medicine,* and the *Proceedings of the National Academy of Sciences*—have adopted a policy of financial disclosure, while others—such as *Nature*—ignore disclosure as unneeded. The latter group insists that the work should be evaluated for itself, not for the author's affiliation, thus virtually erasing the idea of the perceived conflict of interest. Will this interpretation initiate a radical departure from the accustomed legal concept?

There are numerous complex cases involving at least 'perceived conflict' that indeed would require minute contractual details just to be nominally accurate. A satisfactory presentation of such cases here will sidetrack this chapter from its main thrust, and I would simply refer the reader to the literature listed in the footnotes. A few broad samples might suggest a general picture: A journal editor and university professor accepts and rejects articles evaluating a pharmaceutical product in which he/she is financially involved, and all the rejected pieces question the product, while the accepted ones support it; a researcher praises a drug produced by a company in which he is heavily invested; a climatologist denies global warming while not disclosing that he is paid by oil companies as well as the government of an oil-exporting country; corporate sponsors—pharmaceutical companies, for instance—insist on the rights to review, revise, and approve the research reports. Many pressures are successfully resisted, but not always. After all, the development of effective medicines is extremely costly, and since federal and public funding is not always available, industrial research funds are avidly sought. Some projects will bring huge benefits to public health, as well. Nevertheless, the eventual importance of a final product does not safeguard the project from vulnerabilities to compromise. And while most funds are legitimate and honourable, intensified commercialization of research obviously opens more chances of jeopardy.

Finally, does high-tech corporatization benefit the public around the university? Certainly, the industry enjoys the low-cost R & D, funded by the federal taxpayers and offered by the university. The university managers who often sit on the corporate boards receive some remuneration and satisfaction. True also, a good number of start-ups—one out of four—grow into successful companies, and even those that fail can retry, and their trained employees can find positions elsewhere. But what about outside the 'business community?' Science parks undoubtedly generate jobs and incomes. The inflow of high-wage researchers contributes to the growth of shops and markets, in turn creating business in service industries. On the other hand, such rapid urbanization means a steep climb in real-estate values, leading to sprawling housing developments and resulting in traffic congestion. This sets off a vicious circle of further sprawl, traffic jams, and, above all, environmental deterioration. And the infrastructural maintenance for such a development must be entirely funded by the local and state taxpayers. Regarding the corrosive effect of Silicon Valley's indifference toward its surrounding area, an observer has this to say: 'The average home price in San Mateo County is more than $400,000; in Santa Clara County, it's nearly that high. Most of the workforce that drives the high-tech engine spends hour after hour commuting to and from another valley—the Central Valley—because that's where the workers can find affordable housing. Polluted air, over-crowded schools and a yawning disparity between haves and have-nots—all are waste products of high-tech's economic internationalism.' (Scott 1999). Unlike some older cities—say, Pittsburgh, Pennsylvania, or Portland, Oregon—which have grown over decades and centuries, repeatedly adjusting economy and civilization to geography, the high-tech research parks lack the needed softening elements of life, such as walks, parks, landmarks, theatres, old shopping districts, plazas—the space for flaneurs. Instead, shopping malls with their sham–public spaces offer the only meeting ground to the young and to grown-ups alike. Shouldn't the university provide a place for rethinking all this before it's too late?

The corporatization of a university means its globalization in the current economic situation, since crucial corporations are typically transnational. Universities are networked through countless international ties. It is practically impossible, for instance, to find a scholar in any university in any industrial country who has not spent an extensive period of time in at least one foreign institution, either as a student or as a scholar. Visits, exchanges, and conferences are routines of academic life. Publications are often collaborative and transnational, and their circulation is worldwide. Third World engineers and intellectuals are welcomed in the metropolis. Awards such as the Fields Medal and the Pritzker, Kyocera, and Nobel Prizes are, of course, global, as are, increasingly, key academic appointments. Foreign students, once pursued for geopolitical reasons, are now actively recruited for the tuition they bring from rich families in the Third World. Sources of research funding—institutional funding, project support, endowment of chairs, grants, and fellowships—are often cross-border, as we have already seen. This development obviously contributes to a greater circulation of information and understanding along with capital and technology, helping to erase regional and cultural misapprehension and misrepresentation. And it indeed has salutary aspects.

One danger that cannot be ignored altogether, however, is the emergence of a global academic industry that powerfully attracts and absorbs scholars and students. The industry is far from a 'village' envisioned by the administrators of the virtual university; rather, it is a de-territorialized corporation. Transnational scholars, now career professionals, organize themselves into an exclusionary body that has little to do with their fellow citizens, either in their places of origin or arrival, but has everything to do with the transnational corporate structure. As it expands, Novartis is the global model swallowing up administrators, professors, researchers, and graduate students. English, the lingua franca of business, is their standard language. For generations, the goal of the humanities and the social sciences has been advertized as the investigation, interpretation, and criticism of social, cultural, and political relations. But now reality seems to have finally caught up with this facade. The huge impact of the global information and knowledge industry on academic learning that would and should be the most urgent topic of concern was hardly discussed, or even acknowledged, by scholars in the humanities or the social sciences until recent days. Once globalization discourse began, however, terms such as globalization and transnational—together with multiculturalism—have been spreading like any other commodity. In the process, it is being compartmentalized, sheltered, sanitized, and made tame and safe by experts, as if globalization discourse is itself a thriving cultural and intellectual activity. Although some minimal room is still left for serious inquiry and criticism in academia, such space is rapidly shrinking, and the ranks of independent eccentrics are fast thinning. This failure of professors in these 'un-applied' divisions of learning to discuss and intervene in the ongoing commercialization of the university is becoming painfully glaring—at least to some observers. What are the intellectual factors that have brought about such a failure? And what are the external circumstances that have promoted this failure? The deafening silence?

PART II. THE FAILURE OF THE HUMANITIES AS AN AGENCY OF CRITICISM AND INTERVENTION

Recent publications have discussed the link between the global market and the university (Slaughter 1990; Dickman 1993; Levine 1993; Ehrenberg 1997; Graham and Diamond 1997; Kennedy 1997; Noll 1998; Tierney 1997). The 1995 edition of Kerr's *Uses of the University*, for instance, adds new chapters that are deeply worried about the privatization and corporatization of the university. *Academic Capitalism*, by Sheila Slaughter and Larry Leslie (1997), observes that 'the freedom of professors to pursue curiosity-driven research was curtailed by withdrawal of more or less autonomous funding to support this activity and by the increased targetting of R & D funds for commercial research.' It even predicts that 'faculty not participating in academic capitalism will become teachers rather than teacher-researchers, work on rolling contracts rather than having tenure, and will have less to say in terms of the curriculum or the direction of research universities.' (p. 211). And yet these books, solely concerned with the institutional economy, have nothing whatever to say on the humanities, as if this branch of learning had already vanished. On the other hand, books by such humanities scholars as W. B. Carnochan (1993), David Damrosch (1995), William V. Spanos (1993), John Beverley (1993), Michael Bérubé and Cary Nelson (1995), and Neil Postman (1998) have hardly anything specific to say with respect to the entrepreneurial transformation of the university and its impact on the humanities. The two sides are oblivious to each other. Slaughter and Leslie prophesy that 'the concept of the university as a community of scholars will disintegrate further' (p. 243), but the disintegration has already taken place.

In order to reflect on the circumstances around the retreat of the humanities from the line of intellectual and political resistance, I would like to draw here a thumbnail sketch of the postwar intellectual transformation, keeping a close eye on the gradual rejection of the idea of totality and universality in favour of diversity and particularity among the 'progressive' humanities scholars. This ideological shift seeks to rectify enlightenment collectivism, and it is no doubt salubrious. At the same time, it must be recognized that the idea of multiplicity and difference parallels—in fact, endorses—the economic globalization as described in Part I of this chapter.

To return to the 1960s, the worldwide student rebellion was obviously not a unified response to cognate historical events. Mexico City, Paris, Berkeley, and Tokyo each had different contingencies traceable to different histories. And yet, there were certain circumstances that underlay most, if not all, of the campus uprisings: the pervasive effect of the independence movements in the Third World; anger and guilt over colonialism and racism; a generational challenge by students born after Second World War; an intense revulsion to cold war repression both in the East and the West; the newly aroused skepticism about dominant central power, ranging from patriarchy and sexism to statism and straight sex; the growth of the counterculture in defiance of high arts; and, finally, the rejection of Euramerican modernism and enlightenment foundationalism. Such revolts varied in configuration and consequence from society to society, but they were present in some form or other on these strife-torn campuses throughout the world. Further, in a tightening circle of globality, the regional events were interconnected and convergent.

Among the French intellectuals, the consequences of the liberation movements in Vietnam and Algeria were deep and wide, while their historical alliance with Soviet communism was being shattered by Khrushchev's revelation of Stalinism in 1956 and the Soviet intervention in Hungary that same year and Czechoslovakia later on. Marxist humanism was the first to be interrogated after the horrors of postwar discoveries began to sink into European minds. Such skepticism called into question universality of any kind, including Eurocentricity, proposing 'difference' as the cognitive framework, and 'differance' as the strategy. Language was the limit beyond which 'reality' was gradually banished as inaccessible. The postmodern turn thus commenced.

After the Second World War, the pre-eminent intellectual had been Sartre, whose Marxist commitment to humanism, universality, and collectivism was, in fact, already attenuated by his existentialist rejection of the essence and by his at least dormant structuralism. And yet for Claude Lévi-Strauss (1976), whose ethnology replaced Sartrean existential humanism as the most hegemonic of French thoughts, it was the Saussurean linguistic model of difference that was interpreted as providing the ground for liberation egalitarianism. His perceived abandonment of totality as well as universalism, derived as it was from a profound disillusionment with collectivism, centralism, and enlightenment humanism, was instrumental in generating various schools of structuralism and poststructuralism. According to Lévi-Strauss, 'Civilization implies the coexistence of cultures offering among themselves the maximum of diversity, and even consists in this very coexistence' (p. 358). His epistemology of difference that led to the recognition and maintenance of diversity and plurality was powerfully enabling to Third Worldism, Maoism (an alternative Marxism), feminism, antiracism, anti-Orientalism, and antitotalitarianism. More importantly, his challenge to totality and to Eurocentricity had an impact on every branch of learning, from anthropology and sociology, to art, literature, history, politics, and law, among the students and the now dominant poststructuralist theorists, such as Jacques Lacan, Roland Barthes, Louis Althusser, Paul de Man, Jean-François Lyotard, Gilles Deleuze, Félix Guatarri, Michel Foucault, and Jacques Derrida.

Lévi-Strauss's structuralism was a response to the rupture of the long-established tradition of Eurocentricity, and it has played an immensely important role in intellectual history not only in France but also nearly everywhere else in the world to this day. However, it also introduced problems of its own, whose culminating aftermath is now beginning to be felt in this age of the global economy. First, Lévi-Strauss's anthropology is, as the title of one of his later books indicates, 'the view from afar,' because to maintain the diversity of cultures, one should not/cannot intimately identify with any. The result is not only a propensity toward exoticism and superficial knowledge, but uninvolvement, laissez-faire, and indifference regarding the other. Second, diverse cultures are equally unique and autonomous in the sense that there are no common terms in which to compare them: He points out, for instance, 'the absurdity of declaring one culture superior to another' (p. 354). Does he mean that cultures, and ages, should be/are always equally desirable or undesirable? Cognitive relativism is unavoidable, and solipsism and randomness ensue. Third, in Saussurean linguistics, which is construed as based on the lexicographic system of difference, a sign is understood in its relation to other signs but not to its referent. In Lévi-Strauss's application, reference is inevitably lost, and thus 'truth' is assumed to be unrepresentable. The world is now shifted to texts, and history to narratives. Fourth, every culture or age has its own unique terms and discourses, which are thus judged incommensurable across the cultural and historical borders. Fifth, to the extent that the discreteness of diverse cultures is presumed, each individual subject born into a culture is regarded as inescapably determined by it. This is an impossible contradiction to his basic premise of difference, which denies totality and collectivity (is a given culture an undifferentiated totality?); but, more significantly, the subjectship—the individual agency—is disallowed so as to make any political engagement impossible. Finally, because of this erasure of political agency, the diversity of cultures paradoxically surrenders to the hegemonic centre once again—very much as in the so-called global 'borderless' economy.

Obviously, this is a simplification, and it might well be called an American literary and critical interpretation of the transmigration of French structuralism/post-structuralism. Also, the rejection of universality, collectivity, reference, and agency in favour of difference, particularity, incommensurability, and structure can hardly be uniform among the post-structuralists. And yet, as seen in the context of the theorists in the United States, there is an undeniable common proclivity among them to fundamentally reject such totalizing concepts as humanity, civilization, history, and justice, and such subtotalities as a region, a nation, a locality, or even any smallest group. As if breathing together the zeitgeist of division and difference, they each believe that foundational ideas and concepts are historical and cultural constructs—as represented by Thomas Kuhn's 'paradigm' (Weinberg 1998) or Foucault's 'episteme'—and that no all-inclusive judgement or causal explanation can be found. The fear of totality as inevitably totalitarian remains unabated. The theory of difference is not limited to history but extends to social and cultural relations. A totality is differentiated as a majority and minorities, then a minority into subminorities, a subminority into sub-subminorities, and so on. Differentiation and fragmentation never stop by the sheer force of its logic. Such precise identification is a beneficial calibration in the face of crude generalizations that obliterate the distinctions that exist in any category. It helps to fight marginalization and erasure. Yet if the strategy of division and fragmentation is not contained and moderated with the idea of a totality—its context—it may very well lose its initial purpose and end up paradoxically in universal marginalization.

An individual, a group, or a programme requires a totality in which to position itself. Conversely, a totality is not always a monolithic system for the suppression of all differences and marginalities. Specifics and particulars negotiate at all levels with the context and with other specifics and particulars. Likewise, all concepts and ideas may be bound to a specific locale in time and place, but a specific locale in time and place does not produce uniform and identical concepts and ideas. Further, essentialism would be equally present and absent in both totality and particularity.

The contradiction, or antinomy, between totality and particularity is most clearly demonstrated in a debate between Noam Chomsky and Foucault, 'Human Nature: Justice versus Power,' held in 1974. Their disagreement becomes palpable in the second half of the debate, where they argue about the notion of justice. For Foucault, justice is a historical and social invention 'as an instrument of a certain political and economical power or as a weapon against that power,' whereas for Chomsky, it should have/has 'an absolute basis . . . residing in fundamental human qualities.' Foucault disagrees with Chomsky's old-fashioned enlightenment metanarrative on the grounds that it is just one discourse among many. Chomsky speaks not only as a universalist intellectual here but also as one who is committed to the struggle for the suppressed of the world. Chomsky indeed believes that truth and falsehood can be distinguished and that the individual as the subjective agent has a moral responsibility. For Foucault, such claims are merely functions of the desire for power. Chomsky, on the other hand, detects in the Foucauldian abandonment of justice and the truth a cynicism that conceals a moral and political failure behind an elaborate intellectual sophistry (Elders 1974).[7]

The theory of difference has been more enthusiastically embraced in the United States, Canada, and Australia than in European countries because of its long history of a settlement society par excellence, where heterogeneous races and ethnicities have 'coexisted' geographically. The university rebellion of the 1960s began, as we have already seen, with the Civil Rights movement in the late 1950s and early 1960s, and with the rising protest against the war in Vietnam. Further, the United States was founded on the long history of genocide and slavery, whose effects have not yet been erased even in this late date. More recently, the global economy, has vastly intensified migration and exchange, and the promise and the problem of difference have been daily encountered and accommodated. Thus multiculturalism is the urgent issue both of pedagogy and political economy in the university in the United States.

Multiculturalism that rejects the discrimination of marginal groups is a democratic improvement over the majoritarian monopoly that had long suppressed all but dominant history and culture. Under multiculturalism, all sections and factions can claim fair inclusion and representation, and there have been signs of success in several actual social programmes. Affirmative action is a practical programme rooted in a version of multiculturalism that has resulted in an increased participation of women and minorities in both industry and the university. The representation is still far from equitable, and yet one should remember how complete the exclusion of the peripheries was a mere generation ago. Before proceeding to celebration, however, one needs to face the problems.

---

[7] This important debate deserves to be read and discussed extensively. Edward Said's (1983) well-known essay, 'Traveling Theory,' was the earliest I know to discuss, followed much later by Christopher Norris's Uncritical Theory: Postmodernism, Intellectuals, and the Gulf War (1992), esp. 'Chomsky versus Foucault,' 'The Political Economy of Truth,' and 'Reversing the Drift: Reality Regained,' pp. 100–25. Norris's related works, such as What's Wrong with Postmodernism: Critical Theory and the Ends of Philosophy (1990); Deconstruction: Theory and Practice (1991); The Truth about Postmodernism (1993); and Reclaiming Truth: Contribution to a Critique of Cultural Relativism (1996), examine Richard Rorty, Stanley Fish, Jean Baudrillard, and other pragmatic postmodernists, as well as Foucault.

First, there are the revived challenges to the legality of the affirmative action laws that threaten to reduce enrolment of women and minorities once again. Though protected by the present federal laws, the future of such programmes of redress is far from assured. And let me repeat once more: The equalization and inclusion of marginals are still far from adequate in any social category.

More crucially, contradictory currents that converge in the programme of multiculturalism itself must be noted: the greater recognition of alterities, on the one hand, and the exclusionist reaffirmation of self-identity, on the other. The former is the official line of multiculturalism by which the world is perceived to be diverse and one's place to be within this plurality. The principles of diversity and plurality demand that one's own ethnicity or identity be deemed to be no more than just one among many. If this requirement of equal limitation and discipline were accepted by all members of the 'global community,' multiculturalism would make great strides toward the realization of a fair and just human community. Self-restriction, however, is seldom practised for the betterment of general and abstract human welfare—especially when it involves material discipline and sacrifice for the parties involved (Eagleton 1998). Besides, multiculturalism premissed on all particularities of all categories—ethnicity to class, region to development, gender to nationality, poverty to wealth, race to age—is infinitely varied, and even in this age of cross-border mobility, no one is expected to know intimately more than an infinitesimal portion of such variety. Picture the variations: aged and impoverished white lesbian women, rich Korean men who speak no English, gay middle-class Lebanese–American males who are newly jobless with no families. However imaginative, sympathetic, or concerned, one is severely restricted in the ability to know and embrace others. The view is bound to be 'from afar.' When the difference—gap—in wealth is widening, as now, the cross-categorical understanding becomes still more difficult. And the harder the likelihood of coeval encounter proves, the louder the cry for multiculturalism rises. The abstract principle of multiculturalism, an expression of liberal open-mindedness and progressive tolerance, much too often stands in for an alibi to exonerate the existing privileges, inequities, and class differences.

Two other possible perils are inherent in the programme of difference and multiplicity. First, very much like industrial globalization, multiculturalism is preoccupied with the facade of internationalism and cosmopolitanism, helping to form a league of the elite in all regions of the world, while ultimately ignoring the multitudes in hopeless economic isolation and stagnancy. Second, multiculturalism has been paradoxically aloof to the establishment of a transidentity affiliation, and this indifference directly inverts itself into the aggressive rejection of any involvement in the affairs of, for, and by the other. Thus, multiculturalism amounts often to another alibi: Under the pretext of eschewing the 'colonialist' representation of former colonies, it abandons the natives to their 'postcolonial' vacuum and disorder of authority, often a direct result of earlier colonialism itself. There are numerous examples of such developments, the most conspicuous of which are the sub-Saharan countries, where starvation, corruption, pillage, and violence relentlessly continue—while the Northern nations merely stand by without offering assistance. At home, inner cities are their equivalents. Supported by the idea of postcoloniality, the positioning of colonialism as a past event, multiculturalism works nearly as a licence to abandon the welfare of the unprofitable marginals and concentrate on the interests of the dominant. This is what Slavoj Zizek (1997) means when he characterizes multiculturalism as 'the ideal form of ideology of this global capitalism.'

An oppressed and exploited group has the right and responsibility to defend itself, and it requires the firm establishment of a group identity for self-protection. Once survival and self-defence cease to be a desperate necessity, however, identity politics often turns into a policy of self-promotion, or, more exactly, a self-serving sales policy in which a history of victimization becomes a commodity that demands payment. It can pervert itself into opportunism and cannibalism, be it racial, sexual, national, social, or otherwise. In the name of multiculturalism, one privileges one's own identity, while making merely a token acknowledgment of the other's—whom one proceeds to disregard when an occasion for help arrives. It is as if self-identity were an article of private property, which the group—but more likely its elite leadership—claims to own and guard exclusively. Exclusionism is destructive, whether among the rulers or the ruled. Entrepreneurial self-assertion sunders any possible political alliance with other marginal groups into uncoordinated and fragmented promotional drives, which most likely head towards a disastrous defeat in the hands of the far better organized dominant parties. In this connection, it may do well to reflect on what Tzvetan Todorov (1993) suggests as a common human feature: 'The context in which human beings come into the world subjects them to multiple influences, and this context varies in time and space. What every human being has in common with all others is the ability to reject these determinations' (p. 390). I do not believe that such freedom is given to everyone, and yet the wish occasionally to alter them, to assume the identity of another, must surely be a very common experience indeed. The borders between beings must remain passable at least in the imagining.

To return to the corporate use of multiculturalism, privatization and entrepreneurship are valourized in globalism. While the corporate system has no reason—or no profit motive—for eradicating racism and sexism, it has similarly little reason—or little profit motive—for always encouraging racism and sexism. In fact, the corporate system stands to gain under certain circumstances by promoting diversity among ethnic and gender groups as it expands its markets, insofar as it can retain class difference and uneven development—the indispensable capitalist condition for cheap labour. Here, identity politics, to which the idea of diversity often irresistibly leads, can easily be played into the hands of corporate management. Every marginal group will be as exclusive and alienated from all others, as it is led by ethnic spokespersons, each working in a self-sealed entrepreneurship, with its identity as a private investment, as capital. Transnational corporatism needs only low-cost labour, regardless of its ethnic origins and geographical roots. Which ethnicities or regions it comes from is of little consequence (Shiver 1998). In the advocates of exclusionary identity politics, in fact, transnational capitalism, or neocolonialism, finds a soul mate who can stand in as the manager of the group.

In the context of the university's organization, identity politics is bound to create factionalism and fractionalization. But it now has the imprimatur from the philosophy of difference. The multiplicity of perspectives, specializations, and qualifications is intensified with the rage for differentiation. Agreement is ipso facto suspect and unwanted. Internecine disputation is substituted for political engagement. Thus, in a humanities department now, feminists vie with ethnic groups as well as the male of all kinds; among feminists, essentialists contest anti-essentialists; assaults on the 'ludic posties' become the career of 'postludic' academics; post-Marxists reject orthodox Marxists; conventional disciplinary scholars hold in contempt cultural studies writers; novelists despise theorists who can't sell products; theorists look down on creative writers as ignorant and self-absorbed; empirical historians are convinced that theorists are moon-struck obscurantists; queers believe they are the best because their identities are identity-less; formalists are proud of their purity, while they are the targets of derision as hopelessly out of date and out of touch according to the politically engaged; ethnics are opportunists in the eyes of the whites, whereas the whites are both mindless and heartless troglodytes as the marginals see them.

Factions disagree with each other on nearly every topic, be it the BA or PhD requirements, recruitment, and admissions preferences, promotion, tenure, or even the selection of a guest lecturer. The most difficult document to compile in any academic unit nowadays may be the general description of itself, its history and objective, in the form of a handbook or manual. Strife, however, is not the worst of possibilities: At least people are talking to each other—even if they do raise their voices. It is common today to observe a mutually icy-distant silence, which allows everyone to escape into her/his womblike cocoon, talking minimally to the fewest contacts possible. Thus, instead of open discussion and argument at a meeting, perfunctory mail ballots—likely by email—decide issues. Education of undergraduates consists of the mechanical transfer of safe packaged information unsullied by fundamentals and intricacies; graduate education is somewhat more involved, but even that is apt to be left to the students themselves. Uncontaminated as yet, graduate students expect guidance of a general nature in the humanities but often find that the best part of their education is in reading groups they form among themselves rather than in the institutional seminar rooms, where the instructors, full of anxieties over other texts and readings, tend to say nothing of significance. Indeterminacy rules, and it is a poor bargain for those graduate apprentices who must decide on their future in the few years allowed them by the production-dictated rules of their graduate administrators. The administration's pressure towards quantitative production—though no one knows the specifications—heats up the internal mechanics of academia. Nowadays, more frequently than ever, humanities departments are placed in receivership, an academic equivalence of bankruptcy, in which the unit is judged to be incapable of handling itself because of irreconcilable internal dissension (Allen 1998; Scott 1998).

The faculty would rather do the things that might promote their professional careers. Untenured assistant professors are understandably in panic; they may not make it. Furthermore, they know that a financial downturn—real or fabricated—can legally eliminate the programmes they have worked so hard to get into. But before that eventuality takes place, they must first sneak in, even if there is no guarantee of any kind for their long unfathomable future years. Yet the marginalization of the humanities and the social sciences has been terrifying not only for the pretenure faculty but also the supposedly securely tenured professors. The same eventualities face them. They still have many years remaining in their careers, and during these long leftover years, they need to appear confident and attractive at least to their students (customers), if not to their colleagues (business competitors). The sad fact is that many ageing professors are finding it difficult to conceal the lack of a project that fully absorbs their interest and energy, if not passion and imagination. But most choose to evade it. It is pathetic to have to witness some of those who posed as faculty rebels only a few years ago now sheepishly talking about the wisdom of ingratiating the administration—as if such demeaning mendacity could veer the indomitable march of academic corporatism by even an inch. To all but those inside, much of humanities research may well look insubstantial, precious, and irrelevant, if not useless, harmless, and humourless. Worse than the fetishism of irony, paradox, and complexity a half century ago, the cant of hybridity, nuance, and diversity now pervades the humanities faculty. Thus, they are thoroughly disabled to take up the task of opposition, resistance, and confrontation, and are numbed into retreat and withdrawal as 'negative intellectuals' (Bourdieu 1998, pp. 91–9)—precisely as did the older triad of new criticism. If Atkinson and many other administrators neglect to think seriously about the humanities in the corporatized universities, the fault may not be entirely theirs.

If all this is a caricature, which it is, it must nevertheless be a familiar one to most in the humanities now. It is indeed a bleak picture. I submit, however, that such demoralization and fragmentation, such loss of direction and purpose, are the cause and effect of the stunning silence, the fearful disengagement, in the face of the radical corporatization that higher education is undergoing at this time.

In the macromanagement picture, there is little likelihood here of a return to nation-statism, which enabled the construction of a national history, a national literature, a national culture, and a national economy during the major portions of the last two centuries. Obviously, the nation-state structure will not disappear anytime soon, but this does not mean that it is still the fecund soil for intellectual and cultural imagination now. That time is over, and it is glad tidings in several ways. At the same time, now unchecked by national and regional sectioning, control quietly made pervasive and ungraspable in the global economy is even more powerfully effective. And there is hardly any space for critical inquiry and cultural resistance in academia that might provide a base from which to launch a challenge to this seamless domination of capital. Does this mean an end to all oppositionist politics?

As long as extreme inequity in power and privilege persists, there will be discontent and resentment that can ignite at a propitious moment. The opportunity will not arrive by the call from an intellectual leader, of course. When the workers and underclass find it intolerable to live on with the uneven distribution of comfort and suffering, they will eventually rise up. The humanities as we have known it for many decades have ceased to be of use for now. Critics, however, can still discern signs among people and organize their findings into an argument and programme for dissemination. The academics' work in this marketized world, then, is to learn and watch problems in as many sites as they can keep track of, not in any specific areas, nations, races, ages, genders, or cultures, but in all areas, nations, races, ages, genders, and cultures. In other words, far from abandoning the master narratives, the critics and scholars in the humanities must restore the public rigour of the metanarratives. Together with those already mentioned, there are several others whose voices I, for one, would cherish to hearken to. As importantly, we know that in every institution, there are serious minds who quietly keep toiling in their reflection and teaching, often unrewarded and unacknowledged except by their students. They may well be the ones with whom the people will share their future in large measure. What we need now is this powerfully reintegrated concept of society, where diversity does not mean a rivalry of minorities and factions, and resultant isolation. The emerging orientation of scholarship is likely to appear yet opaque and ill-defined for those accustomed to the clear dictates of the nation-state during the colonial, imperial, and cold-war years. It is no mean task in these days to orient one's own scholarship in the university that is being reduced to the exclusive site for R & D. The administrators seem eager to write off the humanities—as an instrument to control minorities, or else merely as a managerial training programme in metropolitan manners, style, and fashion, set aside for the socially 'elite' institutions. We need a new interventional project with which to combat the corporatization of the university and the mind.

The appellation ivory tower, a translation of 'tour d'ivoire,' is a cliché and is as taken for granted as the university itself. Examined closely, however, the designation reveals more than we are accustomed to seeing in it: The modern university is indeed built with ivory, a material robbed from Africa and India, where elephants are now nearly extinct, and thus ivory is contraband.[8] The greatest benefactor of the modern university, upon reflection, may indeed be

---

[8] 'Ivory tower' is a translation of tour d'ivoire, which was first used in 1837 by Charles-Augustin Sainte-Beuve (according to *A Supplement to the Oxford English Dictionary*, vol. 3), and in 1869 (according to Webster's *Third New International Dictionary*). The English phrase first appeared (according to the *OED Supplement*) in Henri Bergson's (1911) *Laughter: An Essay on the Meaning of the Comic*. No explanation is given for the choice of ivory for indicating seclusion from the world or shelter from harsh realities. The fact that no one—as far as I know—has ever detected

King Leopold of Belgium, Queen Victoria's uncle, who may have contributed to the extinction of ten million African lives. We should perhaps never talk about the modern university without recalling Joseph Conrad's *Heart of Darkness*. The late Bill Readings's (1996) excellent book, *The University in Ruins*, is right in its discussion of the humanities. In other aspects, however, today's university is immensely prosperous and opulent. No longer far from the madding crowd, the university is built increasingly among shopping malls, and shopping malls amidst the university. It is no longer selling out; it has already been sold and bought. The deed has been written and signed, and the check already signed, too. But the deed has not been registered, and the check not cashed as yet. To right the situation, to null the transaction and be just to all on earth, we may have to relearn the sense of the world, the totality, that includes all peoples in every race, class, and gender.

REFERENCES

Allen, Charlotte (1998) 'As Bad as It Gets: Three Dark Tales from the Annals of Academic Receivership', *Lingua Franca* 8(2) March: 52–9.

Apollo Group website (nd), www.apollogrp.com.

ARCH Development Corporation (nd), The University of Chicago, *About ARCH*, available at www.arch.uchicago.edu

Arenson, Karen W. (1998) 'For university presidents, higher compensation made it a 'gilded' year', *New York Times*, 18 October.

—— (1998) 'Modest Proposal', *New York Times*, 2 August.

Arnold, Matthew (1932) *Culture and Anarchy*, J. Dover Wilson (ed.) Cambridge: Cambridge University Press.

Atkinson, Richard C. (1996a) *Universities and the Knowledge-Based Economy*, Paper presented at the California State Senate Fiscal Retreat, 3 February, available at www.ucop.edu/ucophome/pres/comments/senate.html.

—— (1996b) 'High Stakes for Knowledge', *Los Angeles Times*, 28 April.

—— (1997a) *The Role of Research in the University of the Future*, Paper presented at the United Nations University, Tokyo, Japan, 4 November 1997, available at www.ucop.edu/ucophome/pres/comments/role.html

—— (1997b) *Visions and Values: The Research University in Transition*, the 19th Annual Pullias Lecture, delivered at USC on 1 March, available at www.ucop.edu/ucophome/pres/comments/pulli.html

—— and Donald Tuzin (1992) 'Equilibrium in the research university', *Change: The Magazine of Higher Learning* (May/June): 21–31.

—— and Edward E. Penhoet (1996) (President and CEO of Chiron Corp.), 'Town and Gown Join Forces to Boost State', *Los Angeles Times*, 31 December.

—— (1998a) 'It Takes Cash to Keep Ideas Flowing', *Los Angeles Times*, 25 September.

in the phrase the connection between academia and ivory, the university and colonialism, might reaffirm the devastatingly accurate denunciation implanted in the phrase.

—— (1998*b*) 'The Future of the University of California', September, available at www.ucop.edu

AUTM (1997) *Licensing Survey, FY 1997.*

Barrow, Clyde W. (1990) *Universities and the Capitalist State: Corporate Liberalism and the Reconstruction of American Higher Education, 1894–1928.* Madison: University of Wisconsin Press.

Berger, Joseph (1998) 'After Her PhD, a Scavenger's Life: A Temp Professor among Thousands', *New York Times*, 8 March.

Bergson, Henri (1911) *Laughter: An Essay on the Meaning of the Comic*, trans. Cloudesley Brereton and Fred Rothwell. New York: Macmillan Company.

Bérubé, Michael and Nelson, Cary (1995) *Higher Education under Fire: Politics, Economics, and the Crisis of the Humanities.* London: Routledge.

Beverley, John (1993) *Against Literature.* Minneapolis: University of Minnesota Press.

Bourdieu, Pierre (1988) *Homo Academicus*, trans. Peter Collier. Stanford, Calif.: Stanford University Press.

—— (1998) 'The Negative Intellectual', in *Acts of Resistance: Against the Tyranny of the Market*, trans. Richard Nice. New York: New Press.

—— and Jean-Claude Passeron (1990) *Reproduction in Education, Society, and Culture*, trans. Richard Nice. Newbury Park, Calif.: Sage.

—— and —— (1979) *The Inheritors: French Students and Their Relations to Culture*, trans. Richard Nice. Chicago: University of Chicago Press.

Bryant, Adam (1998*a*) 'Stock Options That Raise Investors' Ire', *New York Times*, 27 March.

—— (1998*b*) 'Flying High on the Option Express', *New York Times*, 5 April.

—— (1998*c*) 'Executive Cash Machine', *New York Times*, 8 November.

Burress, Charles (1998) 'UC Finalizes Pioneering Research Deal with Biotech Firm: Pie Tossers Leave Taste of Protest', *San Francisco Chronicle*, 24 November.

Business Week (1998) The Good, the Bad, the Ugly of CEO Salaries Scoreboard: Executive Compensation', 20 April, pp. 64–110.

Carnochan, W. B. (1993) *The Battleground of the Curriculum: Liberal Education and American Experience*, Stanford, Calif.: Stanford University Press.

Carter, James (1998) 'Concerns over Corporation Alliance with UC College of Natural Resources', *Berkeley Voice*, 19 November.

Casper, Gerhard (1998) *The Advantage of the Research-Intensive University: The University of the Twenty-first Century*, presented on 3 May 1998, Peking University, available at www.stanford.edu/dept/pres-provost/president/speeches/980503peking.html

Cerny, Joseph (1998) 'UC Research Alliance', letters to the editor, *San Francisco Chronicle*, 7 November 1998.

Chomsky, Noam *et al.* (1997) *The Cold War and the University: Toward an Intellectual History of the Postwar Years.* New York: New Press.

Coale (1998) 'The $50 Million Question', *San Francisco Chronicle*, 23 October.

Council on Governmental Relations (COGR) (1993) *The Bayh-Dole Act: A Guide to the Law and Implementing Regulations*, 30 November, available at www.tmc.tulane.edu/techdev/Bayh.html

Cumings, Bruce (1997) 'Boundary Displacement: Area Studies and International Studies during and after the Cold War', Bulletin of Concerned Asian Scholars 29(1) January–March: 6–26.

Damrosch, David (1995) *We Scholars: Changing the Culture of the University.* Cambridge: Harvard University Press.

Dickman, Howard (1993) (ed.) *The Imperiled Academy.* New Brunswick, NJ: Transaction Publishers.

Eagleton, Terry (1998) 'Defending the Free World', in Stephen Regan (ed.) *The Eagleton Reader.* Oxford: Blackwell.

Economist (1997*a*) 'One World?', 18 October, pp. 79–80.

—— (1997*b*) 'The Disappearing Taxpayer', 31 May–6 June, p. 15, 21–3.

Ehrenberg, Ronald G. (1997) (ed.) *The American University: National Treasure or Endangered Species?* Ithaca, NY: Cornell University Press.

Elders, Fons (1974) (ed.) *Reflexive Water: The Basic Concerns of Mankind.* London: Souvenir Press.

Flanagan, James (1998) 'Southland's Tech Prowess Is in Partnerships', *Los Angeles Times*, 8 March.

Gove, Alex (1995) 'Ivory Towers for Sale', *Red Herring*, August, available at www.herring.com/mag/issue22/tech1.html

Gracie, Sarah (1999) 'Dreaming Spires Wake Up to Business', *Sunday Times*, 6 June.

Graham, Hugh Davis and Diamond, Nancy (1997) *The Rise of American Research Universities: Elites and Challengers in the Postwar Era.* Baltimore, Md.: Johns Hopkins University Press.

Guilbaut, Serge (1983) *How New York Stole the Idea of Modern Art: Abstract Expressionism, Freedom, and the Cold War*, trans. Arthur Goldhammer. Chicago: University of Chicago Press.

Harvey, David (1996) *Justice, Nature, and Geography of Difference.* Oxford: Blackwell.

Honan, William H. (1998) 'The Ivory Tower under Siege: Everyone Else Is Downsized; Why Not the Academy?' Education Life supplement, *New York Times*, Spring, pp. 33, 44, 46.

Johnston, David Cay (1997) 'Tax Cuts Help the Wealthy in the Strong Economy', *New York Times*, 5 October.

Kennedy, Donald (1997) *Academic Duty.* Cambridge: Harvard University Press.

Kerr, Clark (1995) *The Uses of the University*, 4th edn. Cambridge: Harvard University Press.

Koretz, Gene (1997) 'Where Wealth Surged in the 90s', *Business Week*, 25 August, p. 32.

Kreeger, Karen Young (1997) 'Studies Call Attention to Ethics of Industry Support', *Scientist*, 11(7) 31 March: 1, 4–5,

Krimsky, Sheldon (1991) *Biotechnics and Society: The Rise of Industrial Genetics*, New York: Praeger.

Lazarus, Neil (1997) 'Transnationalism and the Alleged Death of the Nation-State', in Keith Ansell-Pearson, Benita Parry, and Judith Squires (eds), *Cultural Readings of Imperialism: Edward Said and the Gravity of History.* London: Lawrence and Wishart, pp. 28–48.

Levine, Arielle and West, Susan (1998) Students for Responsible Research, Department of Environmental Science, Policy and Management, College of Natural Resources, UC Berkeley, Letters to the editor, *San Francisco Chronicle*, 26 November.

Levine, Arthur (1993) (ed.) *Higher Learning in America, 1980–2000*, Baltimore, Md.: Johns Hopkins University Press.

Lévi-Strauss, Claude (1976) *Structural Anthropology*, trans. Monique Layton. Vol. 2. New York: Basic Books.

Lively, Kit (1998) 'What They Earned in 1996–97: A Survey of Private Colleges' Pay and Benefits: The Presidents of Rockefeller, Vanderbilt, and U. of Pennsylvania Top $500,000', *Chronicle of Higher Education*, 23 October.

Locke, Michelle (1998) 'Berkeley Celebrates $25 Million Novartis Grant, but Some Have Questions', *Associated Press*, 23 November, available at www.sfgate.com.

Madrick, Jeff (1997) 'In the Shadows of Prosperity', *New York Review of Books*, 14 August, pp. 40–4.

Martin, Randy (1998) (ed.) *Chalk Lines: The Politics of Work in the Managed University.* Durham, NC: Duke University Press.

McKibben, Bill (1998) 'A Special Moment in History', *Atlantic Monthly*, May, pp. 55–78.

McNeil, Donald G. (1998) 'AIDS Stalking Africa's Struggling Economies', *New York Times*, 15 November.

Melcher, Richard (1998) 'An Old University Hits the High-Tech Road', *Business Week*, 24–31 August, pp. 94–6.

Miller, Mark Crispin (1997) 'The Crushing Power of Big Publishing', *Nation*, 17 March, pp. 11–18.

Miyoshi, Masao (1998) ' "Globalization," Culture, and the University', in Fredric Jameson and Masao Miyoshi (eds) *The Cultures of Globalization.* Durham, NC: Duke University Press, pp. 247–70.

Modern Languages Association (MLA) (1997) *Final Report: MLA Committee on Professional Employment.* New York: MLA. Reproduced in *PMLA* 113 (5) October: 1154–77.

Moretti, Franco (1988) 'The Spell of Indecision', in Cary Nelson and Lawrence Grossberg (eds) *Marxism and the Interpretation of Culture.* Urbana and Chicago: University of Illinois Press, pp. 339–46.

Mydans, Seth (1995) 'Part-Time College Teaching Rises, as Do Worries', *New York Times*, 4 January.

Newman, John Henry, Turner, Frank M. (1996) (ed.) *The Idea of a University.* New Haven, Conn.: Yale University Press.

Noble, David (1999) *The Religion of Technology: The Divinity of Man and the Spirit of Invention.* New York: Penguin, 1999.

Noll, Roger G. (ed.) (1998) *Challenges to Research Universities.* Washington, DC: Brookings Institution Press.

Norris, Christopher (1990) *What's Wrong with Postmodernism: Critical Theory and the Ends of Philosophy.* Baltimore, Md.: Johns Hopkins University Press.

—— (1991) *Deconstruction: Theory and Practice*, rev. edn. London: Routledge.

—— (1992) *Uncritical Theory: Postmodernism, Intellectuals, and the Gulf War.* Amherst: University of Massachusetts Press.

—— (1993) *The Truth about Postmodernism.* Oxford: Blackwell.

—— (1996) *Reclaiming Truth: Contribution to a Critique of Cultural Relativism.* Durham, NC: Duke University Press.

O'Brien, George Dennis (1997) *All the Essential Half-Truths about Higher Education.* Chicago: University of Chicago Press, quoted in James Shapiro, 'Beyond the Culture Wars', *New York Times Book Reviews*, 4 January 1998.

Pochoda, Phil (1997) 'Universities Press On', *Nation*, 29 December, pp. 11–16.

Porter, Roger J. and Malone, Thomas E. (eds.) (1992) *Biomedical Research: Collaboration and Conflict of Interest.* Baltimore, Md.: Johns Hopkins University Press.

Postman, Neil (1998) *The End of Education: Redefining the Value of School.* New York: Vintage.

Readings, Bill (1996) *The University in Ruins.* Cambridge: Harvard University Press.

Reich, Robert B. (1999) 'Despite the U.S. Boom, Free Trade Is Off Track', *Los Angeles Times*, 18 June.

Rosset, Peter and Moore, Monica (1998) 'Research Alliance Debated: Deal Benefits Business, Ignores UC's Mission', *San Francisco Chronicle*, 23 October 1998.

Rothman, Kenneth J. (1993) 'Conflict of Interest: The New McCarthyism in Science', *JAMA— The Journal of the American Medical Association*, 269 (21) 2 June: 2782–4.

Said, Edward (1983) 'Traveling Theory', in *The World, the Text, and the Critic.* Cambridge: Harvard University Press, pp. 244–7.

San Francisco Examiner (1998) 'Bay Area Datelines', 24 November.

Sanger, David E. (1997) 'A Last Liberal (Almost) Leaves Town', *New York Times*, 9 January.

Scott, Janny (1998) 'Star Professors, as a Team, Fail Chemistry: Once a Model, English Department at Duke Dissolves in Anger', *New York Times*, 21 November.

Scott, Steve (1999) 'Silicon Valley's Political Myopia', *Los Angeles Times*, 4 July.

Shapiro, Harold T. (1998) 'University Presidents—Then and Now', Paper presented at the Princeton Conference on Higher Education, March 1996, the 250th Anniversary of Princeton University, included in, William G. Bowen and Harold T. Shapiro (eds), *Universities and Their Leadership.* Princeton, NJ: Princeton University Press.

Shiver Jr., Jube (1998) 'House Lifts Visa Cap for High-Tech Workers', *Los Angeles Times*, 25 September.

Shulevitz, Judith (1995) 'Keepers of the Tenure Track', University Presses Supplement, *New York Times*, 29 October.

Shulman, Seth (1999) *Owning the Future.* Boston: Houghton Mifflin.

Slaughter, Sheila (1990) *The Higher Learning and High Technology: Dynamics of Higher Education Policy Formation*, Frontiers in Education. Albany: State University of New York Press.

—— and Leslie, Larry L. (1997) *Academic Capitalism: Politics, Policies, and the Entrepreneurial University.* Baltimore, Md.: Johns Hopkins University Press.

Solely, Lawrence (1998) 'Higher Education . . . or Higher Profits? For-Profit Universities Sell Free Enterprise Education', *In These Times*, 22 (21), 20 September: 14–17.

—— (1995) *Leasing the Ivory Tower: The Corporate Takeover of Academia.* Boston: South End.

Spanos, William V. (1993) *The End of Education: Toward Posthumanism.* Minneapolis: University of Minnesota Press.

Specter, Michael (1998) 'Urgency Tempers Ethics Concerns in Uganda Trial of AIDS Vaccine', *New York Times*, 1 October.

Todorov, Tzvetan (1993) *On Human Diversity: Nationalism, Racism, and Exoticism in French Thought*, trans. Catherine Porter. Cambridge: Harvard University Press.

United Nations Development Programme (UNDP) (1998) *Human Development Report 1998.* New York: Oxford University Press.

University of California (1998) 'Notice: A Publication of the Academic Senate', 22 (7) May: 1, 3, 4.

University Times, (1998) 'Pitt, CMU Form New Non-profit Corporation, Innovation Works, Inc.', 31 (7) 25 November, available at www.pitt.edu/utimes/issues/112598/06.html.

Veblen, Thorstein (1969) *The Higher Learning in America: A Memorandum on the Conduct of Universities by Business Men*, American Century Edition. New York: Hill and Wang.

Griffith, Victoria (1998) 'High Pay in Ivory Towers: Star Professors Are Subject of Concern', *Financial Times*, 6 June.

Weinberg, Steven (1998) 'The Revolution That Didn't Happen', *New York Review of Books*, 8 October, 48–52.

Weiss, Kenneth R. (1998) 'A Wary Academia on Edge of Cyberspace' and 'State Won't Oversee Virtual University', *Los Angeles Times*, 31 March and 30 July, respectively.

—— and Jacobs, Paul (1998) 'Caltech Joins Rush to Foster Biotech Spinoff Companies', *Los Angeles Times*, 16 September.

William G. Tierney (ed.) (1997) *The Responsive University: Restructuring for High Performance*. Baltimore, Md.: Johns Hopkins University Press.

Winks, Robin W. (1987) *Cloak and Gown: Scholars in the Secret War, 1939–1961*. New York: William Morrow and Company.

Wolin, Sheldon S. and Schaar, John H. (1965) 'Berkeley and the Fate of the Multiversity', *New York Review of Books* 4(3) 11 March, p. 17.

Zizek, Slavoj (1997) 'Multiculturalism, or, the Cultural Logic of Multinational Capitalism', *New Left Review*, 225 (September/October).

PRACTICES AND POLICIES

5

Working through the Work of Making Work Mobile

James Cornford and Neil Pollock

> The hype of our times is that we don't need to think about the work anymore
>
> Bowker and Star (1996)

INTRODUCTION

What does the recent application of information communication technologies (ICTs) in higher education, and particularly the emergence of commercially-oriented, digital, online or virtual universities hold for the future shape of established, campus-based universities? The transformative and increasingly popular view is that, because of the possibility of new and different ways of producing, distributing, and consuming higher education, these new 'place-less' institutions have the potential to reshape traditional university methods, relationships, geographies, and perhaps even 'ethos'. Such a prospect is well captured in the words of Tom Abeles (1998: 606) who describes how: '. . . students who once travelled great distances to listen to lectures of scholars, can now access this knowledge via the world of the internet.' Told in such a manner it is easy to be seduced by suggestions that we are nearing 'the end of campus based education' (Noam 1995: 247–9), that the university's key role and function—the

This paper was first presented at the Economic & Social Research Council 'Virtual Society? Get Real' conference in Berkhampsted, UK, April 2000. This research partially stems from a study of Virtual Universities (funded under the UK Economic & Social Research Council's (ESRC) Virtual Society? Programme) and a study of students as users of information systems (also funded by the ESRC, Grant No. R000223276). We would also like to thank those staff at North Campus, particularly CM, who allowed us to undertake interviews and ethnographic research. We would like to acknowledge the input of our collaborators John Goddard, Frank Webster, David Charles, and in particular Kevin Robins (who contributed some of the main ideas presented here).

creation, preservation, and transmission of knowledge—is to be rapidly usurped by telecommunications networks (broadcasting, cable, Internet, World Wide Web, email, and so on.) (Abeles 1998), or that long established institutions may be turned into 'dinosaurs' overnight (Noam 1995).

For all that has been written about them, however, recent research suggests that new virtual institutions represent a tiny fraction of higher education provision,[1] and that their significance lies, not so much in their real-world number or market share, but in the pressures they are bringing to bear on the mainstream higher education sector to adopt their methods, strategies, technologies, and, perhaps, commercial ethos.[2] Having caught the imagination of policy makers, institutional managers and academic leaders (see, for example, Newby 1999), it would seem that established universities everywhere are embarking upon ambitious plans to translate existing modes of provision into ones that can be delivered via technology and at a distance.[3] Indeed, such is the enthusiasm and activity underway that some suggest a 'blurring of the boundaries between distance education and on-campus teaching' (Johnston 1999: 39). Given that the bulk of the work of building ICTs into higher education is, in fact, taking place in existing and established institutions, then, the question that begs answering is: 'how are traditional universities attempting to come to terms with these new technologies?'

Much of the recent writing on virtual universities is, we feel, limited, assuming either a 'pro' or 'anti' stance, and tending to emphasize only the differences that exist between online and traditional forms of provision.[4] Our focus, in contrast, is a different and necessarily wider one. For us, the notion of a virtual university is useful, not as a depiction of a particular type of institution, nor as a simple choice between one form of university over another, but rather as a description of a series of projects that are being implemented within universities. While there has been much written in recent years about individual ICT projects in higher education, this literature has often tended to skate over the question as to how, and in what form, these projects can be established alongside those social, organizational, institutional and technical aspects of the university which are already in place (an exception is Agre 2000a). In other words, the question to be addressed is: how

---

[1] See the recent report by the CVCP (2000); see also, Middlehurst, R. (2001). Even in the most developed market, the United States, new for-profit universities such as the University of Phoenix constitute 'only 2% of degree enrolments' and 'publicly-listed educational services companies constitute only 3% by value of the billions of dollars spent on education and training in the US' (Ryan 2000).

[2] For instance, in a recent and widely circulated letter by the Higher Education Funding Council for England (HEFCE) the dangers of such 'virtual and corporate universities' eating into the UK higher education market were spelt out. The letter invites universities to respond to this threat by contributing to a new 'e-University' project that will challenge these new entrants. The document can be found on HEFCE's website: http://www.hefce.ac.uk/Pubs/CircLets/2000/cl104_00.htm.

[3] See, for instance, some of the projects mentioned in a special issues of *Futures*, Vol. 30(7), 1998, and *Information, Communication and Society*, Vol. 3(4), 2000, or in a recent issue of *Minerva*, Vol. 39(1), 2001.

[4] Several of the advocates have already been mentioned in the introduction. Some of the critics include David Noble (1998) and Langdon Winner (1998).

ICTs are actually being built *into* universities? What struck us at the outset of our research into this issue was the sheer volume, and the heterogeneous nature, of the work involved in constructing these virtual university projects to sit alongside more conventional forms of provision. Indeed, our central term, and one that is substantially missing from much of the debate, is 'work'.

Whilst many might consider such a discussion in terms of a narrowly technological agenda, by using the concepts and language from the sociology of technology, particularly what has become known as the actor network approach, we maintain a wider notion; one that attempts to recognize the heterogeneity of the effort involved.[5] Given the way technologies like the Internet are often presented in tandem with the future of universities, we believe it useful to sketch out the nature of this work. We present three case studies, each of which discusses the tensions that arise once those building such technologies attempt to complement and, in some cases, replace the work that the existing physical campus and its established organizational and institutional structures undertake on behalf of the University.

In this article, which is part of a wider programme of research carried out in a number of different higher education institutions in the north east of England over the past four years (Cornford 2000; Pollock 2000; Cornford and Pollock 2002; Pollock and Cornford 2000), we focus on projects and initiatives carried out in just one university. The choice of institution, which for the purposes of this article we shall call 'North Campus', was partially influenced by its institutional commitment in relation to the application of the Internet and other web based technologies to higher education; from our work in other institutions, however, we did not find things to be different in kind (although maybe in degree).

THE VIRTUAL UNIVERSITY AS MOBILE WORK

What is a virtual university? How might it differ from a non-virtual or traditional university? Stuart Cunningham and his collaborators, reviewing a range of new new-media related future scenarios for higher education, provide a useful summary of the vision of the virtual university:

Picture a future in which students never meet a lecturer face to face in a class room, never physically visit the on-campus library; in fact, never set foot on the campus or into an institutional lecture-room or learning centre. Such is the future proposed by the virtual university scenario   (Cunningham *et al.* 1998: 179).

The defining feature here is principally an absence. What defines the virtual university, in this vision, is the way in which it presents a future characterized by the *lack* of physical co-presence ('never meet... never physically visit... never set foot on'). And with the need for co-presence removed, so too is the need

[5] For elucidation and examples of the actor network approach see the work of Callon (1986), Latour (1987), Law (1994).

for the specialist site of co-presence, the campus. From this point of view, then, the virtual university is 'the university without walls'. This point cannot be taken too literally: the people who make up the university still have to be someplace (and require the protection of walls), but what is significant is that they no longer all need to be in the *same* place. The virtual university, then, is the 'distributed university'.

What is it that makes this distribution appear possible? At one level, the answer is clear; it is information and, more specifically, communications technologies. Yet, for us, this does not get to the root of the matter. The mere presence of the communications technologies on its own does not permit the distribution of the university. For us, rather, the key point is that these technologies are used to *move* the work of the university around. Most obviously, communications technologies enable this work to be transferred between different locations, linking up students, lecturers, researchers, administrators, technicians, funders, evaluators and assessors without the need for co-presence. But the virtual university also promises to redistribute work tasks in other ways. Work can be shifted around in time as well as space, with materials stored and made accessible 24 hours a day. New divisions of labour between different categories of individuals within the university become possible. Work can be shifted from staff to students (e.g. students can take on responsibility for checking and maintaining some parts of their student records, relieving administrative and academic staff of this task); administrative staff can take on tasks formerly allocated to academic staff and vice versa (see Pollock and Cornford 2001). Finally, we can talk of the possibility of a new division of labour between people and machines as computers can take on much of the laborious work of compilation, storage, and distribution. The virtual university, then, is a new social, technical, temporal, and spatial division of labour in Higher Education—*it is work made mobile*.

THE WORK OF MAKING WORK MOBILE

As we have said, the mere presence of the communications technologies does not allow work to be mobile. Rather, in order to become mobile, work must be transposed into a format that is compatible with the technologies in use. To achieve this compatibility, work must be untangled from its local constraints and stripped of its existing linkages. In short, it must be translated into *information*. Theodore Porter points to this link between the notion of information and that of space and scale.

The creation and use of information needs to be understood first of all as a problem of space and of scale, of getting beyond what is local, personal or intimate and creating knowledge that is, so far as possible, neutral and well standardised. The ideal, in short, is to go beyond perspective, to turn a view from somewhere into a 'view from nowhere'. Businesses and governments, as organizations spreading over large territories, depend on this. So also do scientists and for identical reasons   (Porter 1994).

We might say that the effort of building the virtual university is that of turning work into information and thus making it mobile—the work of making work mobile.

The scale of resource required for this task is increasingly recognized. The upfront costs of the virtual university are large, whether we are talking about administrative systems, systems to support teaching and learning, library catalogues or specialist research facilities (CVCP 2000). But what are these resources required for? Most obviously, it is the hardware and software of the new systems. The technical configuration of those systems and the re-coding of existing materials into a machine-readable form also constitute a portion of the work required. Finally, the costs of training staff and students in the effective use of these technologies must also be accounted for. However, the working of such systems and software into the university demands various other activities, the type and scale of which are not easily appreciated. These range from issues to do with the identity of the university, assumptions about its role, functions, and relationships, to recognizing the underlying sets of assumptions, dispositions, and behaviours—the common sense of the institution, its unexamined 'organizational infrastructure'—on which these are built and depend.

Typically such dependencies are difficult topics to investigate. The primary reason for this is that much of this shared common sense simply remains invisible (until, that is, something happens and we then witness how some of the most basic and taken for granted resources, conventions or categories of modern university life come to the fore). But a second cause is that we simply lack the language and tools to examine how the mundane processes of rolling out new and advanced technologies interrelate with the common sense on which institutions and organizations like universities are constituted.

The notion of 'network building', as developed within the sociology of scientific knowledge and actor network approach, is useful here. For example, through a number of laboratory ethnographies and historical studies, Bruno Latour and his colleagues have painted a picture of the scientific and technological process in which the central actors are treated not simply as scientists or technologists but as multifaceted entrepreneurs or 'heterogeneous engineers' (Law 1994). These actors engage not only in those practices typically thought of as 'scientific' or 'technological' but also in a wide range of political, sociological, and economic processes. In this sense, to understand just how scientific knowledge is constructed or a technology becomes a success, we must follow and observe these innovators as they attempt to enrol others into more or less stable 'networks'. Importantly, for the actor network approach, agency is not restricted to human beings but is expanded to encompass objects, machines, and texts, all of which must also be enrolled and aligned.[6]

---

[6] Callon's (1986) notion of radical symmetry is that no one element (human or nonhuman) in a network is assumed, *a priori*, to be more important than any other; they all, methodologically at least, have equal status.

This metaphor of network building and maintenance is useful for foregrounding all those typically invisible work processes, objects, and actors that are essential in the construction of an enduring network (in Latour's case to describe how scientific knowledge extends itself out of the laboratory to dominate other forms of knowledge, but in our case to describe the introduction of these new technologies into the university). In particular, we want to show how this perspective is useful when considering how new technologies have to wrestle with the inertia of the organizational forms, infrastructures, and practices already in place. As we have suggested, the actor network approach's primary focus is on change—the introduction of new networks—and it has developed a series of terms and concepts (such as *interressement, translation* and *enrolment*) to describe this process. What happens, then, when we try to apply this analytical frame to the processes of constructing virtual Higher Education?

BUILDING THE VIRTUAL UNIVERSITY *INTO* THE TRADITIONAL UNIVERSITY

One of the places in which we became interested during our research was the Learning Development Services (LDS) department of a University near to our own—we will call it 'North Campus'. In particular, we followed and observed the activities of someone we will call Tom. Tom had been working in LDS as a Telematics Development Officer for some years. His official role was to 'enrich the existing teaching and learning provision given to students through increasing the use of ICTs among academic staff'. In one of our first meetings with Tom he told us how recently there had been a number of important changes to his remit and how these had stemmed from the re-orientation of North Campus more generally. Below, he describes his role and the way this is beginning to alter:

What's really interesting is that there has been a massive shift really in what [my boss] and the Vice Chancellor wants us to try and achieve now. My main job as Telematics Development Officer has been enrichment up until now where I have worked with a lecturer trying to put some telematics into their web materials, or move a little bit of their traditional teaching onto the web. About two months ago, [my boss] came down with a directive from above saying that she wants us to get the old print based [courses] that are working well out there in the field and convert them to run on the web, entirely telematically, so that people can log in on one of the browsers like Netscape, run it from anywhere, and be completely stand alone so that they can operate at a distance from the University.

This conversion of the 'old print based' courses—what Tom calls a 'conversion job'—is only one facet of the planned re-orientation underway:

In the last 18 months or so, there's been another big push in the University. We're looking to try and find markets outside the University where we can deal direct with the student. So the student's a bit like an Open University student with us—we interface with them on a one-to-one basis, but mediated through the technologies. We've all been trying—several lecturers in the Computing Department, a few staff in LDS, and one or two other keen individuals dotted around the University—to come up with a model of a package that the student could reasonably be expected to sit down in front of, plough away on their own, and self-study all the way through.

During the period of our research we were able to observe examples from each of these themes. Firstly, in terms of curriculum enrichment, there was a 'virtual seminar' conducted as part of a Photography degree course. Video-conferencing technologies were used to connect researchers and students based in the UK with their counterparts located in other parts of Europe. The idea behind the seminar was that they could present work and ideas to each other and receive feedback much like a traditional seminar. In terms of transferring existing print-based courses to the Internet, there was an 'Information Skills' module taken by over three hundred first year students each year, with the aim of familiarizing them with the technologies, practices, and procedures of the library. Previously run and supervised by library staff, it was to be developed into an online self-study module, available anywhere on campus via the university network. Finally, in terms of a package to attract new students from a distance, there was the design and construction of a credit bearing, self-study module on 'Cyber Culture'.

In order to understand how these projects worked out in practice we followed the progress of Tom and his team. Month after month we sat in on technical sessions and planning meetings as the academic material was gathered, the technology was developed, and the actual form of these initiatives began to take shape. Staff and students willing to be part of the project rollout were identified and enrolled as participants. Yet, just several months after everything had seemingly been put in place, all three projects had, for want of a better word, 'stalled'. The immediate reasons for this are varied: one of the partners pulled out of the video-conferencing project complaining of high telecommunication costs; the library staff could not be convinced that the online version of their Information Skills course was sufficiently improved to warrant its introduction in place of existing methods; and, despite the imagined new markets outside of the University, only *one* student had enrolled to study the Cyber Culture course at a distance.

While these failures might be accounted for in a number of different ways, this is not the primary concern here.[7] Rather we are interested in these initiatives because of the way they usefully highlight the extent and nature of the work that is demanded before these new networks can be knitted into the existing arrangements within North Campus. In the process of making things virtual, the University had to 'rework' and rethink much of what it currently does and reconfigure its relationship with the numerous actors and entities on which it currently depends (cf. Agre 2000*a*). Moreover, it was only when attempts were

---

[7] We certainly do not want to be critical of the staff in the Learning Development Services Department who, despite limited resources, often showed remarkably ingenuity and resourcefulness during their work.

made to abstract courses or activities from the campus—to make them virtual—that the necessity for, and nature of, all of this effort became visible. And with this new visibility, there was the realization of the costs and complexity of seeking to compensate for the work that the various networks already in place so discretely undertake on behalf of the University. To understand these points more clearly, we need to look at each initiative in greater detail. Let us begin with the video-conferencing project.

THE VIRTUAL UNIVERSITY ONLY PARTIALLY EXISTS

The great power and appeal of communication technologies is that they seemingly provide for the opportunity to connect places that have, hitherto, never been connected. The virtual seminar involved four institutions in three countries. It included active participants from the academic staff and postgraduates, as well as a more 'passive' undergraduate audience. The official history of the seminar, as told by those involved in its conception, was that they simply wanted to use video-conferencing to establish 'connections' with universities in other places; the detailed format and rationale for the project, as they saw it, would come later. The actual seminar ran on several different occasions during the academic year and, indeed, as the project developed a number of important outcomes became apparent. First, it was thought that, once the North Campus team had established links with other institutions, it might then be possible to gain access to expertise in areas where they were weak. What really excited the participants at the British University, for instance, was that the technology might allow their more practically orientated undergraduates and postgraduates access to the more theoretically orientated European academics:

We did a pilot this year, and it was about a year in brewing it up. The [Belgian partner] suggested a module of study to follow, and then everyone threw in different papers. Bob and Kath, and someone called Sergio over there, did something for us. Bill wrote a short paper, and a woman from Liege University wrote a paper as well. They took it in turns to present their papers and here we have a calendar of these things [pointing to the screen]. These are the videoconference links, you know, where we link up with the camera and an ISDN line. We gave 20 minutes talks, each person giving presentations, and the students from all four universities sat in and listened to those talks. There was about five minutes at the end of each talk for the students to ask genuine questions to the lecturer who had just spoken. So in a way we have got a way of sharing specialists in that subject.

It was also thought that the presentations might even be useful as 'learning material' for undergraduate students who were the audience in the seminar:

... that was the video conferencing bit, but the web bit is that the lecturers then put the stuff up on the Web. For example, Sergio put his paper up there. The students could dip into it and read it. And then, the last bit—the most important bit, I always think—is the seminar part. The students were allowed to go and email into a giant email box that everybody else can see. So it is like a live, open forum. And the students can start to follow things up. [The emails] get quite long. There were really quite considered contributions.

The compelling aspect of this story is that fairly mundane technologies such as email and video-conferencing appear to make the scenario of the virtual university possible: actors and institutions who never cooperated before are brought together in new alliances and affiliations to produce novel forms of higher education not previously available; work is moved from staff based in one place to those located elsewhere; and, thus, students are able to draw on expertise and knowledge from outside the walls of their own institution.

At the beginning, the seminar had been an extra module for the North Campus students for which they had volunteered (in the other countries it was a core module). Such was its apparent success, however, that it was decided to make it a regular feature and include it as a compulsory aspect of the degree course. Yet, as already mentioned, just a short time before the new academic year was about to commence, and the seminar was to run with a new set of students (and we were beginning to organize ourselves to go and sit-in on a number of these sessions), we were told that there had been some difficulties and it had, therefore, been decided to 'temporarily' postpone the seminar. When we asked as to why this might have happened we were told that partners in the Netherlands had pulled out because the organization allowing them to use a video-conferencing suite had decided to charge them the equivalent of £50 an hour to use it.

While we do not discount this financial story (although the small sums of money involved make us doubt its adequacy), we want to add a further aspect to this. Typically, we understand technologies in terms of what they might afford. Thus it could be suggested that it was the connections afforded by the video-conferencing equipment and email that initially allowed the project to get off the ground, and since other universities with the same technology were assumed to have a similar interest in being connected, the project began to flourish. Yet, the virtual seminar was basically technology-led—based simply on a desire to use video-conferencing within the University. And, as Latour and others remind us, the work of innovation involves not simply a requirement to contend oneself with the 'technological' specifics of the artefact, but just as importantly to manage the simultaneous construction of other (political, sociological, and economic) ties. This work was crucial if the project was to extend its influence within the wider networks of the University. Among other things, this work might include the establishment of an idea or a concept that can link the virtual seminar to the wider institutional goals (its educational aims and mission, and the role technology might play in this). In other words, the seminar lacked a context into which it could be inserted.

In the early phase of the project the goal of connection appeared self-evidently a 'good' and 'necessary' thing without further need of elaboration, and did indeed prove adequate to get the project off the ground. However, once the seminar had to jump a minor financial hurdle, the essentially technical goal of connection proved too weak, in at least one case, to sustain the project. And because the seminar had no wider context or other connections to draw upon, it was unable to negotiate this hurdle.[8] Tom describes how, in a meeting with the European partners to discuss the merits of the seminar and the potential for collaboration with other universities, the partners had decided, in the context of commitments to existing education methods, that the seminar 'wasn't worthwhile'. Interestingly, shortly after this meeting, Tom's own institution also began to question the benefits of financing further video-conferencing projects. Tom again: 'It's funny, at the same time [as the European partners pulled out of the project] in my University I've always had a £3000 budget to spend on anyone who wants to do video-conferencing from my room, and my budget's been cut on that as well'. Indeed, as far as Tom is concerned, just a couple of months after the technology had seemingly brought all these actors together into a network, video-conferencing within his University had 'come and gone'.

In summary, we have discussed what might be described as a failure to extend a network; the seminar was not fully integrated into the University and this lack of context or limited means of connection meant that the project was conceived of and remained simply a 'technical project'. For the actor network approach, a technology only becomes a success when a sufficient network has been built for it. Indeed, as Rudinow Saetnan (1991) points out, without such connections a technology can be said to only 'partially exist'. Finding an adequate way of conceiving of these virtual projects also appears as an issue in our second case study, the Information Skills course, to which we now turn.

WHAT IS A COURSE?

New technologies often demand the rethinking and reworking of the most basic and essential concepts (Kiesler and Sproull 1987). The idea behind the Information Skills course was to take 'old print based material' which was 'working well out there in the field' and convert this to run on the Web. The course could therefore be completely 'stand alone and accessible at a distance from the University'. What became apparent, however, whilst carrying out this 'conversion job' was the extent to which a tension was created in the existing organizational arrangements within North Campus. Seemingly, those established concepts and practices which were in place were not capable of providing the support that these advanced technologies asked of them.

---

[8] For instance, see Sarah Green and Penny Harvey's (1999) account of the different senses of 'connection' as it is typically discussed by technology advocates and, in contrast, how it might be understood elsewhere (as in anthropology or actor network theory). The upshot of their argument is that while technology can be effective at maintaining existing connections or relations between actors it is less good at building new ones. See also Brown and Duguid (2000: ch, 8), where a similar argument is made.

Let us elaborate on what this means through a description of one particular meeting where Tom and Sonia, a programmer from LDS, are demonstrating the new online version of the Information Skills course to one of the assistant directors of the Library, Helen. Helen was responsible for running the existing course and it was she, therefore, who would decide if the online version would get the go-ahead. While we waited for Helen to arrive, Sonia described how she was nervous about the forthcoming meeting. She had spent the whole summer turning the Information Skills material into something that could be put on the web and now she had reached the most crucial stage: the coding work was complete and she and Tom were ready to demonstrate it to Helen. Her nervousness rested on the fact that, while translating the course, she had made some necessary modifications to its format. Until the meeting, Helen had appeared supportive of the idea. In the immediately preceding weeks, however, she had been less forthcoming, both in terms of providing more information about the course and in her attitude and interest.

Towards the end of the demonstration Helen concluded that she liked the package but that, in truth, she was not sure how to proceed with it. Tom's suggestion was to test the package with some of her students over the next few weeks. However, Helen was not convinced that this was how it should be taken forward: as she understood it, no trial could possibly occur until the University had validated the course. What followed was a lengthy discussion about the need for validation. Sonia was convinced that there was no need to put the package through the validation process as, despite her modifications, she believed it was in essence the 'same course'. Helen disagreed: anything that has 'substantial modifications' has to be re-evaluated. For Sonia, however, while the course has been changed, it *was* the same course. The discussion as to whether or not the course was the same or different went on for some time. Indeed, at some points we observed how there was even some ambiguity about what a course, one of the most taken for granted categories of the University, actually *was*.

The problem appeared to be that the project team were not willing to describe the course in *too novel* terms for fear that the online version's genesis from the original Information Skills module would be completely disregarded. It was not simply that, if seen to be completely 'new', the course would have to be re-validated, but that the very processes and procedures for validating an online course would, themselves, have to be created and put in place. At the same time, however, if they used a concept that was too fully rooted to the conventional conception of the course, then they ran the risk of their work never being adopted, as the team believed the library staff would not go to the effort of implementing something that was simply an online version of what they were already teaching. Thus, the project team attempted to deploy a notion of a course that is *simultaneously* old and new: it was both a traditional course and a new virtual university course.

Finally, the meeting broke up and Tom appeared disappointed. It had not gone exactly as he had planned. He was particularly upset that Helen might want to have the course re-evaluated, telling us that in all previous dealings he had managed to avoid dealing with the 'centre' and that he had hoped to do the same this time around as well.[9] Now it would mean much more work for his team and, he thought, the module would probably never be launched. Such confrontations, we found during our research, were commonplace.

THE CYBER CULTURE COURSE IS *TOO* VIRTUAL

Let us finally turn to the Cyber Culture module. Here, too, we witness the demand for various forms of boundary or 'bridging' work between the universities as they are now and the idea of a future institution. In some respects, the Cyber Culture module is the most interesting project we observed as it comes closest to what is most commonly thought of as truly virtual Higher Education: it was a completely new course that took North Campus in a very different direction by targetting new groups of students—those outside the institution. The idea behind this course, to repeat Tom's words, was that his department should become a little 'Open University' that would transact directly with its students through technological means.

In the end, the course was not able to attract 'large' numbers. This is not to say, however, that the course was not used. As well as being a package to be sold on the Internet, it also became a compulsory module on the European Studies degree programme, one taken by traditional campus-based students. Tom describes the logic behind this as being the desire to encourage staff in other departments to become similarly involved and develop their own online courses; as Tom saw it, the Cyber Culture module would serve as a useful device for enrolling other members of staff. Yet, before the module can work to enlist others, it must first enrol the students. Here the team saw a potential problem: how might students accustomed to more traditional forms of teaching and learning react to a fully online course? Tom's experience of similar developments had led him to believe that students could sometimes be sceptical of such developments and as a way of addressing this scepticism right from the outset, Tom and his team had spent a lot of time reworking the course with these users in mind.

The basic problem, as Tom saw it, was that the Cyber Culture module in its existing form was *too virtual* for these particular students. Indeed, the extent to which he considers this a serious issue can be seen from the following description of a conversation where, meeting with two of the University's graphic designers, Tom discussed the design of some printed material that might be incorporated into the Cyber Culture module.

---

[9]   Of course, what Tom was referring to as the 'centre' is among other things the tradition within universities of 'rule by committee'. For a good description of the workings of the committee system, see Lockwood and Davies (1985).

In terms of a fully online course, it will never happen. We will never go electronic. So, we have come to this kind of moment when we feel that we have to try and market—sort of market in inverted commas, but really market without the inverted commas—these materials. Internally for ourselves we have got to persuade—I think that is the best word, it's not too strong a word—persuade students that this is a good route to choose while there is still a choice between using the printed versions and the web versions.

To gain access to the online course, the procedure is simply to issue each student with a World Wide Web address (URL), a username, and a password. However, for the project team, the fear was that a simple slip of paper sent to the student, or an email, containing the necessary information to access the course would not be adequate because it would fail to effectively stand in for, or symbolize, the work which the team and the Institution had put into developing and running the course. This, it was feared, would lead the students to undervalue both the course itself and North Campus's role in creating it. The issue, then, as Tom sees it, is a matter of persuading students of the benefits of these forms of technology and of further developing the package with this relationship in mind. Considerable effort was, therefore, put into finding a suitable way of making this wholly immaterial (virtual) course distinct and significant for its potential users.

The outcome of this effort was the creation of an elaborately packaged floppy disk which prominently displayed the University's logo in order to establish firmly the provenance of the course. The exact problem as Tom sees it is as follows:

It's so difficult you see, because [the online courses] don't exist. I can't bring any to show you. And that is what we want the print [material] to do is to turn them into 'things', and that is why we slipped back to this idea of at least giving them a diskette for the first one, and then we can have students coming along to LDS and we can give them a disk out over the table, over our reception desk.

In short, the success of the virtual course becomes reliant on a functionally redundant physical token—the packaged floppy disk.

This leads us to a more general point about the nature of the virtual university and its relation to the campus. In common with many commentators, and indeed many of those involved in the initiatives that we studied, we began our research with the notion of the traditional place of the university—the campus—as a barrier, as something to be overcome with the aid of ICTs. Indeed, this appears more generally as a powerful trend within the discourse of virtuality. We did not, of course, suppose this represented a total escape from the constraints of geography, but rather that the university could only escape a particular spatial configuration by instituting another: to paraphrase David Harvey (1987), this would be annihilating space and time through a new 'spatial fix'. Thus, we assumed that although the university could become 'dis-embedded' from the campus, it could only do so by becoming re-embedded in some other configuration of places.

Over the period of the research, however, we moved increasingly away from this image of dis-embedding and re-embedding as we were made increasingly aware of the ways in which place—the physical world of the campus—far from being simply a constraint on the activities of the university and its staff and students, performed a number of important, if unacknowledged, functions for them; it is what Phil Agre (2000b) has described as a sort of 'meta-place' that provides all the other places of the university with a common administrative apparatus, physical plant, and, as we have suggested, symbolic resource.

It was only after attempts were made to abstract a course from the campus setting that these roles become visible, and with this visibility came a growing awareness of the complexity of seeking to replace the work that the campus so discretely undertakes (see Cornford and Pollock 2002).

Taking this notion further, we would argue that the effort of substituting for the various forms of work that the campus performs for higher education turns on its head the assumption that universities, as they take-up and use more and more ICTs, will become increasingly 'virtual'. Rather, much of the effort of building these components into the university is concerned with giving them a greater sense of material presence (cf. Wakeford 1999). Tom again: 'It is a hard move, you know, moving from giving away books to, you know, giving away nothing. So, it is like this: hopefully the print will carry that through, give it that sort of solidity and life'.

CONCLUSION

What is particular about our account of why these projects 'stalled'? Three reasons are conventionally put forward for the failure of such initiatives: the technology doesn't work (or doesn't work as expected); staff, in particular teaching staff, actively or passively resist the introduction of the technology which threatens their autonomy (e.g. by removing their control of course construction and use); and, finally, that the costs of such courses are simply too high, at least when they are not spread across a very large number of learners. There is, of course, something in each of these analyses. We would argue, however, that each of these arguments is, in fact, partial and superficial. In none of the cases we looked at did the technology fail. Further, there was no overt staff resistance to the introduction of the courses. On the contrary, all the teaching staff involved were, somewhat to our surprise, more or less keen on the use of the techno- logy, and where there was criticism, this was offered in a 'constructive' manner. Finally, while the issue of costs did emerge frequently in each of the cases, it was the costs of the work of (re)configuring the institution, rather than those of the technology, that eventually emerged as significant. What we would argue, then, is that each of these three reasons can be seen as simply the surface manifestation of a deeper underlying tension between the old and the new: between established technological configurations and the new context of higher education in which they are deployed; between the engagement of staff in the established networks of the university and the possibilities of the new, and the more technologically mediated, networks of the 'online' university; and, finally, the tension between the conventionally accounted costs of course construction, and the revealed costs of (re)creating the context in which virtual courses can survive (including the problems of accounting for these).

Returning to the quotation with which we began this essay, the underlying problem in each case is the sheer volume and complexity of the work required to configure the multiple actors—people, machines, objects, texts, and money—all of which are already enrolled more or less consciously in existing networks.

What form of university is emerging in light of the increasing applications of new Information and Communication Technologies? On the one hand, it is unlikely that there will be an absolute transformation of the university: its core role and functions cannot simply be shifted online overnight; physical places like campuses are increasingly relevant; and there is little evidence to suggest that learners find fully online courses (Hara and Kling 2000) or electronic study resources (Stephens 1999) wholly appropriate to their needs. On the other hand, staff and students are increasingly reliant on information systems, the Internet, and other online technologies to conduct their everyday routines. Indeed, the nature of academic work is changing as scholars find themselves using more technology, and not only within scientific and technological fields (Star and Ruhleder 1996); communication between these scholarly communities is increasingly shaped by the possibilities (and limitations) afforded by e-mail (Walsh and Bayma 1996); new undergraduates increasingly want to complete registration procedures online rather than wait in line at a desk, and so on.

The picture we painted at North Campus is, then, just as equivocal. Despite the early phase where the projects appeared to flourish, albeit only within the close confines of the team and allied groups, what Law and Callon (1995) have called a 'negotiation space', once attempts were made to extend these networks out into the University, or as in the case of the virtual seminar where the Institution enters the space of the project, each 'stalled'. Essentially, the initiatives demanded the rethinking and, more importantly re*working* of relations between a wide-ranging set of actors and entities, many of which were well beyond the imagined scope of the original, technologically conceived projects. The abstraction and distribution of courses and activities from the campus can create new divisions of labour between staff, students, and objects, as well as places. But what is divided must then be reconnected. And this work of reconnection is not simply a matter of establishing a technical linkage.

What is crucial, then, to whichever form(s) of university that may emerge from the encounter with virtual technologies is the 'work' of building the virtual university *into* the traditional university. Pivotal to this has been the effort of the project team and the multi-faceted or 'inter-mediation' role they have played as they have grappled with the various technologies, sociologies, economics, politics, and materialities of campus life. We say intermediation role because the team are 'Janus faced', attempting to face different directions at the same time (Latour 1987). They are trying to build the virtual university from within the constraints and limitations of the traditional university and the issue for them is whether to continue to work with, and try to fit these new online courses and seminars into, existing concepts, arrangements, and infrastructures, or to begin to call into being new and different ones. Such work—this continuous movement back and forth between the existing Institution and the (often mismatched) requirements of the new projects—is slow, complex, and prone to failure. This is because the university, like most institutions, has a large number of well established networks, infrastructures and routines that are not easily recognized or changed (Agre 2000b). The problem Tom and his team, and those like them, face, can thus be seen as a choice between exploring new technological mediated possibilities and the exploitation of old certainties. In other words, the issue for universities as they face the challenges brought about by ICTs is to choose which aspects of their existing institution they should continue to exploit and which of the promises of the new technologies they should begin to explore.

REFERENCES

Abeles, T. (1998) 'The academy in a wired world', *Futures*, 30(7): 606.

Agre, P. (2000a) 'Infrastructure and Institutional Change in the Networked University', *Information, Communication and Society*, 3(4).

—— (2000b) 'Imagining the Wired University', Paper presented at the Symposium on the Future of the University, University of Newcastle, September 2000.

Bowker, G. and Star, S. L. (1996) 'How things (actor-net)work: classification, magic and the ubiquity of standards', Graduate School of Library and Information Science, University of Illinois at Urbana-Champaign, found at http://weber.ucsd.edu/~gbowker/pubs.htm, no page number.

Brown, J. S. and Duguid, P. (2000) *The Social Life of Information*. Boston: Harvard Business School Press.

Callon, M. (1986) 'Some elements of a sociology of translation: domestication of the scallops and the fishermen of St. Brieuc Bay', in J. Law (ed.) *Power, Action and Belief: a New Sociology of Knowledge?* Sociological Review Monograph, Routledge: London.

Cornford, J. (2000) 'The Virtual University is . . . the university made concrete', *Information, Communication and Society*, 3(4).

—— and Pollock, N. (2002) 'The university campus as a "resourceful constraint": process and practice in the construction of the virtual university', in M. R. Lea and K. Nicoll (eds) *Understanding Distributed Learning*. Milton Keynes: Open University Press.

Cunningham, S., Tapsall, S., Ryan, Y., Stedman, L., *et al.* (1998) *New Media and Borderless Education: A Review of the Convergence between Global Media Networks and Higher Education Provision*. Australian Government, Department of Employment, Education, training and Youth Affairs, Evaluations and Investigations Programme, Higher Education Division (http://www.deetya.gov.au/highered/eippubs/eip97-22/eip9722.pdf)

CVCP (2000) The Business of Borderless Education. London: CVCP.

Green, S. and Harvey, P. (1999) 'Scaling Place and Networks: an ethnography of ICT "innovation" in Manchester'. Paper Presented to the Internet and Ethnography Conference, University of Hull, 13–14 December.

Hara, N. and Kling, R. (2000) 'Student distress in Web-based distance education', *Information, Communication and Society,* 3(4).

Harvey, D. (1987) *The Condition of Postmodernity: An Enquiry into the Origins of Cultural Change.* Oxford: Basil Blackwell.

Johnston, S. (1999) 'Introducing and Supporting Change Towards More Flexible Teaching Approaches', in A. Tait and R. Mills (eds), *The Convergence of Distance and Conventional Education.* London: New York.

Kiesler, S. and Sproull, L. (1987) 'The Social Process of Technological Change in Organizations', in S. Kiesler and L. Sproull (eds) *Computing and Change on Campus.* Cambridge: Cambridge University Press.

Latour, B. (1987) *Science in Action.* Cambridge, Massachusetts: Harvard University Press.

Law, J. (1994) *Organising Modernity.* Oxford: Blackwell.

—— and Callon, M. (1995) 'Engineering and Sociology in a Military Aircraft Project: A Network Analysis of Technological Change' in S.L. Star (ed.) *Ecologies of Knowledge: Work and Politics in Science and Technology.* Albany: State University of New York Press.

Lockwood, G. and Davies, J. (eds) (1985) *Universities: The Management Challenge.* Windsor: NFER-Nelson Publishing.

March, J. (1989) 'Exploration and Exploitation in Organizational Learning', *Organizational Science,* 2(1): 71–87.

Middlehurst, R. (2001) 'University Challenges: Borderless Higher Education, Today and Tomorrow', *Minerva,* 39: 3–26.

Newby, H. (1999) 'Higher Education in the 21st Century: Some Possible Futures', Discussion Paper. CVCP: London, March.

Noam, E. (1995) 'Electronics and the dim future of the university', *Science,* 270(13): 247–9.

Noble, D. (1998) 'Digital Diploma Mills: the Automation of Higher Education', *Monthly Review,* 49(a): 38–52.

Pollock, N. (2000) 'The Virtual University as "accurate and timely information"', *Information, Communication and Society,* 3(3): 349–365.

—— and Cornford, J. (2000) 'The Theory and Practice of the Virtual University', *Ariadne,* Issue 24, found at http://www.ariadne.ac.uk/issue24/virtual-universities/intro.html.

—— and —— (2001) 'ERP Systems and the University as an "Unique" Organisation', paper presented to the Critical Management Studies Conference, UMIST, Manchester, UK, July. Available in *Electronic Journal of Radical Organisation Theory* at http://www.mngt.waikato.ac.nz/ejrot/cmsconference/2001/papers_education.asp

Porter, T. M. (1994) 'Information, power and the view from nowhere', in L. Bud-Friedman (ed.) *Information Acumen: The Understanding and Use of Knowledge in Modern Business.* London: Routledge.

Rudinow Saetnan, A. (1991) 'Rigid Politics and Technological Flexibility', *Science, Technology, & Human Values,* 16(4).

Ryan, Y. (2000) 'The Business of Borderless Education: US case studies and the HE response', paper presented to the CVCP conference 'The Business of Borderless Education', 28th March.

Star, L. and Ruhleder, K. (1996) 'Steps Toward an Ecology of Infrastructure: Design and Access for Large Information Spaces', *Information Systems Research*, 7(1): 111–34.

Stephens, K. (1999) 'Notes from the Margins: Library Experiences of Postgraduate Distance-Learning Students', in A. Tait and R. Mills (eds), *The Convergence of Distance and Conventional Education*. London: New York.

Wakeford, N. (1999) 'Gender and the Landscapes of Computing in an Internet Café', in M. Crang, P. Crang, and J. May, (eds), *Virtual Geographies: Bodies, Space and Relations*. London: Routledge.

Walsh, J. P. and Bayma, T. (1996) 'Computer networks and scientific work', *Social Studies of Science*, 26: 661–703.

Winner, L (1998) 'Automatic Professor Machine' (available from http://www.rpi.edu/~winner/apm1.html, downloaded 6 June 1999).

6

The Virtual University: The Learner's Perspective

Charles Crook

There are many reasons given for developing virtual universities. Those most frequently heard concern the ambition of greater social inclusion and the promise of greater cost-effectiveness. It is not so common to hear arguments based upon advancing the quality of the learning experience itself. Nevertheless, some advocates of virtualization indicate high expectations about that experience. For example, it is frequently claimed that virtual learning offers to students a new intellectual independence; it does so by providing them with greater freedom in the management of their studies. Yet, there is little sense that such promises are based upon any principled consideration of how people learn. The academic discipline of psychology is expected to offer insight into these matters. Accordingly, one aim of the present chapter is to consider how our thinking about virtualization might be informed by psychological perspectives. I shall note what these have had to say about the issue of learning, and how this, in turn, has influenced the design of educational technology.

  This chapter also has a second theme. Within the evolving debate about virtual universities, the voice of one particular stakeholder seems strangely absent. I am thinking of the student. It is true that students do participate in research on virtual learning interventions. Accordingly, questionnaires are filled in and tests are taken that furnish data on 'learning outcomes'. Yet, such materials seem to provide only a rather superficial analysis of the student perspective. This lack of probing into how current undergraduates relate to the virtual agenda is odd. Perhaps this is because opportunities for virtual learning have generally catered for students that are 'continuing' or 'lifelong'. However, consideration also must be given to those who make up the bulk of the present higher education constituency: full-time and younger students. The general trajectory of their education will not necessarily be affected by virtualization. For there is no obvious political ambition to break the present contiguity between secondary and tertiary education. In which case, whatever gets done to virtualize universities had better be acceptable to traditional school-leaving undergraduates, because individuals very like them could be populating these new institutions in large numbers. In the second part of this chapter, I shall draw upon my own involvement with research directed at students facing opportunities to take part in more virtual practices.

The chapter is organized as follows. In the next two sections, I configure a position at the intersection of psychology, learning, and information and communication technologies (ICTs). I shall identify the virtual agenda in relation to ICTs and note how psychology has previously guided both popular understandings of learning and practical applications of educational technology. In the third section, I propose that a 'cultural' version of contemporary psychology offers the greatest promise for analysing virtual scenarios. The empirical case for such a perspective will then be made by drawing from my own involvement with projects investigating this area (Crook, forthcoming; Crook and Light 1999; Light, Crook, and White 2000). These findings are described in the second half of this chapter. There, I shall illustrate a cultural perspective on the virtualization of undergraduate learning (the discussion being organized into four sections, around the themes of time, place, social relationships, and materials). I believe that the two resources I have identified above—the students' own voice and the lessons of psychological research—must contribute to the debates exercised in this book. My aim is not a thorough research review: it is more to map a landscape of issues for participating in the virtual education project—as seen by a psychologist.

PSYCHOLOGY, LEARNING, AND TECHNOLOGY

I understand the concept of a virtual university to mean higher education that is more loosely distributed in time and place. Virtual undergraduates will configure programs of study to a more flexible timetable and they will not be obliged to congregate for study at particular places. The possibility of such virtualization is commonly associated with opportunities afforded by new communications technologies. It might be tempting simply to presume that any psychology of virtual learning will simply be the psychology of learning with ICTs. Yet, as others have argued (e.g. Clark 1994), such media do not have direct effects. Where new technology is being adopted, it is important to notice the underlying teaching and learning practices that are guiding the forms of its use. Although there must therefore be a web of causal factors behind activities observed in any particular virtual scenario, I shall nevertheless use ICTs as a way of creating a focus for my own analysis of virtual education here. This will be pursued in two ways. First, in the remainder of this section, I shall review how psychologists have theorized learning, sketching three traditions, each of which have influenced the design of educational technology. Then, in the sections that follow this theoretical sketch, I shall develop more fully one particular strand of theorizing—cultural psychology—by reference to research on student learning.

Behaviourism Cuban (1986) has reviewed the history of teachers and technology, reminding us of how resilient educational practice has been in the face of such new tools. However, the term 'teaching machine' only gains currency towards the end of Cuban's story. It was the psychological tradition of behaviourism that gave authority to this form of device (Skinner 1968). From behaviourism, we derive the idea of learning being a question of acquiring new responses. New responses must be 'shaped' out of an existing behavioural repertoire. This happens as the environment selectively applies rewards to (initially spontaneous) activities, such that they are successively fashioned to match the desired behavioural goal. All organisms were judged to learn in this same way. Accordingly, for a long time, the study of learning famously dwelled on laboratory animals, simply for convenience. The invention of teaching machines made visible what followed from this theoretical perspective on learning. Presenting knowledge in a form that facilitated learning was achieved by analysis and reduction of the domain-to-be-learned. The learner's encounter with that domain was therefore orchestrated as a gradual re-building: a path of rewarded interactions with those components of the domain that had been ordered by the designer/teacher's analysis.

While there is a useful insight in the principle that individuals change and develop according to the consequences of their actions (their 'contingencies' with the world), this principle was not powerful enough to prove very useful in practice. In particular, teaching machines were neither popular nor very successful in the form that this theory encouraged. Behaviourism has declined from its prominent influence. Yet, one legacy is important: it frames learning as a matter of 'acquiring' something (responses).

Cognitivism It is commonly claimed that behaviourism was displaced by cognitive psychology—roughly during the 1960s, and gaining central status in psychology thereafter. While behaviourism rejected the need for postulating hidden (i.e. non-behavioural) psychological processes, cognitivism positively celebrated the role of invisible symbolic structures acting somewhere between stimulus and response. The prevailing metaphor for this theory was 'information processing', for this was a period in which engineering control theory and cybernetics were attracting wide interest. The project adopted by cognitive psychologists became one of modelling how information was detected, discriminated, transmitted, stored, and retrieved by the complex mechanism of the human information processing system. Thus, the human mind was conceptualized as a symbol-manipulating apparatus. Like behaviourism, this perspective also encouraged a distinctive form of educational technology. Design of that technology was inspired by the cognitivist concern with 'knowledge representation'. A seductive challenge was to devise mechanical systems that might diagnose an individual's representational structures for some domain that they wished to learn (say, some area of physics). Once properly specified, such a diagnosis could then be data for an intelligent tutoring system (ITS). The 'syllabus' designed into an ITS would then not resemble the rigid and reductionist formats of the behaviourists' teaching machine. With this new educational technology, the selection of 'problems' for the learner was much more carefully crafted to a theory about that person's existing understandings (and misunderstandings).

The ITSs have had only modest impacts. Diagnosis and utilization of students' putative knowledge structures proved difficult; and simulation of tutorial dialogue proved even more challenging. Again, the fate of educational technology may be a yardstick for judging the psychological perspective that inspired it. While cognitive psychology does well in handling memory (modelling the storage and retrieval of information), it seems to say little about learning and even less about teaching. A certain preoccupation with cognitive architecture renders the learner as relatively passive; moreover, the whole issue of motivation—what engages learners—is seriously neglected. Although cognitive psychology shifts the conceptual vocabulary from behaviour to mind, one important legacy resembles that claimed for behaviourism: namely, a concern for specifying some entity that the learner 'acquires'—albeit in relation to representations, rather than responses.

Constructivism Parallel with the growth of cognitive psychology, has been an increasing interest in theories variously termed 'constructivist'. Such perspectives can moderate the more passive model of learning propagated by some cognitive psychology. This is because constructivism does view the learner as very much an active agent. Within education, Jean Piaget's work has been particularly influential. As such, constructivism has encouraged a view of educational practice as a task of 'facilitating'. Instruction comes to be about orchestrating optimal conditions for learners: conditions that allow active processes of knowledge building. Learning arises from guided exploration of the world consolidated by the student's own reflection upon the consequences of such exploration. The growing influence of constructivist theorizing is evident in the direction taken by educational technology. Experienced commentators (e.g. de Corte 1996) judge there to have been a drift from *instructional* software (such as the teaching machine and the ITS) towards more *pupil-centred* tools that are less directive in their design. A landmark example is the problem-solving language Logo theorized by Papert, with extensive reference to Piaget's constructivism (Papert 1980). If there is a distinctive legacy from this form of theorizing, then it must be its insistence that the learner is self-directed. Thus, the computer in education should become less a teacher and more a 'pupil'—a resource that the learner can control, explore or 'instruct'.

EVALUATING PSYCHOLOGIES OF LEARNING

The value in reviewing these psychological traditions is to help us identify the theoretical assumptions that could be driving current interest in virtual forms of learning. However, such links between theory and practice must be tentatively made. It is not as if the designers of virtual learning environments have been explicitly invoking psychology. However, it is clear from the sketch above that the discipline has been implicated in the design of many other computer-based educational technologies. There is every reason to suppose that psychological theorizing informs the present agenda of virtualization—even if that influence is sometimes tacit and not formally acknowledged.

I wish to identify two particular theoretical themes that are apparent in the arguments that promote virtual practices. They both have roots in the psychology of learning and yet they are both problematical—arguably because of limitations in the scope of the underlying psychological thinking. The first concerns learner autonomy: the expectation that virtualization allows students to take greater control over their own study. The second is more abstract, and its influence is more subtle: namely, a conception of learning that supposes that it involves the 'acquisition' of something.

First, prioritizing learner autonomy clearly resonates with constructivist theories of learning. Practice based on such theories equips learners to achieve understandings through their own exploratory actions. In turn, they may consolidate these experiences by actively reflecting on the logic and consequences of those actions. Virtual learning seems to promise this, insofar as it offers to liberate the student from institutional direction; stressing instead resource-based and independent learning. However, cognitive psychology is implicated along with constructivism. For the credibility of learner independence must depend on the quality of the 'resources' upon which it is based. There is an expectation cultivated by cognitive psychology that the conceptual sophistication of learners is something that might be diagnoseable—thereby locating their exact state of 'readiness' and selecting learning resources to match this well. The MacFarlane report provides a good marker for this. It does so at the very outset, in a chapter that explicitly grounds the committee's deliberations in psychological knowledge about learning. MacFarlane himself, writing later, declares: 'Technology can transform an individual's learning environment by presenting richly structured information to aid the assimilation, by providing highly-structured instantiated knowledge for easy and flexible interactive access, and by generating highly-interactive simulations for experiential learning' (MacFarlane 1998: 83).

Such celebrations of student autonomy typically carry an implicit critique of the status quo in this promise of 'transformation'. By implication, current practices are insufficiently flexible, the student is not interacting, and learning is insufficiently experiential. It is as if the spontaneous curiosity of students is held

back by institutional obstacles: by the slow, resilient and inaccessible procedures of current practice. Learner-oriented technology will liberate students from
some stifling curricular organization. On this model, the design of 'richly structured information' will be guided by cognitive psychology, and the constructivist
student can pursue such resources free from the constraints of timetable and
classroom. Put starkly, 'Online self-learning packages fundamentally question
the traditional role of the educator by giving students greater individual control. Effective learning can be realized by providing a student with a computer,
loading the educational software and walking away' (Gell and Cochrane 1996:
252). However, this liberational vision is a promise needing closer scrutiny.
Psychological theory is relatively silent on whether the orchestration of learning might depend upon traditional communities of peers and tutors. Just as it
has little to say about how easily student learning can actually be scaffolded by
the less-animated formats of learning materials and distance communication.
I shall revisit these concerns later by discussing a more *cultural* theory of student learning—one that is more centrally concerned with the situated nature of
learning and its scaffolds of support.

A cultural form of theorizing can also be derived from consideration of the
second psychological theme that fuels expectations for virtual education. That
theme concerns the metaphor of 'acquisition', an image that pervades all three
psychological theories considered above. It is also an idea that sits comfortably
with the implicit theme of 'delivery' that characterizes resource-intensive modes
of education—such as is associated with virtual learning. It is argued below that
the acquisition metaphor inevitably cultivates a relationship to knowledge that
is more about 'taking in' than 'taking part'.

Within psychology, learning-as-acquisition finds its clearest endorsement in
the behaviourist view that learning is manifested as a repertoire of acquired
responses. It is a seductive notion, for it fits well with our natural intuition that
the mind is a sort of container. This is not merely a common sense idea. It also
captures a core supposition of much cognitive psychology: namely, that the currency of mental life must be particular sorts of entities (representations, say);
then learning, thinking, and remembering, entail no more than the acquisition,
sifting and sorting of those entities. However, neuroscience does not offer much
support for this conception. While the brain admits a coarse localization of function, it does not seem to be structured like a filing cabinet. This, therefore, does
not encourage a view of the mind as a spatial architecture into which knowledge
gets strategically 'placed'. It does not encourage a model of learning in terms of
the 'acquisition' of any such items-for-storage. Bereiter and Scardamalia (1996)
have critically discussed the mind-as-container assumption. They draw attention
to a more appealing alternative for theorizing learning, namely connectionism
(e.g. Rummelhart 1989). Connectionist theories invite us to think of the mind as
primarily an environmental pattern-detecting device. Learning involves recognizing such patterns and thereby adapting to the environment in a 'finding our
way around' manner. For this theory, the canonical and telling achievements of

learning are those arising from routine cultural practices: achievements such as tending the garden, playing poker, navigating a city, being a policeman, parenting etc. Learning is a successful attunement to the environmental structures in which these practices are encountered.

The case for connectionism has not yet been made in terms of some educational technology—although a case has been developed through the construction of learning automata (robots) based upon connectionist design principles. Indeed this perspective tends not to encourage the design of educational tools that are conceived to promote information–delivery relationships with the learner. The connectionist influence upon educational technology is more through the design of learning *environments*: contexts in which technology can be recruited to catalyse engagement of learners with authentic disciplinary practices (e.g. Bereiter and Scardamalia 1992). In such instances, there is played out a different metaphor for learning to that of acquisition. The consequences of learning in these settings seems more a matter of 'participation' than acquisition (Sfard 1998). The notion that instruction involves designing opportunities such that learners may 'come to take part' resonates more with modern connectionism than does the notion that learning is a matter of acquiring representations, and rules for sifting and sorting them.

However, it also resonates with conceptions of learning derived from social anthropology (Lave and Wenger 1991). Within this tradition we find a similar theoretical perspective on educational practice: namely, that it should involve orchestrating students' entry into communities of (disciplinary) practice (Wenger 1998). This more anthropological version of such theorizing is represented within psychology as 'cultural psychology' (Cole 1998). While connectionism is oriented more towards neuroscience for grounding its theories (therefore, tending to build learning automata), cultural psychology is more oriented towards ecology (therefore tending to build learning environments).

In this section, I have dwelt upon the learning rhetoric of student autonomy and the metaphor of acquisition, suggesting that psychological thinking has tended to cultivate these virtualization themes. The argument has converged on the attraction of an alternative psychological theory of learning: one that takes participation as its central concern, and which views study as a form of culturally-embedded practice. Such a cultural psychology could offer a useful reference point for our present concern with evaluating virtual education. That claim is developed in the next section.

LEARNING AND CULTURAL PSYCHOLOGY

Cultural psychology invites us to view mental life as essentially mediated. Human beings everywhere act upon the world through mediational means—artefacts, tools, technologies, social rituals, genres of communication, and so on. The psychology of intelligence is thus concerned with a novel analytic unit: people-acting-with-mediational-means. Intelligence ceases to comprise an in-the-head repertoire of generic processes—skills that psychologists might isolate for study in context-free laboratories. Intelligence becomes a socially cultivated phenomenon—activity that has come to be *distributed* over systems of artefacts and technologies, as well as systems of social organization. It is best cultivated by students taking part in the contexts where such resources are made available.

Learning is of great interest to cultural psychology. The approach is quite naturally concerned with how communities rapidly empower newcomers (children) to take advantage of the historically evolved possibilities available in a local culture. From this perspective, learning becomes a matter of 'enculturation'. Much attention has been directed to how that is achieved within the pre-school years. Indeed, an emphasis on the participatory dimension of learning has often been grounded in observations of how children readily learn the language and social practices of their culture without anything that looks like 'teaching'. This informal learning seems to depend upon the willingness of adults (say, parents) to join in and thereby orchestrate children's interactions around cultural material. This is achieved in such a way as to create episodes of creative activity that could not be achieved by a learner acting independently. Such openings for participation are commonly said to be 'scaffolded' by adults (Wood 1988). Put against agendas for virtual education, this perspective makes a striking claim for the central role of interpersonal support in learning.

The interest of cultural psychologists in educational practice has encouraged research on two particular questions. The first concerns the idea that learning as enculturation must always entail an effort to capture some 'culture of practice': how things get done in the discipline. For example, in the curricula of schooling this might be the culture of mathematicians, chemists, geographers, and so on. The question then arises as to whether schools should reproduce conditions that more closely approximate the practices and values of actual disciplinary communities. A second research interest of cultural psychology dwells on expert–novice (say, parent–child) scaffolding in accounts of learning outside of school. Here, the question is whether interactions among teachers and learners should more closely approximate the dynamic observed in the powerful exchanges of informal or domestic learning. The practical agenda arising from the first question is one of how to construct 'communities of practice' in educational contexts (Brown *et al.* 1989). While the second question invites consideration of whether formal education can import arrangements for 'assisted performance', which some have argued define optimal methods of teaching (Tharp and Gallimore 1988). Each of these cultural psychological concerns can be considered in relation to ICT-intensive versions of virtual education.

Enthusiasts for creating *communities of practice* have found new technology a powerful tool for the design of more authentic learning environments (e.g. Cognition and Technology Group at Vanderbilt 1990). However, such interventions do embed the technology in a strong classroom culture of face-to-face interaction: authentic practice being supported by new and powerful tools, but also being supported by a social context of communication and collaboration. While conventional schooling may be criticized for not giving learners a strong-enough sense of disciplinary participation, these case study interventions show that good approximations are possible (see also Brown 1992). It is less obvious that the distributed social relations of virtual education will be able to deploy techno-logy in ways that claim quite such a degree of authenticity. It will be necessary to debate whether a significant strand of development in educational practice will thereby be sacrificed.

Enthusiasts for *assisted performance* as a learning arrangement may also mobil-ize technology. For computers can provide particularly rich (interactive and resourceful) settings for catalysing an effective episode of such tuition. Perhaps virtual education could also provide such collaborative experiences 'around' technology (Crook 1994). However, it could do so only at considerable expense, because such interpersonal occasions are inherently synchronous and are most naturally managed in learning environments where participants are in close and regular contact. It might be supposed that a substituted form of interaction could be devised for virtual learners, one that involved ICT as a tutorial *partner* for the learner—rather than a catalyst. This is no more than the vision of ITSs mentioned above. The study of learning as social practice has clarified why this is a seriously limited ambition. The capacity for both strategic collaboration and for organized instruction seems to depend upon a uniquely human capacity: in psychology this is often termed 'intersubjectivity' (Rommetveit 1979). Indeed, the distinct-iveness of this capacity accounts for why other species lack anything resembling pedagogy (Premack and Premack 1996). Intersubjectivity refers to the projection of psychological states into other people: it describes an inclination for suppos-ing that the behaviour of others is directed by mental dispositions such as belief, desire, and fear. As will be argued in below, this allows human beings to do the sort of anticipating, predicting, and hypothesizing that underpins the subtle interpersonal process of instruction.

It is now possible to state summarily what follows from this sketch of cultural psychology. It promotes a conception of learning that stresses two designs: parti-cipation in communities of practice and expert-to-novice engagements through scaffolded or 'assisted' performance. I have argued that neither arrangement is easily configured in a virtualized context of learning. Yet, it can be also be argued that neither is very often realized in traditional institutions either (Lave 1991; Tharp and Gallimore 1988). Thus the poor prospect of doing so in virtual settings is hardly a fatal critique. Accordingly, although such ideas may be central to cul-tural psychology's manifesto for educational design, they need not be the main reason for invoking this version of psychology to help our thinking about virtual learning.

Instead, what is provocative about a cultural approach to learning is something more basic: namely, its conception of learning as 'practice'—activity that always entails a dynamic of engagement with cultural resources. Other psychologies tend to promote a conception of cultural context as no more than a background (perhaps this is the common sense understanding). In the case of educational settings, the background is one against which some set of activities we term 'studying' gets played out. So, it is easy to suppose that this context could be radically reconfigured, if only political will and some technology or other invited it. In particular, the *institutions* that orchestrate this context are not recognized as crucial to the principle activity of learning itself. This marginalization of cultural context readily encourages upbeat visions of virtual alternatives. For instance, visions in which 'information technology would be used to provide self-paced and asynchronously-accessed learning support delivered as, when and where the learner needed it. Such support, delivered at a user's request and convenience, would be paid for like any other commodity' (MacFarlane 1998: 86).

One way of casting the role of the institutional context into more familiar language is to invoke the notion of motivation and the particular idea that studying is invariably demanding of us. I have already noted that learner motivation is neglected by the mainstream of psychological theorizing. What is potentially problematic for virtualization is how far the traditional cultural contexts of education help students with the demands of learning: serving to sustain and—where necessary—insulate the activities of study from competing alternatives. Experience and/or career aspirations may supply such motivation among 'continuing' and 'lifelong' learners: indeed, this may underpin the successes of virtual education within such constituencies. However, the traditional school-leaver is a more serious challenge in this respect (Magee *et al.* 1998). Insofar as this is acknowledged in the agenda of virtualization, it is portrayed as merely a skills-training challenge: 'Students will have to be taught how to manage their own learning processes to an unprecedented degree' (MacFarlane 1998: 83). There may be a skills aspect to such self-management. However, at present, the main burden of sustaining study may be carried by the curriculum, rituals and architecture of traditional institutions. This fabric deserves some consideration. It would be helpful to understand more of how it works for the learner and what we might expect to follow from disturbing it. Accordingly, the remaining discussion here moves towards this in relation to four ingredients of culture as we find them in current higher educational settings: *time, place, community*, and *materials*. First, I shall introduce the research context that informs my own commentary around these themes.

A RESEARCH CONTEXT FOR OBSERVING THE CULTURE OF LEARNING

In this second half of the chapter, I shall make reference to a variety of published psychological research in order to identify themes that seem challenging to the virtualization project. However, there is an emphasis on studies with which I have been personally involved. These concern students who have been provided with extended access to learning technologies that are central to virtualization. They are not participating in a fully virtual university but it is a setting where virtualization is in progress. Thus, it furnishes a chance to capture reactions to such resources at a point of transition. Our observations were based upon various methods. Interviewing was one: 45 students drawn from a cross section of the university took part, discussing various aspects of current study practices, as well as perceptions of virtual and ICT-based learning methods (Crook 2001). Half of these students had networked PCs in their study bedroom and half did not.

Networking gave students access to a file server that provided web space for all taught modules in the university. Each of these course sites also offered a text-based conference forum. In addition, the university maintained a further file server dedicated to providing computer-aided learning applications for all disciplines. Finally, at this time, the university library was part of a project that allowed full text of all nominated course reading to be made available at any station on the campus computer network. A group of 26 students with networked study bedrooms and a matched group of 19 without kept detailed diaries of their study practices in this environment. We also took system logs from the PCs of the networked students: this recorded all their room-based computer activity (Crook and Barrowcliff 2001). While not a particularly large sample, every effort was made to recruit a cross section of the whole community—indeed, refusals to participate were infrequent.

THE TEMPORAL ORGANIZATION OF STUDY

Innovators in educational technology often project a somewhat romantic view of the student. So, they may conjure up such ideal notions as 'the insatiable desire of students for more and more information at a higher level of complexity' (Cole 1972: 143). Against this, it is common to set the constraints of current institutional life, perhaps characterizing a system that obstructs the student's spontaneous enthusiasms for knowledge. New technology then may be cast in the role of a resource for lifting such obstructions. Yet, the spontaneous motivation of school-leaving students cannot be taken for granted. Indeed, researchers are often disappointed at not discovering among students a greater commitment or 'thirst for knowledge' when their motives are investigated (Kuh 1993). A study by Newstead (1998) reminds us that a rather small number of undergraduates regard their higher education in terms of such 'personal development' and many (around a third in his sample) see university as merely a stop gap—dominated by the prospects of a vigorous social life. These observations are complemented by Newstead's sobering discovery of the considerable amount of cheating that occurs in the conduct of coursework.

Similar observations are reported from North America, where statistical surveys imply a growing trend towards greater disengagement from study. For example, the percentage of students reporting being 'frequently bored' in class has risen from 25 per cent in 1985 to 36 per cent in 1997 (Sax *et al.* 1997). This phemomenon may be seized upon by virtual innovators. They will often claim to be offering a more active, experiential, and collaborative approach to study—contrasting their vision with an existing system that is said to involve rigid and unstimulating methods. Yet, other North American evidence questions this; suggesting that, across this same period, faculty were engaging in more student-centred practices than ever. They were lecturing less and were doing more class discussion and more group projects (Sax *et al.* 1996).

Together, these various observations indicate that students' natural enthusiasm for study should not be taken for granted. An important issue, then, is whether the new formats of virtual learning will serve to increase, rather than further dampen, motivation to engage. Success will depend in part on whether virtual learning materials can really be made more vivid and stimulating than those which students currently use. This seems fanciful, although the prospect will be discussed further below. Otherwise, success will depend on whether a virtual university is able to cultivate strategies of independent study management among students, or whether it is able to impose them externally. Previously, such study skill training has not met with very striking successes, and, in some cases, has actually led to students developing a more superficial study approach (Ramsden 1987). On the other hand, the external imposition of study regimes does not seem very promising either. Indeed, it seems at odds with the 'flexibility' agenda that has been strongly promoted as a feature of virtual education.

Our own interviews with students suggested that the temporal structure of the traditional curriculum was very important to their capacity for remaining 'on task'. Over 60 per cent of their diary-recorded study time was not timetabled: it was private—and usually solitary—study. In talking about this, students identified the manner in which the formal curriculum imposed a necessary discipline on the management of their activity. At a coarse-grained level of temporal organization, they referred to a strict system of dates and deadlines, admitting that they often worked very close to them. At the finer level, they noted how the organization of a daily routine—lectures, meal breaks and social events—were important in framing their private study episodes. There was a sense in which their accounts suggested that the corporate nature of this pattern motivated some of the individual investments made. Certainly, the pattern of daily life was often punctuated by brief exchanges in which checks were made on how other people were managing with current assignments, reading and other course-related obligations.

It is hard to be confident regarding the significance of this temporal structure. Certainly, it is commonly invoked by students when explaining the management of their own study practices. Its prominence in their conversations about sustaining study does suggest a need to consider whether the temporal 'flexibility' of virtual practices is potentially problematic. However, one further aspect of study time in this community needs mentioning. Our group of students in networked study bedrooms had ready access to a wide range of ICT-based resources of just the kind contemplated by virtual institutions. Their need to respect the temporal order of campus life—by joining in at the sites at which students congregated—should thereby have been reduced. Going to the library, even going to lectures was less necessary, for resources were more to hand. Furthermore, their ability to communicate electronically with others rendered less necessary face-to-face social contacts in these traditional study places. Indeed, these students did use their computers for private study significantly more than their non-networked peers. However, the total amount of time they invested in private study was no more or less than those matched peers. In fact, no aspect of campus life—time in lectures, libraries or other public spaces—was significantly changed by flexible access to more powerful computer-based learning resources. This suggests that the institutional timetable is not readily subverted by easy access to virtual tools. However, this is a point about the resilience of institutional space as much as about institutional routine. We turn to this aspect of the cultural context next.

STUDY AND PLACE

Virtual education fractures the temporal structure of study; and it also loosens up the traditional associations between study and places. At the end of the last section, it was commented that when traditional students were given more virtual learning tools, they were not seduced away from the familiar bricks-and-mortar contexts of their study. I will not dwell further on the significance of this large-scale institutional environment, but, instead, comment on an aspect of the micro-environment of study—an issue that became visible when we considered the way our students organized their activity at the computer desktop.

Although universities do provide a wide range of locations that support private study, most of the students we interviewed reported that they did such work in their own rooms. Moreover, those with networked PCs recorded that significantly more of their room-based study was carried out at their computer. In other words, this technology had become a distinctive point at which study was now focussed. This is the pattern that must be expected for the virtual university student. The learning materials and the communication infrastructure of virtual universities will be focussed on a single technology in just this manner. Moreover, distinguished educational commentators assure us that the present generation of students do expect learning to be situated within this interactive media: 'Unlike those of us who were raised in an era of passive, broadcast media such as radio and television, today's students expect—indeed demand—interaction. They approach learning as a 'plug and play' experience' (Duderstadt 1999).

Full time students have presumably always had to deal with the tensions of segregating their recreational interests from the obligations of study. As suggested in the previous section, the temporal organization of a curriculum and the functional geography of a campus may help them to manage this segregation. Inevitably, the personal spaces in which so much study is concentrated will provide distractions that may sometimes make such self-management difficult. However, students may evolve routines for protecting themselves from competing interests, and students that we interviewed did identify such strategies. Yet, new technology achieves a precarious juxtaposition of both playful and study resources. This single site of activity—the computer desktop—resources both agendas. Detailed system logs from the computers of students in networked study bedrooms revealed much computer activity that had little relation to the formal curriculum. Consequently, over half of these students had commented during interviews that they felt they spent too much time on ICT distractions.

However, the main point is perhaps not the absolute amount of time given over to playful interests. What was more striking was the animated nature of the activity. So, the common expectation that a lot of time might be invested in prolonged game playing was not supported. Rather, the pattern of activity was highly interactive and mobile, in the sense of skipping frequently from one application to another. Typically, the computer desktop was populated with media players, web browsers, email readers, instant messaging software, and news tickers—in addition to tools concerned with study, such as word processors or spread sheets. Such a tightly localized collection of resources with strong interactive affordances necessarily invites a multi-tasking style of engagement. In particular, the networked status of these computers adds the extra temptation of opening up conversational exchanges, as friends logging on elsewhere on the network become visible at the desktop.

Such a fluid style of computer use might be regarded as productive where the focal interest was academic. Agile movement between information sources, or unplanned exchanges with peer collaborators, could be powerful forms of study practice. However, our records indicate that such agility was only occasionally exercised in the interests of formal study. Instead, the strong impression was one of an interactive technology that somewhat undermined sustained periods of engagement with a single academic task or document. The aim here is not to hazard confident predictions of how such students would study if they were part of a virtual university. However, the fact that the key technology of this future is a single site that hosts such a mixed range of applications—playful and more scholarly—is something to be reckoned with. Just as there is a helpful discipline imposed by the temporal organization of the curriculum, so the physical design of traditional learning spaces also affords a framework for study management. Again, the loosening up of existing structures by virtualization is something whose effects deserve closer consideration than it currently enjoys.

STUDY AND COMMUNITY

Conventional universities derive their institutional identity from temporal and spatial orders. However, they also manifest a *social* structure. Learning is organized in relation to the student's participation in a community. Two research traditions have considered the nature of this community, both of which concentrate on the North American case. The first has been associated with those organizations in American colleges known collectively as 'student affairs'. They embrace the more pastoral and extra-curricular care of students and, interestingly, were stimulated in an earlier era by a concern for the growing influence of business and industry on university life (Veblen 1948/1918). The second research tradition is sociological and flourished in the 1960s and 1970s. Partly stimulated by social upheaval in university communities at that time, it dwelt upon understanding how personal identity might be shaped by the broad experience of college (e.g. Chickering 1981; Perry 1970; Sanford 1968).

Both of these traditions are vigorous in stressing the extra-curricular dimension of full-time college experience. Reviews of the literature reinforce an association between progress with learning and campus residence (Pascarella and Terenzini 1991), as well as between learning achievements and the scope of informal contacts with peers and faculty (Astin 1993; Terenzine and Pascarella 1996). Unfortunately, few studies have taken a very fine-grained approach to such matters, such as might reveal more of the social texture mediating the useful benefits claimed. Neither has the nature of the benefit itself been very deeply theorized, say, in terms of clarifying the links between social practice and forms of cognitive development. Once again, care must be taken not to over-romanticize a feature of traditional university experience. The nature of the prevailing undergraduate community may not involve intense and frequent episodes of collaborative working. In fact, evidence suggests that these might be rather rare among undergraduates (Crook 2000). Yet, such an observation should not force the conclusion that academic community is no longer particularly significant (cf. Finnegan 1994).

In our interviews, students confirmed that orchestrated work-related discussions were indeed quite unusual. For example, in an invited consideration of the preceding 24 hours, most students had had some informal study-linked discussion with a peer. But only 15 per cent of those had been by previous arrangement, or the result of actively setting out to find the other person. Most social encounters concerning study were serendipitous and arose as a by-product of routine movements between occasions of organized study. Moreover, not only were such encounters short and improvised, they did not seem particularly probing. Three quarters of them concerned coursework and assignments, and much of what got said seemed to concern the monitoring of corporate progress. In fact, many students made explicit reference to the aim of seeking, via their peers, 'reassurance' about their own study routine. Sharing gripes about lectures and lecturers was another commonly cited theme. A similar pattern arose in relation to encounters with faculty. These were also rarely by arrangement but, nevertheless, 42 per cent of this sample had had at least one unscheduled conversation with a member of staff in the preceding 24 hours. Again, there was a sense of improvization about these staff–student consultations out of class time.

This pattern of engagement with peers and staff is echoed in how these students used electronic communications on campus. It was rare to use email for discussion of study and the electronic discussion conferences associated with course web pages attracted virtually no traffic (Crook 2001). Such communications media seemed to create a formality to exchanges that was at odds with the more unplanned form of campus-based exchange that was sketched above. That formality arises from the textual and asynchronous nature of the computer-based communication. There is no shared context at the point of launching a message; talking in text seems to demand greater care with composition and, if the target is a discussion forum, then the student's contribution remains hauntingly visible thereafter.

None of this should suggest that the communal nature of study is not important. In fact, students were quite clear that they regarded it as precious. However, while academics might prefer that participating in this community should lead to deeper and more extended collaborative conversations than we observed, the fact that the community may not be working in that particular way does not mean that it is not working at all. The dominant pattern of study-related conversations—brief, serendipitous and frequent—seemed very important to these students. We also sensed that, towards the end of the undergraduate period, these encounters were sometimes transforming into more substantial collaborative occasions. In the virtual university, whatever social interaction there might be is likely to be dominated by computer-mediated communication. Yet, it is not clear that text (or even video) conferencing captures what it is that is potent for current students' experience of peer-supported learning. Such collaborative ICT arenas have been largely tested on a different constituency of distance learning students—individuals who may differ a lot in experience and motivation. For any future cohort of (school-leaving) undergraduates, these communication tools may not be capturing the improvized camaraderie that seems to dominate what is currently valued.

STUDY AND ITS MATERIALS

The learning materials to be enjoyed by virtual undergraduates are typically computer-based. They are often promoted in terms of their depth, accessibility, and dynamism or 'richly structured, highly-accessible and interactive machine-resident knowledge' (MacFarlane 1998: 83). Moreover, it is promised that they will be encountered in a student-centred culture: 'Yesterday's classrooms were defined by what the teacher did; tomorrow's classrooms will be defined by what the learner does' (Conway 1998: 203). Indeed, virtual innovators still trapped within conventional settings can unpick traditional formats and advertise their online replacements with a rhetoric of student-centred practice: 'By cancelling traditional lectures as we have done and making the material available online are supporting the ideals of having student-directed and student-controlled learning' (Smeaton and Keogh 1999: 84).

I shall not dwell on the promise of materials offering greater richness-in-content. Certainly, our own sample of students had rather little appetite for the computer-aided learning applications that were on the network, and their interest in course web sites was largely focussed on the downloading of lecture notes, rather than the pursuit of scholarly URLs. Instead, I wish to consider one particular promise that these materials may have within their design. Namely, a capacity for helping students manage their own learning path: a promise to catalyse a form of self-teaching. Again, this comes down to an issue of whether a particular form of cultural structuring (materials, rather than time or space) adequately captures what gets achieved in the existing system.

The language describing online learning materials often suggests ambitions for being exhaustive, accessible, and well structured. Designers may feel that their distance from the user demands that they make particular efforts to be comprehensive—that their commitment to doing so is what will distinguish this species of learning resource from its predecessors. However, research on the effective design of such materials is scarce and some of what is known might be taken to suggest that these apparently laudable ambitions of designers are misguided. The crucial issue concerns how keenly the learner becomes engaged with some material and how far its design maximizes the opportunity for learners to interrogate the 'text' in an active manner. Bjork (1994) has summarized a range of studies suggesting that there is a useful but curious consequence of variability and unpredictability in the design of learning situations. While such inexactness can slow down the pace of learning, it can extend the scope of what finally gets learned. Similarly, McNamara *et al.* (1996) show how a minimally coherent (while still accurate) science text stimulates deeper student processing than that from a maximally coherent text. Such findings seem to echo earlier observations by Lepper and Chabay (1988), who studied how school teachers managed the discourse of classrooms. They compared this classroom talk to the forms of dialogue typically constructed by designers of educational software. The human teachers seemed actively to *avoid* the precision and explicitness of the software.

The core principle here is one that concerns optimizing an invitation for the learner (listener/reader) to engage actively with the presentation—to be led by it to points that demand active reflection in order to create closure. The idea is summarized by McNamara *et al.*: 'In general, researchers have found that people remember information that they have actively generated better than presented information and that they are better able to put such knowledge to use in novel situations' (1996: 3). One possibility is that the capacity to design discourse, assignments or demonstrations such as to leave meaning 'suspended' or 'provocative' in this sense is a capacity that may depend on intimacy of mutual knowledge between presenter and audience. Indeed, this fine-tuning to the learner is perhaps a self-monitoring demand that makes the act of teaching so tiring. The problem for virtual teaching practices may be the difficulty that a fragmented community creates for the construction of such 'common knowledge' (Edwards and Mercer 1987)—and its subsequent exploitation as a platform for instructional communication.

CONCLUDING REMARKS

Speculation about the prospects for virtual universities too rarely embraces psychological conceptions about learning. Psychology may not have made *great* strides in this area but, arguably, there are enough strands of research and theorizing to make a provocative contribution to policy debate. In this chapter, I have been particularly concerned to foreground a culturally influenced form of psychology, arguing that it is especially well matched to the issues at hand. This led to a consideration of virtualization in terms of its disturbance to four aspects of the traditional institutional culture: time, place, community, and materials. If there is a central preoccupation underlying this presentation, it is as follows. Whatever may be achieved with other constituencies of students, we must not take for granted the spontaneous motivation of traditional, school-leaving undergraduates. Insofar as, in some future, they may encounter virtual education, it is important to understand how far the capacity to sustain the demands of deliberate learning depends upon well-honed structures designed into the fabric of current educational institutions.

Orthodox psychologies have not chosen to theorize learning as a form of cultural practice in the sense that has been encouraged here. By doing such theorizing, we are obliged to notice how the activity of learning is embedded in various forms of institutional organization. Here I have considered the influence of such structure in relation to *temporal* patterns of activity, the organization of activity in physical *space*, the social structure of the university *community*, and the design of the *artefacts* mobilized for teaching and learning. In each case, there are grounds for supposing that virtual practices will be hard placed to reproduce similar structurings of activity. This may compromise students' capacity to sustain effectively their engagement with study.

However, if there are valid concerns here, it may be that they could have been detected more easily by simply talking with students themselves. Indeed, it is ironic that, while students are now often regarded as a species of customer, the tradition of interest in customer opinion is rarely applied. During the course of interviews, we asked our forty-five undergraduates about the prospect of studying at a virtual university. In their answers they revealed a clear understanding of the likely technical configuration of such an experience. They also revealed familiarity with arguments of economy and social inclusion that the virtualization project often attracts. However, without exception, they denied any interest in studying in such a manner. The reasons tended to congregate on two issues: first, the idea that successful teaching and learning was inherently a face-to-face experience; and, second, the idea that graduation involved valuable experiences that went beyond those tested in finals examinations. Whatever our reactions to social science research, there may be a neglected resource for planning virtual education in the voice of the principle stakeholder.

REFERENCES

Astin, A. W. (1993) *Four Critical Years: Effects of College on Beliefs, Attitudes and Knowledge.* San Francisco: Jossey-Bass.

Bereiter, C. and Scardamalia, M. (1992) 'An architecture for collaborative knowledge building', in E. De Corte, M. Linn, H. Mandl, and L. Verschaffel (eds) *Computer-Based Learning Environments and Problem Solving.* Berlin: Springer-Verlag.

—— and —— (1996) 'Rethinking learning', in D. Olson and N. Torrance (eds) *The Handbook of Education and Human Development: New Models of Learning, Teaching and Schooling.* Cambridge, MA: Basil Blackwell.

Bjork, R. A. (1994) 'Memory and metamemory: considerations in the training of human beings', in J. Metcalfe and A. Shimamura (eds) *Metacognition: Knowing about Knowing.* Cambridge, MA: MIT Press.

Brown, A. L. (1992) 'Design experiments: theoretical and methodological challenges in creating complex interventions in classroom settings', *Journal of the Learning Sciences,* **2**: 141–78.

Brown, J. S., Collins, A., and Duguid, P. (1989) 'Situated cognition and the culture of learning', *Educational Researcher,* **18**: 32–42.

—— and Duguid, P. (2000) *The Social Life of Information.* Boston, MA: Harvard Business School.

Chickering, A. W. (1981) *The Modern American College.* San Francisco: Jossey-Bass.

Clark, R. E. (1994) 'Media will never influence learning', *Educational Technology Research and Development,* **42**: 21–9.

Cognition and Technology Group at Vanderbilt (1990) 'Anchored instruction and its relationship to situated cognition', *Educational Researcher,* **19**: 2–10.

Cole, M. (1998) *Cultural Psychology.* Cambridge: Cambridge University Press.

Cole, R. I. (1972) 'Some reflections concerning the future of society, computers and education', in R. Chartrand (ed.) *Computers in the Service of Society.* New York, Pergammon Press.

Conway, K. L. (1998) 'Designing classrooms for the 21st century', in D. Oblinger and S. Rush (eds) *The Future Compatible Campus.* Boston: Anker Pulbishing Company.

Crook, C. K. (1994) *Computers and the Collaborative Experience of Learning.* London: Routledge.

Crook, C. K. (2000) 'Motivation and the ecology of collaborative learning', in R. Joiner, K. Littleton, D. Faulkner, and D. Miell (eds) *Rethinking Collaborative Learning*. London: Free Association Press.

—— (2001) 'The campus experience of networked learning', in C. Steeples and C. Jones (eds) *Networked Learning*. Springer.

—— and Barrowcliff, D. (2001) 'Ubiquitous computing on campus: patterns of engagement by university students', *International Journal of Human Computer Interaction*.

—— and Light, P. (1999) 'Information technology and the culture of student learning', in J. Bliss, P. Light, and R. Saljo (eds) *Learning Sites*. Springer.

Cuban, L. (1986) *Teachers and Machines*. New York: Teachers College.

De Corte, E. (1996) 'Learning theory and instruction science', in P. Reimann and H. Spada (eds) *Learning in Humans and Machines*. Oxford: Pergamon/Elsevier Science.

Duderstadt, J. J. (1999) 'Can colleges and universities survive in the information age?' in R. Katz (ed.), *Dancing with the Devil: Information Technology and the New Competition in Higher Education*. San Francisco: Jossey-Bass.

Edwards, D. and Mercer, N. (1987) *Common Knowledge*. London: Methuen.

Finnegan, R. (1994) 'Recovering "academic community"', in R. Barnett (ed.) *Academic Community*. London: Jessica King Publishers.

Gell, M. and Cochrane, P. (1996) 'Learning and education in an information society', in W. Dutton (ed.) *Information and Communication Technologies*. Oxford: Oxford University Press.

Kuh, G.D. (1993) 'In their own words: what students learn outside the classroom', *American Educational Research Journal*, **30**: 277–304.

Lave, J. (1991) 'Situating learning in communities of practice', in Resnick, J. Levine, and S. Teasley (eds) *Perspectives on Socially Shared Cognition*. Washington DC: American Psychological Association.

—— and Wenger, E. (1991) *Situated Learning: Legitimate Peripheral Participation*. Cambridge: Cambridge University Press.

Lepper, M. R. and Chabay, R. W. (1988) 'Socializing the intelligent tutor: bringing empathy to computer tutors', in H. Mandl and A. Lesgold (eds) *Learning Issues for Intelligent Tutoring Systems*. New York: Springer-Verlag.

Light, P., Crook, C. K., and White, S. (2000) 'Learning sites: networked resources and the learning community', *The New Review of Information Networking*, **6**: 187–94.

MacFarlane, A. (1998) 'Information, knowledge and learning', *Higher Education Quarterly*, **52**: 77–92.

McNamara, D. S., Kintsch, E., Songer, N. B., and Kintsch, W. (1996) 'Are good texts always better? Interactions of text coherence, background knowledge, and levels of understanding in learning from text', *Cognition and Instruction*, **14**: 1–43.

Magee, R., Baldwin, A., Newstead, S., and Fulerton, H. (1998) 'Age, gender and course differences in approaches to studying in first-year undergraduate students', in S. Brown, S. Armstrong, and G. Thompson (eds) *Motivating Students*. London: Kogan Page.

Newstead, S. (1998) 'Individual differences in student motivation', in S. Brown, S. Armstrong, and G. Thompson (eds) *Motivating Students*. London: Kogan Page.

Papert, S. (1980) *Mindstorms*. Brighton: Harvester Press.

Pascarella, E. T. and Terenzini, P. T. (1991) *How College Affects Students: Findings and Insights from Twenty Years of Research*. San Francisco: Jossey-Bass.

Perry, W. G. (1970) *Forms of Intellectual and Ethical Development in the College Years.* New York: Holt.

Premack, D. and Premack, J. (1996) 'Why animals lack pedagogy and some cultures have more of it than others', in D. Olson and N. Torrance (eds) *The Handbook of Education and Human Development.* Oxford: Blackwell Publishers.

Ramsden, P. (1987) 'Improving teaching and learning in higher education: the case for a relational perspective', *Studies in Higher Education*, **12**: 275–86.

Rommetveit, R. (1979) 'On the architecture of intersubjectivity', in R. Blakar and R. Blakar (eds) *Studies of Language, Thought and Verbal Communication.* New York: Academic Press.

Rummelhart, D. E. (1989) 'The architecture of the mind: a connectionist approach', in M. Posner (ed.) *Foundations of Cognitive Science.* Cambridge, MA: MIT Press.

Sanford, N. (1968) *Where Colleges Fail.* San Francisco: Jossey-Bass.

Sax, L. J., Astin, A. W., Arredondo, M., and Korn, W. S. (1996) *The American College Teacher: National Norms for the 1995–1996 HERI Faculty Survey.* Los Angeles: Higher Education Research Institute, University of California.

——, ——, Korn, W. S., and Mahoney, K. M. (1997) *The American Freshman: National Norms for 1997.* Los Angeles: Higher Education Research Institute, University of California.

Sfard, A. (1998) 'On two metaphors for learning and the dangers of choosing just one', *Educational Researcher*, **27**: 4–13.

Skinner, B. F. (1968) *The Technology of Teaching.* New York: Meredith.

Smeaton, A. F. and Keogh, G. (1999) 'An analysis of the use of virtual delivery of undergraduate lectures', *Computers and Education*, **32**: 83–94.

Terenzine, P. T. and Pascarella, E. T. (1996) 'Students' out-of-class experiences and their influence on learning and cognitive development: a literature review', *Journal of College Student Development*, **37**: 140–62.

Tharp, R. G. and Gallimore, R. (1988) 'A theory of teaching as assisted performance', in R. Tharp and R. Gallimore (eds) *Rousing Minds To Life.* Cambridge: Cambridge University Press.

Veblen, T. B. (1948/1918) *The Higher Learning in America: A Memorandum on the Conduct of Universities by Business Men.* New York: Hill and Wang.

Wenger, E. (1998) *Communities of Practice.* Cambridge: Cambridge University Press.

Wood, D. (1988) *How Children Think and Learn.* Oxford: Basil Blackwell.

7

New Managerialism: The Manager-academic and Technologies of Management in Universities—Looking Forward to Virtuality?

Mike Reed and Rosemary Deem

INTRODUCTION

This chapter will explore the extent to which ideologies, discourses, and practices associated with 'New Mangerialism' are evident in, and also resisted by,
manager-academics and academics in universities. 'New Managerialism' is a
multi-faceted phenomenon drawing on practices and discourses from the private
for-profit sector. It is argued by theorists to have permeated public sector services and organizations in most western countries (Ferlie *et al.* 1996; Clarke and
Newman 1997*a*; Exworthy and Halford 1999). Management discourses and practices appear to have an increasing presence in UK universities and elsewhere
(Trow 1993; Meadmore 1998; Deem 1998; Deem and Johnson 2000; Marginson
and Considine 2001). The extent and remit of higher education management
is bolstered by declining public funding, state priorities for the sector, and
a shift from an elite to a mass system, as well as by an increased degree of
internal and external control, surveillance and 'self-governmentality'. The latter
are also encouraged by quality assessments of teaching, research, and administration. To some degree, these features are found in almost all publicly-funded

Grateful thanks are due to all the individuals and institutions which participated in the study. We
are also indebted to other members of the research team: Rachel Johnson, Sam Hillyard, Oliver
Fulton, and Stephen Watson. Thanks also to Cheryl Scott, Heidi Edmundson, Teresa Seed, and
Jill Greenwood for their work on tape transcription.

universities in the west, although the complex interplay of 'the local' and 'the global' generates different institutional patterns in national and sub-national contexts (Slaughter and Leslie 1997; Scott 1998; Deem 2001). However, not all the features of managerialism and management found in universities are new (Deem 1998). Rather, hybridized forms of old and 'New Managerialist' discourses, cultures, and practices may be evident. Furthermore, the mere existence of New Managerial discourses in universities, whether hybridized or otherwise, does not necessarily mean that managers whose practices, values, or narratives show permeation by 'New Managerialism' are always aware of this. A minority of our interviewees did demonstrate that they were so aware; most did not.

The chapter draws on data from a recent Economic and Social Research Council funded project (grant R000237661) concerning the implications of 'New Managerialism' for the management of UK universities. Clearly most UK universities already have in place some aspects of virtuality, notably in relation to teaching innovation (Hannan and Silver 2000). However, there has been some suggestion that the UK may be lagging behind other countries in relation to the concept of the borderless university (Middlehurst 2000). We examine our data to see if it can shed any light on this. Three particular aspects of the research data are considered. The first of these relates to interview data on the careers and experiences of those holding manager-academic posts, particularly in those posts, from Dean to Vice Chancellor, positions where most post-holders have chosen to follow a management route. Senior manager-academics are usually particularly heavily involved in making strategic decisions about the future direction of their institutions. Yet the long career path to becoming a manager-academic may mean that whilst, lower down an institution, lots of early and mid-career staff are making use of new technologies, senior manager-academics are often in a late-career stage and some may have little personal experience of new technologies.

The second aspect considered consists of an analysis of the extent of technologies of management and organizational control over other academics and support staff that are currently in use by manager-academics. Such technologies include e-mail and devolved financial allocation mechanisms. As academic institutions grow in complexity and acquire features of private sector organizations, especially in respect of the management of applied research and other entrepreneurial activities (Slaughter and Leslie 1997; Clark 1998; Gray 1999; Marginson and Considine 2001), so the use of new technologies might be expected to increase. In the present chapter we use case study and interview data to explore this, including the views of 'managed' academic and support staff and the accounts of Heads of Department (HoDs) as well as those of more senior post-holders such as Vice-Chancellors (VCs), Pro-Vice Chancellors (PVCs) and Deans. We suggest some support for Robins and Webster's argument that virtuality within universities is already 'present in the present', although we also point out some of the tensions and resistances which may arise from the use of new technologies. The third and final aspect draws on case study material and senior manager-academic interviews to consider the degree to which the management of universities revolves around the day-to-day 'negotiation of order' and 'crisis management'. This too has major implications for the extent to which the senior management of conventional universities is likely to embrace dimensions of virtuality with enthusiasm and encompass it in long-term strategic plans.

Underpinning each of these substantive concerns, a more developed theoretical specification of the concept of 'New Managerialism' and its implications for the emergence of relatively novel forms of organizational control and surveillance in UK universities will be provided. We locate the former within wider debates about the nature and impact of different forms of managerialism in public service organizations, including universities, in the post-1944 era and their capacity to restructure the academic labour process and reconstruct professional academic cultures and identities in ways which seem to 'prepare the way' for the virtualization of universities. However, it is suggested that the crucial importance of historical, cultural, institutional, and organizational factors that mediate the implementation of 'New Managerialist' discourses and practices in complex, and often contradictory ways, cannot be denied.

THE 'NEW MANAGERIALISM' PROJECT

The project was in three phases and was principally concerned with examining the extent to which 'New Managerialism' had permeated the management of UK universities. Investigations began by means of twelve focus group discussions with academics, manager-academics and administrators belonging to a range of learned societies. We gathered respondents' perceptions about what was happening to the management and running of UK higher education. In phase two we carried out semi-structured interviews with manager-academics from Heads of Department (HoD), through Deans, to PVCs and VCs, at 12 pre-1992 and post-1992 UK universities. We conducted 135 interviews with manager-academics. The term manager-academic is preferred to the term academic manager, as the latter could refer to professional administrators as well as academics holding management. We also interviewed 29 senior administrators in order to find out whether administrators saw themselves and manager-academics working for common aims. We wanted to explore whether administrators were a source of 'New Managerial' influences on higher education. The manager-academic interviews covered careers and selection mechanisms, training and support for management, work and home life balance, management practices and routines, views about change, work anxieties, and pleasures, attitudes towards institutional management and organization, recent developments in the external context of UK higher education, and issues related to management and gender processes. Our sampling strategy included both women and men respondents and a cross section of subject disciplines. Nevertheless, we do not claim that our interviewees are necessarily typical of all manager-academics in UK universities. Finally, in phase three, we selected a small number of institutions for more detailed study. We made our choice of four universities based on size, type (pre or post-92 institution), location, number of site(s) and academic emphasis. We also chose universities where the current VC had been in post for at least three years. We first conducted a similar range of interviews with manager-academics and senior administrators as in phase 2. We then collected and analysed documentation from each institution (e.g. mission statements, operating statements, corporate plans, published teaching reviews, annual reports), did some general observation on site and conducted interviews and focus groups with a broad range of university employees (including support staff).

'NEW MANAGERIALISM' IN THE PUBLIC SERVICES

The imposition of 'New Managerialism' has been much studied in public services from health (Ferlie *et al.* 1996) to local government and schools (Exworthy and Halford 1999), but has been little examined in higher education except very recently in Australia (Marginson and Considine 2001). The concept of 'New Managerialism' informing our research project can be defined in relation to three overlapping elements. First, as a generic *narrative of strategic change* which is constructed and promulgated in order 'to persuade others towards certain understandings and actions' (Barry and Elmes 1997: 433) in relation to the established governance and management of universities. Second, as an emergent but *distinctive organizational form* that provides the administrative mechanisms and managerial processes through which this theory of change will be realized. Third, as a *practical control technology* through which strategic policies and their organizational instrumentation can be transformed into practices, techniques, and devices that challenge, or substantially modify, established systems of 'bureau-professionalism' (Clarke and Newman 1997: 68–70).

Taken as a package of cultural, organizational, and managerial interventions, 'New Managerialism' constitutes an alternative model of governmental and institutional order for higher education within the UK to that which has existed under the traditional compromise between corporate bureaucracy and professional association from the mid-1940s onwards (Smith and Webster 1997; Jary and Parker 1998). The latter shaped the post-Second World War development of British higher education to the extent that it facilitated a viable trade-off between managerial control and professional autonomy as exemplified in the organizational logic and practice of 'professional bureaucracy' (Mintzberg 1979). 'New Managerialism' radically questions the terms on which that compromise was originally struck, by questioning the *endemic* lack of external accountability, internal managerial discipline, and routine operational efficiency (Ackroyd *et al.* 1989). 'New Managerialism' draws on a body of literature that legitimates the exercise of managerial prerogative within the modern private and public corporation (Child 1969; Anthony 1986; Enteman 1993). The justification for this is based on claims relating to the universal specialist expertise assumed to reside in 'management' as a general capacity overriding specific 'professional' or craft skills and knowledge (Locke 1989, 1996; Glover and Tracey 1997). However, 'New Managerialism' is also part of quasi-market-based managerialism mobilized right across the public sector (e.g. in health or in social services) as an institutional logic that both reduces the power of professionals (Ackroyd *et al.* 1989; Exworthy and Halford 1999) and ends the organizational inertia characteristic of corporate bureaucracy (Pollit 1993; Pollitt and Bouckaert 2000).

'New Managerialism' has entailed a number of interrelated changes in structural design and operating systems which in turn allow a more tightly integrated regime of managerial discipline and control radically different from the untidy but stabilizing compromises of bureau-professionalism (Harrison and Pollitt 1994; Hood 1995; Clarke and Newman 1997; Webb 1999). At the same time, professionals are subjected to a much more rigorous regime of external accountability in which continuous monitoring and audit are dominant (Kirkpatrick and Lucio 1995; Power 1997; Morgan and Engwall 1999). A consistent emphasis on the detailed monitoring and evaluation of 'quality' standards has emerged as the overriding priority within a public sector remodelled on private sector commercial enterprise and its concern with 'total quality management' (Kirkpatrick and Lucio 1995). The needs and demands of the 'customer', rather than the 'provider', have come to be regarded as paramount (Du Gay and Salaman 1992; Du Gay 1996). The 'cultural revolution' that 'New Managerialism' sets in motion requires a technology of workplace control, within a restructured governance and management structure, in order to make it a viable programme of change, grounded in a set of practices and devices focused upon the highly complex task of re-engineering the labour process within and through which public sector professionals and managers do their work (Reed 1995, 1999). 'New Managerialism' strives to transform the organizational culture within which this re-engineered, professional/managerial labour process is embedded. Re-engineering the professional labour process is attempted through a number of devices such as financial monitoring, quality audit, performance measurement, and work rationalization. The needs and demands of the 'customer', rather than the 'provider', come to be regarded as paramount (Du Gay and Salaman 1992; Du Gay 1996). 'New Managerialism' has produced a series of interconnected strategies and practices for restructuring public services focused on work intensification, service commodification and 'control at a distance', allowing the state to choose when, where, and how it might intervene (as for example on top-up fees for undergraduate students). However, some have argued that these changes are also likely to lead to 'the emergence of schisms within the public service class between "old-style" professionals who use the language of welfare and care and "new-style" senior managers and professionals who use the language of markets and efficiency' (Webb 1999: 757).

WHO ARE THE MANAGER-ACADEMICS?

Work on the importance of subject disciplines to academic identities is well established (Clark 1987; Becher 1989; Huber 1990), so we ensured that our interviewees came from a wide range of disciplines. Though disciplines have different market positions and priorities, in general, we did not find that the accounts of management practices and cultures varied significantly by discipline. Indeed, this is consistent with research on academics in general, which has found attitudes to university management and governance remarkably similar across the disciplines (Fulton 1998; Henkel 2000). However, we identified very few women in senior manager-academic posts, and a similar situation is evident for the system as a whole (Brooks 1997; Eggins 1997; Woodward and Ross 2000; Deem and Ozga 2000). What was distinctive about our respondents related to their motivations for taking on a management role and their tenure of office. About half of our interviewees were in temporary posts and except at PVC level, this was mostly in the pre-1992 universities. The manager-academics we interviewed had entered management roles by three main routes. The first was the career track route (a minority of our respondents, mostly in post-1992 universities), where an early-career decision is taken to pursue a management role. This group self-identified as managers and generally worked in institutions where established traditions of managerialism were evident. Motivations for becoming a career-track manager included enjoying management, exercising power and institutional politics, becoming dissatisfied with teaching and research, and seeking a higher salary. Here is a typical description of a career track manager's route:

I rose through the ranks as it were and . . . I was Senior Lecturer, Principal Lecturer, Course Director for the major undergraduate course there, Head of Postgraduate department. Then Dean, I think, unless there was another Head of Department's job in between. And I had a couple of um, a couple of sort of side trips, I ran what was then the Faculty of Health & Social Sciences for a while um, for a few months, and I worked as an assistant to the previous Director at the Polytechnic, um for a short while. Then as I say I became Dean down there and then the Pro Vice-Chancellor left so I applied for the job and got it.   (PVC, post-1992 university)

The second route identified was the reluctant-manager route, especially typical of HoDs in the pre-1992 institutions, where such roles are usually temporary. Some had been coerced into taking on the job and others agreed for fear that someone else might make a worse HoD. This reluctance is at odds with much of the literature on 'New Managerialism', which assumes that managers not only want to manage but wish to assert their right to manage. For reluctant managers, motivation often came from seeing staff and students succeed and obtaining good scores in teaching or research assessment. Finally, there is what we have termed the 'good citizen' route, where an individual chooses to take on a more senior management role (e.g. at PVC level), often at quite a late career stage, in order to give something back to their institutions. This last route may be declining, as manager-academic roles occur earlier in careers. This group also had reservations about regarding themselves as managers. Furthermore, the three routes we identified are also permeable, as this account shows:

> I was one of two Professors in the Department, one of whom, my colleague was the Head of Department who decided he wanted to stand down after a fairly short time . . . so in a sense I was Hobson's Choice for being HoD. And it wasn't a role I was particularly looking for, or a role I particularly welcomed, but I recognised that somebody had to do it and I was probably the best person to do it. And that was 10 years ago . . . Now having done that for some years I was then approached by the Vice-Chancellor to become a Pro Vice-Chancellor, that was about going on for 5 years ago. Again I don't think I gave the offer a great deal of consideration, I just thought, well if he wants me to do it, I'll do it and so I have continued to do it. I wouldn't say, I'm not a reluctant, I'm not trying to pretend I'm a reluctant manager. . . . But um, yes, these things just I think it happens to most of us, it just happens.   (PVC, pre-1992)

Thus Webb's distinction between old-style professionals and new-style managers, as found in local government reforms, was revealed within the manager-academic ranks rather than between academics and manager-academics (Webb 1999).

It was also the case that relatively few manager-academics above the level of HoD showed significant interest in developments in the concept of virtual universities, except where they were already researching or teaching in the field of telematics or informatics. We found few senior equivalents of enthusiasts such as this HoD:

> We are into, we started to do a lot of long distance learning, using the web much more . . . with globalisation, with running courses abroad, you know we sort of see ourselves as the hard core of full-time students but a sort of virtual department most of the time. It's all exciting, we've got great plans.   (HoD Art & Design, post-1992 university)

In some occupational fields, greater acquaintance with new technologies might come through training or staff development. However, it would seem that much of the involvement of academics in new technologies has occurred on a self-taught basis. We found that this was also so for learning about management. Just over a third of the manager-academics in our sample had received any special training for their roles. Nevertheless, most of our respondents were able to articulate how more minor administrative experiences as well as teaching and research had helped prepare them for management.

> Specifically, I think, my training as a scientist has been useful in a number of ways, one is that I think a scientific training, and it's not only true of scientific training, but I think any academic discipline gives you the ability to think or should give you the ability to think logically through things. So you can be presented with quite a complex situation, you ought to be able to analyse that, find out what the component parts are and come to some conclusion about that. I think having a numerical background is useful in terms of dealing with financial issues, you know, just being able to read a balance sheet. But you don't claim

to be an accountant but you can sort of tell whether the figures add up. Um, I think um, the fact that as an academic you deal with a lot of individuals. Um, if you just think of the turnover of students that there are, you are constantly meeting new people, er and that's very useful as well. Um, because someone comes into your room with an issue or a problem you've got to weigh up very quickly how significant is this, is it an individual problem, is this person really representing a much wider er, issue or what? So I think all those skills are very useful. Clearly other skills like um, you know, if you have written scientific papers or published anything in fact, it doesn't have to be scientific, that's useful in preparing reports and the like, or making a case for something. So I think all of those skills are very useful.   (Dean of Science, post-1992 university)

But we need to bear in mind that such experiences may not necessarily have included much exposure to new technologies. Most interviewees had consciously sought out opportunities to facilitate their own informal learning, often by seeking out colleagues in similar roles, whether in their own or a nearby institution or through a learned society. This kind of learning was not always well supported, or even recognized, by institutions. Yet opportunities to ensure, for example, that manager-academics with little experience of new technologies met those who had more experience, in a non-threatening context outside a formal meeting, may not occur by accident. Like school governors who hark back to their own schoolday memories, successes and failures (Brehony and Deem 1995), manager-academics are likely to draw upon their own experience of academic life in undertaking their management roles. Thus those with little or no experience of virtuality are highly unlikely, without any other intervention, to make this part of their management practice or strategic planning. In addition, though some argue that this is changing, a good number of senior manager-academics (PVC level and above) whom we interviewed had reached the more senior ranks at a relatively late stage in their careers. Even at Dean level, where especially in the post-1992 sector there were earlier-career post-holders, there was little dissimilarity in the backgrounds of most of our sample. They had almost all come through the academic ranks, rather than coming in from outside, as did many managers in the late 1980s and early 1990s UK health service reforms (Flynn 1992; Ferlie et al. 1996; Mark and Dopson 1999; Flynn 2000). Although a minority of our respondents had industrial experience, it was often a long time ago and not, therefore, in our view, a source of 'New Managerial' ideologies. However, some of our sample had undoubtedly benefited from the greater opportunities available to managers now, compared with when they had embarked upon their academic careers. In addition, many of the recent external changes to UK higher education—massification of undergraduate student intakes, declining public funding, regular assessment of teaching and research, and emphasis on quality management—have allowed those manager-academics who wish to do so, to present themselves as having no choice but to become more directive of staff whose performance appears not to be up to scratch:

I think, I think in professional life you end up having to do things which you don't like. Um, so for example, to take the obvious example, the beginning of last year, a group of a hundred of my colleagues were offered PRCS*, they weren't forced out, they were offered PRCS. And the university is going to get a lot tougher about performance. Now obviously that's tough . But if I then look at myself and my own life and my own career and what I do and what I believe in, um, I would have to say those people have not performed i.e. if you are then going to be absolutely blunt about it, they haven't fully done what they are paid for doing. And in a tougher world they might well have been dismissed for not fulfilling a contract or whatever else. So the fact that many of them, I mean, many of them I like, one or two of them are personal friends. Um, the fact that some of those people were deeply dismayed by what happened, I'm sorry about it, I mean, I am not a vindictive person   (PVC, pre-1992 university).   *Premature Retirement Compensation Scheme

Though the audit culture (Power 1997; Shore and Wright 1998), has probably not invaded higher education to any greater extent than other public services, higher education in the UK had previously experienced a period largely free of audit and assessment (Parry 2001). So the arrival of the audit culture has perhaps been seen differently by academics, especially in the light of other changes to their working conditions and morale (Halsey 1992; Fulton 1996; Enders 2001). Manager-academics who wish to become more directive of staff performance may be assisted by the current tendency towards greater emphasis on team-work in higher education, even in non-science subjects, that many of our focus group respondents commented upon. We now turn to an exploration of the kinds of technologies of control at the disposal of manager-academics in the current conjuncture.

NEW TECHNOLOGIES AND MANAGEMENT CONTROL IN UNIVERSITIES

Much emphasis in the debates on 'New Managerialism' is placed on the increasing tendency of managers to use specific control mechanisms in order to monitor the workloads and performances of staff. For some writers, the most significant change to internal operating systems lies in the increasing emphasis given to performance target-setting and management against predetermined operational efficiency norms and strategic effectiveness outcomes (Smith 1993). Within the context of much more intrusive and pervasive performance management, a consistent emphasis on the detailed monitoring and evaluation of 'quality' standards in service delivery and outcomes emerges as the overriding priority. This can then be embedded within a public sector management ideology and practice remodelled on private sector commercial enterprise and its concern with 'total quality management' (Kirkpatrick and Lucio 1995). The programme of structural and operational reforms entailed in the ideology of 'New Managerialism' is argued to coerce public sector managers and professional service providers into a more meaningful and direct engagement with their relative competitive position, within an increasingly fragmented and uncertain market environment. Higher education undoubtedly has the uncertain external environment and universities are also very aware of their market position. But there some of the similarities to other public services may end.

First, we found that the universities in which we conducted our research were culturally often very different from each other (reflecting different histories, niches, and locations as well as institutional values), including within, as well as between, the pre-1992 and post-1992 sectors. There was little sign of the institutional isomorphism identified in other public organizations subjected to 'New Managerialism' (DiMaggio and Powell 1991; Clarke and Newman 1997; Brock *et al.* 1999). Second, academics, unlike some other professionals in public employment, still retain a relatively high degree of autonomy over their work, despite challenges to that autonomy (Henkel 2000). Hence the kinds of control mechanisms which are suitable for use with academics may well be different to those in use by other public service managers. A good many of our respondents spoke of the need to use 'carrots' rather than 'sticks', or used the term 'herding cats', and in general emphasized subtle persuasion and the necessity of personal negotiation with individual staff, or the use of peer-pressure, to persuade academics that they want to do something which they may not wish to do. This was so amongst our respondents at all levels:

I've found committees haven't worked. We have a rather silly situation here that the building is far from ideal and we can't join together socially, meet and exchange views . . . So I spend an awful lot of my time going round visiting people on one excuse or another and just seeing how things are . . . it's time-consuming but you've got to do it.   (HoD Humanities, pre-1992)

Probably too much of my week is actually spent in planning meetings of one sort or another . . . we've been going through this process of faculty consultation and change, meetings that should have been once a month were almost becoming once a week or once every two weeks.   (HoD Management, post-1992 university)

You have to adopt a more enthusiastic, you know, management by influence rather than management by power, which is the first thing you, you, you know, you learn very quickly, but you know they're very different managerial styles and that was certainly an advantage of moving into HE, because I certainly brought in a very different mind-set.   (PVC with industrial experience, post-1992)

Such time-consuming activities may help to explain the long hours that many interviewees reported spending on their management tasks (Deem and Hillyard 2001). But of course persuasion and negotiation are very 'old technologies' in universities. What evidence is there of the use of new technologies in management?

We found that the majority of comments on new technologies from our respondents in all three phases were about email, resource allocation models, and data-bases containing student information or indicators of research activity. Email is now in widespread use in universities. It is not necessarily a technology of management control in any very overt sense (though all universities screen all incoming and outgoing emails) but it does allow manager-academics to exercise some remote control over staff and send information or requests without organizing a meeting. Some welcomed email as a means of facilitating communication:

People don't have too much problem with email. We actually have a faculty directive which went through the faculty board about a year and half ago, with it all communications should be via the email and we do virtually everything including we have scanned in all the university's forms, admissions forms and everything. It doesn't stop the paper coming but most of it comes from the centre and not the faculty. (Dean, applied science, post-1992 university)

Email also enables work to be done directly by manager-academics that previously might have been undertaken by secretarial staff. It permits rapid communication with all staff by manager-academics that may indirectly add to the intensification of work. A number of our manager-academic respondents had reservations about email because of its workload implications:

I use email a lot for administration and I read and send it all myself but sometimes I feel it is a bit too open—I was recently away for 5 days in Washington and when I came back I had over 400 messages. (HoD science, pre-1992 university)

At the same time, as this respondent notes, email is not just a management tool. It may also be a way of allowing staff not in management roles (and importantly also students) to ask questions and seek advice from manager-academics in their own timeframe, thus redressing a very unequal power balance between managed staff and managers. Email is not, however, available to all. In the phase 3 case studies, people like porters and library assistants pointed out that whilst senior management sent out much information via email, they had no email or web access and thus did not receive these bulletins. In this respect, manager-academics who retained a personal touch and spent time trying to see people were preferred to those who mainly communicated via email:

The previous VC walked about the campus a lot—the current VC uses email all the time. (case study data from support staff focus group, pre-1992 university)

Thus, the virtual university may have its drawbacks if new technologies are not available to all or are resisted by some staff.

Resource allocation models and associated devolved financial management and student data-bases were the other major forms of new control technology used by our manager-academics. Devolved resources also affect the emphasis placed on different aspects of the organizational forms of universities as organizations, since the cost-centre level also then acquires a new significance. Most universities within which we conducted research had both information software and resource allocation models using spreadsheets, often accompanied by a range of other performance indicator data. For HoDs, such technologies were not infrequently regarded as a source of frustration rather than a useful tool:

We've got a computer system within this university called Resource*, that's supposed to give us student information and when we do our annual monitoring of information about students that we take in and how they progress, it's always wrong! The information that goes into the damn computer is put in by humans. When it comes out it's gobbledegook. You know and I can tell exactly how many students I've got going in and when it comes out you think, 'There's no resemblance to what has enrolled!' And then you get at the centre, 'Oh, well that's what comes out of Resource' and I say, 'Resource! It doesn't work!' Now, if I had and could implement one change, I would take that computer system and I'd stick it somewhere and roll it down into a hill in a ditch.   (HoD Health, post-1992 university) *Name of system has been anonymised

HoDs were also often the recipients of the control-potential of resource allocation models, since the information was frequently used to monitor the performance of their departments:

You are expected to deliver as far as the directorate is concerned, so for example, hit student targets, generate external income, raise the research profile, there all part and parcel of what you're expected to achieve. And at the same proper time you know from the troops that some of those things are almost impossible to do given all this resource constraints that have been imposed. And there is a degree of frustration on occasions that you can't make those two ends meet.   (HoD applied science, post-1992)

Um, I guess with it being a very, very, competitive university for survival of departments for getting research funds, keeping up your FTE's, um, if the department's not run properly then you're all in serious trouble.   (HoD science, pre-1992)

Data-bases and spreadsheet-based performance indicators were not only used to monitor department and faculty performances. From both phase 2 interview data and phase 3 case study material, it was apparent that these forms of inform- ation storage were also used as a tool for assessing how individual staff were performing. Typically, such data were compiled initially in relation to external demands such as the Research Assessment Exercise but then used for wider management purposes, as this PVC relates:

There was an episode in my first year where, in the aftermath of the '96 RAE . . . where we had the question of how that would be followed up in terms of a kind of research version of appraisal.   (PVC, pre-1992 university)

However, as the same respondent noted, these kind of exercises can lead to other problems:

I think I under-estimated the need to sort of be in constant communication with the trade unions on that. As I said it wasn't my mistake alone but I would certainly have done that differently in retrospect.

It is likely that computerized information will increasingly be used as a man- agement tool. As theorists of 'New Managerialism' have noted, the ideology of market-based managerialism and the programme of organizational reform that it legitimates and instigates both require a practical configuration of techniques, devices and tools if they are to be operationalized 'on the ground' (Mitchell 1999; Rose 1999). Unlike paper-based information, computer-stored data makes it much easier to compare departments or individuals with each other. Further- more, it can rapidly be updated and also circulated to many different audiences, thus bringing in an element of peer-pressure. It can be time-consuming for staff at lower levels to challenge the data and often difficult to find out who input which elements of that data. However, there is also the possibility that financial and student-information systems also enable staff to see who is subsidizing whom, unlike the more opaque manual systems which they replaced. In phase 1, some focus group respondents, particularly from the humanities, felt that greater transparency could lead to greater openness and enhanced collegiality between the subsidized and non-subsidized departments. Indeed arts and humanities are typically in the former group. In the UK these disciplines have suffered considerably from a shift in funding to favour lab-based subjects from the late 1990s onward. Nor is this just a UK phenomenon (Pan 1998). However, in phase two only a minority of other respondents agreed with the view that transparent budgets fostered openness. This Dean, from a faculty that was highly successful, both financially and academically, was definitely atypical:

One of the things I have learnt as a Dean is to think more corporately and I think all of the Deans now have. When I first became Dean we were quite frequently seen as competitors and I was in actual fact I think had an attitude of 'I conquer' at that time. Nowadays we tend to think much more corporately, for instance, I am thinking particularly in terms of the different profitability of the faculties. Dept X for instance in this faculty is the most profitable in the university, generating a surplus of about to £2,500,000 to £3,000,000 every year, which we see nothing of because it goes in to the centre, but what it does, it subsidises the deficits in areas like humanities. Now I think we decided some years ago that we were not unhappy with that, the university should have some cross organisation, you don't want a university that doesn't have a history department and not every area has the same opportunities to generate income.   (Dean, maths/information science, post-1992 university)

More usually, the view was that financial models allowed departments and faculties that were profitable, to nurture resentment because others took the money away from them:

Some of my colleagues um, are feeling quite de-motivated because of the fact that for many years we have been under-resourced. Um, the resource allocation model, I only have had sight of it now as Head of School . . . I'd probably get my knuckles wrapped photocopying it, but I'm happy to read off the figures to colleagues. So, there is a perception that we have been used as a cash-cow for the university and for the Faculty and as a result of that the member of staff who's faced with the final year class of 300 and the practicality of ensuring good teaching, looking after the students, dealing with things the way we should have done, has left colleagues feeling a little bit ground down, well quite substantially ground down. Equally, when we're asked to do something we are promised that resources will follow and the hysterical laughter of that phrase brings about in colleagues.   (HoD management, pre-1992 university)

Hence the introduction of new control technologies into universities brings with it new problems, as well as helping senior manager-academics to get a firmer grip on the activities of their staff. Resistance to such technologies may well prove to be greater than to the previous more subtle forms of control used by manager-academics, not least because there is a much greater degree of self-surveillance involved (something of which our phase three respondents were very much aware). Some HoDs felt uncomfortable about this:

I think this whole more intrusive culture that people aren't left to just get on with it in the way that they were ... certainly in the past there wasn't enough accountability. But I feel that we have now perhaps swung too far in the other direction ... there perhaps is too much monitoring and too much written reporting and so that is a bit of a dilemma, being asked to implement that on the one hand whilst having misgivings about it. (HoD humanities, pre-1992 university)

Other researchers have noted that the responses to change from managed staff in universities are very varied (Trowler 1998). At the same time, Reed has pointed out that the shift from somewhat bureaucratic but essentially overt management controls as found in bureau-professionalism (Clarke and Newman 1997) to those which rely more heavily on the indirect 'gaze', as in some publicly funded and private sector organizations, does not necessarily empower those employees involved (Reed 1999). In higher education, the search for clarity and transparency by means of systems using new technology may put more onus on individuals to perform than did the looser and less information-based forms of management control which new technologies partially replace. Despite the apparent popularity of better information flows with some of our phase 3 respondents (many of whom wanted universities to be more open and democratically run), these very flows may exacerbate as well as ease power dynamics and tensions. Indeed it is possible that these tensions, added to the constantly changing external environment for UK higher education, may well have the effect of making strategic management of higher education more difficult.

CRISIS MANAGEMENT OR STRATEGIC DIRECTION?

A great deal of recent research on the *implementation* of the change strategy, programme of organizational restructuring and control technology redesign associated with 'New Managerialism' suggests that, to date, practical outcomes are rather more ambiguous and contradictory than its *emergent theory of change*. As such, the research literature on implementation indicates that the emerging leitmotiv is '*hybridization*'—of institutional structures, organizational forms, control technologies and occupational cultures, and work identities and relations (Ferlie *et al.* 1996; Kean and Scase 1998; Brock *et al.* 1999; Exworthy and Halford 1999; Pollitt and Bouckaert 2000). It is the combination and recombination of 'the old' and 'the new' within what we might call 'soft bureaucracy' that seems to define the contemporary trajectory of institutional and organizational restructuring within the public sector (Flynn 1999; Reed 1999; Courpasson 2000; Flynn 2000). In part, this might be interpreted as the necessarily, piecemeal and long-term nature of public sector change. It might also be viewed as the outcome of an inevitable confrontation between the ideology of 'New Managerialism' and the reality of its operational translation into organizational and professional practice. This confrontation unavoidably produces all sorts of endemic contradictions and tensions—between intensified market competition and institutional stability, between more detailed and intrusive managerial control and effective professional practice, etc.,—that have to be coped with in some way or another on a localized, everyday basis. Thus, in universities, for instance, the Research Assessment Exercise puts pressure on manager-academics who are research active and those who are mainly teachers, even though both are essential to the continued survival of higher education and despite the loss of morale and career prospects that this may entail for those labelled 'teaching only'. While public sector institutions and organizations have always been hybridized combinations of 'markets', 'bureaucracies', and 'networks', the dissemination and implementation of the package of reforms associated with 'New Managerialism' has drastically exacerbated the endemic contradictions and tensions that they contained. This may have generated an organizational response in which 'New Managerial' cultures and control technologies have been selectively 'grafted on', in an adaptive and piecemeal fashion, to pre-existing structures and cultures of bureaucratic and professional power. Where this has happened, as in higher education, bureaucratic and professional power are being incrementally diluted, dispersed and displaced by the ideological, institutional, and organizational reforms that 'New Managerialism' has initiated. We saw some evidence of this in our research, as reported in the last section, though we also noted resistance to it.

In this section, our focus is upon the extent to which manager-academics working in the sixteen universities which were the subject of our research were driven by strategic considerations or by response to crises. In our phase 3 case studies, many respondents contended that universities lacked strategic direction and were blown about both by external changes and by internal indecision. One research fellow in social science at a medium-sized traditional, pre-1992, university expressed it thus:

The university is floating on loop-holes without an organisational structure. Managers do not know what is going on on campus.

This was not an isolated criticism. A group of secretarial staff at the same institution said of it:

It's chaotic and desperate. One part does not know what the other is doing. Managers know less than union reps who have access to [Governing body] minutes. There is very slow decision-making—3 years is average. It's a dinosaur.

In a post-1992 institution some similar concerns were expressed:

It's a numbers culture. You adjust the definitions to fit the thing you want to make. The spin is 'changing things to suit' but the fact is that fewer people who are actually subject specialists can deliver.   (NATFHE trade union representatives)

In a second post-1992 institution, the difficulty of achieving strategic change was compared with an oil-tanker and a dispersed frigate by a recently appointed dean of social sciences:

You know to turn the ship round is a hell of a job. It was presented to me when I was talking to people at the interview as like trying to change the direction of an oil tanker, you do it, and five miles down stream you see some movement. At first I said 'I don't think you've got that amount of time quite frankly, the current context in higher education, you've only got five miles and if you equate miles to years you haven't got time'.   (Dean of Social Sciences, post-1992 university)

The notion of crisis-management echoed some comments made in focus group discussions, including by more senior managers:

One of [the] business members of the University Council said, um, at I think the last Council meeting that he'd never realised what complicated institutions universities were totally round the board. And it was he that pointed out that, he said that 'I'm accustomed to working in institutions which can shed staff, err, more or less at will, which can set their own, err, err, err, price which can determine the quality of their product'. Now, universities are in contrast to this. I can't shed staff at will, because an awful lot of, well, certainly academic staff have got old contracts. Well, I can do it, but it would cost such a fortune that it would back up the institution. And I can't set a price for the services that are being offered, it's set for me by the Government. We live in a world of never, never and live in a world of administrative crisis.   (VC, learned society focus group)

In phase 2 interviews such reservations were still expressed but usually in a fairly optimistic manner so that challenges were seen as there to be dealt with rather than as obstacles to strategic change. However, our data are based mainly on interviews and what people describe themselves as doing may not be very close to what they actually do. A recent study of University Chief Executives suggested that such individuals do typically talk about their involvement with strategic decision-making when interviewed (Bargh *et al.* 2000). The researchers identified the main aspects of this strategic decision-making as being about academic issues. There are, it is noted, two dimensions to this—one concerned mainly with enabling the institution to meet the demands of external accountability and the other more focused on the values and ethos underlying higher education. The latter might be expected to be in flux as universities move from an elite to a mass system. However, Bargh *et al.* found in their work-shadowing of university chief executives that management of and response to crises often took over from the longer term strategic work of those chief executives. This must be borne in mind for our data too. Certainly our senior respondents talked of their involvement in strategic decision-making, despite the difficulties faced:

Clearly I would never want finance to drive a university, it mustn't. The university has to be driven by a set of academic values and vision. But it's going to be constrained by resources. What you must never let happen is . . . a university to be driven, its agenda set by the inevitable shortage of resources which exists in every university in the country now. (VC, post-1992)

Well, one of our strategic objectives and I would say first amongst them all um, is that the next RAE, and like everybody else in the world, we want to get a raft of 5's . . . I think it's a realistic objective because we've got nothing less than a 4 last time. But we didn't get any 5's. So what we're looking to do is to ratchet it up everywhere from the 4's to the 5's in terms of research, or at least in the vast majority of them. Now, and that I think is probably, if you had to prioritise the objectives that we're aiming to, that's probably gonna come out number 1 on virtually everybody's list because of the implications that it has beyond 2001, and not just the direct funding implications either, because of the implications it would have for staff recruitment, student recruitment, um ability to be chosen as an academic partner with um, companies and so on and so forth. So it really is very important that we get that.   (PVC, pre-1992 university)

However, most manager-academics were also aware that their plans could easily be blown off-course by government policy changes, volatile international student markets, failure to sustain research income and the steady decline in the unit of resource per home student. Furthermore, there was widespread awareness that year on year efficiency savings had also reduced the capacity of universities as organizations to cope with the unexpected:

We've become such a sort of lean organization that we only cope with the day to day business and any disturbance to that caused by a need for additional information, to respond to Government initiatives, HEFC[1] initiatives and those sorts of things, are, they cause massive perturbations in our systems, because something else doesn't get done and then we discover that something else was rather important as well.   (Dean, applied science, post-1992 university)

You're always trying to do more with less, because you know HEFC funding is being cut by 3 or 4 per cent a year. You're always trying to do more with less and that becomes very wearing on the staff and so that I think consistently is the difficult issue to manage.   (HoD, social science, post-1992 university)

'You could say that academics are being asked to do more & more for the same amount of money & institutions have to do more & more for the same amount of money & the money now comes with, you know, far more strings to it than previously.   (PVC, pre-1992 university)

The very people who are implementing changes to higher education recognize that their own practices and conditions are also changing very rapidly and in ways not always very consistent with long-term strategic decisions about their institutions. The effort involved in thinking about, for example, the effects of globalization or becoming a virtual university, is not assisted by the constant search for resources and the need to make fresh economies every academic year. 'New Managerialist' theory argues that new realities can only become institution-alized in the form of the 'entrepreneurial firm' once the structural and cultural restraints embedded in bureaucracy have been swept away by the global com-petitive pressures and cultural demands generated by the inexorable movement towards the 'new economy'. Thus, a putative 'paradigm shift' in the international

---

[1] This is used as a generic term as to use the actual initials would increase the risk of identification of institutions and individuals.

economy, corporate structures and organizational cultures (Korten 1995; Clarke and Clegg 1998; Clegg *et al.* 1999) provides the wider context in which the reforms associated with 'New Managerialism' can be located. Professional bureaucracy cannot be saved; it is irreparably damaged by its inherent limitation and its inability to move with the times. A new moral order is gradually established. But in the universities we researched, the new order seems to be struggling too, not least perhaps because it still retains so many elements of the old order, including many academics who have yet to embrace the concepts of 'family' and 'team' rather than the fragmentary and often pluralistic identities associated with occupationally and functionally-based professionalism (Casey 1995).

CONCLUSION

In this chapter we have explored the extent to which 'New Managerialism' has permeated the management of UK universities and the effects that this might have on the move of higher education towards virtuality. To the extent that 'New Managerialism' has taken hold in higher education, it has done so very much in a hybridized form, building on old forms of management and authority and adding new elements (including virtuality). However, the research goes beyond this to look at who becomes a manager-academic. Our data point to the various career-profiles of senior manager-academics and the strong possibility that many of those currently in post have relatively little experience of new technologies. Nevertheless, contemporary manager-academics are making more use of new technologies in their management. Often, this is justified initially on the basis of meeting the requirements of external agencies, but can then be used for other internal purposes such as monitoring research activity or financial performance. When used in this way, new technologies have the potential to be more invasive and to emphasize self-governmentality, whether at a unit or individual level. This was recognized by some of our case study respondents, many of whom felt they had acquired more responsibility but not more power. The context in which decisions are made is also relevant to an understanding of the ease with which virtuality may sweep the management corridors of UK universities. The uncertain and constantly changing external environment of those universities means that strategic decision-making has to occur side by side with more mundane activities and more importantly, urgent crisis management. This seems consistent with other reports on the slow progress of UK universities in coming to terms with the effects of globalization and virtuality (Middlehurst 2000).

We have also tried to show the extent to which what is happening in the UK universities we researched is consistent with or at odds with wider theories about 'New Managerialism' in public services. It is apparent from our investigations that academic and support staff not in management roles regard higher education as having undergone a significant shift towards 'New Managerialism' in respect of resource-dependency, emphasis on management of the academic labour process rather than academics working with academics, and adoption of new control technologies such as computer stored performance data and email. However, both academic responses to this and the situation as described by manager-academics contains evidence of the development of highly hybridized forms of management in their universities. Even though new languages describing what is done in universities are beginning to develop as they are elsewhere in public services (Shore and Roberts 1995; Shore and Wright 1998), they are only slowly being accepted and only by some staff. This is consistent with evidence about the reworking of academic professionalism (Henkel 2000) around traditional elements of academic life, and the view that academics themselves are becoming more differentiated from each other despite pressures towards convergence caused by the ending of the binary line in 1992 (Fulton 1998). Some cultural re-engineering of UK higher education has clearly been attempted but we have yet to find out if it has succeeded. If it does, it may be that it restricts the thinking potential of university staff rather than freeing them up to think about new ways of running higher education, along the lines that Sennett (1998) has discussed, in a wider context of changes to work:

The revolt against routine, the appearance of a new freedom is deceptive. Time in institutions and for individuals has been unchained from the iron cage of the past, but subjected to new, top-down controls and surveillance. The time of flexibility is the time of a new power. Flexibility begets disorder but not freedom from restraint.   (Sennett 1998: p. 59)

REFERENCES

Ackroyd, S., Hughes, J., *et al.* (1989) 'Public Sector Services and their Management', *Journal of Management Studies*, 26(6): 603–19.

Anthony, P. (1986) *The Foundation of Management*. London: Tavistock, 1986.

Bargh, C., Bocock, J., *et al.* (2000) *University Leadership: The Role of the Chief Executive*. Buckingham: Open University Press.

Barry, D. and Elmes, M. (1997) 'Strategy Retold: Toward a Narrative View of Strategic Discourse.' *The Academy of Management Review*, 22(2): 429–52.

Becher, T. (1989) *Academic Tribes and Territories*. Buckingham: Open University Press.

Brehony, K. J. and Deem, R. (1995) 'School governing bodies: reshaping education in their own image.' *Sociological Review*, 43(1): 79–99.

Brock, D., Powell, M., *et al.* (eds) (1999) *Restructuring the Professional Organisation*. London: Routledge.

Brooks, A. (1997) *Academic Women*. Buckingham: Open University Press.

Casey, C. (1995) *Work, Self and Society after Industrialism*: London, Routledge.

Child, J. (1969) *British Management Thought*. London: Allen and Unwin.

Clark, B. (1987) *The Academic Life: Small Worlds, Different Worlds*. Princeton: Carnegie Foundation for the Advancement of Teaching.

—— (1998) *Creating Entrepreneurial Universities: Organisational pathways of transformation*. New York & Amsterdam: Elsevier.

Clarke, J. and Newman, J. (1997) *The Managerial State: Power, politics and ideology in the remaking of social welfare*. London: Sage.

Clarke, T. and Clegg, S. (1998) *Changing Paradigms: The Transformation of Management Knowledge for the 21st Century*. London: Harper Collins.

Clegg, S., Ibarra-Colado, E., *et al.* (1999) *Global Management: Universal Theories and Local Realities*. London: Sage.

Courpasson, D. (2000) 'Managerial Strategies of Domination: Power in Soft Bureaucracies', *Organisation Studies*, 21(1): 141–62.

Deem, R. (1998) 'New managerialism in higher education—the management of performances and cultures in universities', *International Studies in the Sociology of Education*, 8(1): 47–70.

—— (2001) 'Globalisation, new managerialism, academic capitalism and entrepreneurialism in universities; is the local dimension still important?', *Comparative Education*, 37(1): 7–20.

—— and Hillyard, S. (2001) 'Making time for management—the careers and lives of manager-academics in UK universities', in G. Allan, G. Crow, S. J. Heath, and G. Jones (eds) *Times in the Making*. Basingstoke: Macmillan/Palgrave.

—— and Johnson, R.J. (2000) 'Managerialism and university managers: building new academic communities or disrupting old ones?', in I. McNay (ed) *Higher Education and its Communities*. Buckingham: Open University Press. 65–84.

—— and Ozga, J. (2000) 'Transforming post compulsory education? Femocrats at work in the academy.' *Women's Studies International Forum*, 23(2): 153–66.

DiMaggio, P. and Powell, W. (1991) 'Introduction', in P. DiMaggio and W. Powell (eds) *The New Institutionalism in Organisational Analysis*. Chicago: University of Chicago Press.

Du Gay, P. (1996) *Consumption and Identity at Work*. London: Sage.

—— and Salaman, G. (1992) 'The Cult(ure) of the Customer', *Journal of Management Studies*, 29(4): 616–33.

Eggins, H. (ed) (1997) *Women as Leaders and Managers in Higher Education*. SRHE. Buckingham: Open University Press.

Enders, J. (ed) (2001) *Employment and Working Conditions of Academic Staff in Europe*. Frankfurt am Main: Gewerkschaft Erziehung und Wissenschaft.

Enteman, W. (1993) *Managerialism: The Emergence of a New Ideology*. Wisconsin: University of Wisconsin Press.

Exworthy, M. and Halford, S. (eds) (1999) *Professionals and the New Managerialism in the Public Sector*. Buckingham: Open University Press.

Ferlie, E., Ashburner, L., *et al.* (1996) *The New Public Management in Action*. Oxford: Oxford University Press.

Flynn, R. (1992) *Structures of Control in Health Management*. London: Routledge.

—— (1999) 'Managerialism, professionalism and quasi-markets', in M. Exworthy and S. Halford (eds) *Professionals and the New Managerialism in the Public Sector*. Buckingham: Open University Press.

—— (2000) 'Soft Bureaucracy, governmentality and clinical governance: theoretical approaches to emergent policy', *Soft Bureaucracy, Governmentality and Clinical Governance: Theoretical Approaches to Emergent Policy*. Unpublished Paper given to ESRC Seminar Series on Governing Medicine, Bradford, November.

Fulton, O. (1996) 'Mass Access and the End of Diversity? The Academic Profession in England on the Eve of Structural Reform', in P. Altbach (ed) *The International Academic*

Profession: Portraits from Fourteen Countries. Princeton, USA: Carnegie Foundation for the Advancement of Teaching.

—— (1998) 'Unity or fragmentation, convergence or diversity? The academic profession in comparative perspective in the era of mass higher education', in W.G. Bowen and H. Shapiro (eds) *Universities and their Leadership.* Princeton: Princeton University Press.

Glover, I. and Tracey, P. (1997) 'In Search of Technik: Will Engineering Outgrow Management?', *Work, Employment and Society*, 11(4): 759–76.

Gray, H. (ed) (1999) *Universities as Wealth Creation.* Buckingham: Open University Press.

Halsey, A. H. (1992) *Decline of Donnish Dominion : The British Academic Professions in the Twentieth Century.* Oxford: Clarendon.

Hannan, A. and Silver, H. (2000) *Innovating in Higher Education.* Buckingham: Open University Press.

Harrison, S. and Pollitt, C. (1994) *Controlling Health Professionals: The Future of Work and Organisation in the NHS.* Buckingham: Open University Press.

Henkel, M. (2000) *Academic Identities and Policy Change in Higher Education.* London: Jessica Kingsley.

Hood, C. (1995) 'Contemporary Public Management: A New Global Paradigm?', *Public Policy and Administration*, 10(2): 104–17.

Huber, L. (1990) 'Disciplinary Cultures and Social Reproduction', *European Journal of Education* 25(3).

Jary, D. and Parker, M. (1998) *The New Higher Education: Issues and Directions for the Post-Dearing University.* Stoke on Trent, Staffordshire: Staffordshire University Press.

Kean, L. and Scase, R. (1998) *Local Government Management: The Rhetoric and Reality of Change.* Buckingham: Open University Press.

Kirkpatrick, I. and Lucio, M. (1995) *The Politics of Quality in the Public Sector: The Management of Change.* London: Routledge.

Korten, D. (1995) *When Corporations Rule the World.* London: Earthscan Publications.

Locke, R. (1989) *Management and Higher Education Since 1940.* Cambridge: Cambridge University Press.

—— (1996) *The Collapse of the American Management Mystique.* Oxford: Oxford University Press.

Marginson, S. and Considine, M. (2001) *Enterprise University in Australia. Governance, Strategy and Reinvention.* Cambridge: Cambridge University Press.

Mark, A. and Dopson, S. (eds) (1999) *Organisational Behaviour in Health Care: The Research Agenda.* London: MacMillan.

Meadmore, D. (1998) 'Changing the culture: the governance of the Australian pre-millenial university', *International Studies in the Sociology of Education*, 8(1): 27–46.

Middlehurst, R. (2000) *The business of borderless education : UK perspectives—analysis and recommendations.* London: Committee of Vice Chancellors and Principals.

Mintzberg, H. (1979) *The Structuring of Organisations.* Englewood Cliffs, New Jersey: Prentice Hall.

Mitchell, D. (1999) *Governmentality: Power and Rule in Modern Society.* London: Sage.

Morgan, G. and Engwall, L. (eds) (1999) *Regulation and Organisations: International Perspectives*, London: Routledge.

Pan, D. (1998) 'The Crisis of the Humanities and the End of the University', *Telos* (111 Spring 1998): 69–106.

Parry, G. (2001) 'Reform of Higher Education in the United Kingdom', in B. Nolan (ed.) *Public Sector Reform: An International Perspective*. Basingstoke: Macmillan.

Pollit, C. (1993) *Managerialism in the Public Services*. Oxford: Blackwell.

—— and Bouckaert, G. (2000) *Public Management Reform: A Comparative Analysis*. Oxford: Oxford University Press.

Power, M. (1997) *The Audit Society*, Oxford: Oxford University Press.

Reed, M. (1995) 'Managing Quality and Organisational Politics: TQM as a Governmental Technology', in I. Kirpatrick and M. Martinez-Lucio (eds) *The Politics of Quality in the Public Sector*. London: Routledge: 44–64.

—— (1999) 'From the "Cage" to the "Gaze": the dynamics of organisational control in late modernity', in G. Morgan and L. Engwall (eds) *Regulation and Organisations: International Perspectives*. London: Routledge. 17–49.

Rose, N. (1999) *Powers of Freedom: Reframing Political Thought*. Cambridge: Cambridge University Press.

Scott, P. (ed) (1998) *The Globalisation of Higher Education*. Buckingham: Open University Press.

Sennett, R. (1998) *The Corrosion of Character: The Personal Consequences of Work in the new Capitalism*. London: Norton and Company.

Shore, C. and Roberts, S. (1995) 'Higher Education and the Panopticon Paradigm: Quality Assurance as a "Disciplinary Technology"', *Higher Education Quarterly*, 27(3): 8–17.

—— and Wright, S. (1998) 'Audit Culture and Anthropology: Neo-Liberalism in British Higher Education', *Journal of the Royal Anthropological Institute*, 5(4): 557–75.

Slaughter, S. and Leslie, G. (1997) *Academic Capitalism*. Baltimore: John Hopkins.

Smith, A. and Webster, F. (eds) (1997) *The Postmodern University? Contested Visions of Higher Education in Society*. Buckingham, Open University Press.

Smith, P. (1993) 'Outcome-Related Performance Indicators and Organisational Control in the Public Sector,' *British Journal of Management*, 4(3): 135–52.

Trow, M. (1993) *Managerialism and the Academic Profession: The Case of England*. Stockholm: Council for Studies of Higher Education.

Trowler, P. (1998) *Academics Responding to Change: New Right Education Frameworks and Academic Cultures*. Buckingham: Open University Press.

Webb, J. (1999) 'Work and the new public service class', *Sociology*, 33(4): 747–66.

Woodward, D. and Ross, K. (2000) *Managing Equal Opportunities in Higher Education*. Buckingham: Open University Press.

8

Exporting Management: Neo-imperialism and Global Consumerism

Yiannis Gabriel and Andrew Sturdy

INTRODUCTION

The transfer of knowledge across societies is not a recent phenomenon and does not require the movement of electrons in cyberspace. In earlier societies, religious missionaries and mercenaries ('soldiers of fortune') were key agents of the diffusion of religious and military knowledge, respectively. Explorers and navigators acted as disseminators of scientific and technical knowledge, along with stories, legends, and myths from distant lands. Some of this knowledge assumed the form of gifts, exchanged by representatives of different cultures, while some was traded for money or goods. Throughout the Cold War, the transfer of knowledge in the guise of charitable donations became a powerful weapon and/or inducement, as the super-powers tried to recruit other countries to their way of life and of thinking and doing (cf. Locke 1989; Djelic 1998). Donations of knowledge, like other charity, aimed to make the receiver gratefully dependent on the giver. At the same time, it helped fuel the economic and ideological power of the US especially. Today, similar initiatives are under way in the name of 'development' and 'progress'. Receiving states, for their part, are becoming more sensitive or 'wise' to the dangers of neo-imperialism and dependence. In recognition of their own identities and, in many cases, growing economic power, such states may seek to assert themselves in various ways. Donor agents cannot take for

We gratefully acknowledge the comments on earlier drafts of this chapter from colleagues, including Barry Wilkinson and Bill Harley. This chapter is based upon the authors' experiences of teaching and running an MBA course whilst working at the University of Bath. The material presented here consists of a revision and re-working of an earlier article—Sturdy, A.J. and Gabriel, Y. (2000) 'Missionaries, Mercenaries or Car Salesmen?—MBA Teaching in Malaysia', *Journal of Management Studies*, 37(7): 979–1002.

granted the gratitude of the receiver. Instead, there is more likely to be an ambivalence of attraction and repulsion towards new ways signalled by the transfer of knowledge.

Not all transfers of knowledge followed the dynamics or rhetoric of gifts and donations. Long before the Cold War was over, a process of *commodification* of knowledge had begun. This takes many forms, such as books, videos, consultants' services, and educational packages. Knowledge became a major export industry for industrialized countries, not altogether unlike that of material commodities. Key actors here were government appointed advisers, firms of consultants (e.g. in engineering or information technology), and educational and training institutions. One feature of commodification was the segmentation of knowledge into discrete packages or qualifications, which could be purchased, with producers and consumers meeting as 'free' agents within 'free' markets. The MBA (Master of Business Administration) can be seen as probably the most globally recognizable such package, available both in domestic and export markets. Suppliers try to make their MBAs desirable and consumers try to get good (use/symbolic/exchange) value for money. While some view the MBA as signalling the demise of education as a vocation, others celebrate or assert the 'efficiency' and 'choice' brought to 'sovereign' students.

Administrators are coming to recognize that their educational campuses need to grow like the other new means of consumption to thrive. The high school has been described as resembling a shopping mall. The university, too, can be seen as a means of educational consumption . . . (so far) ineffective compared to . . . cruise ships, casinos and fast food restaurants.   (Ritzer 1999: 24)

In this chapter, we will explore the view that management education in general, and MBA programmes in particular, can be seen as a type of consumption. Following a selective review of relevant literature on knowledge diffusion as consumption and neo-imperialism, we will discuss our observations as lecturers on an MBA jointly run with a local organization—the Malaysian Institute of Management (MIM). Drawing primarily on our reflections and observations of teaching and administration experiences and of the attitudes and experiences of students, we shall address the following research question: To what extent does the consumption perspective do justice to the complexities of the diffusion of management knowledge? Does the MBA represent a prototype for the globalization of higher education? What, if any, forces oppose it? And what are the implications of expanding commodification in higher education? By using an analogy with that most emblematic of consumer products, the motor car, we will see how far the consumption paradigm in its different forms takes us and at what point the purchasing and use of knowledge demands different assumptions from those of other goods and services. In doing so, we also provide insight into the ambivalence surrounding the transactions between teachers and students. In addition, by identifying a number of commonalities with experiences of teaching in the UK, our analysis highlights some of the contradictions resulting from the commodification and consumption of MBAs in a wider context. Overall, we are hoping to provide a critical analysis of the dominant consumption discourses of management education as well as an empirical insight into the dynamics of overseas teaching and learning which draws particular attention to the national identity of management ideas in diffusion.

MANAGEMENT KNOWLEDGE DIFFUSION AS CONSUMPTION

There is now a large and growing literature on different aspects of the diffusion and learning of management ideas and ('best') practices within and between organizations, sectors, and nations. This growth can be linked to a number of interrelated developments such as the increased profile and popularity of prescriptive management communicators from the USA (e.g. writers, consultants); the continued demand for solutions to perceived crises in competitiveness, particularly in established or hitherto protected markets; increased neo-liberal ideological legitimation for management; globalization (e.g. IT); and theoretical shifts which have attached primacy to knowledge and cultural diversity (e.g. post-modernism; post-colonialism). Key debates in this growing literature are mainly concerned with the agents, processes, constraints, conditions, and directions of knowledge diffusion (e.g. see Clegg and Palmer 1996; Stallings 1995; Clark and Fincham 2001). Other areas are less developed: these include managers' use of new ideas in their organizations (cf. Watson 1994), the desirability and beneficiaries of diffusion (Dore 1996; Easterby-Smith 1997), and our own area of interest—the commercialization of university management education. Two features of diffusion, which are of interest to our discussion, but remain relatively under-researched, are neo-imperialism and commercialization. Both are particularly pervasive in international management education discourse and our own experience.

The neo-imperialist quality of management diffusion is well-captured by Kostera (1995), who uses the metaphor of missionaries, 'heathens', and religion to explore the spread of Western management ideas by lecturers and consultants to the peoples of Eastern Europe. While the style of delivery may be more or less 'culture sensitive', the ideological messages or 'myths' are the same—'hard work', 'economizing', and the 'free market' (*ibid*: 343). Kostera restricts her label of missionaries to those with ready-made knowledge packages and pursuing material interests, explicitly excluding those who come for other reasons or wish to work closely with local partners. This highlights a different dimension of the transfer of management knowledge, one that goes beyond the missionary zeal of individuals and views diffusion as a market process through which knowledge, as a commodity, is traded.

This approach is complemented by Huczynski's (1993) study of gurus and other agents of diffusion as part of a broader 'productivization' of management ideas in the UK. Here, ideas are transformed and packaged—like 'milk into dairy products'—to be marketed, sold, and consumed by managers (also seen as 'retailers') and other employees (Huczynski 1993: 217; see also Anthony 1977). This involves branding, promotion, product development, and the development of marketing strategies for different markets. Frequently, such a perspective presents diffusion as uni-directional—consumers as gullible victims (Thomas 1993; Sturdy 1997a) and, therefore, suppliers such as Western educational establishments as somewhat unscrupulous. But the paradigm of consumption can take a more interactive form. With the proliferation of both management ideas ('fads') and educational packages and escalation of media coverage, consumers can become more discriminating and demanding (e.g. Ramsay 1996). The opposite view, then, to that of the consumer as victim is that of a consumer as a sovereign agent, capable of distinguishing between different products on offer and exercising choice to get best value for money. Higher education students in the UK, for example, are conceived as increasingly 'sophisticated' customers, capable of separating fact from hype and value from image. Modularization enables such students to exercise further choice, selecting those courses whose design, content, and delivery suit their needs. As Lyotard (1984) has observed:

The relationship of the suppliers of knowledge and the users of knowledge, to the knowledge that they supply and use, is now tending, and will increasingly tend to assume the form already taken by the relation of commodity producers and consumers to the commodities that they produce and consume—that is, the form of value.   (Lyotard 1984: 4)

Compared to some other areas of knowledge (e.g. philosophy, history), management ideas and education rapidly acquire commodity characteristics, not least because of the financial value increasingly claimed and extracted. Unlike reading Rousseau or Proust, reading Michael Porter or Tom Peters, or at least 'knowing' their ideas, has come to be seen as a *sine qua non* for today's practising manager or business-person, whether in the UK or in Malaysia. Furthermore, unlike reading works of philosophy or history, Western management knowledge displaces other, longer standing, locally produced forms of management know-how in the interest of increased efficiency, better quality, and enhanced competitiveness. Thus, within the broad and diffuse process of producing and transforming management ideas, the MBA has come to be viewed as the standardized package of management education. It is strongly associated with student instrumentalism (aimed at achieving practical, tangible, and even measurable results), smart packaging from lecturers and concomitant marketing from educational institutions for home and overseas markets. It can be claimed that the almost universally recognized initials of the MBA have come to represent a guarantee of management competence throughout the world—at one and the same time, the standard and the elemental commodity in this growing market.

CROSS-NATIONAL DIFFUSION AND THE NATIONAL IDENTITY OF KNOWLEDGE

Debates on the *cross-national* diffusion of management knowledge have long oscillated between divergence and convergence (e.g. Hirst and Thompson 1992). The latter is reflected in the view of globalization as straightforward Westernization of local practices and cultures (cf. Robertson 1992; Bauman 1998). Perhaps as a reaction to this popular and simplistic view, emphasis on local distinctiveness and resilience ('embeddedness') is currently assuming a somewhat dominant position in organization theory (Sorge 1991). Accordingly, attention is focused on *obstacles* to cross-national diffusion (Biersteker 1995).

Resistance against new Western ideas and practices in the area of management is due to many factors and should not automatically be attributed to cross-national diffusion (Sturdy 2001). Nevertheless, the journeys of management ideas and systems across continents or nations has never been unproblematic and there is a long history of resistance by individuals and organizations to such ideas—from Taylorism to service smiles—explicitly on the basis of their foreign or national origin. This has contributed to the barriers and time lag in diffusion. Littler (1982) notes how, despite being promoted as a universal ('scientific') practice, Taylorism was initially resisted by British managers and engineers, not simply on the grounds of being inappropriate for Britain, but because it was seen as American. Indeed, such stances may inform practitioners' accounts which give ostensibly more 'rational' objections to new practices (Cox and Cooper 1985). Similarly, Kogut and Parkinson argue from the cases of the 1920s France and Germany that diffusion is more likely where related practices are already being developed locally and that these 'indigenous roots' are stressed by promoters at the expense of foreign origins (Kogut and Parkinson 1993: 186). Smith and Meiksins (1995) argue that, as Taylorism became increasingly accepted, it lost its national label:

> With the passage of time, the competitive advantage of the methods and the creation of a layer of diffusion agents ... Taylorism lost its national status and entered textbooks as a universal practice. This was because it was not simply an American capitalist ideology—a cultural contingent—but a way of organising from a dominant state, hence one tied to capitalist advance, and by capitals with the power to internationalise, diffuse and impose their 'solutions' on other nations. (Smith and Meiskins 1995: 260)

By contrast, in some cases the politicization of local identity may highlight the foreign origin of methods. For example, Chanlat (1996) documents changes in management education in Quebec since the 1960s based in part on a conscious assertion of local identity and concomitant resistance to Anglo, then American, definitions of management knowledge. More generally, the recent emergence and diffusion of post-colonialism, whereby multiculturalism and difference are celebrated, may serve to reinforce local identities and sensitivities over neo-imperialism. Thus, concern about what appears as the individualistic and masculinist character of Western management ideas can inhibit or prevent their uncritical appropriation (Jacques 1996).

In Malaysia, resistance to UK, US, and Western ideas and practices is evident not simply on the basis of its former colonial status, but from a state-led effort to construct a unifying national and/or 'Asian' identity and culture to support economic growth and political stability among different ethnic groups.[1] This is evident in the quite recent and high-profile government hostility to Western currency speculators (Jayasankaran 1997). More generally, the government *seeks to* regulate and maintain some control of the activities of foreign companies and business visitors. This is sometimes achieved by requesting that new foreign investment is channelled through international joint ventures (Sturdy 1997*b*). Similarly, efforts to transform or translate imported knowledge and practices to the local contexts are increasingly encouraged, such as in the case of 'Islamic management' (Mendoza 1991).

Under these circumstances, then, current management ideas may not be 'neutralized' nationally as easily as it appears to have been the case with Taylorism. Yet, the core paradox for much of south-east Asia is that the appetite for US management ideas remains strong, even as the myth of 'one best way' is challenged (Clegg *et al.* 1996; Locke 1996). Indeed, resistance to US ideas is typically juxtaposed with the lure of potential economic growth and symbolic status to be derived from the practices associated with successful nations. As we shall see, there remains a strong demand for, and faith in, Western, especially American, management knowledge in Malaysia. Of course this by no means guarantees complete diffusion in the light of countervailing forces. In fact, the overall response to Western management ideas and practices is one of intense *ambivalence*. There appears to be hunger, but the available food is bitter-sweet to taste. It is not simply a case of economic pull–cultural push (away), for the two cannot be separated. The culture itself contains mixed and contradictory messages: Western management ideas are at the same time fashionable, 'effective', and 'modern', but also potentially divisive, dangerous, and smacking of neo-imperialism.

Within this pronounced ambivalence, there are considerable variations in responses to Western management ideas and practices across individuals,

[1]   The Malaysian population of around 20 million comprises 62.4% Malays and other 'indigenous' people (Bumiputera), 29.1% Chinese and 8% Indians (Bank Negara 1994). In addition, there are thousands of 'guest' workers from Indonesia and Bangladesh, many of whom reside without legal status or protection. Given this ethnic mix and Malaysia's colonial background, English is still used as a lingua franca for many despite the state's promotion of the local Bumiputera language, Bahasa. Relatedly, there are positive action policies to support Bumiputera interests against an established ethnic division of labour whereby the Chinese dominated business and the Malays, the public sector. Seeking political stability is a key feature of policies designed to attract foreign investors. Apart from general legislation such as that restricting rights to public assembly, it has been achieved in part by tough industrial relations laws since the 1970s, including restrictions on collective bargaining and special provision for foreign companies (Aun 1982; Ayadurai 1992; Guyton 1995). Clearly, the image of stability has been tarnished by the recent demonstrations in Kuala Lumpur over the prosecution of the Deputy Prime Minister.

groups (e.g. business elites), organizations and economic sectors. In particular, the receptivity of MBA students to foreign management ideas is not typical of other managers nor, almost certainly, of the population as a whole. For example, in research conducted by one of us in both local and multinational companies in Malaysia, the younger aspirant generation of managers who were more likely to have been educated abroad or have an MBA were less likely to resist Western management practices (Sturdy 1997*b*).

MBAs IN MALAYSIA

That the teaching of management is a major export business for Western countries, notably the USA, Great Britain, and Australia, is not hard to establish (Tysome 1999). The advertisements for MBAs in the Malaysian press compete for space with advertisements for cars, watches, and cosmetics. These MBAs are commonly sponsored jointly by a Malaysian institution, and a British, Australian, or American university. While still 'underdeveloped' within Malaysian universities, management education enjoys very high status. Entire hotel and conference complexes have been built to accommodate business education, and sometimes visitors from three or more foreign universities may be involved in separate residential programmes at the same hotel at the same time.

Like many consumer goods, the MBA is publicized for its utility value but much of its value lies in its symbolism. The cost of MBAs has a strong correlation to the status they accord their student or the owner. Some courses can be almost completely managed at a distance through the Internet and/or by correspondence. As other chapters in this volume show, these offer the student invisible or non-interpersonal contact with the source of educational authority. Other courses are programmes taught predominantly or, like ours, partly by local lecturers but approved, examined, and underwritten by Western universities and staff. In some cases, overseas universities have set up their own campuses in Malaysia with mixed local and ex-patriate staff. Finally, it is possible that there may also be 'phoney' MBAs, just like the pirate designer objects that fill street markets.

Until the recent economic crisis, MBA graduates have strongly increased their earning power and have been able to move from job to job. This seems to be an important 'fact'. In a country which, until very recently, suffered acute labour shortages, especially in management jobs,[2] the addition of the MBA letters after one's name immediately and substantially increased one's earning capacity. In many respects, then, an MBA in Malaysia is a commodity, which can be seen as part of a burgeoning process of conspicuous consumption. But it is also

---

[2] On the basis of government statistics for 1995, the labour market was described as 'tight' with the economy 'virtually operating at a full employment level' (2.8% unemployment) such that 'shortages were experienced in most major sectors in the economy, particularly in the skilled labour categories' (Bank Negara 1996: 254). Of course, the recent regional and national economic crisis has undermined the labour market power felt by skilled employees.

an investment—while the status accorded to the owner is important, it also translates into future earnings.

It is a curious fact that in a country where the British rule is greatly under-played in their national history in favour of 'Asian values' and economic miracles, many espouse, with great enthusiasm, Western management and business edu-cation. To be sure, the practices associated with earlier management doctrines of capitalist countries were adopted by their ideological opponents for example, Stalinist Russia took on Ford's assembly lines as a rational doctrine of effective production. However, this situation does not readily conform to that of con-temporary Malaysia. Western consumption is embraced by substantial sections of the population. For many people, branded Western goods, styles as well as their simulations and fakes, are cherished, and this is seemingly unencumbered by inhibitions of a religious or stylistic nature—for example, being branded 'nouveau-riche' or profligate. Indeed, while some forms of consumption (e.g. alcohol) are regulated or discouraged by the state, the government seems to actively encourage consumption:

The urge to spend is very much in conformity with the overall pro-consumption envir-onment prevailing in the country . . . penetrating every level of the society, both rural and urban. . . . the values and habits of material acquisition are being aggressively promoted, especially in the media, which happens to be (mostly) controlled by the government. (Talib 1995: 211–12, 214)

In the educational marketplace, the success of foreign-sponsored or foreign-validated MBAs can be linked to the presumed quality and associated controls offered by the foreign institutions. This involves a modicum of competence on the part of the teaching staff, but perhaps more importantly, an image of integrity in the award of the degrees. Concern over the integrity of both home and overseas awarding institutions is heightened by the government's recent increased atten-tion to quality control and certification (Hazman Shah 2000). Such regulation may reinforce the status of Western involvement—some programmes require an expert overseas adviser—while recognizing the scope for abuse and corruption.

THE CURRICULUM (THE 'PRODUCT')

Management education packages in Malaysia seem to be highly standardized with similar course structures and methods. Although students may be taught and assessed more heavily, there is little in the curricula to differentiate them from most MBA programmes in the West. However, 'sensitive' issues such as gender or ethnicity may be treated more carefully or even excluded (cf. Sinclair 1997). It is telling that, in a country where the study of Islamic and (more recently) 'Asian' civilization is part of every undergraduate programme, no great acknow-ledgement of local cultures is yet made in MBA programmes. To be sure, 'culture' features in OB courses and elsewhere, but is taught usually through Hofstede's typology or through the catch-all sobriquet of the Confucian ethic. It is possible that Australian universities, due to their intermediate geographical position, may increasingly provide a greater regional, if not entirely post-colonial, 'flavour' in course content. More generally, some changes are occurring as expatriate lecturers develop research and consultancy interests in the region. Furthermore, local institutions increasingly demand some tailoring of curricula, fuelled by their own increasing purchasing power as consumers. However, the programmes continue to be conducted mainly by white males and exclusively in English, the language of business education in Malaysia as in most other places.

Beyond the Malaysian context, the MBA generally is probably the university course most often seen as a commodity with a definite, and sometimes precisely calculable, financial (cf. 'academic') value for both students and institutions. This is especially so for foreign institutions running MBAs in countries like Malaysia—their motive seems to be primarily and increasingly financial. They may be promoted to and by government agencies (e.g. British Council) as tools for economic and political 'development' and, within the curriculum, the promise may be to solve organizational problems in a rational/superior way. However, in attracting students, for instance, through advertizing and presentations in educational fairs, a different sales pitch is adopted: 'Smelly breath? Try *Colgate* mouthwash'; 'Problems with your career? Get an MBA'.

It is tempting to compare MBAs with another high profile commodity that carries powerful symbolic resonances—cars. In Malaysia as elsewhere, *aspiring classes* invest much meaning in the cars that they purchase. Unlike the pride shown by many in the supposedly 'home-grown' *Proton* which is also an export product, this group often derides it and even apologises ('It's only a Proton, I'm afraid'). They value foreign, especially European, cars in much the same way as they appear to value foreign management education. In business as well as within the university system, those with a US, UK, or Australian qualification are favoured, especially as the government has scaled down the numbers of people it supports financially to study abroad.[3]

Foreign cars, like MBAs, are much more highly priced compared to local products. They are seen as better quality and better designed. They are associated with wealth and success generally, but there are variations depending on the marque's prestige or national reputation. Even from the same producer, there may be differences in value, especially if the product is assembled locally (e.g. by analogy, MBAs taught by correspondence) and/or with only local labour (MBAs by licence). While the status value may be based on perceptions

---

[3] There are some exceptions in the relative value attached to home and foreign institutions. For example, some of the former, such as University Sains Malaysia, are very highly regarded. In terms of business education, however, home-based products generally have only developed recently. Moreover, the role of overseas institutions is shifting with the establishment of their own campuses in Malaysia. Some commentators even point to a growing market for Western universities (e.g. Tysome 1999).

of tradition (the age of the organization), an assessment of quality is increasingly sought through consumer rankings in the media. As is evident in the UK, students engage in seemingly obsessive comparisons between the prestige of different institutions, aided and abetted by 'official' leagues. Finally, as we have noted, producers are unlikely to make many modifications to the product for the local circumstances. Not only would this require more resources, but, to do so—changing the name of a model for instance—might detract from its perceived value. However, as we shall see in the following section, such modifications to MBAs could have the opposite effect.

THE CONSUMERS

In the same way as it is commonplace to regard MBAs as a commodity, MBA students generally are easily and often stereotyped as the most instrumental educational consumers of all. Although this is only part of the picture, Malaysian students also display a strong awareness that they (or, often, their companies) are paying a relatively high price for the 'Bath MBA'. Their queries outside of the classroom reflect a concern about the status of Bath in comparison to other UK universities. The money seems to be a source of psychological discomfort and possibly conflict, as they often laugh or joke when they broach this subject. In a series of sketches which they performed as an 'ice-breaking' exercise, the winner was the one in which the MBA director's interview, supposed to establish the intellectual suitability of students, concluded with the question 'And how are you going to pay?'

The students appear enthusiastic about acquiring knowledge and determined to make the most of their contact with foreign lecturers. They ask questions fluently inside the classroom, something that creates in the lecturer a sense that they are genuinely curious and that they understand well what they are being taught. Many of the questions are probing and the students are not satisfied with general or ritualistic answers. Outside the lecture theatre, lecturers continue to be bombarded by questions from the students—these may range from the finer points of the theories introduced to highly practical matters, like: 'Should I go ahead with the product launch?', 'Should I fire my chauffeur?', 'How can we find a franchisee in the UK?'

How do Malaysian students use the knowledge that they acquire? Here, some of the diffusion literature mentioned earlier may be useful. Some of it highlights differences in the form (e.g. behavioural, cognitive, and affective) and extent of learning, and relates them both to different forms of knowledge (e.g. tacit, 'strategic', 'systemic', and 'technical') and socio-economic contexts (Child and Rodrigues 1996; Lillrank 1995; Lam 1997; Guillen 1994; Argyris and Schön 1974). Some authors in the management education literature have explored culturally specific preferred learning (and teaching) styles such as the *supposed* passivity and deference in South East Asia (e.g. Simon and Davis 1996; Warner 1991; Johnson 1991; Richards 1997; Hofstede and Bond 1988).

Such perspectives are now quite familiar and are evident in the Malaysian media. They are also echoed by the students. For example, a selection of their essays on Western management teaching suggests that some find it hard to criticize teachers and ideas on the basis of ancient cultural traditions.

> The passive learning style in business education and training is inherited from the Malaysian school system where 'the teachers are considered as "sifus" (a Chinese term for reverent and expert masters of any particular profession), the "all knowing", and the students . . . absorb the knowledge imparted like a sponge. . . . Where students disagree with the teacher, the *'predominant' Asian value of respect for elders precludes confrontation*. Instead, they may silently reject the idea without much critical thinking or, because of our high collectivism attitude, may agree with the idea without really understanding it. (emphasis added)

Cultural factors from the more recent colonial period (as well as economic development and policy concerns) are drawn on to explain the national appetite for Western management.

> . . . the current Malaysian business leaders are still very much influenced by the colonialist style of learning whereby everything taught by Western and Western-trained teachers is considered superior and can be taken wholesale.

> Despite being independent for the past 40 years, the British/Western technology and management style is still highly respected

> (student essays)

In keeping with the view that certain kinds of knowledge are more or less socially (i.e. locally) embedded, there do seem to be differences across courses. The apparently more 'concrete' or 'technical' knowledge (accounting, information systems, marketing) is, as is often the case in the UK, received with a degree of respect, albeit also with considerable anxiety—will they be able to answer the exam questions and survive the course? The 'human disciplines' create greater ambivalence as one might expect, particularly in a cross-national context. The anxiety, which they cause, is less like that generated by the prospect of an assault course and more like that generated by finding oneself in an alien and dangerous territory. Indeed, students, at least when set an essay on the topic, are not slow to criticize the lack of relevance of the material which they are taught to their particular national, cultural, *and* economic contexts.

> Assignments and exams are set based on Western business context. Western universities fail to customise their training programs and syllabi to meet the requirements of the Malaysian operating environment (e.g. most companies are SMEs in growth). On the other hand, the Western style is too confrontational, bureaucratic, rigid—it emphasises too much the individual. It can have adverse consequences for Eastern cultures that value relationships, trust and moderation.

Yet most of these well-known Western management approaches do not appear to work here (however, local or translated management materials are not widely available).

... much of what the lecturers teach has little relevance to the objectives, the needs, and the motivations of, as well as the opportunities and problems encountered by managers in developing countries.

(student essays)

Not all student criticisms should be interpreted as *negative* reactions to cultural imperialism. Our own experience of Malaysian students suggests that, in many ways, their responses to Western management education are not unlike those of their Western counterparts. For example, a concern with explicit *business* relevance, in the form of case studies, for instance, is a priority.

Consider the scenario of MBA students falling asleep whilst the management lecturer expounds the latest theories. As soon as a case study is mentioned, there is an immediate response. Case studies are in fact stories about businesses which makes them such effective teaching tools.

(student essay)

Similarly, some criticisms concern teaching failings such as inadequate or tokenistic student participation in the classroom. Such expectations may well be partly derived from their current and previous (e.g. undergraduate) experience of Western institutions. Indeed, and as intimated earlier in relation to the diffusion of post-colonialism from the West, some students are able to articulate concerns with the help of the very staff or ideas which they criticize. With 'faddism', for example, many students borrow elements of Western critical management thinking from the syllabus and local media (e.g. newspapers) to critique the type of package available to them.

With the present day easy accessibility to knowledge, media and personnel it will be difficult to find totally unquestioning followers. They may be quiet in word, but certainly not in mind.

... as the level and quality of education improves, the mechanical way of teaching becomes no longer suitable as students begin to ask questions more often and no longer display a very accepting attitude to whatever is being taught.

(student essays)

Thus, the approach adopted by Malaysian students to the knowledge they acquire seems to be increasingly that of 'sophisticated' consumers. They engage seriously with some ideas which they view as having relevance in their business, they are intrigued by others which appear to open interesting possibilities, they are disturbed by some which seem to run against their own experiences, and they dismiss quite a few as irrelevant or wrong. Yet, such criticisms only contribute to the general picture of ambivalence noted earlier. Notwithstanding individual and other variations, they run alongside the considerable enthusiasm for Western management ideas.

To what extent then does the consumption of educational packages resemble that of motorcars? There are extensive similarities in our students' attitudes towards their MBA and towards the cars which they purchase. First, there is a similar discomfort about paying a high price for a product whose qualities are not entirely known, and whose suitability for the local conditions is questionable. Equally, there is a concern that the high status of the product is maintained and that its prestige justifies the price premium—the product therefore should not be associated with a lower class of customer. Third, there is a concern that the suppliers are not offering an inferior package to the ones which they sell in their home markets. In all of these respects, there is a tension shared by the MBA student and the purchaser of a prestige motorcar—a tension that arises from paying both for a badge and a product/service. The badge is important, but the badge alone, the MBA letters or the BMW logo, does not justify the price, however much prestige and status it accords its owner. The product itself must be demonstrably good, at least as good as that sold in the home markets. At the same time, some modifications to the product must be made, in acknowledgement of the special local conditions. These modifications may be more important for reasons of pride rather than practicality. Fourth, there is a reluctance to criticize the product that they have purchased, even where its flaws are quite evident. Finally, one might detect a sense of unease (disloyalty?) over the buying of a foreign product at all, which sits uncomfortably with the more visible appetite for, and celebration of, its symbolic appeal.

If in all these respects, MBA students act in ways analogous to those purchasing any expensive foreign good, there are several unique qualities that set the MBA apart, as a high price commodity. Assessment, in particular, generates certain anxieties that are rarely encountered as regards other commodities. Yet, even these anxieties may have their parallel in the consumer who buys a sports-car and is beset by worries, like 'Am I good enough a driver to handle it?' Where we discerned a marked departure from the Western consumer paradigm in our students is in their determination to establish relations of mutual respect with their lecturers. In informal conversations, students are keen to inform visiting staff about Malaysia and portray it in a positive light, perhaps in an effort to counter the imbalance in information exchange. They want their lecturers to express an interest in their own country—that they are not uninterested imperialists, but that they want to learn too. This echoes Kostera's (1995) account, cited earlier, of Polish responses to Western management education. It is very far from the students' intention to relate to their lecturers as they may relate to sales staff, even if what they receive from them is a product. To this end, students emphasize non-commercial elements in the relationship, insisting on having their photographs taken with their teachers and often presenting them with presents, cards, and other tokens of personal esteem. These elements depart from the mostly impersonal cash nexus that underpins Western consumerism. They introduce a gift exchange aspect to the relationship, one that is often formalized with the offer of formal gifts by students to their lecturers. These are typically objects of local handicraft and culture as if to emphasize the value of the local inherent in the student's gift as against the lecturer's global knowledge.

THE TEACHER AS DIFFUSER

Western lecturers teaching in Malaysia find themselves in a perplexing situation. Their knowledge and position is infinitely more respected in Malaysia than in their own country—titles (Dr or Professor) according them a status approaching that of a guru. During their stay in Malaysia, they typically enjoy a standard of living considerably higher than that of an average family summer holiday. Expensive hotels, club class air travel, taxis everywhere and a general sense of being able to do things without the normal careful budgeting and penny-counting. Albeit for a very short time, they live the life of expatriates whose skills command much greater value than 'back home'. They receive gifts, they are entertained and shown considerable hospitality by the students as well as by the Malaysian partners. Moreover, they typically return home better off, having saved on living expenses and, often, received an extra payment or 'disturbance allowance'. At the same time, however, the novelty and enjoyment of such an experience quickly wear off. For many, there is insufficient time to adjust and any payment received does not compensate for soul-less (and sometimes unfinished) international hotels, jet lag, formal social events and being removed from the responsibilities and satisfactions of home. Once again then, ambivalence tends to result.

Lecturers arrive armed with their lecture notes, overhead transparencies and bullet points, pet stories and vignettes, all the comforting impedimenta of their professional lives and, maybe without surprise, they discover that 'they work' when practised on Malaysian students. 'Culture is no problem here', if anything the students are, or appear to be, even more impressed and interested than students at home. The tricks work. Yet, we have a sense that lecturers tend to exaggerate somewhat the degree of 'customer' satisfaction with their courses. They may also reassure themselves with the perception that their own teaching is theoretically more sophisticated than that of some of the local lecturers. Certainly, some of us may also feel discomfort in the role of disseminator of flawed, Western-based ideas and practices, especially when some students appear to receive them as the final word of wisdom. Indeed, it is important to note that the North American content within course syllabi is culturally alien to most lecturers as well as to the Malaysian students. All the same, we have a sense of responsibility, both towards our students and as standard-bearers of our university, and pride ourselves on satisfying our students. Accordingly, we may localize our course contents in minor ways or share our misgivings with the students, thereby perhaps reinforcing theirs. We may also try to be sympathetic to what we perceive to be the religious and socio-political sensitivities of the students, much more so than at home.

However, few, if any, of the visiting lecturers, have the remotest idea about Malaysian cultures beyond the interpretations they make of material artefacts. This is, perhaps, unsurprising given the brevity of visits and the extent of other responsibilities. Nevertheless, virtually none know any of the many languages used in Malaysia other than English. They can hardly distinguish their students' family name from their first name and they rarely master any of the local titles of address. Once they leave Malaysia, the majority can hardly claim to have anything more than a skin-deep familiarity with its cultures and people, even if they are also engaged in research.

It is tempting to view the MBA lecturer abroad not so much as a missionary or a mercenary but rather as a car salesperson, who earns income from sales to a soft market. Money is made for the organization and the salespersons receive a commission. While they do not rely solely on this for a living, for their own (e.g. occupational) self-identity and addressing customer anxieties at least, they have an interest in 'talking up' their organization and presenting some belief in the product. As noted earlier, it is unlikely that any major modifications to the product for the local circumstances will be made. However, some custom-ization may occur to enhance the selling process, suggesting that the overseas market is important, valued, and not taken for granted. Local staff may be hired, in addition to the manufacturer's own experts who also may have some local knowledge. Similarly, in the encounter with customers, superficial gestures or local references might be made. The car seller may explain how—'this car is . . . used by government Ministers . . . fitted with heat resistant tyres to cope with the climate'. In a similar way, a lecturer might link McGregor's Theories X and Y to Confucius as well as Rousseau, Fen Zei as well as Hobbes.

POWER AND CONSUMPTION — THE LIMITS OF THE CONSUMPTION PARADIGM?

In the preceding sections, we have explored our perceptions from teaching in Malaysia by viewing the MBA as a commodity, similar to foreign car. We examined the product (curriculum), the consumers (students) and the produ-cers/sellers (teaching staff). Little has been said about the links between these elements or about associated power relationships. Some might see this as the point at which the consumption paradigm starts to break down or, at least, become fragile. But consumers and consumption do not represent a single paradigm. They may be understood in different ways, many of which have widely diverging and problematic assumptions (see Gabriel and Lang 1995). For example, the neo-liberal notion of a 'free and sovereign consumer', choosing among alternatives, is flawed in a number of respects *whatever the product or service*—it assumes an undersocialized actor and open competition (Knights *et al.* 1994; Keat 1994; Dixon 1992). How well do such assumptions hold in the case of educational services (e.g. Legge 1995)? Two issues in particular set the educational consumer apart from the mythical 'sovereign consumer' of material commodities—*selection and assessment*. An individual may wish to 'purchase' a Harvard MBA, but may find it difficult to be admitted on one, however wealthy. Furthermore, having been admitted, he/she may find that they never attain the object of adding those prestigious letters after their name.

There are other forms of consumption where the purchaser is subject to some form of assessment by producers and/or their regulators to qualify for access— insurance, credit cards, guns, and membership of certain clubs. In these areas, as with *some* MBAs, the assessment may be somewhat tokenistic, a ritual which furthers the symbolic value of the product. For the students, however, assessment is not a minor but a major part of the MBA package. It is a source of much anxiety and worry. In class, the students appear to be attentive, interested, and thirsting for answers. When asked how they approach their studies, many describe the MBA as a course to be 'survived', more than as a voyage of pleasure, discovery, or learning. (These latter qualities emerge more in the *post hoc* accounts of alumni members.) In practice, only a few students fail to survive, yet there is no doubt that the individual's experience on an MBA programme is as much that of being judged and assessed as it is that of assessing and judging.

When we started working on this chapter we wondered whether our roles as management lecturers in Malaysia could be viewed as akin to those traditional agents of cross-cultural knowledge diffusion, missionaries, and mercenaries. It soon became clear that MBA teachers neither display the ideological fervour of the former nor experience the personal risks and hardships of the latter. A more appropriate metaphor for our role was suggested by the more mundane figure of car exporters and salesmen, who sell a 'prestige' product to an emerging market. The analogy of the car as commodity throws into sharp relief some features of the MBA. Like cars, MBAs are undoubtedly status symbols, which may be used to raise their owner's prestige or earning power. They are also signifiers of differ- ence, bestowing meaning to infinitesimal variations, and becoming embedded in individuals' identities. Price is a very important dimension of signification— high price bestows value. Packaging is another very important dimension—the opulence of the buildings, the prestige of the instructors, the lavish resourcing in educational 'technology'.

Moreover, the car captures the 'imported goods' quality of the MBA 'market'; foreign goods, at least from certain nations, are seen as superior, authentic- ated by prestigious institutions, regarded as superior in credibility, integrity, and expertise than local ones. Yet, they also generate some anxiety—lest they prove less good than they are meant to be. Purchasers of imported goods face the consumer's perennial dilemma between being a trend-setter and finding him- self/herself conned by smart foreigners and losing part of one's social (local) identity.

Yet, despite its pervasiveness, the consumer paradigm, at least in its neo-liberal form, cannot capture adequately the full complexity of power relations involved in the provision of MBAs. These unfold at three interdependent levels, the inter-national, the institutional and the personal/interpersonal. At the international level, the provision of MBAs can be likened to a wholesale rather than retail form of commodity exchange. The importing country, like the wholesale purchaser, has some degree of power over the supplier provided that there are alternative suppliers. In this way, the supplier is forced to control price, achieve a minimum of quality and, yet, at the same time, ensure that a majority of the students go through the programme successfully. At this level, assessment functions as the crest of the contradiction—it is meant to ensure quality control and yet must not lead to poor value for money, in the form of rejects, students failing. At the inter-national level, the export of MBAs undoubtedly serves to reinforce the West's ideological dominance, even if this may, on the fringes at least, include the new 'one best way' of celebrating the 'local'. Whatever the moral and economic fail-ings of the West, its management education as well as its cars continue to be objects of value.

At the institutional level, power relations are more ambiguous. The Western university setting up an operation in Malaysia must satisfy all the bureau-cratic, 'developmental', and political requirements which the authorities require. A profit-making opportunity appears to be littered by bureaucratic hurdles and what may seem as local sensitivities. One way for Western universities to deal with these obstacles is to find a Malaysian partner. In such cases, they also par-tially divest themselves of some powers (e.g. selecting the students, setting the fees, deciding on the curriculum). They do, however, engage in an elaborate institutional power game with their partner/sponsor, where it is never clear nor fixed who has the 'upper hand'.

Power relations at the inter-personal level are even more complex. It is here that the commodity paradigm is both the sharpest, but also the most problem-atic. Students do indeed purchase a service, a commodity. Like a haircut, but unlike a car, an MBA is a non-transferrable commodity. Yet, at the same time, in purchasing the initials, the students enter a bargain—money alone cannot buy the initials, 'learning' has to be involved. This may generate ambivalence. At one level, learning is a free bonus, riding on top of the MBA initials. But learning has a sting in its tail—assessment. Assessment suddenly spoils the MBA con-sumer idyll. The self-same consumer who features as the 'sovereign king' (sic) in much of the marketing theory the students learn, with all his/her pampered demands for service, quality, and choice, finds himself/herself reduced to the standing of an infant, performing, being observed, judged, and criticized. One may regard this as part of the payment that the student makes, in order to get his/her MBA. He/she must pay not just with money, but also with his/her will-ingness to undergo this arcane rite of passage into MBAhood. This then is the point where a financial transaction becomes a more explicitly political one and where the control—resistance dialectics at all three levels can be seen acted out. Where most Malaysian MBA students differ considerably from their Western counter-parts is in the added ambivalence which they experience. Not only does the desired product come with a sting in the tail, but it comes from quarters inextricably linked with colonial exploitation and oppression, of doubtful moral and spiritual integrity. Finally, the knowledge itself is seen as, at least in part, threatening to local know-how, identity, and pride.

CONCLUDING COMMENTS — FROM CAR SALESMAN TO ENTERTAINER

Does it matter if MBA students are increasingly consumerist in their orientation? Over the past twenty years, rampant consumerism has fuelled a major international expansion for business education. It would not be an exaggeration to say that the MBA provided a financial lifeline to universities suffering under public sector cutbacks, creating employment for a whole class of academics from different disciplines, some old, some new. Undoubtedly, less propitious academic disciplines have been cross-subsidized by the success of management education. Moreover, the market mechanism has introduced many welcome quality controls in areas of higher education that needed them. Today's paying student–consumer is treated with much greater respect than the average student of yesteryear. Finally, management education may have consolidated the rise of a more enlightened class of managers, who use a common language and share concerns and ideas.

The downside of this development is not difficult to discern. A wide-spread standardization of the educational package, an emphasis on presentation at the expense of content, a constant preoccupation with league tables, an unwillingness to experiment with new course designs are all costs of escalating consumerism in the field of business education. In some cases, quality has suffered as universities have been prepared to enrol customers who are unable or unwilling to act as students. Furthermore, a wide range of divisions has been introduced in higher educational establishments, with MBA students enjoying physical facilities that are denied other students, even within business schools. Among teaching staff, it is frequently those teaching MBAs who enjoy status and material benefits, for their ability to satisfy these most demanding of customers. But the worst of all may be this: a vocabulary of crass salesmanship has now taken root in educational establishments, with institutions vying to outshine each other in brash brochures, aggressive presentations in MBA fairs, and creative manipulation of statistics and league tables. Snobbery, envy, flattery, and contempt are rife in a system where infinitesimal distinctions of merit and prestige translate into massive differences in fees and salaries. These are eroding the fundamental values of liberal education, the values of free and impartial inquiry, of pastoral care for students, of collegiate relations among academics and researchers, and of education as a force towards enlightenment, emancipation, and social progress.

166 YIANNIS GABRIEL AND ANDREW STURDY

Throughout the 1990s, in academic conferences, meetings, and publications there was constant talk about 'the MBA bubble bursting'. The likeliest forces to bring this about were the increasing saturation of the market and consequent devaluation of the entire MBA concept as well as the establishment of corporate universities, aimed at teaching a curriculum tailor-made to the needs of the company, not dissimilar to McDonald's 'Hamburger University'. The bubble has still to burst, although among many academics, there is a sense of hubris which will sooner or later invite its nemesis. Currently one of the most far-reaching developments lies in the increasing involvement of academic publishers in providing MBA materials over the Internet. These include not only course hand-outs and curricula, but case studies, textbook extracts, and other reading material, mock examinations, lecture notes, and so forth. Several publishers are approaching university and departmental Heads with contractual offers as well as dealing with individual lecturers offering this 'service' free, where the only commitment is to 'adopt' a particular textbook. The potential for further standardization brought about by such developments is matched by the erosion of the authority of the lecturer as expert. Instead, the role of the lecturer might move in the direction of merely enacting material put together by higher authorities, ending up as an actor or, more fittingly, an entertainer.

REFERENCES

Anthony, P. D. (1977) *The Ideology of Work*. London: Tavistock.
Argyris, C. and Schön, D. A. (1974) *Theory in Practice*. San Francisco: Jossey Bass.
Aun, W. M. (1982) *The Industrial Relations Law of Malaysia*. Kuala Lumpur: Heinemann.
Ayadurai, D. (1992) *Industrial Relations in Malaysia*. Kuala Lumpur: Butterworths.
Bank Negara (1994) *Money and Banking in Malaysia*. Kuala Lumpur: Bank Negara.
—— (1996) *Annual Report, 1995*. Kuala Lumpur: Bank Negara.
Bauman, Z. (1998) *Globalization—The Human Consequences*. Cambridge: Polity.
Bierstecker, T. J. (1995) 'The "triumph" of liberal economic ideas in the developing world', in B. Stallings (ed.) *Global Change, Regional Response: The New International Context of Development*. Cambridge: Cambridge University Press.
Chanlat, J.-F. (1996) 'From cultural imperialism to independence', in S. R. Clegg and G. Palmer (eds), *The Politics of Management Knowledge*. London: Sage.
Child, J. and Rodrigues, S. (1996) 'The role of social identity in the international transfer of knowledge through joint ventures' in S. R. Clegg and G. Palmer (eds), *The Politics of Management Knowledge*. London: Sage.
Clark, T. and Fincham, R. (eds) (2001) *Critical Consulting—Perspectives on the Management Advice Industry*. Oxford: Blackwell.
Clegg, S. R. and Palmer, G. (1996) 'Introduction' in S. R. Clegg and G. Palmer (eds). *The Politics of Management Knowledge*. London: Sage.
—— *et al.* (1996) 'Management knowledge for the future: innovation, embryos and new paradigms' in S. R. Clegg and G. Palmer (eds) *The Politics of Management Knowledge*. London: Sage.

Cox, C. J. and Cooper, C. L. (1985) 'The irrelevance of American organizational sciences to the UK and Europe', *Journal of General Management*, 11(2): 27–34.

Dixon, D. F. (1992) 'Consumer sovereignty, democracy and the marketing concept', *Canadian Journal of Administrative Science*, 9(2): 116–25.

Djelic, M.-L. (1998) *Exporting the American Model—The Post-war Transformation of European Business*. Oxford: Oxford University Press.

Dore, R. (1996) 'Conclusion', in S. Berger and R. Dore (eds) *National Diversity and Global Capitalism*. London: Cornell University Press.

Easterby-Smith, M. (1997) 'Disciplines of organizational learning: contributions and critiques', *Human Relations*, 50(9): 1085–113.

Gabriel, Y. and Lang, T. (1995) *The Unmanageable Consumer—Contemporary Consumption and its Fragmentations*. London: Sage.

Guillen, M. F. (1994) *Models of Management*. Chicago: University of Chicago Press.

Guyton, L. (1995) 'Japanese FDI and the transfer of Japanese consumer electronics production to Malaysia', *Journal of Far Eastern Business*, 1(4): 63–97.

Hazman Shah, B. A. (2000) 'ISO 9000 and quality assurance in educational institutions in Malaysia', *Malaysian Management Review*, 35(1): 31–50.

Hirst, P. and Thompson, G. (1992) 'The problem of globalisation', *Economy and Society*, 21(4): 357–96.

Hofstede, G. and Bond, M. H. (1988) 'The Confucius connection: From cultural roots to economic growth', *Organizational Dynamics*, 16(4): 4–21.

Huczynski, A. A. (1993) *Management Gurus*. London: Routledge.

Jacques, R. (1996) *Manufacturing the Employee—Management Knowledge from the 19th to 21st Centuries*. London: Sage.

Jayasankaran, S. (1997) 'Two-edged sword—anti-American mood angers US but helps Mahatir', *Far Eastern Economic Review*, November 27.

Johnson, H. (1991) 'Cross-cultural differences: implications for management education and training', *Journal of European Industrial Training*, 15(6): 13–16.

Keat, R. (1994) 'Scepticism, authority and the market' in R. Keat, N. Abercrombie, and N. Whiteley (eds) *The Authority of the Consumer*. London: Routledge.

Knights, D., Sturdy, A. J., and Morgan, G. (1994) 'The consumer rules? The rhetoric and reality of marketing', *European Journal of Marketing*, 28(3): 42–54.

Kogut, B. and Parkinson, D. (1993) 'The diffusion of American organizing principles to Europe' in B. Kogut (ed) *Country Competitiveness: Technology and the Organizing of Work*. Oxford: Oxford University Press.

Kostera, M. (1995) 'The modern crusade: the missionaries of management come to Eastern Europe', *Management Learning*, 26(3): 331–52.

Lam, A. (1997) 'Embedded firms, embedded knowledge: problems of collaboration and knowledge transfer in global cooperative ventures', *Organization Studies*, 18(6): 973–96.

Legge, K. (1995) *HRM—Rhetorics and Realities*. London: Macmillan.

Lillrank, P. (1995) 'The transfer of management innovations from Japan', *Organization Studies*, 16(6): 971–89.

Littler, C. R. (1982) *The Development of the Labour Process in Capitalist Societies*. London: Heinemann.

Locke, R. L. (1989) *Management Education and Higher Education Since 1940—The Influence of America on West Germany, Great Britain and France*. Cambridge: Cambridge University Press.

Locke, R. L. (1996) *The Collapse of the American Management Mystique*. Oxford: Oxford University Press.

Lyotard, J.-F. (1984) *The Postmodern Condition: A Report on Knowledge*. Manchester: University Press, quoted in Huczynski, *Management Gurus*. London: Routledge.

Mendoza, G. (1991) *Management—The Asian Way*. Philippines: Asian Institute of Management.

Ramsay, H. E. (1996) 'Managing sceptically' in S. R. Clegg and G. Palmer (eds) *The Politics of Management Knowledge*. London: Sage.

Richards, D. (1997) 'Developing cross-cultural management skills: experiential learning in an international MBA Programme', *Management Learning*, 28(4): 387–407.

Ritzer, G. (1999) *Enchanting a Disenchanted World: Revolutionizing the Means of Consumption*. London: Sage.

Robertson, R. (1992) *Globalization: Social Theory & Global Culture*. London: Sage.

Simon, L. and Davies, G. (1996) 'A contextual approach to management learning—The Hungarian case', *Organization Studies*, 17(3): 269–89.

Sinclair, A. (1997) 'The MBA through women's eyes', *Management Learning*, 28(3): 313–30.

Smith, C. and Meiksins, P. (1995) 'System, society and dominance effects in cross-national organisational analysis', *Work, Employment and Society*, 9(2): 241–67.

Sorge, A. (1991) 'Strategic fit and the societal effect: interpreting cross-national comparisons of technology, organization and human resources', *Organization Studies*, 12(2): 161–90.

Stallings, B. (1995) *Global Change, Regional Response: The New International Context of Development*. Cambridge: Cambridge University Press.

Sturdy, A. J. (1997a) 'The consultancy process', *Journal of Management Studies*, 34(3): 389–413.

—— (1997b) 'Global diffusion, generic barriers: customer service culture initiatives in Malaysian retail banking', EGOS Conference paper, Budapest.

—— (2001) 'The global diffusion of customer service: reasserting generic barriers and contradiction', *Asia Pacific Business Review*, 7(3):

Talib, R. (1995) 'Credit and consumer culture in Malaysia', in R. Talib and T. Chee-Beng (eds) *Dimensions of Tradition and Development in Malaysia*. Petaling Jaya: Pelanduk.

Thomas, A. B. (1993) 'Sacred cows and other animals', *Times Higher Education Supplement*, 26 November.

Tysome, T. (1999) 'Hard sell in an Asian market', *Times Higher Education Supplement*, 26 February.

Warner, M. (1991) 'How Chinese managers learn', *Journal of General Management*, 16(4): 66–84.

Watson, T. J. (1994) 'Flavours of the month and the search for managerial control', Labour Process Conference paper, Aston University, 23–25 March.

9

Saving the Soul of the University: What Is To Be Done?

Lee Benson and Ira Harkavy

To begin this action-oriented, real-world, strategic, problem-solving chapter, we sketch a futurist good news/bad news scenario.[1] In our scenario's optimistic version, the twenty-first century becomes the global Democratic Century—the century in which the *irrepressible* information and communication (ICT) revolution powerfully contributes to the worldwide democratization, civic engagement, and action-oriented social responsibility of universities. In turn, socially responsible and engaged, participatory action-oriented, democratic universities powerfully contribute to the worldwide democratization of cosmopolitan

[1] This chapter draws freely on a considerable number of works we have published elsewhere, beginning in 1991. Given our space restrictions, since our previously published works provide fuller documentation for many of the arguments made in this chapter, we think it necessary to provide only a 'barebones' form of documentation here. Our earlier published works include: Lee Benson and Ira Harkavy (1991) 'Progressing beyond the welfare state', *Universities and Community Schools*, **2**: 2–28; Ira Harkavy and John L. Puckett (1991) 'Toward effective University Public School partnerships', *Teachers College Record*, **92**: 556–81; Lee Benson and Ira Harkavy (1994) '1994 as turning point: the University-assisted Community School idea becomes a movement', *Universities and Community Schools*, **4**: 5–8; Lee Benson and Ira Harkavy (1994) 'Anthropology 210, Academically Based Community Service, and the Advancement of Knowledge', *Universities and Community Schools*, **4**: 66–9; Ira Harkavy and John L. Puckett (1994) 'Lessons from hull house for the contemporary urban university', *Social Service Review*, **68**: 299–321; Lee Benson, Ira Harkavy, and John Puckett (1996) 'Communal participatory action research as a strategy for improving universities and the social sciences: Penn's work with the West Philadelphia improvement corps as a case study', *Educational Policy*, **10**: 202–22; Lee Benson and Ira Harkavy (1997) 'Universities, colleges, and their neighboring communities', *Universities and Community Schools*, **5**: 5–11; Lee Benson and Ira Harkavy (1997) 'School and community in the global society', *Universities and Community Schools*, **5**: 16–71; Ira Harkavy and Lee Benson (1998) 'Deplatonizing and democratizing education as the bases of service learning', in R. A. Rhoads and J. Howard (eds) *Service Learning: Pedagogy and Research*. Josey-Bass, pp. 11–19; Lee Benson, Ira Harkavy, and John L. Puckett (1999) '1998 as turning point', *Universities and Community Schools*, **6**: 3–6; Ira Harkavy (1999) 'School–community–university partnerships: effectively integrating community building and education reform', *Universities and Community Schools*, **6**: 7–24; Lee Benson

communities and societies committed to the worldwide abolition of poverty and racism. Greatly compressed, woefully oversimplified, that's our futurist, optimistic, good news scenario.

In our pessimistic, ultra-Left Marxist, *bad news scenario*, a radically different outcome materializes. The twenty-first century becomes the global Commodification-of-Everything Century in which the irrepressible ICT revolution powerfully broadens, deepens, and accelerates the commodification of universities. In turn, thoroughly commodified universities, tightly controlled and operated by Social Darwinist technocratic entrepreneurs in academic clothing, powerfully accelerate the commodification of societies and the worldwide intensification of poverty, inequality, and racism.

The ultra-left Commodification-of-Everything scenario sketched above simply updates, of course, the nightmare vision of capitalist dehumanization passionately denounced by Karl Marx and Friedrich Engels in the 1848 *Communist Manifesto*. Updated for our pessimistic twenty-first century scenario, it envisions a world in which *Social Darwinist capitalism* has completely triumphed. In that commodified world, universities, like all other institutions, function as amoral, 'nakedly' for-profit corporations that produce and sell commodities (broadly conceived to include all types of services and cultures). Universities do that because, to quote rather than paraphrase, the 1848 *Manifesto*,

no other nexus [remains] between man and man than naked self-interest, than callous 'cash payment' . . . [The triumphant bourgeoisie has] drowned the most heavenly ecstasies of religious fervor, of chivalrous enthusiasm, of philistine sentimentalism, in the icy water of egotistical calculation . . . [and] stripped of its halo every occupation hitherto honored and looked up to with reverent awe . . . [and] converted the physician, the lawyer, the priest, the poet, the man of science, into its paid wage-laborers.[2]

Or, as Eric Fromm subsequently summarized the *Manifesto*'s dehumanization thesis, in *Escape from Freedom*: in a fully capitalist world, 'Man does not only sell commodities, he sells himself and feels himself to be a commodity.'[3]

In all likelihood, of course, what actually happens to universities and societies in the twenty-first century will locate them somewhere on a continuum between the opposite poles of complete *Democratization* and complete *Commodification*. As we conceive Democratization and Commodification, they represent

and Ira Harkavy (1999) 'University-assisted community schools as democratic public works', *The Good Society*, **9**: 14–20; Lee Benson, Ira Harkavy, and John L. Puckett (2000) 'An implementation revolution as a strategy to fulfill the democratic promise of university–community partnerships: Penn-West Philadelphia as an experiment in progress', *Nonprofit and Voluntary Sector Quarterly*, **29**: 24–45; Lee Benson and Ira Harkavy (2000) 'Higher education's third revolution: the emergence of the Democratic Cosmopolitan Civic University', *Cityscape: A Journal of Policy Development and Research*, **5**: 47–57; Lee Benson and Ira Harkavy (2000) 'Integrating the American system of higher, secondary, and primary education to develop civic responsibility', in Thomas Ehrlich (ed.) *Civic Responsibility in Higher Education*. Phoenix, Arizona: Oryx Press, pp. 174–96.

[2] Dirk J. Struik (ed.) (1971) *Birth of the Communist Manifesto*, New York: International Publishers, pp. 91–2.

[3] Eric Fromm (1941) *Escape from Freedom*. New York: Rinehart Press, p. 4.

ideal-type 'fields of force' pulling universities and societies in opposite directions. Which field will actually prove most forceful in the twenty-first century? That depends. Depends on what? Given the central societal role universities have played since 1945, it depends to a great extent on what universities (i.e., all 'post-secondary' institutions) actually do—and fail to do—with the ICTs now developing exponentially. But what will determine how universities actually use ICTs in the twenty-first century?

As is well known—more precisely, should be well known—human technologies are not facts of nature, human technologies are social constructions. Since they are social constructions, they cannot be 'socially neutral'.[4] It follows, therefore, that good answers to critical questions about how universities will use ICTs in the twenty-first century will depend on answers to a much more basic set of questions.

WHAT ARE UNIVERSITIES, WHAT DO THEY DO, WHAT SHOULD THEY DO, WHAT WILL THEY ACTUALLY DO IN THE TWENTY-FIRST CENTURY?

What kinds of institutions have universities been? What kinds of institutions are they now? What kinds of institutions will they become in the twenty-first century? What will be their primary goals, or primary set of interrelated goals? Do universities now advance or retard democracy? How can universities best advance democracy? Who will benefit from them, who will not? Who will win the battle for the 'soul of the university'?

Like human technologies, universities do not exist in nature. The 'idea of the university' is a social construction. Human beings construct and operate universities, human beings determine what kinds of institution universities should and will be, what they should and will be good for, *who should and will benefit from them*. Moreover, universities are anything but autonomous institutions. They have never achieved the high level of autonomy they (frequently) claim to be necessary for their proper functioning. Wishful thinking and bold assertions to the contrary, universities do not constitute self-contained, self-regulating, 'closed systems', impervious to pressures originating in the complex 'environments' (broadly conceived, e.g. other universities) which 'surround' them and in which they must function. Particularly during the late twentieth century when they became increasingly important societal institutions, their internal operations and decisions have invariably been influenced (determined?) by an increasingly wide range of external 'forces'.

Given the post-1945 Electronic Revolution which transformed the world into a 'Global Village', given the recent invention and exponential expansion of the

---

[4] Kevin Robins and Frank Webster (1999) *Times of the Technoculture: from the Information Society to the Virtual Life*. New York: Routledge, p. 4.

Internet and World Wide Web, it seems virtually self-evident that all universities are now more-or-less significantly affected by an increasingly wide range of
developments occurring almost anywhere in the world. Alas, the following pessimistic conclusion seems equally self-evident: *On balance, those developments,*
particularly since the 1980s and 1990s, have powerfully accelerated the worldwide
tendency towards university commodification.

Should our pessimistic observation and assessment (developed in detail below)
be dismissed as merely a Leftist, agitprop, gross distortion of complex reality?
No. To briefly support its credibility here, it only seems necessary to cite two
remarkably revealing, remarkably significant, articles recently published in the
Chronicle of Higher Education. Datelined Washington, 20 February 2001, the
first article summarized the gloomy valedictory speech that Stanley Ikenberry
delivered in his role as the 'departing president' of the American Council on
Education (American umbrella organization of higher education).[5]

Market forces are in danger of pushing the leaders of colleges and universities out of
the driver's seat at their institutions, the departing president of the American Council on
Education said here Monday at the group's annual meeting. [and warned]... that *higher*
education risks becoming a mere commodity [emphasis added].... [Among other threatening developments] Mr. Ikenberry said he worries about corporate sponsorship of research
and the commercialization of intellectual property.... He urged leaders in higher education to push back harder against the forces of commercialization... and to do their best to
protect the 'integrity of the core academic enterprise'.

Datelined Melbourne, Australia, 28 February 2001, the second Chronicle article
demonstrates that members of the 'academic masses' (our somewhat facetious
term), as well as elite leaders of the academic Establishment, are highly alarmed
about the accelerating tendency towards university commodification. Under the
banner headline, 'Australian Students Protest Plan for Global University', the
article summarized the student protest as follows:

Students at Australian universities are attacking a plan to create a global on-line university
called Universitas 21, charging that the reputations of the universities involved would be
threatened.

The National Union of Students backed protesters who demonstrated outside Queens-
land University's council meeting last week. ... The union's national education officer,
Kate Davison, said Universitas 21 was another push by university officers and 'profit-driven
corporations' to further deregulate the international education system... Universitas 21 is
negotiating with *Thomson Learning to provide on-line course design, content development,*
and testing and assessment [emphasis added].... Alan Gilbert, Melbourne's vice chancellor, told a meeting of Melbourne's deans last week that setting up the on-line university
would initially cost $25 million in American currency. Member institutions will be asked to
pay $500,000 to $5 million each. ... *Revenue of $500 million is projected by the tenth year,*

---

[5]   David L. Wheeler (2001) 'Market forces in danger higher education, the party ACE President
says', *Chronicle of Higher Education*. 28 February.

with the profits being split between Thomson Learning and each of the member institutions [emphasis added].[6]

Given the dangers rhetorically warned against by President Ikenberry and actively protested against by Australian students, what can academics do to 'push back harder against the forces of commercialization'? Put another way, what *specifically* is to be done by democratic-minded academics to counter and reverse the worldwide tendency to accelerate and expand the commodification of higher education in the twenty-first century?

To answer that question, to begin the process of developing an action-oriented, real-world strategy capable of solving the anti-commodification, 'what is to be done problem' sketched above, we primarily focus on American universities, the only ones we know reasonably well. Despite that disclaimer, since the strategy we propose essentially derives from Francis Bacon's seventeenth century grand vision of universal progress, non-American academics may find that it has some relevance for them.

Francis Bacon and the 'Charitable' Pursuit of the 'True Ends of Knowledge'

It is not possible to run a course aright when the goal itself is not rightly placed.   Francis Bacon, *Novum Organum* (1620)

Lastly, I would address one general admonition to all, that they consider what are the true ends of knowledge, and that they seek it not either for pleasure of the mind, or for contention, or for superiority to others, or for profit, or fame, or power or for any of these inferior things, but for the benefit and use of life; and that they perfect and govern it in charity. For it was from lust of power that the angels fell, from lust of knowledge that men fell; that of charity there can be no excess, neither did angel or man ever come in danger by it.   Francis Bacon, *The Great Instauration* (1620)

As his biographers strongly emphasize, Bacon became convinced, at an early age, that the contemplative, idealist philosophies and theories of learning, knowledge, and science propagated by the ancient Greek 'wise men' were false. They not only were false, they had powerfully worked against—and continued to work against—human progress. Convinced of that truth, convinced that his lifelong mission was to win acceptance for it, Bacon dedicated himself to overthrowing the persistent, pernicious, dominance of Plato and Aristotle in Western thought and education.[7]

To discredit and displace Plato and Aristotle, doctrinaire 'ancients' whose ideas and methods Bacon sardonically characterized as 'fruitful of controversies but barren of works', he 'trumpeted' the necessity to develop a *morally inspired, morally controlled*, modern experimental science of inquiry. Diametrically opposed

---

[6] Geoffrey Maslen (2001) *Chronicle of Higher Education.* 28 February.

[7] For illuminating analyses of Bacon, see among other numerous recent works, Perez Zagorin (1998) *Francis Bacon.* Princeton, NJ: Princeton University Press, and Markuu Peltonen (ed.) (1996) *The Cambridge Companion to Bacon.* New York: Cambridge University Press. See also our discussion of Bacon in Lee Benson and Ira Harkavy (1991) 'Progressing beyond the welfare state,' *Universities and Community Schools*, **2**: 4–5.

to the ancient Greek tradition of individual philosophers fruitlessly, egotistically, engaging in idealist, contemplative, 'barren' controversies and disputations, Bacon proposed development of an all-encompassing, continually evolving, modern experimental science of inquiry based on the integrated, large-scale organization of collaborative work. Designed to achieve the 'total reconstruction of sciences, arts, and all human knowledge,' it would actively, purposefully, *plan and implement the integrated production and use of knowledge* for the glory of God and the 'relief of man's estate'.

Inspired and captivated by Bacon's grand vision, and convinced, like John Dewey, the great modern proponent of action-oriented, real-world, problem-solving inquiry and participatory democracy, that Bacon was the true 'prophet' of the idea of progress and the 'real founder of modern thought', we modestly propose a gradualist, anti-commodification strategy that essentially calls, in the long run, for the radical reinvention of American universities. Somewhat more specifically, we call upon American universities to reinvent themselves, to become democratic, virtuous, *organizationally integrated*, moral/intellectual institutions, dedicated to practical realization of two Baconian-inspired true ends:

- education for virtue
- advancement of learning and knowledge for the moral and material betterment of *all* human beings, everywhere in the world.

Put still another way, to counter the present pernicious tendency to use the ICT revolution as a powerful means to accelerate the worldwide commodification of universities, we call upon American universities to reverse that process. By reversing that process, we mean using the ICT revolution to help them function *collaboratively and democratically, not competitively and autocratically*, as Neo-Baconian, Neo-Deweyan, moral/intellectual institutions dedicated to the 'betterment of humanity', to the 'relief of man's estate'.

Given their present ferociously competitive orientation (obsession?) and their ruthless, contradictory, simultaneous pursuit of 'pure research' and crass commodification, given their present tendency towards centralized 'managerial' decision making and control, how in the world can we expect American universities to answer our 'call' positively? Does our proposed 'revolutionary' strategy simply demonstrate that we are Leftist 'nuts' afflicted by, suffering from, delusionary utopianism, or what, following Shakespeare, might be stigmatized as 'Glendowerism'? (In *Henry IV*, Shakespeare had Hotspur deliver the classic putdown to the self-aggrandizing Glendower, who boastfully proclaimed that he could 'call spirits from the vasty deep'. Hotspur's putdown: Why, so can I, or so can any man; But will they come when you do call for them?).

When we 'call upon' American universities to reinvent themselves, do we naively convict ourselves of 'Glendowerism'? Not really. As emphasized above, we view universities as *social constructions*, not *social organisms*. So of course we do not really call upon *universities* to reinvent themselves. We have simply used that shorthand formulation for brevity's sake. More accurately stated, our strategy *calls upon all democratic-minded American academics*—faculty, administrators, staff, students, irrespective of rank—to unite and work for the reinvention of universities as the best way to 'exorcise' what might (somewhat facetiously) be termed the 'Specter' of Commodification now 'haunting' them—the Specter growing ever more menacing as a result of the ICT revolution.

On balance, to-date, American universities have strongly tended to use ICTs as though their only (or best) use is as powerful instruments of commodification. Appropriately, intelligently, progressively used, however, ICTs can function as powerful instruments of democratization. But ICTs will only be used that way, we contend, if democratic American academics recognize that commodification now constitutes so great a 'real and present danger' that to overcome it they must unite in a movement powerful enough to ultimately bring about the radical reinvention of American universities.

That's a big, very big, 'if' of course. Does our even posing it as a possibility demonstrate that we must be suffering from delusionary utopianism? Sceptical critics might charge that the highly heterogeneous group of 'democratic-minded academics' our strategy relies upon to function as agents of radical change have long been, and are now, bitterly divided by (almost) countless internal quarrels. Except for the wishful thinking long characteristic of American 'progressives' and 'leftists', what reason exists to imagine that bitterly divided 'democratic-minded academics' can be united in an anti-commodification movement powerful enough to radically reinvent American universities? A good question. To answer it, we invoke a well-known, well-supported, powerful proposition: Unambiguous, visible, seriously threatening *out-group hostility tends strongly to produce in-group cohesion.*

As we will show below in some detail, what Stanley Ikenberry stigmatized as the 'market forces . . . pushing' university commodification (e.g. 'outsourcing' of functions, abolition of tenure, low-paid 'adjuncts', faculty 'accountability', universities as 'brand names', students as 'consumers') were gaining strength before the ICT revolution got well underway in the 1980s and 1990s. But, as noted above, as the ICT revolution has primarily been used to-date, it has powerfully strengthened those 'market forces'. Strengthened them so greatly, made them so visible, in fact, that President Ikenberry felt compelled to warn against them in his valedictory speech to the American Council on Education. Given the quintessential Establishment character and highly influential role of the ACE, it seems reasonable to believe that President Ikenberry's Paul Revere-like warning ('the Commodifiers are coming', 'the Commodifiers are coming') represented a critical turning point in the emerging movement to mobilize American academics against the powerful forces of commodification now visibly, increasingly, threatening 'the integrity of the core academic enterprise'.

As we will show below, that commodification threat has now become so great, so visible, that a reasonable possibility exists that democratic American academics will recognize that it is imperative for them to resolve, or at least suspend, the internal conflicts that now greatly weaken their ability to resist it effectively. Once they recognize that, our strategy assumes, they then may see the need to participate wholeheartedly in a movement designed to restore and develop further the humanistic ideals, civic purposes, and democratic goals, or, in William Sullivan's elegant summary phrase, the 'animating sense of [public] mission' which inspired and energized American universities during their pre-First World War formative period of great intellectual growth and development.[8]

To develop and support our 'anti-commodification' resistance strategy in some detail, as well as support our proposition that American universities now constitute the primary site of battle for the Good American Society, we begin by sketching a highly compressed, highly oversimplified, history of some relevant aspects of American higher education since its Harvard College origins in 1636.

ACCELERATING COMPETITION AND COMMODIFICATION IN THE AMERICAN HIGHER EDUCATION SYSTEM, 1636–2001

'Do I contradict myself? Very well then, I contradict myself. I am large. I contain multitudes.' Thus sang Walt Whitman in *Song of Myself*. Flamboyantly, arrogantly, characterizing himself as the personal embodiment of the democratic country whose contradictions he celebrated and gloried in, Whitman has long been hailed as the quintessential American poet.[9] Breathtaking in its self-centred arrogance, Whitman's celebration of his country as Whitman writ large, nevertheless caught an (the?) essential truth about America. It is large. It contains multitudes. Like Whitman, therefore, America contradicts itself.

Suppose we grant that America is—and always has been—contradictions. It then becomes much easier to understand the remarkable contradictions increasingly built into the American higher education system, past and present, as American society has become increasingly contradictory and commodified. Before the American Revolution (more-or-less accidentally) broke out in 1776, nine colleges had been founded in the British colonies scattered along the Atlantic seaboard. According to the well-regarded authors of a *History of American Colleges and Universities*,[10] 'probably the single most important factor explaining the founding of the colonial colleges' was the determination of the competing, intermingled, religious denominations to secure a 'literate, college-trained

---

[8] William M. Sullivan, 'Keynote Address', at the conference of Philadelphia Higher Education Network for Neighborhood Development, Swarthmore College, 23 October 1997. See also Professor Sullivan's illuminating book, *Work and Integrity*. New York: Harper Business Press, 1995, *passim.*

[9] See the highly perceptive discussion of Whitman in Peter Conn (1989) *Literature in America*. Cambridge: Cambridge University Press, pp. 210–16.

[10] The full citation of the book on which we're relying for our discussion of the colonial colleges is John S. Brubacher and Willis Rudy (1976) *Higher Education in Transition: A History of American Colleges and Universities, 1636–1976*, 3rd edn. New York: Harper & Row. Our quotations are from pp. 3–9.

clergy'. They used the founding of Harvard College to support what we regard as their considerably exaggerated, over-general proposition that the 'Christian tradition was the foundation stone of the *whole intellectual structure* [emphasis added] which was brought to the New World'. In addition to a college-trained clergy, that tradition called for educating religiously orthodox 'professional men in fields other than the ministry and public officials'.

Having emphasized the Old World origins of American colleges, the authors then pointed to the critical discontinuities that came about when the 'medieval university tradition' was transferred to the radically unmedieval American environment. Because the American colleges were 'desperate' to attract tuition-paying students and local patrons, in sharp contrast to Oxford and Cambridge, they never 'prescribed specific doctrinal tests in religion for admission or for the granting of degrees'. Moreover:

In order to attract more students in the face of stiffened competition from other colleges, and to enlarge the basis of their financial support [emphasis added], these colleges had to stress in their public pronouncements interdenominational policies and practices. Here again, this was very different from the situation confronting the English universities.

As the quotations suggest, to a far greater extent than anywhere else in the world, intense and undisguised competition for students, distinguished professors, financial support, and institutional prestige was built into the American higher education system from the start. However, unlike the authors we have been quoting, we believe that religious diversity and denominational competition only partially explain the competitive nature of the American higher education system and the complex set of contradictions increasingly produced by institutional competition. Speaking very broadly (and loosely), even before the 1776 Revolution, American 'society' (i.e. the thirteen British colonies) constituted, in relative terms, by far the most capitalist economy, society, and culture in the world. In that uniquely capitalist 'New World' environment, leading members of newly settled, newly forming, local communities competed fiercely with leading members of other communities in a wide variety of ways, for a wide variety of group and individual reasons.[11]

For our purposes, we need only note that the founding of colleges was a significant form of community competition. Colleges, it was anticipated, would bring more than religious and educational benefits to a local community, they would bring economic (and a wide variety of other) benefits. The Brown brothers of Providence, Rhode Island, provide a particularly clear—and crass—statement of anticipated economic benefits. Appealing for support to 'the businessmen of Providence and . . . surrounding towns', they promised that:

Building the college here will be the means of bringing great quantities of money into the place, and thereby greatly increasing the markets for all kinds of the country's

---

[11] For the uniquely capitalist character of the American economy, society, and culture, see the magisterial analysis in Thomas C. Cochran (1972) *Business in American Life: A History*. New York: McGraw-Hill, pp. 1–42 and *passim*.

produce, and consequently increasing the value of estates to which this town is a market.[12][13]

Summarily and oversimply stated, what we characterize as 'contradictory capitalist motives', not simply traditional medieval Christian motives, inspired and shaped the contradictory origins and increasingly contradictory development of the American higher educational system. To make that point, we now sketch a highly oversimplified account of the founding and early history of what eventually became our own university, the University of Pennsylvania.

BENJAMIN FRANKLIN AND THE ABORTIVE BACONIAN REFORMATION OF HIGHER EDUCATION IN AMERICA

During his lifetime (1561–1626), Francis Bacon's ideas had little impact. By the 1640s and 1650s, however, largely as a result of the Puritan Revolution, Bacon's 'new philosophy' had become highly influential in England and elsewhere in Europe. To quote from the introductory chapter in the recent *Cambridge Companion to Bacon*:

Bacon's conviction that the advancement of science was an effective means to assuage humankind's sufferings and improve its state found eager response in republican England.... The full translation of these ideas into action, in the founding of the Royal Society after the Restoration of 1660 represents . . . Bacon's deification as a philosopher and the final victory of the Baconian project of *collaboration, utility* and *progress* [emphasis added]. Another high point in Bacon's ... [reputation] occurred in the eighteenth century, when the French *philosophes* revered him as the most important propagandist of science . . . Bacon's methodological precepts [also] received an enthusiastic response from the English epistemologists of the early nineteenth century.... [Though Bacon's reputation declined somewhat thereafter] it is widely acknowledged that his boldly ambitious ideal of the leading role of an operative science in the transformation of the conditions of humankind's life became, soon after his death, a central part of the Western philosophical heritage. And it is not too much to say that there remains today much that Bacon would recognize as part of the program he inaugurated.[13]

Much may remain today of the programme Bacon inaugurated. But certainly not the vital moral parts necessary to realize his quintessentially 'charitable' vision of the 'true ends of knowledge' and the 'advancement of learning'. *Demoralized Bacon, Frankensteinian Bacon*, is essentially what remains today of his utopian programme for the moral, material, and scientific progress of humanity. Among many reasons for that lamentable condition, we believe that a major one is vividly illuminated by the failure of Benjamin Franklin's attempt to institute a Baconian reformation of higher education in eighteenth-century Philadelphia.

Like John Dewey, another native son of Puritan New England, Franklin viewed Francis Bacon as one of the great figures in world intellectual history.

---

[12] Thomas C. Cochran (1972) *Business in American Life: A History*. New York: McGraw-Hill, p. 35.
[13] Peltonen (ed.) *Cambridge Companion to Bacon*, pp. 23–4.

Transplanted to Philadelphia, Franklin was an ardent Baconian. Contemptuous of medieval scholasticism, passionately devoted to the 'modern experimental philosophy', Franklin continually worked, in a variety of ways, to implement this basic Baconian proposition: Morally inspired, morally controlled, effective, collaborative organization is mandatory if learning and knowledge are to help achieve the 'relief of man's estate'.[14]

In 1743, having already founded a municipal circulating library (among other innovations), Franklin proposed to establish two Baconian-inspired organizational innovations. One eventually became the present-day 'American Philosophical Society, held at Philadelphia, for Promoting Useful Knowledge', the other, the University of Pennsylvania. Franklin's 'Proposal for Promoting Useful Knowledge Among the British Plantations in America' was essentially modelled after the British Royal Society. But his other organizational proposal was much more original—in fact, genuinely revolutionary. No copy of the 1743 version of that proposal is known to exist. But, according to Edward P. Cheney, the great historian of the University of Pennsylvania, the 1749 published version, *Proposal Relating to the Education of Youth in Pensilvania*, represented a severely watered-down compromise forced on Franklin by timid associates fearful of any departure from the classical collegiate curriculum. Using a variety of documents, however, Cheyney was able to reconstruct Franklin's original unwatered-down ideas:

He would have had an education utilitarian rather than cultural, *entirely in the English language* [emphasis added], though following the best models in that language, devoting much attention to training in thought and expression. It should include mathematics, geography, history, logic, and natural and moral philosophy. *It should be an education for citizenship* [emphasis added], and should lead *to mercantile and civic success and usefulness* [emphasis added].

Writing in 1940, Cheyney, a long-time Penn student and professor, then observed sardonically: 'It is unfortunate that it was never tried.' Alas, except rhetorically and in some limited respects, Cheyney's sardonic observation remains valid in 2001.

If the college envisioned by Franklin had been instituted, it would have exemplified in real-world practice the Baconian ideal of experimentally, collaboratively, acquiring, transmitting, and pursuing learning and knowledge for the 'betterment of humanity', for 'the relief of man's estate'. Put another way, Franklin's proposed college would primarily have functioned as a modern, effectively integrated, moral–intellectual institution dedicated to public service and practical implementation of the seventeenth- and eighteenth-century Commonwealth philosophy. As Franklin conceived it, the moral and intellectual components of the modern Baconian College he envisioned were symbiotic, interrelated, inextricably intertwined, and interactive.

---

[14]   Our discussion of Franklin in this section essentially summarizes the analysis in Benson and Harkavy, 'Progressing beyond the welfare state', *Universities and Community Schools*, **2**: 6–8.

Viewed in historical perspective, Franklin's proposed New World reformation of higher education clearly aimed to give concrete organizational form to Bacon's fervent 'admonition' that utilitarian, scientific, experimental inquiry should fundamentally be morally inspired, controlled, driven. 'What are the true ends of knowledge' and learning and why should they be sought, both Bacon and Franklin asked? In Bacon's seventeenth-century cautionary formulation (so brilliantly illuminating and terrifying in the twenty-first century), learning and knowledge should be sought neither for 'pleasure of the mind, or for contention, or for profit, or fame, or power, *or for any of these inferior things* [emphasis added].' Stated more positively, in Franklin's eighteenth-century terms, the advancement of learning and knowledge should be sought to 'Do Good to Men'. But for that to happen, Franklin emphasized, John Locke's prescription for education must be obeyed: ''Tis *VIRTUE*, then, direct *VIRTUE*, which to be *aim'd at* in Education.'[15]

Unlike the appeals made for all the other colonial colleges, Franklin's proposal to establish a college in Philadelphia, it is critical to note, did not appeal for support on religious grounds. But it also did not appeal for support only on the Baconian and Lockean high-minded grounds sketched above. On the contrary.

Through less blatantly than the Brown brothers in Providence, Franklin clearly pointed out that an Academy would bring significant economic benefits to Philadelphia.[16] Succinctly stated, though Franklin envisioned a college dedicated to 'education for virtue' (our term), he thought it necessary to argue that it would also produce 'education for profit' (again our term). Whether consciously or not, Franklin opportunistically chose to ignore the contradictions and tensions inherent in any educational institution designed to pursue such radically different aims. (As we emphasized above, America is contradictions—and Franklin was American to the core.) In the event, however, as the college in Philadelphia was actually conducted, it strongly tended to produce neither education for virtue, nor for profit.

Soon after the college began operations in 1751, Franklin left Philadelphia on a variety of missions that essentially kept him in Europe for more than thirty years. During Franklin's long absences, the men who controlled and conducted the college were strongly committed, both in theory and in practice, to the traditional classical model. Nothing resembling Franklin's proposed Baconian reformation of higher education, therefore, was ever put into practice in Philadelphia (or anywhere else, to our knowledge).

As we will show later, our close study of Frankin's failed experiment has helped shape and improve (we hope) our plan to realize a Neo-Baconian reformation (i.e. reinvention) of American universities. Here we need only note that Franklin's failure forcefully demonstrated to us that for such a reformation to succeed, its

---

[15] For Franklin's invocation of John Locke, see Franklin's 1749 *Proposal*, conveniently reprinted in John Hardin Best (ed.) (1962) *Benjamin Franklin on Education*. New York: Teachers College Press, pp. 150–1.

[16] For the letters Franklin had published to promote his *Proposal* see *ibid*, pp. 124–6.

proponents will have to think and work hard and skilfully to overcome a basic contradiction deeply embedded in the American educational system: Though calls for educational innovation are as 'American as apple pie' and tend to win rhetorical approval ('make it new', Ezra Pound famously commanded American poets), they strongly tend to be powerfully resisted and/or distorted in practice. Franklin, in effect, invoked that proposition to explain the failure of his Baconian experiment.[17]

Shortly before he died in 1790, Franklin angrily denounced the Trustees of what by then had become in remarkably convoluted ways (which we still suffer from in 2002) the University of Pennsylvania. Their disastrous 'Deviations' from his original plan, Franklin charged, their deceptions and bad faith, had produced an institution criticized severely by 'the Publick' and suffering financially from the 'great loss of Revenue' brought about by their terrible 'mismanagement'. Instead of conducting the institution along the lines of the highly innovative English school he had called for, they had conducted it as a traditional college based on the outmoded 'Latin and Greek' languages wholly unsuited to 'such a country as ours'.

Why had the Trustees followed so disastrous a reactionary course? Franklin's answer to his own question invoked, in effect, the general historical theory of intellectual and institutional inertia which John Dewey later invoked to explain his own failure to bring about progressive innovations in the American schooling and political systems. To quote Franklin's summary statement of the 'historical inertia theory' (which he may well have gotten from Francis Bacon):

there is in mankind an unaccountable prejudice in favor of ancient Customs and Habitudes, which inclines to a Continuance of them after the Circumstances which formerly made them useful, cease to exist.

From academic study and long, painful personal experience, we are convinced that, in basic respects discussed below, that general theory holds particularly true for American universities.

JOHNS HOPKINS AND THE DEVELOPMENT OF THE UNIQUELY CONTRADICTORY AMERICAN RESEARCH UNIVERSITY

We have previously emphasized that local community building played a critical role in the founding of colonial colleges. After the Revolution, to again cite the *History of American Colleges and Universities*, a 'vast multiplication' of colleges occurred. Not only were colleges founded by religions denominations fiercely competing for status, members, and financial support; they were viewed as important economic assets in the fierce competition among rival local

---

[17] For Franklin's letter denouncing the Penn Trustees on the ground that they had deviated from and ruined his original plan for the Academy, see *ibid*, pp. 171–4.

communities, 'real estate speculators', and newly constructed railroads trying to attract migrants to the communities and regions they served.[18]

As part of that competition, the term 'university' had occasionally been used before 1876 (the centenary year of the American Revolution). But the first 'real' American university was Johns Hopkins. Unreflectively, uncritically, unwisely, Hopkins, trying to imitate the prestigious German university model—a model based on an overall schooling system and societal structure, culture, and history radically different than the American—hoped to achieve national status, prestige, and resources by devoting itself to faculty research and graduate instruction. Accordingly, the original plan for Hopkins excluded undergraduates. But strong local protests from leading Baltimoreans forced a compromise. Quite reluctantly, the would-be German-style university allowed undergraduates to be admitted. Marvellously foreshadowing the later history of American research universities, undergraduate education at Hopkins, from its start in 1876 was viewed as a highly regrettable, but highly necessary, means to achieve the real university ends, reputation-building faculty research and advanced graduate instruction.[19]

Viewed in historical perspective, Hopkins constituted a uniquely contradictory innovation in world higher education. When critically and systematically analysed rather than unreflectively celebrated, Hopkins splendidly exemplifies the mistransference fallacy in tragicomic action. By the mistransference fallacy we mean taking something that works well in one system and environment and mechanically transferring it to become part of a radically different system and environment. Democratic America, boisterously celebrating the centenary of its Revolution in 1876, was hardly the autocratic Prussia of 1810 in which Count Wilhelm von Humboldt had created the University of Berlin 'to help restore Prussian self-confidence' after Napoleon had destroyed 'the Prussian army at Jena and Auerstadt, with dramatic and momentous consequences for the Prussian state.[20]

Metaphorically speaking, what Hopkins did was to superimpose *something like* a Platonic German university on top of a classical English-type American liberal arts college. That uniquely contradictory research university model, alas, became the model for all subsequent American universities, with disastrous consequences that we continue to suffer from badly today.

Predictably, the highly dysfunctional combination of German research university and American liberal arts college resulted in the 'hybrid' American research universities, particularly after they expanded greatly in number, size, and specialized functions, becoming increasingly affected and distracted by severe

---

[18] Brubacher and Willis, pp. 59–64.

[19] *Ibid.*, pp. 178–82. See also the insightful analysis of Johns Hopkins in Laurence R. Veysey (1965) *The Emergence of the American University.* Chicago: University of Chicago Press, pp. 158–65 and *passim.*

[20] For an illuminating discussion of the founding and *Platonic elitist nature* of the University of Berlin, see Rosalind M. Pritchard (1990) *The End of Elitism?*, New York: St. Martin's Press, pp. 12–58.

internal conflicts and contradictions. The research component dedicated itself to increasingly specialized, increasingly fragmented, scholarship and services (i.e. Clark Kerr's 'multiuniversity'). The college component, unequivocally in mission statements though far less so in practice, dedicated itself to general education, character building, and civic education for a democratic society. After 1876, much of the history of American higher education can essentially be summed up in two oversimplified, deliberately overstated propositions:

1. As American society expanded exponentially in size and wealth and as America became the dominant world power, the internally contradictory, ferociously competitive, American research university became the overwhelmingly dominant form of American higher education, powerfully influencing, in complex ways, all other components of the American schooling system.

2. Within the highly fragmented, highly specialized, highly competitive, American 'multiuniversity', the research component became increasingly dominant. Undergraduates increasingly came to be regarded essentially as 'cash cows' in the present and potentially rich and generous alumni in the future. Their primary function was to help justify and finance faculty research and graduate instruction in increasingly specialized academic departments and schools fixated on their members gaining institutional, national, and international prestige, power—and cash.[21]

Having deliberately overstated those two propositions in highly unflattering but essentially accurate terms, it is critical to amend them somewhat: Before the First World War broke out and sharply undermined the optimistic 'idea of progress' so strongly held in America, the rapid 'rise' of American research universities owed much to the deeply felt conviction that they were playing significant, in fact, indispensable, roles in the increasingly progressive development and democratization of American society. To support that observation, as well as draw 'useful' lessons and 'usable knowledge' from it, we now sketch some significant pre-1914 developments at the University of Chicago and at the Wharton School of the University of Pennsylvania.

WILLIAM RAINEY HARPER, JOHN DEWEY, AND THE FORMATIVE PERIOD OF THE UNIVERSITY OF CHICAGO[22]

Democracy has been given a mission to the world, and it is of no uncertain character. I wish to show that the university is the prophet of this democracy, as well as its priest and

---

[21] For a devastating analysis of undergraduate education in research universities, see Boyer Commission on Educating Undergraduates in the Research University (1998) *Reinventing Undergraduate Education: A Blueprint for America's Research Universities*. Stony Brook, NY; State University of New York at Stony Brook publication.

[22] Our analysis of Harper and Dewey in this section is based primarily on our discussion in Lee Benson and Ira Harkavy (1999) 'University-assisted community schools as democratic public

its philosopher; that in other words, the university is the Messiah of the democracy, its to-be-expected deliverer.   William Rainey Harper, *The University and Democracy* (1899)

Democracy is the soul of America—its charter myth, its ultimate end-in-view (Dewey). In this chapter we argue, therefore, that a Neo-Deweyan conception of participatory democracy should constitute the soul of the overall American schooling system, particularly its most strategic component, the research university. Has it been? Is it now? Rhetorically to some extent, to a very limited extent practically. For us the question then becomes: How do we get there (participatory democracy) from here (rhetorical democracy)? As historians we 'naturally' turn to history to help answer that question.

Around the turn of the twentieth century, William Rainey Harper, the first president of the University of Chicago, and John Dewey, its most noteworthy scholar, placed schooling at the centre of American intellectual and institution-building agendas. We follow their lead, stand on their shoulders, work to realize their vision, and try to progress beyond them by overcoming their contradictions.

Plato was the philosopher Dewey most liked to read. Though he admired Plato, their worldviews differed radically. For our purposes, we need only note two basic differences: Plato's worldview was aristocratic and contemplative, Dewey's was democratic and activist. Despite their many differences, in certain crucial respects, Dewey shared Plato's views about the relationships between education and society.

Like the ancient Greek philosopher, Dewey theorized that education and society were dynamically interactive and interdependent. It followed, then, that if human beings hope to develop and maintain a particular type of society or social order, they must develop and maintain the particular type of education system conducive to it. Stated in negative propositional form: no effective democratic schooling system, no democratic society. Stated positively: to develop and maintain a democratic society, human beings must develop and maintain an effective democratic schooling system.

While at the University of Chicago, Dewey tended to act on that theoretical proposition. And in our forthcoming book, *Progressing Beyond John Dewey*, we argue that Dewey's ten years (1894–1904) at the University of Chicago constituted his most intellectually productive period. But to a much greater extent than has been generally recognized, we also argue, Dewey's ideas about education and society benefited from the great importance William Rainey Harper, the president of the University of Chicago, placed upon his university's active engagement with the severe problems confronting its dynamically growing city, particularly its public school system. Criticized by a university trustee for sponsoring a journal focused on pedagogy in *pre-collegiate schools*, for example, Harper emphatically proclaimed: 'As a university we are interested above all else in pedagogy.'

works', *The Good Society*, **9**: 14–20, and in our chapter, 'Integrating the American system of higher, secondary, and primary education to develop civic responsibility', in Ehrlich (ed.) *Civic Responsibility and Higher Education*, pp. 174–83.

Harper's devotion to pedagogy logically derived from two propositions central to his vision for the University of Chicago in particular and American universities in general.

1. 'Education is the basis of all democratic progress. The problems of education are, therefore, the problems of democracy.'
2. More than any other institution, the university determines the character of the overall schooling system. To quote him: 'Through the school system, the character of which, in spite of itself, the university determines and in a larger measure controls . . . through the school system every family in this entire broad land of ours is brought into touch with the university, for from it proceeds the teachers or the teachers' teachers'.

Given those two propositions and the messianic role Harper assigned the American university as the 'to-be-expected deliverer' of American democracy, he theorized that the major responsibility of American universities is the performance of the overall American schooling system. If the overall American schooling system does not powerfully accelerate 'democratic progress', then American universities must be performing poorly—no matter whatever else they are doing successfully. 'By their [democratic] fruits shall ye know them', was the Baconian performance test Harper prescribed for the American university system.

Long before Clark Kerr hailed the post-Second World War American 'multi-university' as the most important institutional innovation of the mid-twentieth century, Harper, in effect, viewed the new type of urban 'Great University' he worked to create in Chicago as the most strategic organizational innovation of modern society. According to Harper's organizational theory of democracy in industrializing societies, the schooling system functions as the leading societal subsystem. Its continuing development and effective integration is mandatory, therefore, to produce democratic progress. To help achieve his democratic goal, Harper envisioned that his university would function as a cosmopolitan, community-engaged, 'Great University'. A far more skilful and pragmatic analyst and practitioner of power than Dewey, for Harper the 'new urban' university would be the strategic agency to help America realize and fulfil its democratic promise by helping to bring about a democratic 'Implementation Revolution' (our term). Other university presidents enthusiastically seized the opportunity to improve the quality of life in American cities. But Harper saw much farther and went much further than his presidential colleagues when he predicted that an institutional transformation would result if American universities engaged in planned interactions with their urban environments and served as 'the democratic expression of urban civilization'.

During his ten years at Chicago, Dewey's work, directly and indirectly, was powerfully influenced by Harper's vision, programme, and wide-ranging activities. As is well known, Dewey also significantly benefited from associating closely with Jane Addams and the other Hull House settlement workers struggling to improve the quality of life in their local community. At the turn of the twenti-eth century, among other creative innovations, feminist settlement leaders such as Addams in Chicago and Lillian Wald in New York City pioneered the trans-fer of social, health, cultural, and recreational services to the public schools of American cities. In effect, they recognized that though there were very few settle-ment houses, there were very many public schools. Inspired by their innovative ideas and practical community activities, in 1902, Dewey presented a brilliantly prophetic, highly influential address, 'The School as Social Centre', to a national conference of the National Educational Association.

Viewed in historical perspective, Dewey's address clearly adumbrated some of the key ideas and principles of the very loosely organized community school 'movement' which thereafter episodically rose, fell, and, in the form of a newly created national organization, Coalition for Community Schools, is today rising again in the United States. Summarized oversimply, Dewey predicted that the schooling system would increasingly function as the strategic subsystem to solve the complex problems of the increasingly dynamic and complex industrial, post-industrial, and information societies produced by the post-1800 economic and communication revolutions. Neither the 'free market' nor the 'government', he claimed, would be able to cope effectively with the complex societal problems of the twentieth century. Which institution, or combination of institutions, could? The *local community*, Dewey answered.

Specifically, how would the local community carry out those unprecedented responsibilities? Primarily through the *neighbourhood public school*, Dewey answered. The neighbourhood school would serve *all* the residents of the neighbourhood, not simply the children, and would provide the 'lifelong learn-ing' (today's term for Dewey's concept) and new skills needed to cope with dynamic change; it would be comprehensively organized to function as an easily accessible social centre 'for all classes of whatever age'.

In essence, Dewey's creative reconstruction of social and political theory envi-sioned the neighbourhood school functioning as a publicly owned site, a publicly controlled and organized catalyst, to provide lifelong learning and help create the local *democratic coalitions* of residents and organizations required to solve the multitude of problems continually emerging in advanced industrial societ-ies. Unfortunately, soon after his address to the National Education Association, Dewey quarrelled with Harper (and others) over the operation of the remarkably comprehensive School of Education which Harper had finally succeeded in cre-ating to implement his long-held vision of a highly integrated schooling system, from kindergarten to university. As a result of those quarrels—which exempli-fied the internal conflicts built into American universities—Dewey mistakenly decided to leave a university directly and actively engaged in the problems of its city for the traditionally scholastic Department of Philosophy at Columbia University.

Dewey's departure from Chicago, we are convinced, was a tragic mistake that had devastating consequences for the American schooling system in the twentieth century. It was a tragic mistake because, among many other reasons, after moving to Columbia, Dewey failed to act on the powerful community school idea he had advocated in 1902 and which an increasing number of contemporary universities (including our own) are now trying to revive and implement. Moreover, shortly after Dewey left for Columbia, Harper died. With Harper's death, the visionary School of Education he had created turned sharply away from democratic pedagogy and instead became a major advocate and stronghold of scientistic, bureaucratized schooling. In more general terms, after Harper died, the University of Chicago increasingly functioned as the antithesis of the 'Messiah' of democracy—the role which he had envisioned and advocated. To a considerable extent, however, that transformation stemmed from disastrous changes in the American university system which Harper himself had helped bring about.

As we have emphasized repeatedly, America is contradictions. Harper, like Ben Franklin and Walt Whitman, was quintessentially American. Until now, we have discussed Harper's role as messianic advocate of democracy. But Harper was simultaneously a ruthless 'captain of erudition', as Thorstein Veblen characterized the academic entrepreneurs who, at the turn of the twentieth century, built America's universities by tapping into the great fortunes of the 'captains of industry' ('robber barons') who had built America's great business corporations.[23]

Succinctly characterized, Harper was both a democratic prophet and a ruthlessly entrepreneurial practitioner of the innovative, undisguised, 'ungenteel' style that led Veblen to stigmatize university presidents as 'captains of erudition' who competed fiercely for faculty, students, prestige, power, publicity—and cash. Veblen hardly exaggerated. The qualities he attributed to entrepreneurial university presidents are strikingly similar to those we find in glowing tributes to Harper written by one of his closest associates and most admiring biographers.[24]

More than any other university president, Harper raised to a new, much higher level of intensity and 'normalcy', the competitive style characterizing American higher education from its colonial college beginnings, and helped render the 'community of scholars' rhetoric increasingly oxymoronic.[25] In effect, Harper legitimated undisguised competition and, in the process, radically transformed American higher education, *on balance*, increasingly for the worse. In his influential history, *The Emergence of the American University*, Laurence R. Veysey emphasized that:

... the effect of imitative competition upon the pattern of the emerging American university *permanently* [emphasis added] undid all sorts of more creative hopes. Bidding constantly

[23] Our analysis of Harper as 'captain of erudition' appears here for the first time.
[24] Thomas Wakefield Goodspeed (1928) *William Rainey Harper: First President of the University of Chicago*. Chicago: University of Chicago Press, pp. 109–10, 124–5, 147–8.
[25] Frederick Rudolph (1990 ed.) *The American College and University: A History*. Athens, Ga.: University of Georgia Press, pp. 349–51. See also Veysey, *The Emergence of the American University*, op. crit., pp. 366–80 and *passim*.

against one's neighbors for prestige and support, one soon found limits placed upon the freedom peacefully to implement unusual or experimental ideas.[26]

'Imitative competition' did much more than inhibit creativity in American higher education, it multiplied and intensified the system's contradictions and the alienation produced by accelerated commodification, particularly after 1945. But before we discuss post-Second World War developments, it seems best to locate them in historical perspective by first discussing the contradictions between democratization and commodification as they manifested themselves at the University of Pennsylvania during the Progressive Era (roughly 1900–16).

THE WHARTON SCHOOL OF THE UNIVERSITY OF PENNSYLVANIA

Founded in 1881, the Wharton School of Finance and Economy was the first business school in the world.[27] Lacking any precedents to guide them during its early years, the faculty of the Wharton School understandably held sharply different views about what its curriculum and goals should be. By the early 1890s, however, Edmund James and Simon Patten had gained firm control of the school and innovatively developed it as 'both a business college and a place for advanced study in social science'.[28]

Both James and Patten had been students of Johannes Conrad at the University of Halle during the 1870s and both strongly believed in the activist State developed and promoted by the German school of political economy. Accordingly, they both viewed the State as a 'positive factor in material production' and aggressively followed:[29]

... German models in setting forth a program for labor, agriculture, and the allocation of natural resources. They recommended improved sanitary and industrial conditions, higher wages, shorter hours, and the provision of opportunities for 'mental and moral growth'. They called for conservation laws to protect, preserve, and create forests, for the establishment of agricultural experiment stations, for government subsidies to stimulate the production of desirable crops, and for the dissemination of information about natural resources and the best means of developing new industries.

In sharp contrast to their German teachers, however, James and Patten, American to the core, strongly opposed 'autocratic monopolies' and favoured their regulation. As progressive American democrats, they envisioned a 'national economy

---

[26] *Ibid.*, pp. 330–2 and *passim*.

[27] 'Foreword', in Steven A. Sass (1981) *The Pragmatic Imagination: A History of the Wharton School: 1881–1981*. Philadelphia: University of Pennsylvania Press, p. XIX.

[28] For the German academic training and general orientation of James and Patten, see Daniel M. Fox (1967) *The Discovery of Abundance: Simon N. Patten and the Transformation of Social Theory*. Ithaca, New York: Cornell University Press, pp. 32–43.

[29] *Ibid.*, p. 38. For an informative discussion of German political economy, Patten's academic training, family background and personal experiences, and the early history of the Wharton School, see *ibid.*, pp. 1–43.

of smaller industries so distributed as best to utilize our material resources.' Like Joseph Wharton, who endowed the school, they strongly criticized and sharply opposed English-style atomistic, *laissez-faire* capitalism. Accordingly, they worked hard and innovatively to create what became the American Economic Association and to have it function as a highly progressive professional association serving both 'science and social reform'.

Patten was an impressively original thinker. Committed to reform ideas both by family background and youthful experience, he developed a highly progressive, optimistic theory of abundance which directly challenged the age-old pessimistic doctrine, 'the poor ye shall always have with you.' According to Daniel N. Fox, his admiring biographer, Patten powerfully transformed Western social theory in the early twentieth century by changing the dominant 'frame of reference' and bringing about the 'discovery of abundance'.[30] After James and Patten won firm control of the Wharton School, it expanded rapidly in size, scope, accomplishments, and influence. In 1895, however, James, like many other leading academics, was lured to the University of Chicago by its charismatic president, William Rainey Harper. After James left for Chicago, Patten became the School's dominant figure. Under his direction and inspiration, it blossomed into a 'complex institution with a national and even international reputation'.[31]

Given Patten's highly progressive philosophy and theoretically informed activist practice in the grand tradition of Francis Bacon and Penn's founder, Ben Franklin, Joseph Wharton's original mandate was 'stretched beyond recognition'. Rather than primarily concentrating on the management of private business corporations, Wharton increasingly placed heavier emphasis on 'wider fields' of public service and its outstanding faculty gave them 'distinguished coverage'. Instituted by the president of Bethlehem Steel (Joseph Wharton's highly prosperous firm) to train high-level executives to manage large-scale, for-profit enterprises, in actual practice, the Wharton School 'graduate[d] about equally businessmen, teachers and public servants of various kinds. ...'[32] In effect, a school to improve the *management* of American business simultaneously became a school to improve the *regulation* of American business.[33] During the Progressive Era, Wharton probably was the most progressive, most innovative 'school of social science' anywhere in the world—and much more progressive than the University of Pennsylvania as a whole.

Summarily stated, James, Patten, and most of the Wharton faculty held far more progressive views than did either the Philadelphia elites, who served as Trustees of the University of Pennsylvania, or the members of the 'not especially high-minded [Wharton] student body', who strongly tended to be far more interested in 'useful business training' and in 'campus fun and games' than in

[30] *Ibid.*, pp. X–XI. [31] *Ibid.*, pp. 41–3.
[32] For an illuminating, amusing, and somewhat critical account of the early Wharton School, see the memoir by Rexford G. Tugwell (1982) *To The Lesser Heights of Morningside: A Memoir.* Philadelphia: University of Pennsylvania, pp. 3–70. The quotation on the occupations of the graduates of the Wharton School is from pp. 5–6. [33] *Ibid.*, pp. 5–6.

the 'uplift or intellectual excitement' that the faculty worked hard to provide. Predictably, the contradictions between democratization and commodification at Wharton were too great to last for long. Particularly after one of the great figures in Penn's history, Charles C. Harrison, resigned as Provost in 1911, the contradictions grew increasingly sharp and came to a climax during the 1914–15 academic year when the Trustees arbitrarily fired, 'without formal charges or a proper hearing', Scott Nearing, 'the most vocal champion of the progressive cause at Wharton'. Though their arbitrary action 'prompted a huge and instant protest', the trustees prevailed and in 1917 succeeded in delivering:[34]

> ...a culminating blow to progressivism at Wharton. In 1917, Simon Patten reached the age of retirement—sixty-five. The trustees customarily extended the tenure of distinguished faculty.... But the board saw Patten as the source of Wharton's mischief and was anxious to see him go; it refused to continue his contract and terminated his [entire] connection with the university.... In the aftermath of the Nearing affair and the disgrace.... [inflicted on] Patten, a stench lay over the University. The scandal prevented the Wharton School from attracting any first-rate, critical mind to replace Patten and it raised serious questions about the future of the institution. In 1917, the school lost its intellectual, a man who lived for ideas. *Thereafter it had to make do with professionals, men who lived off ideas* [emphasis added].

Wharton survived, of course, and later prospered handsomely. We have cited the Wharton case, among other reasons, because it vividly supports and exemplifies this basic proposition: The 'forces pushing' the commodification of American universities were powerful and active long before the 'virtual university' developed in the 1980s and 1990s and long before Stanley Ikenberry warned against them in his valedictory presidential speech to the American Council on Education in February 2001.

WORLD WARS, COLD WAR, AND ACCELERATING UNIVERSITY COMMODIFICATION, 1914–89

Dreadfully compressed, oversimplified, and overstated, we now sketch the commodification process afflicting American universities and American society from 1914 to 1989. Generalizing in extremely broad terms, the horrors of the First World War, the corrosive disillusionment after 1918, the traumatic series of events after the Great Depression began in 1929, all combined to undermine optimism and stimulate pessimism. Compared to the pre-1914 era of progressive hope and enthusiasm, the intellectual and political 'climates of opinion' in Western societies changed remarkably.

---

[34] For a detailed account of the early history of Wharton, the conflict between its progressive faculty and reactionary Trustees and Provost after 1911, see Sass, *Pragmatic Imagination*, pp. 91–161. The quotations in our text below are from pp. 118–26, 137–9.

Caustically attacked as naively unrealistic and societally dysfunctional, once dominant progressive social and political theories lost much of their power to influence opinion, policy, and action. Formerly progressive American social scientists notoriously jumped on board the scientistic pseudo—'value-free' bandwagon. And professors of all types sought refuge in scholastic Ivy-Covered Towers from the increasing numbers of 'frivolous and anti-intellectual' students who cluttered-up college campuses. American college attendance increased largely during the 1920s. That increase has been taken at face value and mistakenly viewed as though it were a valid measure of increased university democratization. But for most students 'college life' centred around intercollegiate athletics, fraternities and sororities, and various other forms of 'campus fun'. Even after 1929, to quote Page Smith's angry indictment of American higher education, little changed.[35]

... the universities showed little inclination to respond to the onset of the Great Depression. If one were to judge from the typical university curriculum, there was little, if any, recognition that the nation was entering the greatest crisis since the Civil War. On the university campuses it was business as usual.

The outbreak of the Second World War, of course, brought considerable change, particularly after Pearl Harbor catapulted America into the war. We strongly agree with Stuart Leslie, however, that it was primarily the Cold War—and its extraordinarily complex consequences, direct and indirect, short term and long term—that 'redefined American science' and both quantitatively and qualitatively accelerated and deepened the commodification of American universities after 1945.[36]

To place that complex development in historical perspective, Leslie emphasized that during the Second World War, to a far greater extent than during the First World War, universities had:

... won a substantial share of the funds [going into wartime mobilization], with research and development (though not production) contracts that actually dwarfed those of the largest industrial contractors... Vannevar Bush, the chief architect of wartime science policy and a strong advocate of university research, was the man behind the change.

Bush engineered that change as director of the powerful wartime Office of Scientific and Development. Late in 1944, President Roosevelt, highly impressed

[35] Our summary of the 1920s and the impact of the Depression is taken largely from the summary account in Page Smith (1990) *Killing the Spirit: Higher Education in America*. New York: Penguin Books, pp. 131–5.

[36] Stuart W. Leslie (1993) *The Cold War and American Science: The Military–Industrial–Academic Complex at MIT and Stanford*. New York: Columbia University Press, pp. 1–13; Donald E. Stokes (1997) *Pasteur's Quadrant: Basic Science and Technological Innovation*. Washington, DC: Brookings Institution Press, pp. 2–24. In our judgment, Stokes' book is an extraordinarily important analysis of both the postwar disastrous conflict between 'basic and applied research' set off by Bush's 1945 report *Science, the Endless Frontier* and the age-old conflict between 'basic science and technological innovation' which continues to-date to plague American higher education and the American schooling system in general.

by its accomplishments, asked Bush to look ahead and draft a long-term plan for postwar science. Bush delivered his famous (notorious?) report, *Science, the Endless Frontier* in 1945. General agreement exists that, since 1945, it has profoundly, fatefully, influenced American's science policy. For our particular purposes, the chief importance of Bush's 'Basic Science Manifesto' (our term) is that, as Stuart Leslie has convincingly shown in, *The Cold War and American Science: The Military-Industrial Academic Complex at MIT and Stanford*, it rapidly produced what we (again oversimply) characterize and stigmatize as the Big Science, Cold War, Entrepreneurial, Commodified, American Research University System. *On balance*, we contend, that system transformed all of American higher education for the worse.

To credibly support our critical assessment would take a long book, probably a long series of long books. In this chapter, we can do little more than crudely assert and superficially support two basic propositions:

1. The post-1945 commodification of American higher education—including the development, in all their different stages and forms, of for-profit and (nominally) non-profit 'virtual universities'—is best attributed to the complex combined effects of policies and actions resulting from Bush's 'Endless [research] Frontier' Manifesto and pre-1945 American history. To pun a phrase, we are (largely) what we have been. That's our pessimistic bad news proposition.

2. Our optimistic good news proposition takes this form: American history is contradictions. It is, therefore, much more than the commodification bad news alluded to in our first proposition. From its seventeenth-century beginnings, the history of New World America has, *in part*, always signified, embodied, and advanced progress. That's why it seems reasonable to believe that, despite their contradictions and limitations, the progressive ideas and legacies of Benjamin Franklin, William Rainey Harper, John Dewey, Simon Patten, and countless others not cited in this chapter (e.g. Jane Addams), can be used to help democratic-minded American academics successfully resist and overcome the commodification now threatening them so visibly.

To suggest that credible evidence exists for our optimistic proposition, we now sketch some of the many hopeful 'signs of the times' that could be used to support it.

THE POST-1989 EMERGENCE OF THE DEMOCRATIC, COSMOPOLITAN, CIVICALLY AND SOCIETALLY ENGAGED COMPONENT OF THE AMERICAN UNIVERSITY SYSTEM

While the Cold War was being fought, the commodification of American higher education could be resisted only feebly, and only in a few atypical places. The fall of the Berlin Wall in 1989 and the crackup of the Soviet Union in 1991, however, more-or-less marked the end of the Cold War (though its residual effects and echoes, of course, continue to be felt today). The end of the Cold War, we contend, provided the necessary conditions for the 'revolutionary' emergence of what we (clumsily) call 'a Democratic, Cosmopolitan, Civically-and-Societally Engaged American University System'. As envisioned by its proponents, the distinctive mission of the post-Cold War new type of university had two interrelated goals: (1) realization of the *practical*, not simply *rhetorical*, advancement of democratic schooling; (2) realization of the *practical*, not simply *rhetorical*, democratic promise of America for *all* Americans.

How can the *idea* of the new type of university be credibly explained? Largely (though again oversimply) as a defensive response to the increasingly obvious, increasingly embarrassing, increasingly immoral contradiction between the increasing status, wealth, and power of American higher education—particularly its elite research university component—and the *increasingly unnecessary, pathological, state of American cities*.[37]

Early in the twentieth century, Simon Patten had brilliantly observed and theorized that 'abundance for all' was now possible, that all Americans could enjoy a decent standard of living, *provided* that seriously outmoded dysfunctional societal arrangements and habits of mind were changed. By the late twentieth century, the advance of science, technology, and knowledge far surpassed the levels that had been achieved in the early twentieth century. In principle, Patten's far-sighted vision was now much more easily attainable than when he had first 'discovered abundance'. Why hadn't Patten's vision been realized in practice, other than the historical inertia, the 'unaccountable Prejudice in favour of [outmoded] ancient Customs and Habitudes', which Benjamin Franklin had bitterly denounced in 1789 to account for the defeat of his proposed Baconian reformation of higher education?

To paraphrase Oliver Goldsmith's late eighteenth-century lament for the *Deserted Village*: while American research universities in the late twentieth century flourished as never before, 'ill fared the American city, to hastening ills a prey'. If American research universities really were as great as they claimed to be, if they really were the best in the world and not simply the least bad, why did so much poverty and misery exist in America, why were American cities so pathological? After the Cold War ended, the contradiction became increasingly obvious, troubling, indefensible, immoral.

In short, it was the manifest contradiction between the *power* and the *performance* of American higher education that sparked the emergence of the *idea* of the Democratic Cosmopolitan Engaged University (although not anything like its practical realization). Accelerating external and internal pressures forced

---

[37] Most of our previous writings cited in fn. 1 above deal with the development of the Democratic, Cosmopolitan, Engaged University. In particular, see our articles and essays in Volumes 5 and 6 of *Universities and Community Schools*, in 1997 and 1999, and in Ehrlich (ed.) (2000) *Civic Responsibility in Higher Education* Phoenix, Arizona: Oryx Press.

research universities to recognize (very, very reluctantly) that they must—and could—function as cosmopolitan institutions simultaneously engaged in advancing universal knowledge and improving the well-being of their local geographic communities, that is, the local ecological systems which symbiotically affect their own 'health' and functioning. Put another way, after the Cold War ended, the combination of external pressure and enlightened self-interest spurred American universities to recognize that they could, indeed must, function simultaneously as universal and as local institutions of higher education—democratic, cosmopolitan, civic institutions not only *in* but *of* and *for* their local communities.

To reduce (if not avoid) misunderstanding, we emphasize that it is still 'very early days' for the changes we have alluded to above. But things are changing, in the right direction. One indicator of positive change is the accelerating number and variety of 'higher eds'—a much less cumbersome term than 'higher educational institutions'—which now publicly proclaim their desire to collaborate actively with their neighbouring public schools and local communities. Predictably, public proclamations of collaboration, to-date, far surpass tangible interactive, mutually respectful and beneficial collaboration. Nevertheless, progress is being made.

Much greater progress would be made, we maintain, if democratic-minded academics clearly recognized that the danger of accelerating university commodification is now so great that to resist it they must resolve, or at least suspend, the internal quarrels that now divide them. For that to happen, however, we think it mandatory that they develop and accept an inspiring *positive vision* of the role that American universities are capable of playing in the twenty-first century. The main elements of that vision have already been developed, we have suggested, by such passionate advocates of progress as Francis Bacon, Benjamin Franklin, William Rainey Harper, John Dewey, Simon Patten, Jane Addams, and countless others. A shorthand way to summarize and combine the different contributions made by those advocates of progress, we believe, is to call for the reinvention of American universities so that they function as democratic virtuous, organizationally integrated, Neo-Baconian, Neo-Deweyan, moral/intellectual institutions dedicated to the 'betterment of humanity', the 'relief of man's estate'.

To indicate that the reinvention of American universities which we advocate is not an 'impossible dream', not a product and comic example of delusionary utopianism, we now sketch recent developments at the University of Pennsylvania.

PENN, UNIVERSITY-ASSISTED COMMUNITY SCHOOLS, AND COMMUNAL PARTICIPATORY ACTION RESEARCH

To be a great university we must be a great *local* university [emphasis added].   Shirley Strum Kenny, President, State University of New York Times, Stony Brook, *New York Times* (18 August 1999)

To a considerable extent, our proposed American system of higher education derives from general theories developed by John Dewey. We have to confess, however, that we knew almost nothing about his theories when we began work in 1985 to improve university–community relationships. We knew nothing, for example, about Dewey's work on the Dewey Problem (our term for it), that is, the problem of constructing *democratic, cosmopolitan, neighbourly communities.* And we knew nothing about the community school ideas which Dewey had brilliantly sketched in 1902 while he was working with William Rainey Harper and Jane Addams in Chicago.[38]

Over time, we have come to believe that the establishment, development, and maintenance of university-assisted community schools is the best strategy to solve the Dewey Problem, that is, how to construct democratic, cosmopolitan, neighbourly communities. How we got there from where we started in 1985 demonstrates, we are convinced, that Baconian action-oriented, real-world problem-solving, not Platonic scholastic research, is by far the best strategy to advance learning and knowledge.

Ironically, and instructively, when we first began work in 1985 to change university–community relationships, we did not envision it in terms of schools, real-world problem-solving teaching and learning and research, or universities as highly strategic components of urban ecological systems. What immediately concerned us, and what gave us reason to think that Penn's traditionally indifferent (hostile?) attitude towards its local community might change for the better, was that West Philadelphia, Penn's local community, was rapidly and visibly deteriorating, with devastating consequences for the University. West Philadelphia's deterioration, we realized, might be used to spur Penn to creative action to overcome it. But what specifically could Penn do and how could it be induced to do it? (Necessity *sometimes* is the mother of invention.)

Committed to undergraduate teaching, convinced by our personal experiences during the 1960s that undergraduates might function as catalytic agents to help bring about university change, we designed an Honors Seminar which aimed to stimulate undergraduates to think critically about what Penn should do to remedy its 'environmental situation' (broadly conceived). For a variety of reasons, the president of the university, Sheldon Hackney, himself a former professor of American history deeply interested in and strongly moved by the 1960s, agreed to join us in giving that seminar in the Spring 1985 semester. The seminar's title suggests its general concerns: 'Urban University–Community Relationships: Penn–West Philadelphia, Past Present, and Future, As a Case Study'.

When the seminar began, we literally knew nothing about the history of community school experiments and had not given *any thought* to Penn working with public schools in West Philadelphia. For present purposes, we need not recite the complex, painful processes of trial, error, and failure which led us, President

---

[38] We discuss—at length—the beginning of our work in 1985 and its evolution, thereafter, in the numerous items cited in fn. 1 above.

Hackney, and our students to see that Penn's best strategy to remedy its rapidly deteriorating 'environmental situation' was to use its enormous internal and
external resources to help radically improve West Philadelphia public schools
and the neighbourhoods in which they are located. Most unwittingly, during the
course of the seminar's work, we reinvented Dewey's community school idea!

Public schools, we came to realize (more or less accidentally) while working
to improve the quality of life in West Philadelphia, could function as core community centres for the organization, education, and transformation of entire
neighbourhoods. They could do that by functioning as neighbourhood sites for a
West Philadelphia Improvement Corps (WEPIC) consisting of school personnel
and neighbourhood residents who would receive strategic assistance from Penn
students, faculty, and staff. Put another way, the seminar helped invent WEPIC
to help transform the traditional West Philadelphia public school system into
a 'revolutionary' new system of university-assisted, community-centred, community problem-solving, schools, open day and night, throughout the entire
year, not simply to educate school children but to deal with the entire range
of problems affecting all the residents of the communities in which schools are
located.

Previous experiments in community schools and community education
throughout the country had depended primarily on a single university unit,
namely, the School of Education, one major reason for the failure, or at
best limited success, of those experiments. The WEPIC concept of university
assistance was far more comprehensive and involved both assistance from,
and mutually beneficial collaboration with, *the entire range of Penn's schools,
departments, and administrative offices.* The core component of the university-
assisted community school idea is, however, theory-guided, theory-testing,
action-oriented, strategic real-world problem-solving, academically based, community service courses and seminars. Implementing and progressing beyond
Ben Franklin's Baconian-inspired ideas for the reformation of American higher
education, those courses and seminars simultaneously aim to improve both
the quality of life in West Philadelphia and the quality of teaching, learning,
research, and service in all the twelve Schools which constitute the University of
Pennsylvania.[39]

At present, approximately 100 such courses, and seminars, working with
schools and community organizations, have been developed and are 'on the
books' at Penn, with forty-three being offered during the 1999–2000 academic
year. Moreover, an increasing number of faculty members, from an increasingly
wide range of Penn schools and departments, are now seriously considering how
they might revise existing courses, or develop new courses, which would enable
their students to benefit from innovative curricular opportunities to become

---

[39]   For our discussion of Professor Francis Johnston's highly important role in the development
at Penn of what we call 'strategic, academically-based community service', see, in particular,
Benson and Harkavy, in *Universities and Community Schools*, 4: 66–9, Benson and Harkavy in
Ehrlich (ed.) *Civic Responsibility*, pp. 187–9.

active learners and creative real-world problem solvers, and *active producers*, not simply *passive consumers*, of knowledge.

THE CENTER FOR COMMUNITY PARTNERSHIPS AND PRESIDENTIAL AND FACULTY LEADERSHIP

Encouraged by the success of the university's increasing engagement with West Philadelphia, in July 1992, President Hackney created the Center for Community Partnerships. To highlight the importance he attached to the Center, he located it in the Office of the President and appointed one of us (Ira Harkavy) to be its director (while continuing to serve as director of the Penn Program for Public Service created in 1988).[40]

Symbolically and practically, creation of the Center constituted a major change in Penn's relationship to West Philadelphia/Philadelphia. The university as a corporate entity now formally committed itself to finding ways of using its truly enormous resources (broadly conceived, e.g. student 'human capital') to help improve the quality of life in its local community—not only in respect to public schools but to *economic and community development in general.*

Very broadly conceived, the Center is based on the assumption that one efficient way for Penn to carry out its academic missions of advancing universal knowledge and effectively educating students is to function as a 'cosmopolitan community school of higher education'. Stated somewhat more specifically, Penn's research and teaching would focus on universal problems, for example, schooling, health care, economic development, as those universal problems *manifest themselves locally in West Philadelphia/Philadelphia.* By efficiently integrating general theory and concrete practice, Penn would symbiotically improve both the quality of life in its local ecological community and the quality of its academic research, teaching, and learning. Put another way, the Center assumes that when Penn itself is creatively conceived as a 'cosmopolitan community school', it constitutes, in the best sense, both a *universal* and a *local* institution of higher education.

The emphasis on *partnerships* in the Center's name was deliberate; it acknowledged, in effect, that Penn could not try to go it alone, as it had long been (arrogantly) accustomed to do. The creation of the Center was also significant

---

[40] For the creation of the Center for Community Partnerships in 1992, its subsequent development, and the large-scale expansion of Penn's work with West Philadelphia's public schools and neighbourhood, see *ibid.*, pp. 188–93. For the most recent 'testimony' concerning the great value of the Center and is effective integration of Penn's 'three-pronged mission of research, teaching, and service', see the Dean's Column written by Samuel Preston, Dean of the School of Arts and Sciences, in *Penn Arts & Sciences*, Winter 2001, p. 2. The magazine goes to all alumni of the School and almost the entire issue is devoted to the work of the Center and the courses which it has brought into operation and which function, to quote Dean Preston, as 'the very embodiment of [Ben] Franklin's insistence on linking the theoretical with the practical'.

internally. It meant that, *at least in principle*, the president of the University would now strongly encourage all components of the University to seriously consider the roles they could appropriately play in Penn's efforts to improve the quality of its off-campus environment. Implementation of that strategy accelerated after Judith Rodin became president of Penn in 1994. A native West Philadelphian and Penn graduate, Rodin was appointed in part because of her deeply felt commitment to improving Penn's local environment and to transforming Penn into *the* leading American urban university. (America is *competition* and contradictions.)

Rodin made radical reform of undergraduate education her first priority. To achieve that far-reaching goal, she established the Provost's Council on Undergraduate Education and charged it with designing a model for Penn's undergraduate experience in the twenty-first century. Following the lead of Penn's patron saint, Benjamin Franklin, the Provost's Council emphasized the action-oriented union of theory and practice and 'engagement with the material, ethical, and moral concerns of society and community defined broadly, globally, and also locally within Philadelphia'. The Provost's Council defined the twenty-first century undergraduate experience as:

... provid[ing] opportunities for students to understand what it means to be active learners and active citizens. It will be an experience of learning, knowing, and doing that will lead to the active involvement of students in the process of their education.

To apply this Franklinian-inspired orientation in practice, the Provost's Council designated academically based community service as a core component of Penn undergraduate education during the next century.

Presidents and Provosts can provide leadership. But it is faculty members who develop and sustain the courses and research projects which durably link a university to its local schools and community. More specifically, it is through faculty teaching and research that the connection to local schools and communities is ultimately—and durably—made. We gave high priority, therefore, to increasing the number and variety of academically based community service courses. Thanks in large measure to President Rodin's strong support, their number has grown exponentially; from 11 when the Center was founded in 1992 to approximately 100 in the Fall of 2000.

Given its fundamentally democratic orientation, the Center has worked towards increasingly higher levels of participation by community members in problem identification and planning, as well as in implementation.[41] To put

---

[41] Almost from the beginning of our work, we have emphasized that one of our main objectives is to demonstrate both the theoretical and the practical superiority of what we view as Baconian–Franklinian–Deweyan 'communal participatory action research' compared to 'Scholastic Social Science' or 'Pure Social Science', as we derisively label them. For our analysis of the radical differences between those two different orientations to the 'advancement of knowledge', as well as how *communal participatory action research* differs from the *participatory action research* orientation developed by William Foote Whyte and Kurt Levin (from whom we have learned a great deal), see Benson and Harkavy, in *Universities and Community Schools*, **2**: 14–27.

it euphemistically, this has not been easy to do. Decades of community distrust of Penn, based on decades of community-destructive actions and inactions on the part of Penn, take significant effort and time to reduce. The Center's work with WEPIC has focused on health and nutrition, the environment, conflict resolution/peer mediation, community performance and visual arts, school/community publications, technology, school-to-career programmes, and reading improvement. Each of these projects varies in the extent to which they engage public school students, teachers, parents, and other community members in each stage of the research process. The Center's *overall* effort, however, has been *consciously* democratic and participatory.

As WEPIC and related projects have grown and developed, and as concrete, positive outcomes for schools and neighbourhoods have continued to occur, community trust and participation have increased. It would be terribly misleading, however, if we gave our readers the impression that town-gown *collaboration* has completely—or even largely—replaced the town-gown *conflicts* which characterized Penn community relationships before 1985. It has not.

Penn is a leading American research university. Given the ferociously competitive nature of the American academic system, particularly as it developed after 1945, Penn feels compelled to compete ferociously with its rivals. As a result, it inevitably subjects itself to *all the pressures for commodification academic competition entails*. Stated in propositional form, our basic argument can be summarized as follows: *Competition among American universities tends strongly to produce both university commodification and university-community conflict.*

That proposition's validity seems virtually self-evident to us. Granted its validity, it seems understandable, in fact predictable, that Penn administrators and faculty members frequently feel forced to pursue polices which either: (1) result in serious conflicts with West Philadelphia residents; (2) sharply distance Penn from serious concern with the serious problems which West Philadelphia residents have had to confront since the end of the Second World War.

To help support our highly complex proposition, we again use the Wharton School as a case study.

WHARTON AND THE FEROCIOUS CONFLICT DRIVING THE COMMODIFICATION OF AMERICAN BUSINESS SCHOOLS AND UNIVERSITIES IN THE GLOBAL ERA

In 1996, *The Economist* (US edition) published a revealing article, 'Re-Engineering the MBA', which glowingly recited the major accomplishments of the Dean of the Wharton School, Thomas Gerrity. To suggest its main thesis, we quote the article's opening paragraphs:[42]

Anyone who meets the Dean of the Wharton Business School expecting an unworldly academic who lives for nothing but ideas is in for a surprise. Thomas Gerrity is as smooth as they come, immaculately tailored and perfectly coifed. He litters his conversation not with scholarly references but with business buzz words even referring to his university's president as 'the CEO'.

Mr. Gerrity's business patois is not just affectation. He is one of a new breed of deans: businessmen who have been roped back into academia in order to force business schools to practice what they preach.

What forced the change? Why did Wharton 'allow itself to be reinvented'? Here is the article's one word answer to its own questions:

Competition. In November *1988 Business Week started publishing a ranking of business schools* [emphasis added]. It unearthed massive discontent, with students complaining that professors were not interested in anything other than research, and recruiters worrying that the schools produced technical wizards who knew nothing about the real world and were incapable of working in teams. Ever since then deans have had a license to tamper with the syllabus.

As we write this article in March 2001, Wharton, to maintain its lead over its numerous hard-driving competitors in the United States (and elsewhere throughout the world) is building a massive, hugely expensive 'Cathedral of Mammon'—the derisive label bestowed upon it by envious non-Wharton professors themselves highly engaged in severe competition with 'colleagues' (sic) in other universities. To suggest why Wharton can afford to, *and feels compelled to*, do that (and a lot more), we quote from two recent articles in *The Daily Pennsylvanian*, Penn's student newspaper. Under the banner headline, 'With $320 million in pocket, Wharton fundraising goes on', the paper proudly reported:[43]

In its continuous efforts to remain the nation's top business school, Wharton is closing in on its multi-million fundraising goal.

According to Wharton officials, the school has secured over $320 million of the $425 million it hopes to raise by June 2003 in the Campaign for Sustained Leadership.

The reporter then went on to quote the current dean on why Wharton could *never* afford to rest its laurels:

'It is imperative that we equip ourselves to remain the innovator in business education', Wharton Dean Harker said in a statement. 'This campaign effort will assure our ability to remain at the forefront of business schools for the 21st century', Harker said.

---

[42] 'Re-engineering the MBA. Dean of the Wharton Business School Thomas Gerrity seeks to reform business schools', *The Economist (US)*, 13 April 1996. Among (almost) countless articles on the competition among business schools and Wharton's leading role in that competition, see the lengthy article congratulating Wharton for having 'once again [in 2000] finished No. 1 in *Business Week's* ranking of the best B-Schools', in *Business Week*, 2 October 2000.

[43] *Daily Pennsylvanian*, 28 February 2001.

Two weeks earlier, the *Daily Pennsylvanian* had published an article celebrating Harker's accession to the deanship:[44]

Harker has embarked on the expansion of the Wharton name, most notably in the creation of Wharton West, a satellite campus that will open in San Francisco this fall.

And under Harker's tenure, the Wharton School has also been lending a hand to business schools outside U.S. borders, serving advisory roles to Singapore Management University and the soon-to-open Indian School of Business.

In the era of global competition and global corporations, it is not surprising that the competitive pressures which force American schools of business to function, in effect, as 'global corporations', have accelerated greatly. And it is not surprising that, in countless short- and long-term, direct and indirect, ways, the commodification of Wharton has strongly tended *to accelerate commodification and internal conflict throughout the University of Pennsylvania.*

Penn, we emphasize, is anything but unique. More or less the same process is occurring at business schools and universities throughout the country. We have focused on the Wharton case because we know it best and because it seems highly significant to us. Among other things, it demonstrates that while the *visionary idea* of the Democratic, Cosmopolitan, Civic University was emerging in the United States during the 1980s and 1990s, the *harsh reality* of the commodified university was developing much more strongly. Only if those directly contradictory developments are clearly recognized and understood, we contend, can an effective strategy be devised to strengthen what might be called the 'forces pushing' *democratization* and weaken the 'forces pushing' *commodification*. To indicate that such a strategy might be devised, that the victory of commodification is not inevitable, we cite a much more hopeful 'sign of the times' at Penn.

PRESIDENT RODIN'S VISION OF PENN AND WEST PHILADELPHIA AS A 'BELOVED COMMUNITY'

On 20 January 2000, Penn held an 'Interfaith Program' in honour of Martin Luther King, Jr. As part of that programme, President Rodin presented one of us (Ira Harkavy) with 'the Faculty Award for bringing Academically Based Service Learning into reality'. We cite that award because it testifies to the importance Penn now rhetorically gives to action-oriented, community problem-solving teaching, learning, and research. Far more significantly, President Rodin chose that occasion to deliver an extraordinarily visionary speech, 'Martin Luther King's Challenge: Service to Society'. Among other reasons, we quote freely from that speech because it represents by far the strongest commitment she, or any senior

---

[44] 'Wharton dean leads global growth', *Daily Pennsylvanian*, 14 February 2001.

Penn official, has ever made to the idea that the 'University and the City . . . stand on common ground, our futures very much intertwined'.[45]

More than 30 years after his earthly journey ended in Memphis, the Reverend Dr. Martin Luther King, Jr. remains a part of the light by which we chart our ongoing struggle for justice and human dignity for all . . . Dr. King *never* stopped witnessing for justice. He never stopped working to create what he called a 'beloved community'.

I am sure that were he with us today, Dr. King would compliment universities like Penn for producing brilliant, imaginative doctors, lawyers, scholars and scientists who press the envelopes of their disciplines and profession. He would commend us for conducting research that yields important advances in the health sciences and other fields.

But he would also say that it is not enough. It is not enough to expand the intellect and talents of our students if we fail to rouse their souls to serve others and engage them in the larger issues of the day. Nor is it enough, he would say, for us to make great discoveries in the lab and develop theoretical solutions to society's problems if we do not use them to tackle the kinds of challenges we face every day.

Dr. King would be right. But I also believe he would be right at home at Penn, whose founder professed a similar philosophy of education that *today guides us more than ever* [emphasis added].

Dr. Franklin declared that 'the great aim and end of all learning is service to society'. For Penn, society begins *right here* in West *Philadelphia—right here in this beloved community that we are building together* [emphasis added] . . . .

During his life, Martin Luther King, Jr. was a supreme challenger. He challenged the nation to change unjust laws. He challenged a U.S. president to forsake war. And he challenged each of us to love and serve humanity as best we can.

By meeting Dr. King's challenge and rallying to his call, each of us can help make Penn *the* national model for building a beloved community.

We would be less than candid if we failed to observe that President Rodin's heartfelt, visionary speech nevertheless ended on the institutional competitive note more-or-less obligatory for all American university presidents since William Rainey Harper first sounded it in the 1890s. (It simply now goes with the presidential territory.) And we would also be less than candid if we failed to observe that President Rodin knew, of course, that on 20 January 2000, Penn and West Philadelphia did not *really* constitute anything like Dr. King's 'beloved community'.

The purpose of visionary speeches is not to describe present reality, *it is to inspire people to change present reality for the better.* Just as Dr King's historic 1963 'I have a dream' speech eloquently, inspiringly, envisioned a glorious future day when racism would be overcome in America, President Rodin's speech, in effect, eloquently, inspiringly, envisioned a glorious future day when

---

[45] Part of President Rodin's speech was published in the *Almanac*, 25 January 2000. The *Almanac* is Penn's official magazine of record. The reference in our text to the 'University and the City . . . stand on common ground' statement is from Penn's official *Annual Report* for 1987–88. For the radical change that statement represented in Penn's relationship to West Philadelphia, see Benson and Harkavy, *Universities and Community Schools*, 2: 13–14.

university–community conflict would be overcome and Penn–West Philadelphia would indeed constitute (something like) 'a beloved community'.

We quoted President Rodin's speech for two reasons: (1) It strongly signified that the powerful pressures for university commodification notwithstanding, the idea *of the democratic, cosmopolitan, civic university is alive and growing at Penn (and at many other American universities)*; (2) the visionary strategy informing President Rodin's 'beloved community' speech honouring Dr King reinforces our conviction that to overcome university commodification, American academics must *themselves* be powerfully moved by an inspiring democratic vision of what American universities and American society should be. Before developing that argument in our concluding section, we cite another hopeful 'sign of the times', the accelerating national progress of the University Civic Responsibility Idea.

THE UNIVERSITY CIVIC RESPONSIBILITY IDEA BECOMES A NATIONAL MOVEMENT FOR THE ADVANCEMENT OF AMERICAN DEMOCRACY

We cannot overemphasize the point that the accelerating changes in Penn's relationship to its local schools *are not atypical, not unique to Penn*. More or less similar changes throughout the country testify to the emergence of a University Civic Responsibility Movement—a national movement to construct an organizationally integrated, optimally democratic schooling system, as the optimal means to advance American democracy.

A convenient way to suggest the rapid development of that movement during the 1990s is to contrast its relatively flourishing condition today with the devastating indictment against American universities that President Derek Bok of Harvard brought in 1990. In a highly influential book, he indicted American universities for failing to do what they should have been doing 'to help our country cope more effectively with a formidable array of problems'. Less than a decade later, however, that condition had significantly changed for the better.

On 18–20 June 1998 a national conference on *Higher Education and Civic Responsibility* was held in Tallahassee, Florida. Co-sponsored by the American Council on Education and Florida State University, the conference brought together leaders from a wide variety of higher education institutions. The conference had two primary purposes:[46]

... first, to help set the agenda for a new National Forum on Higher Education and Civic Responsibly being initiated by the American Council on Education; and second, to survey

---

[46] See our discussion of the conference in Benson and Harkavy, *Universities and Community Schools*, **6**: 3–4. The book by Derek Bok cited above is, *Universities and the Future of America*. Durham, NC: Duke University Press, 1990. The entire book repays careful study but see, in particular, its 'Preface' and 'Introduction'.

the higher education landscape for the best programs involving civic responsibility. The Forum's goals will be to strengthen higher education's civic role both in educating students and in institutional service to communities.

The conference was a great success. To build on its success and help develop a coordinated national movement to increase the number of colleges and universities working to improve the quality of life in their local communities and the moral and civic education of their students, the American Council on Education published a book of essays in 2000 on *Civic Responsibility and Higher Education*. Its publication constituted a 'hard' indicator of the accelerating growth and development of the idea that universities (broadly conceived, i.e. all institutions of higher education) must assume significant responsibility for the well-being of the local communities in which they function as highly strategic corporate citizens.

In the Preface to *Civic Responsibility and Higher Education*,[47] its editor, Thomas Ehrlich, observed that it focused on two central questions: (1) What does civic engagement mean; (2) What can colleges and universities do to promote it? Having posed those questions, Ehrlich then summarized the volume's contents as follows:

The essays in this volume should be of significant interest to everyone troubled about American democracy and its future, as well as about the future of higher education in this country. The authors have written with particular attention to college and university faculty and administrators and what they can do to educate their own students to be responsible citizens. No less important, these essays provide important insights on *how campuses themselves can be engaged citizens of their communities* [emphasis added]. But the volume is also written for a larger audience of those concerned about how to reverse the decline of civic engagement in the United States. The authors not only diagnose the reasons why higher education has been primarily on the sidelines during this decline, *but also propose concrete steps to change that reality* [emphasis added].

As that summary suggests, the volume focused on what 'engaged' colleges and universities could do to promote democratic citizenship in America and how they could best function as 'engaged citizens of their community'. Given those purposes and the 'Establishment' auspices under which the volume was published, it is understandable that, except in very oblique ways, the essays strongly tended not to focus on the critical problem which concerns us in this chapter, namely, what is to be done to resist and overcome the commodification of higher eds while they are trying to promote democratic citizenship and civic engagement. We turn now to that problem.

---

[47] Ehrlich (ed.) *Civic Responsibility Higher Education*, pp. vi–x.

WHAT IS TO BE DONE? LOOKING BACKWARDS CRITICALLY
TO MOVE FORWARD CONSTRUCTIVELY

We have repeatedly observed that the commodification of American higher education is accelerating rapidly and now seriously threatens both the vocations and the livelihoods of American academics. And we have sketched the long history of competition and commodification in American society and in the American higher educational system which it has shaped and which, in turn, has shaped it.

Until now, however, we have deliberately neglected to point out that American professors are not wholly innocent victims of institutional 'forces' beyond their control. Beginning in the 1890s, *American academics as a collective group*, not simply presidents and administrators, have increasingly played the competitive game whose logical outcome is the academic commodification which now severely threatens them. Far from resisting intense competition in 'the Academy', professors have strongly tended to accept it as a more-or-less 'natural' good thing, particularly since 1945. And acceptance and legitimization of accelerating competition in the 'community of scholars', of course, only further legitimated accelerating competition as the 'natural' state of society at large.

True, as commodification accelerated during the 1980s and 1990s, professors increasingly have voiced doubts about the benefits of academic competition. But only with accelerated commodification has it come to be widely and openly acknowledged that egoistic, self-centred and self-aggrandizing competition among professors, not simply lofty intellectual disagreement, plays a large role in the (almost) countless quarrels that angrily divide the multitudinous American 'community of scholars'. At all levels of 'academia', within universities and among universities, within schools and departments and among schools and departments, within disciplines and among disciplines, within professorial and among professorial ranks, the competitive ranking and rating game has strongly tended to be played enthusiastically, indeed fiercely, rather than resisted determinedly.

To our knowledge, no systematic studies have been made. Anecdotal evidence suggests, however, that the destructive consequences of academic competition are now being increasingly recognized—and not simply by members of the 'lower ranks', (e.g. graduate students). Though hard to document, we believe that a major reason for the rising professorial criticism of academic competition is the impact of the ICT revolution on what might be called the 'speed-up' and 'deskilling' of 'academic labour'. Once applied primarily to factory workers, those terms seem to many observers increasingly applicable to 'academic labourers'. Other chapters in this volume probably deal with those phenomena in much greater detail and much greater authority than we can. For our purposes, we need only quote a recent article in the *Chronicle of Higher Education* by Arthur E. Levine, the president of Teachers College of Columbia University.[48] (Anecdotal reports indicate that the article has attracted a great deal of attention and aroused a great deal of anxiety.)

Ominously and authoritatively titled, 'The Future of Colleges: 9 Inevitable Changes', the article began by specifying several widely recognized 'forces' pushing those changes forward.

Several major forces today have the power to transform the nation's colleges and universities. Those of us who work in higher education are already all too familiar with those forces: shifting demographics, new technologies, the entrance of commercial organizations into higher education, the changing relationships between colleges and the federal and state governments, and the move from an industrial to an information society. In addition, the convergence of publishing, broadcasting, telecommunications, and education is blurring the distinction between education and entertainment. *A variety of knowledge producers will compete to create courses and other education services, to develop new ways to distribute knowledge, and to engage larger audiences* [emphasis added].

For our purposes, we need only focus on one of the 'inevitable' changes President Levine foresees as a result of what might be called the 'new means of production and distribution of higher education' and the 'new producers and distributors' who own and/or control them. In effect, the inevitable result he foresees will be an extraordinarily stratified system of academic labour: A few richly rewarded 'superstars' at the top and a very large number of routinized, underpaid workers in the lower 'proletarian' ranks to carry out the relatively menial tasks still necessary in the new, highly advanced (technologically and organizationally), system of 'course' production and distribution.

Viewed positively, President Levine's article performed a valuable service. Like Stanley Ikenberry's valedictory speech to the American Council on Education which we quoted above, in effect, his article sounded an alarm, a warning bell in the night: 'The Commodifiers are Coming, the Commodifiers are Coming, you must do something to stop them'.

Viewed negatively, however, President Levine's article exemplified what we view as the disastrous, timorous, post-1918 American academic tendency to shun 'advocacy' and simply 'raise', 'analyse', 'address' problems—but carefully evade proposing concrete solutions which, at minimum, might stimulate sustained, intensive, systematic work that, in time, might lead to better solutions. That's what we try to do in this section.

We are convinced that commodification is a real and present danger which confronts American academics and which they must directly confront. We are also convinced that to resist commodification effectively, democratic-minded American academics must truly recognize that it is a real and present danger against which they must 'unite and fight' (to invoke a once familiar American progressive slogan). To do that effectively, however, we contend, they must be

---

[48] Arthur E. Levine, 'The Future of Colleges: 9 Inevitable Changes', *Chronicle of Higher Education*, 27 October 2000.

powerfully inspired by a 'grand vision'. What should that grand vision be? What is to be done to realize it? Hard questions.

RADICALLY REINVENTING AMERICAN UNIVERSITIES TO TRANSFORM THEM INTO NEO-BACONIAN, NEO-DEWEYAN, INSTITUTIONS

Our primary purpose in this concluding section is agenda setting, not detailed planning for step-by-step operational action and decision making. Before we propose some specific actions that we believe democratic-minded academics should take to begin the process of radically reinventing American universities, we need to clarify our terms, *Bacon's Problem, participatory democracy, Neo-Baconian, Neo-Deweyan.*

By *Bacon's Problem*, we mean the problem of creating the necessary conditions to optimally realize the humane use of science and technology. Somewhat more specifically and phrased in question form, this is our definition of what we think can be usefully identified as *Bacon's Problem: How can human beings organize, produce, advance, and practically use knowledge so that the 'advancement of learning' contributes optimally to 'the relief of man's estate?'* John Dewey never actually used the specific term 'participatory democracy'. But that seems to be the best term yet devised to summarize his complex, vaguely stated, but powerful set of democratic ideas, including his democratic theory of human nature. To clarify the term, as well as Dewey's ideas about democracy, we quote from Robert Westbrook's illuminating biography:[49]

Among liberal intellectuals of the twentieth century, Dewey was the most important advocate of participatory democracy, that is, of the belief that democracy as an ethical ideal calls upon men and women to build communities in which the necessary opportunities and resources are available for every individual to realize fully his or her particular capacities and powers through participation in political, social, and cultural life. This ideal rested on 'a faith in the capacity of human beings for intelligent judgment and action if proper conditions are furnished', a faith, Dewey argued, 'so deeply embedded in the methods which are intrinsic to democracy that when a professed democrat denies the faith he convicts himself of treachery to his profession'.

Having clarified (somewhat) the terms, *Bacon's Problem* and *participatory democracy*, we now go on clarify what we mean by the terms, *Neo-Baconian* and *Neo-Deweyan.*

As noted in an earlier section, to solve what we label Bacon's Problem, Bacon 'trumpeted' the need to develop a morally inspired, morally controlled, all-encompassing, continually evolving, experimental science of inquiry.

---

[49] Robert Westbrook, *John Dewey and American Democracy.* Ithaca and London: Cornell University Press, 1991 pp. XIV–XV.

His proposed science of inquiry would be based on the integrated, large-scale organization of collaborative work appropriately designed to solve, at different levels of generality and specificity, the vast array of problems human beings must confront and solve in their quest for long, healthy, happy lives.

What form did Bacon's utopian proposal for large-scale organization of collaborative work take, who would create, control, direct, and maintain that organization, who would decide the appropriate division of responsibility and labour, as well as decide the priorities and schedule of the real-world, problem-solving activities central to his natural and moral philosophy?

Living, thinking, acting, and writing in the early seventeenth century, in his *New Atlantis* utopian fable, Bacon naturally answered all those hard questions in highly elitist terms. To begin with, a wise, all-powerful king would create the basic organization. Once created, 'Salomon's House' would henceforth be generally controlled and directed by a small, elite group of wise, benevolent 'Fellows', subdivided into smaller subgroups with highly specialized responsibilities requiring highly specialized talents. Though benevolently exercised, their power would essentially be unlimited and they would select their own successors.

The Fellows would determine priorities for the interrelated, highly differentiated set of problems which had to be solved to assure long, healthy, happy lives for all members of Bensalem, the 'country' (i.e. society) governed by the Fellows of 'Salomon's House'. They would also set the general parameters for the rational division of collaborative work needed to produce specified goods and services, as well as to continually advance theoretical and practical knowledge.[50]

Obviously, the virtuous, democratic system of American universities we call for would have a radically different structure of power, control, and operation than Bacon's seventeenth century elitist 'Salomon's House' of Fellows. Baconian in its dedication to experimental, active, *collaborative*, real-world problem-solving, it would be Deweyan in the general democratic theory of human nature that informs its operations and *participatory democratic* in its structure of power, control, and organization. In short, our proposed Neo-Baconian, Neo-Deweyan system of American universities would select and integrate the best ideas of Bacon and Dewey and adapt them appropriately to help develop and implement a participatory democratic twenty-first-century American society.

It seems neither feasible nor necessary to call now for any changes in the highly complex legal structure which presently controls the American higher educational system. Somewhat sardonically, we do make one 'radical' proposal: We call on all higher eds to *take their own mission statements and rules of governance seriously* and act intelligently and appropriately to realize them in practice.

Lest we be accused of Glendowerism, we now propose a specific strategy democratic-minded academics might follow to begin the process of moving their own institutions in the direction of becoming the Neo-Baconian, Neo-Deweyan

---

[50] See the clear, illuminating description and analysis of Salomon's House of Fellows, by RoseMary Sargent, 'Bacon as an advocate for cooperative scientific research', in Peltonen (ed.) *Cambridge Companion to Bacon*, pp. 146–71.

institutions sketched above. That strategy can first be stated in general propositional form: *All higher eds should explicitly make solving the problem of the American schooling system their highest institutional priority; their contributions to its solution should count heavily both in assessing their institutional performance and in responding to their requests for renewed or increased financial support.* Actively helping to develop and implement an effective, integrated, optimally democratic, pre-K through higher ed schooling system should become the collaborative primary mission of, *and primary performance test for,* American universities and colleges. Unless universities are radically reinvented to radically reinvent the overall American schooling system, we contend, no other proposal to raise significantly the level of American democracy can succeed.

Primary mission, of course, does not mean *sole* mission. Obviously, American higher eds now have—and will continue to have—important missions other than collaboratively helping to solve the problem of the American schooling system. If space permitted, we would try to show in detail how those other missions would benefit greatly from successful collaborative work on the schooling problem. Here we restrict ourselves to barebones statement of three corollary propositions: (1) given the radically disruptive, complex consequences (e.g. political, economic) of the extraordinarily rapid development of information societies throughout the world, given the critical role schooling must play in such societies, solving the schooling system problem should now constitute American society's highest priority; (2) solving the overall problem of the schooling system must begin with changes at the higher ed level; (3) if higher eds genuinely take responsibility for solving the overall schooling system problem and effectively use their great resources to realize that goal in their local communities, in the long run, directly and indirectly, they will secure *much greater resources than they now have to carry out all their important missions.*

How can American higher eds be induced to act on and implement that general proposition? *One institution at a time, in order to build a movement.* Less cryptically, we call on democratic-minded academics opposed to commodification *to unite with other members of their own institution and concentrate on getting it to accept and implement the general proposition outlined above.* As our discussion of the University Civic Responsibility Movement and Penn's work with West Philadelphia public schools was designed to show, more-or-less successful efforts to implement that general proposition are now being made throughout the country.

What we have essentially done in this chapter is to propose what we regard as a long-term, locally-oriented, practical strategy to unite academics opposed to commodification in a positive national movement to change their institutions in specific ways—specific ways which are in the enlightened best interests of their institutions and the communities in which their institutions are located.

Put another way, to conclude this chapter, we have answered the 'What is To Be Done?' question by adopting and adapting the general strategy of the environmental movement: *Think nationally (and globally), act locally.*

10

Commodity and Community: Institutional Design for the Networked University

Philip E. Agre

INTRODUCTION

Information technology and its uses unsettle the university as an institution. Institutions are shaped by the practicalities of information, and they exist largely to mitigate information problems (Melody 1987). Now, however, we are confronted with radically improved technologies of information. It stands to reason that the university as an institution will change. But how? Proposals are strikingly diverse. Some proposals treat the university as a purveyor of human capital; they envision a micromarketplace in learning services. Other proposals treat the university as a site for the pooling of knowledge; they envision the Internet as a tool to amplify this pooling on a global basis. Each type of proposal isolates one feature of the university as we know it today. Call them the commodity model—the university as a competitor in a marketplace—and the community model—the university as an idealized microcosm of society. Despite the inherent tension between them, the commodity and community models have always coexisted in the institutional design of the university. And no matter how radical the changes in technology become, I will argue that the university must continue to manage this tension.

THE COMMODITY MODEL

The university is understood under the commodity model when people speak of higher education as an 'industry' (e.g. Duderstadt 1997), or of the 'competitive

I appreciate helpful comments by Paul Duguid and Camille Kirk. This Chapter is reprinted with the kind permission of the Society for College and University Planning (www.scup.org).

advantage' of universities (Daniel 1996: 67–85), or of 'just-in-time' education that can be consumed in increments anyplace a student happens to be (Dolence and Norris 1995: 4; Halal and Liebowitz 1994: 22; Perelman 1992: 22). Educational services are the principal commodity, with students as the customers. But other commodities are involved as well, such as the intellectual property generated by research. In the university as we know it, students actually purchase a large bundle of commodities: not just years' worth of interconnected classes, but career counselling, athletic facilities, library services, and much else. Competition among universities is already vigorous, but it is competition among bundles, and also to some degree among choices within a bundle.

If precedents from corporate banking and other industries are a guide, however, Internet-mediated competition will lead to unbundling as competitors arise to provide particular elements of the bundle more efficiently (Evans and Wurster 2000). A new market structure might emerge, segmented by some combination of subject matter and educational philosophy. Individual courses might be purchased à la carte (Dolence and Norris 1995: 46), and complementary services such as access to digital libraries might be purchased from separate firms. That, anyway, is the picture that emerges from a radicalization of the commodity model.

A radicalized commodity model would also surely hold consequences for the higher education workforce, including professors (Neubauer 2000; Skolnik 2000). Lectures, for example, are widely regarded as an endangered species that can easily be replaced by video or interactive multimedia. Faculty might be deskilled in such a scenario, reduced effectively to the status of teaching assistants who tutor students on the material in the video (Noble 1998). Or their skills might be expanded, as they become responsible for managing the ever more complex educational programmes being pursued by the students they advise (e.g. Dolence and Norris 1995; Halal and Liebowitz 1994: 23).[1]

From a commodity perspective, the faculty's role is strictly a matter of value added. If well-produced multimedia content can find an audience in the millions, then it can be sold very cheaply (Agre 1999); as a result, every increment of one-to-one interaction between students and teachers may add a significant proportion to the overall cost of an education. The most appealing technology-intensive educational programme that requires ten hours of student–teacher interaction might be quite different in its structure from the most appealing such programme that requires twenty hours. But will students pay the extra cost to get the virtues of the more labour-intensive programme? That is how the commodity model would frame the question.

---

[1] Many authors, such as Duderstadt (1999: 15) and Tsichritzis (1999: 97, 99) imagine a division of labour between star teachers whose lectures are brought into classrooms through technology and rank-and-file teachers who actually interact with students. 'Universities need to decide the areas for which they will be global content providers' (Tsichritzis 1999: 100).

THE COMMUNITY MODEL

The university has also been viewed as a community. It is through the community model that the university upholds norms of collegiality, provides a forum of debate, and maintains structures of democratic governance. From this perspective, the university is not an artificial bundle but an organic whole that refracts the tensions and controversies of the larger society.

It is unclear, and usefully so, where the boundaries of the university community lie. Is each university a community unto itself, or do communities form along disciplinary lines, or do the universities of the world form a single cosmopolitan community? All are clearly true to some degree, and the institution is designed to manage this multiplicity. Universities and disciplines recognize one another's degrees, at least ritually. Research disciplines are global communities, the famous invisible colleges that cut across the boundaries of universities (Crane 1972), and Alpert (1985: 253) remarks on 'the power exercised by the national disciplinary communities in setting the standards and scholarly goals of American universities'. University governance deliberately assembles committees from faculty who work in entirely different fields. Visiting speakers from other universities are accorded ritual deference. Students are positioned as probationary members of the community, with graduation paradoxically a ritual assumption of full membership and a rite of departure at the same time.

When students do graduate, most of them will join professions that form communities of their own. Some professions have stronger senses of community than others, as evidenced by strong collective identities, active professional societies, involvement in political activities, meaningful accreditation of professional programmes, and requirements for continuing education (Abbott 1988; Derber 1982; Larson 1977). From the perspective of information technology and institutional design, the linkages between the university and these larger communities are crucial.

Brown and Duguid's (1998a) community-of-practice framework generalizes these ideas, and suggests that the Internet will be used to make the communities stronger and, in a sense, more real. Communities of practice correspond to disciplines, occupations, and professions: experimental physicists are a community of practice, and so are urban planners, cardiologists, and social historians. But communities of practice also arise spontaneously whenever people have common concerns and a way to share their knowledge (Orr 1996). As the name suggests, a community of practice shares not simply a body of knowledge but a complex of practices: ways of working, writing, speaking, teaching, learning, organizing, and pursuing a career (Toulmin 1972). To join a community of practice is not simply to learn something; it is also to become someone. In addition to acquiring knowledge, one acquires an identity (Lave and Wenger 1991). Learning, on this view, is a matter of immigration and acculturation.

Brown and Duguid (1998*a*: 46) call communities of practice the 'essential and inevitable building blocks of society', and the community-of-practice theory makes numerous predictions about the institutional dynamics of knowledge. Because knowledge is bound up with practices, knowledge can be transferred more efficiently within a community than across the boundaries of different communities (Brown and Duguid 2000). This transfer of knowledge does not happen automatically; most communities of practice have institutions, both formal and informal, for producing and sharing knowledge. By facilitating these institutions, the Internet helps communities of practice to develop more robust mechanisms of collective cognition (Agre 1998). It becomes easier to pursue professional relationships and collaboration at a distance (Finholt and Olson 1997; Wulf 1993; cf. Star and Ruhleder 1996). This development will have both positive and negative consequences. The benefits are clear enough in the efficiency of knowledge production. But as communities of practice grow closer, they may become insular, or they may tear apart the cross-disciplinary bonds within local university communities (Agre 2000).

From the community-of-practice perspective, 'the central thrust of any attempt to retool the education system must involve expanding direct access to communities, not simply to credentials' (Brown and Duguid 1998*a*: 46). The natural consequence of this approach to education is that the university will take advantage of the distance-spanning capacities of the Internet to negotiate closer relationships with the various professions. As new forms of community interaction become possible, each profession's ongoing community life might become more integrated with lifelong learning at the university. The point is not that individual students will take continuing education courses at a distance, though that will surely happen. The point, rather, is that the profession's very institutions (conferences, journals, social networks, everyday information-seeking, and collaboration) may grow together with the disciplinary community of practice of the university. This already happens in engineering fields where practitioners attend research conferences, and when those conferences are organized by professional societies rather than societies devoted specifically to research. But the process can be deepened through shared libraries and new structures of consulting. Universities can develop new forms of instruction in which students learn in an organized way while immersed in their own work settings, and professional institutions of publication and peer review can be extended to occupations that have not historically organized their own conferences and journals.

HOW THE MODELS COMPLEMENT ONE ANOTHER

The commodity and community models complement one another, and the university has always combined them in complicated ways. In many early universities, individual scholars attracted students based on their own reputations, and were paid accordingly. Scholars with ill-attended lectures could starve. To this day, competition helps to maintain standards and encourages programmes to communicate a coherent philosophy. Students vote with their feet, and everyone has an interest in affiliating with the programmes that have the best people. Competition in the academic labour market is a force for high intellectual standards. On a more basic level, university communities consume many commodities in their daily operation: pencils and computers, janitorial services and online services. But the community also supports the market: the most basic mechanism of academic community is peer review, and the magazine reputation rankings that increasingly drive the agendas of professional schools (e.g. Alpert 1985: 255) are (in part) a kind of peer review. The professional networks that communities cultivate also facilitate competition by spreading reliable information about the quality of individuals and programmes. Requirements to publish in the research literature obligate teachers to remain current in their fields; peer review within a discipline also provides each university with an efficient way to evaluate the research work of its faculty. In each case, the research community reduces the need for an administrative hierarchy.

The balance between commodity and community, however, is not uniform. For freshmen, the main priority is socialization into the university community as a whole, not into a particular disciplinary community. This is one reason why it makes more sense to outsource introductory major courses (that is, contracting with an outside firm to offer Chemistry 101 and Sociology 101 on a distance basis using multimedia courseware packages) than to outsource freshman core courses or major courses at the senior level—assuming that it makes any sense at all. (Other reasons include the low level of faculty interest in such courses and the potential for economies of scale.) Working professionals, on the other hand, are already socialized into their discipline, and so their continuing education can presuppose that socialization. This is one reason why distance education makes more sense for continuing education than for entry-level professional degree programmes. (Other reasons include working professionals' greater access to computing equipment and lesser ability to travel.) The community model makes more sense when students are being socialized into a community of practice, and the commodity model makes more sense when they are not.

The commodity and community models also play complementary roles in the university's production and use of intellectual property. Intellectual property law does not give authors absolute control over their writings, or inventors absolute control over their inventions. Intellectual property protections are limited, in part, because certain aspects of a writing or invention simply cannot be turned into a commodity. Copyright law can protect a text against unauthorized copying, but it cannot protect the ideas in the text against unauthorized thinking. Patent law, likewise, provides an inventor with legal tools to prevent unauthorized persons from practising the invention, but it cannot prevent anyone from being inspired by the invention to create a different invention. Indeed patents are made public precisely to promote that downstream inspiration. In economic terms, these non-commodity aspects of intellectual products are called public goods: everybody can use them, and nobody can be prevented from using them once they know about them. The commodity model thus provides incentives for creative work, but it does not provide incentives for the production of public goods. Fortunately, the community model does provide such incentives: whereas the commodity model rewards the creation of texts and inventions with money, the community model rewards the creation of ideas with credit in the literature (Latour and Woolgar 1986; Merton 1957). Where the commodity model provides its rewards through the market, the community model provides them through peer review and the obligation to cite prior relevant work. Both models, commodity and community, must function correctly for the university system to work.

Intellectual property disputes map the boundary between commodity and community. The complementarity between the two models is always being renegotiated, and it can shift. Thus, many observers have expressed concern about the commodity model's steady invasion of the institutions of research as proprietary interests shape research agendas and hinder the publication of research results (Press and Washburn 2000; Slaughter and Leslie 1997). Many university faculty, particularly in scientific and technical subjects, establish parallel lives, using commodity institutions to extract monetary capital from their research and community institutions to extract academic capital—credit and stature in their field. Universities have sought to manage the tensions that these arrangements inevitably bring, not least by formalizing the university's relationships with industrial firms that collaborate on research projects. The obvious danger is that the commodity logic of the market will undermine the community institutions of research. The integrity of those community institutions ought to provide a clear test for the admissibility of proposed extensions of the commodity model. In particular, it is a fallacy to argue that wealth is always increased by strengthening intellectual property rights, since the wealth created by intellectual property is equal to the sum of its value as a commodity and its value as a public good (cf. Cohen 1998). An intellectual property regime that interferes with the institutions that create public goods would probably decrease wealth rather than increase it.

If the commodity model can invade the university community, the boundary can also move in the other direction. Open-source software employs a peer review model similar to that of academic research. Open-source products such as Apache already have a strong position in the Internet server market, and the open-source operating system Linux is a credible competitor to Microsoft in some market niches. This development may seem paradoxical from the perspective of the commodity model: if nobody owns the code, where is the incentive to create it? Raymond (1999) argues that the paradox dissolves once one understands that, even with a huge industry selling powerful software packages, the vast majority of code is actually written by user organizations for their own in-house purposes of integration and maintenance. This code would be hard to sell, but it is easy to share. The institutions of open-source software facilitate this sharing by providing quality control through peer review. Organizations that have similar software needs thereby form themselves into a community to provide those needs on a cooperative basis, and companies such as Cygnus and Red Hat arise to provide complementary services on a commodity basis. Just as the commodity model is limited in its spread by the inherent limits of commoditization (new technologies make it easier to install toll booths on formerly public roads, but any attempt to turn ideas into commodities would be impossible to administer in practice), the open-source community model is limited to those niches where incentives are structured to encourage sharing.

THE MODELS COMPARED

To understand how the relationship between the commodity and community models may evolve, it is also helpful to compare them.

The commodity and community models are both challenged by diversity. For the commodity model, the issue is economies of scale. When customers are homogeneous, fewer fixed costs are required to produce goods that everyone wants. When consumers are heterogeneous, businesses and industries must find ways to segment the market to achieve economies of scale within each segment while still approximating each consumer's wants. With information goods like multimedia courseware, the pay-offs from a one-size-fits-all product are enormous. Small market segments are likely to be ill-served: the fixed costs of production can be distributed among so few customers that prices are likely to be high.[2] Present-day universities cross-subsidize less remunerative areas of study in the name of human knowledge as a whole, but a radical unbundling of university teaching would eliminate these cross-subsidies and the beneficial side-effects they produce.

Communities, for their part, thrive on commonality. Shared worldviews and customs facilitate communication, coordination, and solidarity. But just for that reason, communities can become exclusionary. Even when a discipline does not overtly discriminate, its culture can be biased. A strong disciplinary culture might provide a ritual foundation for working together and sharing knowledge, but it also makes life harder for people whose personality does not fit the norm. It is

---

[2] It is true, as Evans and Wurster (2000) among others have observed, that interactive multimedia can alleviate this problem by adapting itself to the needs of particular students. But this extensibility only goes so far. Interactive multimedia courseware to teach papyrology will always be a niche market, if it is economically feasible at all. Even when courseware products can be designed to accommodate a variety of learning styles, the resulting code and content will be more complex. The incremental costs of providing this additional complexity must themselves be recovered somehow, and a competing product could be produced and sold more cheaply by focusing more tightly on the largest market segments.

also likely to close off avenues of research that do not fit in symbolic terms with the culture. For example, a cultural emphasis on abstraction is useful when it provides a common theoretical language, but a field can be impoverished if it discounts more concrete styles of thought. What is more, an excessive degree of integration within a disciplinary community can suppress diversity of philosophy and organization among the different university departments in the field (Alpert 1985: 269). Every community needs ongoing critical reflection about whether its culture and practices are based on shared values that are legitimate, or whether they are outdated or arbitrary.

The commodity and community models suggest different ideas about knowledge and, therefore, about lifelong learning. Whereas the commodity model regards knowledge as a 'thing' that can be bought and sold in discrete units, the community model regards knowledge as a provisional turn in a dialogue. Commodities are modules of capital, but communities shape the identities of their participants and encourage emotional investments. Commodities are acquired in zero-sum transactions, but communities depend on lasting bonds of reciprocity. Each view has its elements of descriptive and normative truth. Neither view is adequate.

The commodity and community models each include self-regulatory mechanisms, and these mechanisms have complementary strengths and limitations. The commodity model regulates itself through competition, but this self-regulatory mechanism fails when consumers cannot readily obtain enough information about the commodities and their sellers. Asymmetrical information about the goods can lead to situations of adverse selection, a type of market failure whereby low-quality goods push out high-quality goods because consumers cannot tell the difference until it is too late (Akerlof 1970). The community model regulates itself through peer review, but this mechanism fails when narrow circles of like-minded peers are allowed to review one another for extended periods. The institutions of research are therefore designed to provide several types of peer review, some of them more wide-ranging than others. (Examples include journal and conference refereeing, promotion and tenure reviews, programme planning at funding agencies, and articles that senior scholars write about neighbouring fields.) Despite their surface dissimilarities, each of these self-regulatory mechanisms has an internal structure into which individuals must be socialized. Both market cultures (Smelser and Swedberg 1994) and research cultures (Humphreys 1997) vary across national traditions.

Both models present dangers of monopoly in a networked world. Although the Internet is often described as the herald of Adam Smith's idealized market, globalization of both political economy and computer networks interact to increase economies of scale. The Internet makes it easier to coordinate activity in a large global firm, and the increasing worldwide homogeneity of language, law, and technology rewards firms that can distribute their fixed costs on a global basis. Other things being equal, the likely consequence is increasing concentration in a variety of industries (Bryan *et al.* 1999). In the case of higher education, an organization such as the Open University that is equipped to distribute educational services on a global basis could emerge as a natural monopoly—probably not for higher education as a whole, but certainly for the segments where its greatest competence lies, and where economies of scale are greatest. (On the Open University see Daniel (1996).)

The community model can lead to monopoly because of the economic virtues of enclosing a community of practice in a single organizational framework (Brown and Duguid 1998*b*). In a fragmented world, organizations that promote innovation and learning do not capture the full value of their investment because researchers in other organizations can benefit from the ideas as they become publicly known. But if all of the world's geneticists, for example, worked for a single organization, then only that organization would be capable of benefitting from most of the public goods that the geneticists create. Thus, as communities of practice become more integrated through real-time network connections, they may become increasingly distinct in organizational terms as well.

The institutions of commodities and communities are both decentralized in many ways. Markets operate through the interactions of numerous buyers and sellers within a framework of legal rules and customs, and the overall result of those interactions would be impossible to predict or design (Hayek 1963; North 1990). Academic communities can likewise operate with little central coordination because of the incentives that peer review creates. But in each case, the picture is more complex than it seems. Economies of scale produce great concentrations of economic power, and one excellent example is the small number of textbooks that dominate lower-division undergraduate courses. Network effects—tendencies towards homogeneity that derive from customers' needs for compatibility—also produce concentrations of economic power (Shapiro and Varian 1998). Examples in the realm of market commodities include stock exchanges, which thanks to the Internet are rapidly consolidating on a global basis (Varian 2000), and standards for information technology such as Microsoft Windows. Examples in the realm of academic communities include theoretical languages such as that of Michel Foucault, which apart from their intellectual virtues become widely used because they provide a lingua franca for researchers investigating diverse topics. Both the commodity model and the community model, then, reflect a continuing tension between forces for centralization and decentralization.

Finally, the commodity and community models are similar in the considerable incentive-shaping role of government. The legal system, for example, sets rules for markets, not only in the form of controversial regulations but also in the historical development of commercial law. Government research funding is likewise a powerful force in the development of academic communities. The internal politics of civilian and military funding agencies obviously shapes the research agenda, but more subtly the policy of awarding research grants directly to researchers strengthens the role of academic departments at the expense of the university administration (Alpert 1985).

INSTITUTIONAL DESIGN

The institutional design of the university, then, has always combined elements of the commodity and community models in complex ways. Yet most of the visionary proposals for the information-age university emphasize one model or the other, or they mention both models without a clear plan for integrating them. Perelman (1992: 205–14), for example, advocates a radically commoditized vision of education based on 'microvouchers' for the purchase of small increments of learning services. Along the way, he also endorses the community-of-practice theory (Perelman 1992: 142–6). Yet apprenticeship within a community is a lasting commitment, not something that can be purchased in increments. Starting from the community-of-practice theory, Brown and Duguid (1998a) envision competition among a plurality of 'degree granting bodies' (DGBs). These DGBs occupy the entire spectrum from modern-day research universities with physical campuses to distributed organizations with no geographic locality, physical facilities, or permanent instructional staff. Yet Brown and Duguid's proposal, in its generality, abstracts away from nearly every question about the institutional relationship between commodity and community in the new order. It is not even clear that diverse institutional forms can coexist (DiMaggio and Powell 1991).

How will the university manage the tension between commodity and community in a time of dramatic technological change? It is too early to tell, but we can do a thorough job of asking the question. To start with, information technology creates little that is new in the world. Instead, applications of information technology tend to amplify existing forces (Danziger *et al.* 1982). People shape the technology to let them do more of what they already have incentives to do. The Internet is already being used to amplify both the commodity and community aspects of the university. These trends will continue, and the two models of university life will need to find some new accommodation.

The shape of this new dispensation, however, is not foretold. Many scenarios are possible. Marxists and capitalists, at least of the cruder varieties, imagine progress as an inexorable march of commoditization. Both ideologies imagine that the endpoint of commoditization is utopia, and they both advocate revolutions to that end, even if they disagree on the details. The university might undergo radical commoditization in many ways. Here are four possible scenarios:

Political. Legislatures may be persuaded that the commodity and community models are opposites, that the community model represents the collectivist past, and that the commodity model represents the libertarian future. Any number of government policies could help make this invidious tilt towards the commodity model into a self-fulfilling prophecy.

Technological. Although quantitative improvements in information technology are predictable, in qualitative terms the technology is exceedingly malleable.

The architecture of future educational technologies will be affected by the inter-play of many institutional factors. The design of the wired university is, in other words, political. 'Reinforcement politics' (Danziger *et al.* 1982) is the process by which the dominant political coalition in an organization inscribes its interests into the workings of new information technologies, and new technologies of higher education could be shaped the same way.

Economic. For-profit education companies distribute commodities based on public goods (namely, ideas) that were developed by universities that combine the commodity and community models. If these new competitors manage to impose the commodity model on higher education as a whole, they will under-mine the mechanisms that produce the public goods. The new competitors would be parasitic upon the public goods without cross-subsidizing them.

Cultural. Many students, especially those who grew up in working-class envir-onments where discrete job skills put food on the table, may only be able to imagine the commodity model. This emphasis on vocational job skills is strong among undergraduates even at public research universities. If higher educa-tion companies arise solely on commodity-model lines, then students who do not understand the community aspects of their career—being socialized into a profession's ways, joining professional networks, participating in collective pro-cesses for generating and propagating new knowledge—may make bad market choices that, taken in aggregate, destroy the hybrid institutions of the university.

Despite these fourfold dangers, however, the community model will not die, for the simple reason that knowledge lives in communities. Communities of practice are spontaneous results of commonalities in people's lives. They are increasingly valued by industry (Wenger and Snyder 2000), and many of them are well-institutionalized. Research will continue to be organized around them. If the commodity and community models become disarticulated, then severe institutional pathologies may result, but it is hard to imagine either side dis-appearing altogether.

Indeed, a serious recommitment to the community model may address the hardest problems of institutional transition. The same peer-review mechan-isms that create powerful incentives to conduct original research might also be employed to repair the university's oft-alleged bias against teaching (Cuban 1999). The university community might found a 'teaching literature' that oper-ates using the same principles as the research literature, with refereed teaching journals to which any teacher can submit articles. Different journals would arise to reflect different philosophies of teaching, but each would encourage faculty to design each course as a research project in itself, thereby formalizing what Boyer (1990) has famously called 'the scholarship of teaching'. Promotion and tenure could be based on the sum of one's teaching and research productivity as measured by the journals, or even by their product, as well as peer review of the individual's record as a whole.

That said, institutional design is almost a contradiction in terms. Social theorists have increasingly come to see institutions as emergent phenomena that sustain themselves and evolve over long periods through processes that transcend the consciousness of any individual (e.g. Hodgson 1999; Powell and DiMaggio 1991: 8–9). New institutions do not take hold unless they are congruent with the underlying culture, and institutional change projects face a culture that has long been reinforced by the existing institutions (Offe 1996). This is one reason why institutions often remain stable for centuries. Old institutions can be discredited when their values collapse, or when they cease to deliver practical benefits to their participants (Offe 1996). But new institutions require a broad consensus, and this consensus must run deep: not just shared ideas but a shared way of life.

New institutions evolve in various ways, but ultimately they are shaped by contending interests. A pure commodity model would suit many organized interests, and a pure community model would no doubt suit many others. Every institution is a routinized accommodation among interests (Knight 1992), and the institutional design of the networked university will arise in the same way. But interests can be misunderstood. Those who wish the university to survive will uphold the values of community against the invasion of commodity, but they will also manage the tension rather than try to eliminate it.

REFERENCES

Abbott, Andrew (1988) *The System of Professions: An Essay on the Division of Expert Labor.* Chicago: University of Chicago Press.

Agre, Philip E. (1998) 'Designing genres for new media', in Steven G. Jones (ed.) *CyberSociety 2.0: Revisiting CMC and Community.* Newbury Park, CA: Sage.

—— (1999) 'The distances of education', *Academe*, 85(5): 37–41.

Akerlof, George A. (1970) 'The market for "lemons": Quality uncertainty and the market mechanism', *Quarterly Journal of Economics*, 84(3): 488–500.

Alpert, Daniel (1985) 'Performance and paralysis: The organizational context of the American research university', *Journal of Higher Education*, 56(3): 241–81.

Boyer, Ernest L. (1990) *Scholarship Reconsidered: Priorities of the Professoriate.* Princeton, NJ: Carnegie Foundation for the Advancement of Teaching.

Brown, John Seely and Duguid, Paul (1998a) 'Universities in the digital age', in Brian L. Hawkins and Patricia Battin, (eds) *The Mirage of Continuity: Reconfiguring Academic Information Resources for the 21st Century.* Washington, DC: Council on Library Resources.

———— (1998b) 'Organizing knowledge', *California Management Review*, 40(3): 90–111.

———— (2000) *The Social Life of Information.* Boston: Harvard Business School Press.

Bryan, L., Fraser, J., Oppenheim, J., and Rall, Wilhelm (1999) *Race for the World: Strategies to Build a Great Global Firm.* Boston: Harvard Business School Press.

Cohen, Julie E. (1998) 'Lochner_ in cyberspace: The new economic orthodoxy of "rights management" ', *Michigan Law Review*, 97(2): 462–563.

Crane, Diana (1972) *Invisible Colleges: Diffusion of Knowledge in Scientific Communities.* Chicago: University of Chicago Press.

Cuban, Larry (1999) *How Scholars Trumped Teachers: Change Without Reform in University Curriculum, Teaching, and Research, 1890–1990.* New York: Teachers College Press.

Daniel, John S. (1996) *Mega-Universities and Knowledge Media: Technology Strategies for Higher Education.* London: Kogan Page.

Derber, Charles (ed.) (1982) *Professionals as Workers: Mental Labor in Advanced Capitalism.* Boston: Hall.

Dolence, Michael G. and Norris, Donald M. (1995) *Transforming Higher Education: A Vision for Learning in the 21st Century.* Ann Arbor: Society for College and University Planning.

Duderstadt, James J. (1997) 'The future of the university in an age of knowledge', *Journal of Asynchronous Learning Networks*, 1(2) On the Web at <http://www.aln.org/alnweb/journal/issue2/duderstadt.htm>.

—— (1999) 'Can colleges and universities survive in the information age?', in Richard N. Katz (ed.) *Dancing With the Devil: Information Technology and the New Competition in Higher Education*, Jossey-Bass.

Danziger, James N., Dutton, William H., Kling, Rob, and Kraemer, Kenneth L. (1982) *Computers and Politics: High Technology in American Local Governments.* New York: Columbia University Press.

DiMaggio, Paul J. and Powell, Walter W. (1991) 'The iron cage revisited: Institutional isomorphism and collective rationality in organizational fields', in Walter W. Powell and Paul J. DiMaggio (eds) *The New Institutionalism in Organizational Analysis.* Chicago: University of Chicago Press.

Evans, Philip and Wurster, Thomas S. (2000) *Blown to Bits: How the New Economics of Information Transforms Strategy.* Boston: Harvard Business School Press.

Finholt, Thomas A. and Olson, Gary M. (1997) 'From laboratories to collaboratories: A new organizational form for scientific collaboration', *Psychological Science*, 8(1): 28–37.

Halal, William E. and Liebowitz, Jay (1994) 'Telelearning: The multimedia revolution in Education', *The Futurist*, 28(6): 21–6.

Hayek, Friedrich A. (1963) *Individualism and Economic Order.* Chicago: University of Chicago Press.

Hodgson, Geoffrey M. (1999) *Evolution and Institutions: On Evolutionary Economics and the Evolution of Economics.* Cheltenham: Elgar.

Humphreys, S.C. (ed.) (1997) *Cultures of Scholarship.* Ann Arbor: University of Michigan Press.

Knight, Jack (1992) *Institutions and Social Conflict.* Cambridge: Cambridge University Press.

Larson, Magali Sarfatti (1977) *The Rise of Professionalism: A Sociological Analysis.* Berkeley: University of California Press.

Latour, Bruno and Woolgar, Steve (1986) *Laboratory Life: The Construction of Scientific Facts.* Princeton: Princeton University Press. Originally published in 1979.

Lave, Jean and Wenger, Etienne (1991) *Situated Learning: Legitimate Peripheral Participation.* Cambridge: Cambridge University Press.

Melody, William H. (1987) 'Information: An emerging dimension of institutional analysis', *Journal of Economic Issues*, 21(3): 1313–39.

Merton, Robert K. (1957) 'Priorities in scientific discovery: a chapter in the sociology of science', *American Sociological Review*, 22(6): 635–59. Abridged version reprinted as Chapter 22 of *On Social Structure and Science*, edited by Piotr Sztompka, Chicago: University of Chicago Press, 1996.

Neubauer, Deane (2000) 'Will the future include us? Reflections of a practitioner of higher education', in Sohail Inayatullah and Jennifer Gidley (eds) *The University in Transformation: Global Perspectives on the Futures of the University*. Westport, CT: Bergin and Garvey.

Noble, David (1998) 'Digital diploma mills: the automation of higher education', *Monthly Review*, 49(9): 38–52.

North, Douglass C. (1990) *Institutions, Institutional Change, and Economic Performance*. Cambridge: Cambridge University Press.

Offe, Claus (1996) 'Designing institutions in East European transitions', in Robert E. Goodin (ed.) *The Theory of Institutional Design*. Cambridge: Cambridge University Press.

Orr, Julian E. (1996) *Talking About Machines: An Ethnography of a Modern Job*. Ithaca: ILR Press.

Perelman, Lewis J. (1992) *School's Out: Hyperlearning, the New Technology, and the End of Education*. New York: Morrow.

Powell, Walter W. and DiMaggio, Paul J. (eds) (1991) *The New Institutionalism in Organizational Analysis*. Chicago: University of Chicago Press.

Press, Eyal and Washburn, Jennifer (2000) 'The kept university', *The Atlantic Monthly*, 285(3): 39–54.

Raymond, Eric S. (1999) *The Cathedral and the Bazaar: Musings on Linux and Open Source by an Accidental Revolutionary*. Cambridge, MA: O'Reilly.

Shapiro, Carl and Varian, Hal (1998) *Information Rules: A Strategic Guide to the Network Economy*. Boston: Harvard Business School Press.

Skolnik, Michael (2000) 'The virtual university and the professoriate', in Sohail Inayatullah and Jennifer Gidley (eds) *The University in Transformation: Global Perspectives on the Futures of the University*. Westport, CT: Bergin and Garvey.

Slaughter, Sheila and Leslie, Larry L. (1997) *Academic Capitalism: Politics, Policies, and the Entrepreneurial University*. Baltimore: Johns Hopkins University Press.

Smelser, Neil J. and Swedberg, Richard (eds) (1994) *The Handbook of Economic Sociology*. Princeton: Princeton University Press.

Star, Susan Leigh and Ruhleder, Karen (1996) 'Steps toward an ecology of infrastructure: design and access for large information spaces', *Information Systems Research*, 7(1): 111–34.

Toulmin, Stephen (1972) *Human Understanding*. Princeton: Princeton University Press.

Tsichritzis, Dennis (1999) 'Reengineering the university', *Communications of the ACM*, 42(6): 93–100.

Varian, Hal R. (2000) 'Boolean trades and hurricane bonds', *Wall Street Journal*, 8 May, p. 42.

Wenger, Etienne (1998) *Communities of Practice: Learning, Meaning and Identity*. Cambridge: Cambridge University Press.

Wenger, Etienne and Snyder, William N. (2000) 'Communities of practice: the organizational frontier', Harvard Business Review 78(1): 139–45.

Wulf, William A. (1993) 'The collaboratory opportunity', *Science*, 13 August: 854–5.

PROSPECTS AND POSSIBILITIES

11

Marketizing Higher Education: Neoliberal Strategies and Counter-Strategies

Les Levidow

> Underlying the market orientation of tertiary [higher] education is the ascendance, almost worldwide, of market capitalism and the principles of neoliberal economics.   (World Bank report, Johnstone *et al.* 1998)

> Along with healthcare, education is one of the last fortresses to be stormed. A broad market-oriented reform of the public service of education is underway.   (Moyoto Kamyia, *UNESCO Courier*, December 2000)

INTRODUCTION: MARKETIZATION AGENDAS

Higher education has special stakes for ruling ideologies and strategies. Universities represent the needs of the state and capital as the needs of society, while adapting the skills of professional workers to labour markets. Despite this role, often spaces are created for alternative pedagogies and critical citizenship.

Acknowledgement
My interest in these issues was raised by 'Reclaim our Education', a conference of the Campaign for Free Education in August 2000 at the University of East London. This conference led me to emphasize higher education in a later talk, 'Neoliberal Technologies and Collective Resistance', at the INPEG Counter-Summit (Initiative against Economic Globalization), 22–24 September 2000 in Prague, just before the IMF–World Bank meeting there. I would like to thank the organizers of both events for the opportunity of presenting my ideas there. For helpful comments on the text, I would like to thank Richard Barbrook, Liz Delowee, Anne Gray, Alv de Miranda, David Harvie, Nico Hirtt, Bronwyn Holland, David Margolies, Korinna Patelis, Glenn Rikowski and two anonymous referees of *Education and Social Justice*, which published a similar article in spring 2001, Vol. 3(2): 12–23, <http://www.trentham-books.co.uk>

As part of that long-standing conflict, marketization tendencies have a long history. Student numbers have increased, while teaching has been under-resourced and so appears as an 'inefficiency' problem, to be solved by standardizing curricula. Knowledge has been packaged in textbook-type formats, so that students become customers for products. As a US critic once remarked, 'the various universities are competitors for the traffic in merchantable instruction' (Veblen 1918: 65).

Recent tendencies have been called 'academic capitalism'. Although university staff are still largely state-funded, they are increasingly driven into entrepreneurial competition for external funds. Under such pressure, staff devise 'institutional and professorial market or market-like efforts to secure external monies' (Slaughter and Leslie 1997).[1]

Beyond simply generating more income, higher education has become a terrain for marketization agendas. Since the 1980s universities have been urged to adopt commercial models of knowledge, skills, curriculum, finance, accounting, and management organization. They must do so in order to deserve state funding and to protect themselves from competitive threats, we are told. Moreover, higher education has become more synonymous with training for 'employability'.

These measures threaten what many people value in universities, for example, the scope for critical analysis. Marketization agendas have provoked new forms of resistance around the world. An extreme case was the 1999–2000 student occupation of UNAM, the Autonomous National University of Mexico, which became a test case for potential privatization of all public services.

Recent conflicts over educational values have intersected with debates over Information and Communication Technology (ICT). ICT is designed and used in ways which favour some agendas rather than others. In the ruling ideology, marketization imperatives are attributed to inherent socio-economic qualities of ICT. If accepted as inevitable, this scenario becomes self-fulfilling.

The resulting conflicts can be analysed within wider neoliberal strategies for reshaping society on the model of a marketplace. The original nineteenth-century liberalism idealized and naturalized 'the market' as the realm of freedom; its militants pursued this vision through land enclosures and 'free trade', while physically suppressing any barriers or resistance as unnatural 'interference'. By analogy, today's neoliberal project undoes past collective gains, privatizes public goods, uses state expenditure to subsidize profits, weakens national regulations, removes trade barriers, and so intensifies global market competition. By fragmenting people into individual vendors and purchasers, neoliberalism imposes greater exploitation upon human and natural resources.

---

[1] For such pressures on teaching, other relevant analyses include: Agre (1999, 2000); Dutton (1996); Smith and Webster (1997). Also relevant are marketization pressures on academic research, which has its own critical literature, for example, Demeritt (2000); Evans (2001); Harvey (1998); Harvie (2000); Monbiot (2000: ch. 9).

As this chapter will argue, neoliberal strategies for higher education have the following features:

(1) all constituencies are treated through business relationships;
(2) educational efficiency, accountability and quality are redefined in accountancy terms;
(3) courses are recast as instructional commodities;
(4) student–teacher relations are mediated by the consumption and production of things, for example, software products, performance criteria, etc.

Neoliberal strategies have been devised for marketizing higher education on a global scale. Each geopolitical context provides an extreme case or component of more general tendencies. It is important to draw links among those contexts and among critical perspectives for analysing them. To do so, this chapter proceeds as follows:

(1) the 'information society' as a paradigm for ICT in education;
(2) the World Bank 'reform agenda' for the self-financing of higher education;
(3) Africa, where higher education is being forcibly marketized and standardized through financial dependence;
(4) North America, where some universities attempt to become global vendors of instructional commodities;
(5) Europe, where state bodies adopt industry agendas of labour flexibilization as an educational model, in the guise of technological progress;
(6) the UK, where ICT design becomes a terrain for contending educational agendas; and
(7) global implications for counter-marketization strategies.

Overall the chapter develops concepts of fetishism and reification in order to analyse how neoliberal strategies promote their own socio-political models as the only possible future. The analysis aims to inform counter-strategies and alternatives.

'INFORMATION SOCIETY' PARADIGM

Training 'Knowledge Workers'

Central to the neoliberal project are concepts of the 'information society' and the 'knowledge economy', which derive socio-political imperatives from technological change. According to the 'info-society' paradigm, the management, quality, and speed of information become essential for economic competitiveness. Technological and market modernization become conceptually linked in a forced march towards an inevitable future. This scenario leaves the government only the management task of 'finding security and stability in a world pushed ever faster forward by the irresistible forces of history and human invention', according to Prime Minister Tony Blair (quoted in Robins and Webster 1999: 45).

In the 'info-society' paradigm, ICT is dependent upon highly skilled labour; we are told that together they will be used in order to increase productivity and to provide new services. On that basis, ICT is promoted for greater access to life-long distance learning. Consequently, 'the workers of tomorrow will be able to recycle themselves at their own expense during their free time', as one critic argues (Hirtt 2000: 13).

A related concept is the 'knowledge economy'. This suggests that greater 'human capital' will be necessary to enhance worker creativity, to use inform-ation productively, to raise the efficiency of the service economy, to achieve economic competitiveness and thus to maintain employment. In effect, 'human capital' individualizes skills that can exist only in a social collectivity or network; thus the concept fetishizes social skills as properties of individuals (for a critique, see Fine 2000).

According to the 'knowledge economy' scenario, jobs will have a greater requirement for 'transferable skills' and cognitive capacities.[2] Labour markets will face a skills shortage, and workers will need reskilling so that they remain flexibly employable in a labour market beset by insecurity. Therefore, societies must invest more in 'human capital'.

Yet many jobs are following contrary trends. 'Knowledge' workers face an overload of information to evaluate, spend more time dealing with it, and thus may have even lower efficiency than before. An information overload may even reduce capacity for new ideas. In any case, it is difficult to demonstrate such input–output correlations in practice (Garnham 2000).

Moreover, job specifications have generally not increased the requirement for cognitive capacities. Nevertheless many employers have required workers to have qualifications beyond those needed to carry out the job. As a student lamented, 'You have to work harder to get a worse and worse job' (quoted in Ainley and Bailey 1997).

This 'qualification inflation' is due to excess supply rather than any inherent demands of the job. In the USA, for example, skill levels have risen while wage levels have fallen for comparable jobs (Gottschalk 1998). Indeed, job structures often reduce 'knowledge' to information-processing, rather than require the skill of evaluating information, much less producing new knowledge.

As qualification inflation devalues university degrees, the 'employability' agenda attributes unemployment, under-employment, or job insecurity to indi-vidual deficiencies. The putative remedy is flexible, frequent reskilling which

---

[2] Although this may be true, such skills are associated in practice with elite educational institu-tions and their characteristic student intake. Training in 'transferable skills' would be interpreted by employers as compensatory education for deficient individuals (Robins and Webster 1999: 175–87). Such skills have no inherent relation to ICTs.

supposedly will help graduates to find new jobs, and perhaps even to bargain for higher salaries. Although this outcome may be realized for some professional workers, they face a perpetual responsibility to retrain themselves as a pre-condition for employment.

Further to neoliberal ideology, universities must raise their own productivity in order to survive. They must package knowledge, deliver flexible education through ICT, provide adequate training for 'knowledge workers', and produce more of them at lower unit cost. While this scenario portrays universities as guiding social change, there is evidence of a reverse tendency: that they are becoming subordinate to corporate-style managerialism and income-maximization. For neoliberal strategies, the real task is not to enhance skills but rather to control labour costs in the labour-intensive service sector, for example, education (Garnham 2000).

ICT can relate people to each other and define skills in various ways. Some networks are designed to facilitate electronic exchanges among students (e.g. Passerini and Granger 2000). ICT usage can help to democratize educational access, for example, by helping students to learn at their own pace, or by creating 'virtual communities' of interest in particular issues. Alternatively, it can help to commodify and standardize learning, for example, by extending the authoritative approach of textbook-based knowledge (Johnston 1999).

According to some educators who design internet-based courses, their use can lower personal contact and thus reduce student motivation: 'Many students need the personal interaction', so they readily lose interest. Thanks to ICT, 'We have cleverer ways in which we can search for information, but it still needs to be filtered, sifted', that is, interpreted (interviews quoted in Newman and Johnson 1999). Neglected here is a fundamental question: to seek and evaluate information for what purposes?

Ideological Roles

While the 'info-society' paradigm has been rightly criticized as ideological, it does more than simply to mis-represent reality. Its language serves to naturalize particular practices as objective imperatives. Indeed, not simply the language but also the practices themselves are ideological. Their role can be analysed as fetishism and reification, as sketched here. Let us examine neoliberal accounts of technology, skills, and efficiency.

According to the Director-General of the WTO, 'There are technical reasons for the acceleration of trade in services, especially in the area of information technology'. Through electronic transmission, local services have been 'transformed into internationally tradeable products' such as education services, he argues (Moore 1999). In his account, some current tendencies are projected into an inevitable future, to which we must adapt through rules for trade liberalization. A political agenda is fetishized as an inherent property of electronic media.

Of course, info-tech does facilitate long-distance access to diverse educational materials and accreditation of student achievement, yet this technical capacity could take many social forms.

The forms matter because the neoliberal account is not merely rhetorical: its agenda can be promoted through technological design as well as language. According to one analyst, computer systems are designed by selecting a metaphor (rather than others) and translating it into hardware or software: 'And this is where technology can become ideological: if you believe that information technology as such inevitably brings markets, or hierarchies, or freedom, or modularity, or conflict, or God-like control over human affairs, then you may not even recognize that you have choices' (Agre 1999). Potential choices are pre-empted by fetishizing the preferred metaphor as a property of technology.

ICT exemplifies how knowledge is codified and embedded in technologies. As human qualities are fetishized as properties of things, those things acquire human-like qualities—for example, smart weapons, environmentally clean products, precise techniques, efficient computers, etc. This fetishism is not a false appearance. Rather, it is a real process of investing qualities in things— for example, by designing a social metaphor into technology, by standardizing particular knowledges, by embedding those knowledges in the design—thus favouring some purposes rather than others. By such means, greater control can be shifted to those who exploit or manage labour.

Control can be structured in impersonal and indirect ways. Behind the rhetoric of 'quality control', teachers are being displaced by putative experts in standardized quantitative methods of performance measurement (Klausenitzer 2000). Teachers themselves may internalize and implement such methods. Consequently, social relations take the form of relations between things—for example, between the producers of educational software and their consumers.

These dynamics have analogies to commodity exchange, whereby social relations are actively reified as relations between things. 'To the producers, the social relations between their private labours *appear as what they are*, i.e. they do not appear as direct social relations between persons in their work, but rather as material relations between persons and social relations between things' (Marx 1976: 163). This reification coincides with attempts at extending commodity exchange to more areas of social activity, for example, by measuring transactions according to standard criteria.

Such measures as performance indicators tend to marketize social activities, thus subordinating professional judgements to accountancy. The neoliberal project has 'sought to create simulacra of markets governed by economic or para-economic criteria of judgement in arenas previously governed by bureaucratic or social logics: the new techniques were those of budgets, contracts, performance-related pay, competition, quasi-markets and end-user empowerment' (Rose 1999: 146). Such techniques turn services into simulacra of commodities, for example, by subjecting the content to input–output criteria, regardless of whether the products of labour are literally sold as commodities.

Indeed, 'efficiency' criteria presuppose standardization. Modern bureaucracy homogenizes diverse, heterogeneous qualities into universally comparable ones, thus allowing social qualities to be quantified. This process is 'the precondition of calculable *efficiency*—of universal efficiency . . .', argued Marcuse (1978).

Moreover, technology is specially designed for such purposes: 'Specific purposes and interests . . . enter the very construction of the technical apparatus' (*ibid.*). In developing machinery, 'the social characteristics of their labour come to confront the workers, so to speak, in a capitalized form; thus machinery is an instance of the way in which the visible products of labour take on the appearance of its masters' (Marx 1976: 1055).

Thus alien purposes are embedded in technology, albeit with a pretence of neutral efficiency. New technologies are designed for managing, disciplining, exploiting, and/or expelling human labour, as various critics have argued (e.g. Robins and Webster 1985). In more recent history, such strategies have been extended from the production of commodities to the reproduction of labour power for capital. Not surprisingly, then, controversy often erupts over the criteria for technological design and efficiency.

In the case of higher education, then, we can ask: efficiency for what qualities, values, and social relations? information for whose interests and control? With such questions in mind, the dominant policy language can be analysed as both ideological and material. It provides weapons to naturalize, impose, and legitimize an agenda of marketizing social relations.

WORLD BANK 'REFORM AGENDA'

As promoted by the international financial institutions, trade liberalization generates a virtuous circle of market access, technology, efficiency, etc. As the neoliberal worldview asserts;

Markets promote efficiency through competition and the division of labour—the specialisation that allows people and economies to do what they do best. Global markets offer greater opportunity for people to tap into more and larger markets around the world. It means that they can have access to more capital flows, technology, cheaper imports, and export markets.   (IMF 2000)

On the contrary, as many critics have argued, trade liberalization is generally designed to serve capitalist profitability. It throws people into more intense competition with each other on a global scale, thus preventing people from deciding collectively 'what they do best' and what kind of economic relations to develop with each other.[3] Prime agents are the IMF and World Bank, which elaborate the

---

[3] Consider the story of how IMF–World Bank policies have led Mozambique to shut down its facilities for processing cashew nuts. Contrary to the IMF quote above, the neoliberal project readily blocks technological capacity and market access when their main beneficiaries are local populations rather than multinational companies. See the article by Joseph Hanlon, www.jubilee2000uk.org/policy-papers/roape10400.htm.

strategies of their paymasters in the dominant OECD countries. In the neoliberal project, US capital serves both as a prime driving force and as a model for its imitators or partners elsewhere.

For several years the World Bank has been promoting a 'reform agenda' on higher education. Its key features are privatization, deregulation, and marketization. According to a World Bank report:

The reform agenda . . . is oriented to the market rather than to public ownership or to governmental planning and regulation. Underlying the market orientation of tertiary education is the ascendance, almost worldwide, of market capitalism and the principles of neoliberal economics. (Johnstone *et al.* 1998)

From a neoliberal standpoint, what is the problem—and opportunity? As a private good, higher education is in limited supply, not demanded by all, and is available for a price. Consumers (business and industry) are 'reasonably well informed', while the providers (administrators and faculty) are 'often ill informed—conditions which are ideal for market forces to operate'. Fulfilling the demand, therefore, requires measures to make higher education completely self-financing.

Having defined the problem in this way, the report identifies the traditional university and its faculty members as the main obstacles to a solution:

Radical change, or restructuring, of an institution of higher education means either fewer and/or different faculty, professional staff, and support workers. This means lay-offs, forced early retirements, or major retraining and reassignment, as in: the closure of inefficient or ineffective institutions; the merger of quality institutions that merely lack a critical mass of operations to make them cost-effective; and the radical alteration of the mission and production function of an institution—which means radically altering who the faculty are, how they behave, the way they are organized, and the way they work and are compensated. (Johnstone *et al.* 1998)

This diagnosis identifies teachers and their traditional protections as the obstacle to market-based efficiencies. In its future scenario, higher education would become less dependent upon teachers' skills. Students would become customers or clients. As the implicit aim, private investors would have greater opportunities to profit from state expenditure, while influencing the form and content of education. Business and university administrators would become the main partnership, redefining student–teacher relations.

The World Bank report soon became a political weapon for recasting academic freedom as a commitment to neoliberal futures. University administrations have sought to characterize academic freedom as a duty 'to uphold the balance' between 'the spiraling demand for higher education on the one hand, and the globalization of economic, financial and technical change on the other'. At a UNESCO conference in October 1998, this conflict was ultimately fudged by declaring that faculty members should enjoy 'academic freedom and autonomy conceived as a set of rights and duties, while being fully responsible and accountable to society' (documents quoted in CAUT 1998*b*).

Presumably the university administrations meant 'accountable' to a neoliberal globalization agenda, not to the forces resisting it. Indeed, academic accountability often means subordination to accountancy techniques. In response to these attacks, professional societies have defended academic freedom as a right of free expression.

Although the World Bank agenda has little support among educators, some elements may be implemented. Its extreme proposals may inadvertently help us to understand marketization agendas which are being driven by wider political-economic forces around the world. Let us survey Africa, North America, and Europe as different examples and components of a global neoliberal project.

AFRICA: SAPs FOR RECOLONIZATION

Higher education has become a casualty of the overall neoliberal policies imposed on highly indebted countries of the South. By the late 1970s these countries faced a 'balance of payments' deficit for many reasons—for example, because their main exports suffered a world decline in prices, while oil imports became more expensive. As their governments could no longer repay even the interest on the national debt, their currency lost value, and they were denied credit for further imports.

The IMF and World Bank turned these national debts into an opportunity to impose Structural Adjustment Programmes (SAPs) in the 1980s. Indebted governments were required to reduce spending, to privatize industry and services, to cheapen labour, to open up markets to multinational companies, to relax controls on capital movements, to weaken environmental and labour protection laws, to devalue their currencies, etc.

'Growth-oriented loans' were granted to countries which accepted those 'conditionalities'. According to the World Bank, such measures would help governments reduce budget deficits, reduce the balance-of-payments deficit, control inflation, and thus create conditions for resumed growth. In practice, local industries were driven out of business, many jobs were lost, rural people lost their access to cultivable land, and fees were imposed for health and education services. The main 'growth' has come from people working more in order to pay more than before for goods or services—apart from the 'growth' of multinational companies buying up local assets on the cheap (see examples in FGS 2000).

Consequently, higher education has suffered in all Southern countries, especially in Africa, which was singled out for special treatment. According to World Bank reports on African countries, investment in higher education was benefiting mainly the social elites there, and it had a lower social return than investment in primary education. As yet another conditionality, they were told to reduce funding of higher education, in the name of both egalitarian and efficiency criteria. The costs were transferred to private households, for example, through student fees or education vouchers (Klausenitzer 2000). Thanks to SAPs, governments would have an opportunity to 'increase the efficiency of resource use', declared World Bank consultants.

That neoliberal agenda had different motivations from the publicly stated ones. African governments were regarded as too weak to discipline labour for foreign investors and thus as inadequate managers of public services. More importantly, university faculty and students there were foremost critics of SAPs, often catalysing wider political opposition. In many cases universities were invaded by repressive forces or simply shut down (Federici *et al.* 2000).

Given the great resistance, the neoliberal strategy was to create means by which African universities could be intellectually recolonized, in at least two senses. The general effect of SAPs, combined with tuition fees, effectively limited university access to an elite—far more so than beforehand. Eventually the World Bank acknowledged the worsening quality of African higher education, though not its own responsibility for this outcome. As a remedy, the World Bank promoted 'capacity building' there through direct funding. Through this financial dependence, African universities could be pressurized to change their educational content along lines acceptable to the World Bank (*ibid.*).

In the name of development, the World Bank and UNESCO have sponsored an African Virtual University. It links several African educational institutions with teachers from well-known ones elsewhere, through live digital satellite TV broadcasts and video tapes. Courses emphasize ICT and marketing skills (www.avu.org), perhaps appropriate to neoliberal development models.

Under neoliberal constraints, then, universities substitute new staff, standardize curriculum materials, and marginalize local knowledges. Meanwhile governments repress resistance to such 'reforms'. Within Africa and elsewhere, resistance has been publicized by the Campaign for Academic Freedom in Africa (CAFA 1995–99).

By contrast to Africa, the neoliberal agenda in Western countries promotes corporate appropriation of state subsidy, rather than its reduction. The African case may inadvertently illuminate the more subtle colonization of higher education there, mediated by ICTs.

NORTH AMERICA: COURSES AS INSTRUCTIONAL COMMODITIES

In North America many universities have adopted entrepreneurial practices. They act not only as business partners, but also as businesses in themselves. They develop profit-making activities through university resources, faculty, and student labour (Ovetz 1996).

Within an entrepreneurial agenda, universities have developed on-line educational technology, that is, electronic forms of course materials. Of course, this medium could be used to enhance access to quality education, and to supplement face-to-face contact, as some European universities have been doing for a long time. In North America, however, the aims have been clearly different—namely, to commodify and standardize education.

Those aims have been resisted by students and teachers. For example, in 1997 UCLA established an 'Instructional Enhancement Initiative', which required computer web sites for all its arts and sciences courses. Its aims were linked with a for-profit business for on-line courses, in partnership with high-tech companies. Similar initiatives at York University led to a strike by staff, backed by the students. They raised the slogan, 'the classroom versus the boardroom' (Noble 1998). Critics have held conferences to devise opposition strategies (e.g. Winner 1998).

What problem was the new technology supposed to solve? After university rules were changed to permit profit-making activities, their research role was commodified. Substantial resources were shifted from teaching to research activities, which were expected to result in patents and royalties. With less staff time devoted to teaching, student–teacher ratios increased, thus increasing the burden on them both. This result of profit-seeking was represented as an inherent problem of educational inefficiency.

From that standpoint, the logical solution is to increase efficiency by standardizing course materials. Once lectures are submitted to administrators and posted on webpages, these materials can be merchandized to other universities. Better yet, the course-writing can be outsourced on contract to non-university staff. By transferring control to administrators, the technology can be designed to discipline, deskill, and/or displace teachers' labour.

This approach changes the role of students, who become consumers of instructional commodities. Student–teacher relationships are reified as relationships between consumers and providers of things. This marginalizes any learning partnership between them as people.

Students readily become objects of market research. In Canada, for example, universities have been given royalty-free licences to Virtual U software in return for providing data on its use to the vendors. When students enrol in courses using this software, they are officially designated as 'experimental subjects', who grant permission for the vendor to receive all their 'computer-generated usage data' (Noble 1998).

A marketization model can be extended to sell courses, potentially to anyone in the world. Even third parties can sell new commodities which redefine educational skills. For example, by 1998 IBM's Lotus Corporation had already sold its Total Campus Option software to more than a million students. The company hoped that these future workers would thereby acquire 'a Lotus brand preference and relevant skills: the campus is the starting point of the sales cycle to the corporate world with whom we conduct business'. From these extreme cases of private universities and computer companies, we can better recognize more subtle forms in Europe.

EUROPE: ICT FOR FLEXIBLE LEARNING

The European education debate has been ideologically framed by the supposed imperatives of an 'information society'. This is conceptualized differently by 'market' models versus 'social' models of Europe (de Miranda and Kristiansen 2000). Dominant so far has been a neoliberal agenda of individual flexibilized learning for labour-market needs.

ERT Agenda

A neoliberal agenda has been promoted effectively by the European Round Table (ERT) of Industrialists since the 1980s (Balanyá *et al.* 2000). Its problem-definitions have been adopted by leading politicians and European Union officials. In particular the ERT has sought to change the form and content of education.

The ERT has regarded education and training as 'strategic investments vital for the future success of industry'. European business 'clearly requires an accelerated reform' of educational programmes. Unfortunately, however, 'industry has only a very weak influence over the programmes taught', and teachers 'have an insufficient understanding of the economic environment, business and the notion of profit' (ERT 1989; also ERT 1998).

They further argued: 'As industrialists, we believe that educators themselves should be free to conduct the same kind of internal searches for efficiency without interference or undue pressures exerted on them'. European industry has responded to globalization, but 'the world of education has been slow to respond', the authors lamented. As a remedy, 'partnerships should be formed between schools and local business' (ERT 1995).

More recently they have promoted Information and Communication Technology as an essential learning tool—in schools today and for work tomorrow. As the key virtues cited, ICT opens up the world of knowledge, allows individual enquiry, and powerfully motivates learning (ERT 1997). Also important is the link with 'life-long learning', necessary for Europeans to remain employable amidst the changes brought by global competition (ERT 1995, 1997, 1998).

ICT has a more specific role in the neoliberal business agenda, as critics have argued (Hatcher and Hirtt 1999). First, it facilitates the individualized and flexibilized learning which is required for the modern worker, who must become individually responsible for managing his/her own human capital in the workplace. Second, ICT diminishes the role of the teacher—a desirable change, for example, because teachers have 'an insufficient understanding' of business needs, and because their present role hinders 'internal searches for efficiency', as the ERT complained.

European Commission: Industry Needs

As President of the European Commission, Jacques Delors basically accepted a neoliberal diagnosis in his 1993 White Paper on 'Growth, Competitiveness, Employment'. Identifying the future as an 'information society', it counselled adaptation to inexorable competitive pressures: 'The pressure of the market-place is spreading and growing, obliging businesses to exploit every opportunity available to increase productivity and efficiency. Structural adaptability is becoming a major prerequisite for economic success', for example, by disseminating the skills essential for ICTs (CEC 1993: 92–3).

Moreover, the White Paper mandated the public authorities 'to remove the remaining regulatory obstacles to the development of new markets'. Although not specifically mentioning education, it welcomed marketization of public services:

The ordinary citizen can have access to 'public services' on an individual basis, and these will be invoiced on the basis of the use made of them. Transferring such services to the market-place will lead to new private-sector offers of services and numerous job-creation opportunities. (*ibid.*: 94)

Within that framework, European Commission documents and official speeches have put forward arguments similar to the ERT's. According to the chief of the Directorate-General which funds research, the ICT market is 'too weak and penalises our industry'. Therefore, support is necessary to 'give our market the dimension which our industry needs' (Cresson 1995). By using such language, society's needs are either ignored or else are equated with industry's needs.

Soon the supposed threat was made more explicit: 'It is doubtful if our continent will keep hold of the industrial place it has achieved in this new market of multimedia if our systems of education and training do not rapidly keep pace' (CEC 1996). For the solution, government must subsidize the European ICT industry.

At the Amsterdam Summit, national governments undertook to promote 'flexible labour markets', so that the EU can 'remain globally competitive'. Accordingly, the EU Council recommended 'a restrictive restructuring of public expenditures... to encourage investment in human capital, research and development, innovation and the infrastructure essential to competitiveness'. It encouraged 'training and life-long learning' in order to improve 'the employability of workers' (EU Presidency 1997).

Since then, official documents have promoted 'citizen education' for future workers to participate better in labour markets. They have foreseen and even welcomed a decline in the dominant role of educational institutions:

Even within the schools and colleges, the greater degree of individualisation of modes of learning—which are flexible and demand-led—can be considered as supplanting the formulas that are too heavy and dominated by the provider. It announces the consequent decline in the role of the teacher, which is also demonstrated by the development of new sources of learning, notably by the role of ICT and of human resources other than teachers. (CEC 1998)

Through such language, the empowerment of vendors and business partners is represented as greater freedom for students. A student–teacher learning relationship is potentially replaced by a consumer–producer relationship.

Further steps towards marketization appeared in the Bologna Declaration (1999), signed by twenty-nine European ministers of education, though outside any statutory framework. The Declaration was a set of measures to increase the international competitiveness and thus to enlarge the market share of the European higher education system. It undertook to create a European Higher Education Area as a means to promote citizens' mobility and employability; this could be achieved through 'greater compatibility and comparability' among curricula across countries. Although these measures could benefit some students, an implicit agenda is to standardize education as a global commodity. Exemplifying the EU's democratic deficit, moreover, the plan was drafted without involving student organizations (Oosterlynck 2001).

UK: THE UNIVERSITY AS A BORDERLESS BUSINESS

As the vanguard of the neoliberal project in Europe, the UK epitomizes pressure towards marketizing higher education. As academics there have found since the 1980s, many developments have 'eroded the protection from pressures to render their work more commensurable with the commodity form of value' (Wilmott 1995: 995).

The government has pressed for a substantial increase in student numbers, while providing little increase in funds. Under pressure from the Research Assessment Exercise, many university departments have shifted resources from teaching to research, while seeking more research funds from industry. For both those reasons, there have been less resources for student–teacher contact, and thus greater pressure to standardize curricula and assessment criteria. Similar pressures come from formal assessment exercises which require teachers to produce explicit 'learning aims and outcomes'.

Students have become more subject to accountancy versions of educational values. In the late 1990s the government abolished maintenance grants for most students and introduced tuition fees. As these changes led students into greater debt than before, they felt under pressure to choose academic programmes which would lead to more highly-paid jobs, rather than arts or humanities programmes, for example.

Student protests have opposed tuition fees, while linking this burden to more general dependence upon private finance: 'In providing this funding, business is assuming more direct and indirect control of our education system . . . . Students should not be forced to choose on the basis of what [courses] businesses are prepared to make available', argues the Campaign for Free Education (CFE 2000).

In some ways, the problem is even worse: namely, that universities themselves act more like businesses. Their marketization agendas link two neoliberal meanings of flexibility. First, student-customers (or their business sponsors) seek learning for flexible adaptation to labour-market needs, for example, through skills expected to increase productivity. Second, global competitors flexibly design and sell courses according to consumer demand, so universities must anticipate and counter such competition and support the 'world education market' (Nunn 2002).

Just-in-time Learning

For many years, such a competitive threat has been linked with ICTs. 'In due course, just-in-time electronic education, delivered to your living room by commercial companies, will undermine the most hallowed names in higher education' (Michael Prowse, *Financial Times*, 20.11.95). As an Australian vice-chancellor warned his UK counterparts, non-universities will provide electronic courses, offer degrees and not bother with being accredited, 'thus competing with universities in the education market' (quoted in McLeod 2000).

To protect themselves, while of course extending consumer opportunity, universities must commodify educational goods as individual learning packages. The London School of Economics has founded two electronic-education ventures. According to the chairman of UNext.com, 'We are developing just-in-time interactive learning because we believe that employed adults throughout the world have a hunger for education'. Free markets are ideally suited to the task of creating 'on-line learning solutions', which require a large amount of financial and human capital, he argues (Rosenfeld 2000).

Perhaps taking that logic further, one neoliberal militant has declared: 'Higher education is now a no-value commodity unrelated to real costs and no basis whatsoever for an effective and efficient business . . . the future is always best left in the hands of discerning customers close to the marketplace' (Hills 1999). Again, university corporatization is represented as greater freedom for the student as customer.

According to the UK's committee of university executives, the solution is to abolish borders between the university and business, as well as those between domestic and international 'markets' for educational goods. The executives promote internet-based delivery as a key means to become a 'borderless business'. Going further than the ERT diagnosis, they describe the university as already a business, albeit a deficient one which must be fixed according to corporate principles:

[Universities must create] new systems of operation which disaggregate function, increase specialisation and where outsourcing is a strong feature. It follows that universities need

to give priority to identifying their core business, niche opportunities and specialist functions . . . . (e.g.) consistent delivery through a customer-focused approach to education and
training; a widening of educational values to include company certification, learning outcomes relevant to the workplace, personal development and flexibility.   (CVCP & HEFCE
2000)

According to the executives' chief, Prof. Howard Newby, universities 'are
an integral part of the knowledge-based economy', thus echoing a neoliberal
paradigm. 'At present we seem to be rather like the British motor industry in
the 1960s—on the brink of participating in a global market, but poorly organised to take advantage of the opportunities available'. He identifies changes in
undergraduate delivery: from a 'just-in-case' general intellectual training, to a
more flexible 'just-in-time' ethos, and then to 'just-for-you' forms of learning
(Newby 1999).

Newby emphasizes opportunities as much as threats. In his account, critical
analytical skills are to be supplanted by life-long adjustment to the needs of a
flexibilized labour market. Extending a business logic, he advocates government
investment in higher education as 'a sector which is absolutely central to the
development of the UK as a prosperous and competitive knowledge-based economy'. He also advocates performance-related pay in order to modernize 'our
human resources management'. Thus accountability is reduced to performance
indicators which throw teachers into competition with each other.

e-University

Complementing that scenario, university executives cite threats from foreign
competitors to justify internet-based courses. According to sponsors of the
electronic-University, 'The project is designed to give UK higher education the
capacity to compete globally with the major virtual and corporate universities
being developed in the United States and elsewhere'. The preliminary business
model 'recommended that pedagogic support should be embedded within learning materials, and that supplementary on-line support might be negotiated for
individual students at a price'. This proposal generated debate about what types
of social interaction must be designed into the product in order to find customers
(see detail in HEFCE 2001).

In planning an e-University, some educators emphasize that high quality cannot be achieved at low cost. Partly for this reason, many UK universities formed
a holding company for jointly evaluating and selecting course material, so that
they do not compete among themselves for students. At the same time, commercial criteria may play a role in defining students as 'market demand' for some
types of content rather than others. A private-sector partner will handle 'the
commercial aspects of content procurement to match demand', among other
aspects (McLeod 2000). It aims to 'offer high brand value' for a 'global professional workforce' and 'corporate universites wishing to access a fast growing

international market for higher education and training' (cited in Nunn 2002). Such arrangements may readily conflate the needs of business and society, for example, through 'flexible learning' for the labour market.

Electronic media have a double-edged potential. They can broaden access to quality material and social networks which enhance critical citizenship, but only if the design emphasizes resources for creative student–teacher and student–student interaction. Given the political will, argues one academic, scholarly values 'may survive in the multi-media environment. But the tension between digitized means and these values may sharpen as learning becomes more commodified' (Harris 2000). The effect on education depends on the social design of electronic media and the social forces which shape them.

CONCLUSION: WHAT GLOBAL COUNTER-STRATEGIES?

In order to develop effective counter-strategies, it is necessary to analyse the various forms of marketization and their links. While only some forms extend commodity exchange, they all extend accountancy criteria for valuing education and its human products. The 'investment' metaphor readily becomes literal. Universities and their staff may be held accountable for delivering the dividends in measurable terms (Demeritt 2000: 309).

Marketization Strategies

Marketization strategies should be understood as both ideological and material at the same time. As analysed above, here are some key features.

1. *Efficiency as progress*   In neoliberal ideology, employment insecurity is attributed to a deficiency of 'human capital' appropriate for the 'information society'. This problem is cited to justify curricula for adapting students to labour-market needs. Educational 'reforms' are presented as universal progress on grounds that they enhance efficiency, extend access, flexibly customize the content for individual needs, facilitate learning through ICT, provide account-ability to students and society, yield a better return on state investment, etc. These benefits are to be measured according to 'human capital' criteria, or even according to money transactions. Whether they are literal or metaphor-ical, accountancy methods define the efficiency of educational progress, thus naturalizing marketization.

2. *Commodification*   Prospective students are represented as custom-ers/markets in order to justify commodifying educational services. Knowledge becomes a product for individual students to consume, rather than a collabor-ative process for students and teachers. Individualized learning both promotes and naturalizes life-long re-skilling for a flexibilized, fragmented, insecure labour market. By standardizing course materials, moreover, administrators can reduce

teachers to software-writers or even replace them with subcontractors. Through ICT, neoliberal agendas take the apparently neutral form of greater access and flexible delivery. In all these ways, student–teacher relations are reified as relations between things, for example, between consumers and providers of software.

3. *Neoliberal Globalization*   A global competitive threat and opportunity is invoked to justify commodifying all institutional arrangements. People are actively linked around the world through new market relations—as business partners, competitors, patrons, clients, customers, assessor-consultants, etc. This neoliberal internationalism is promoted within and across countries. As SAP conditionalities forcibly marketize and standardize higher education in Third World countries, people there may become more willing customers for instructional commodities elsewhere, for example, through distance education. Perhaps as a self-fulfilling prophecy, this marketization intensifies (or even creates) the competitive pressures from which universities needed protection in the first place.[4] Moreover, if Western academics fill gaps left by SAPs in Third world countries, then they may collude in re-colonising the curriculum there, unless they ally with local people who promote alternative agendas.

Counter-strategies

In response, what counter-strategies are being developed? Students and teachers have opposed plans to replace human contact with software products, while demanding educational access as a right rather than a commodity. As a defensive approach, teachers' organizations have re-asserted their professional prerogatives as experts in educational content, and they have defended academic freedom against state interference disguised as societal 'responsibilities'.

However, research questions or curricula cannot be entirely autonomous from the wider struggle over public resources, ruling ideologies, and class interests. More imaginative efforts will be needed to counter the neoliberal agenda. In particular:

1. *Demonstrating links among neoliberal forms*   Marketization measures extend far beyond formal requirements of SAPs. The pressures take more subtle forms—for example, ideological language, funding priorities, public–private partnerships, tuition fees, cost-benefit analysis, performance indicators,

---

[4] Another potential weapon is the General Agreement on Trade and Services (GATS), which dates from the founding of the WTO in 1994. In the area of service delivery, GATS aims to remove any restrictions and internal government regulations that are regarded as 'barriers to trade' (Lucas 1999; WDM 1999; Hirtt 2000; Rikowski 2001). Some Western governments have suggested that trade liberalization would help their own universities to penetrate foreign markets. Some academic managers have favourably linked this aim with internet-based courses (e.g. Newby 2001). Although that may be true in some cases, the fundamental aims are for multinational capital to colonize education, to influence the curriculum and to appropriate public subsidies. Marketization measures anywhere will provide encouragement and models for GATS.

curriculum changes, new technology—which often conceal the ultimate implications. Critics need to demonstrate how all these aspects are linked, how they change the content of academic work and learning, and how they arise from efforts to discipline labour for capital, as part of a global agenda.

2. *Linking resistances across constituencies and places* Neoliberal strategies are turning us all into fragments of a business plan, for example, competitors, partners, customers, etc. In response, we need an international network for several purposes: to link all targets of the neoliberal attack worldwide, to circulate analyses of anti-marketization struggles, to enhance solidarity efforts, and to turn ourselves into collective subjects of resistance and learning for different futures. Such networks need to span all relevant constituencies (teachers, students, NGOs), as well as the geographical regions which are supposedly competing with each other.

3. *De-reifying Information and Communication Technology* ICTs can be designed in ways which either facilitate a marketization agenda, for example, by reifying student–teacher relations—or else hinder marketization, for example, by enhancing critical debate among students and with teachers. In that vein, we need to distinguish between various potential designs for ICT, in order to de-reify them as social relations. For example, Computer-Supported Cooperative Learning (CSCL) techniques are being developed to retain the collective aspects of learning at a distance. Although the internet is widely used for distributing critical analyses, we need to ensure that these analyses are included and used imaginatively in accredited courses.

4. *Developing alternatives* It is inadequate simply to oppose marketization or to counterpose whatever existed beforehand. Resistance would be strengthened by developing alternative pedagogies which enhance critical citizenship, cultural enrichment and social enjoyment through learning. These efforts could also stimulate debate over how to define our collective problems and aspirations, beyond making our labour more readily exploitable.[5] In such ways, academic freedom can be linked with public debate over potential and desirable futures.

REFERENCES

Agre, P. E. (1999) 'The distances of education', *Academe*, 85(5): 37–41, also at http://dlis.gseis.ucla.edu/pagre/
—— (2000) 'Commodity and community: institutional design for the networked university' *Planning for Higher Education*, 29(2): 5–14, also at http://dlis.gseis.ucla.edu/pagre/
Ainley, P. and Bailey, B. (1997) *The Business of Learning: Staff and Student Experiences of Further Education in the 1990s*. London: Cassell.
Balanyá, Belén, *et al.* (2000) *Europe Inc.: Regional & Global Restructuring and the Rise of Corporate Power*. London: Pluto Press (co-authored by Ann Doherty, Olivier

---

[5] See for example Hill 1999; McLaren 2000; Rikowski 2001.

Hoedeman, Adam Ma'anit, and Erik Wesselius; see Corporate European Observatory, http://www.xs4all.nl/~ceo).

Bologna Declaration (1999) Joint Declaration of the European Ministers of Education, published by the Association of European Universities, <http://www.esib.org/prague/documents/bologna_declaration.htm>, commentary at <http://www.crue.upm.es/eurec/bolognaexplanation.htm>

CAFA (1995–99) *Campaign for Academic Freedom in Africa* bulletin, email caffentz@usm.maine.edu, Dinavalli@aol.com

CAUT (1998*a*) 'World Bank promotes its agenda in Paris', Canadian AUT webpage, http://www.caut.ca/English/Bulletin/98_nov/lead.htm

CEC (1993) 'Growth, competitiveness, employment: the challenges and ways forward into the 21st century', *Bulletin of the European Communities*, supplement 6/93. Brussels: Commission of the European Communities.

——(1996) 'Accomplishing Europe through education and training'. Brussels: Commission of the European Communities, http://europa.eu.int/comm/education/reflex/en/homeen.html

——(1998) 'Education and active citizenship in the European Union', http://europa.eu.int/comm/education/citizen/citiz-en.html

CFE (2000) 'Winning the arguments: a briefing by the Campaign for Free Education', http://members.xoom.com/nus_cfe, email cfe@gn.apc.org

Cresson, E. (1995) Speech on Socrates programme, Tours, 3 March.

CVCP & HEFCE (2000) *The Business of Higher Education: UK Perspectives.* London: Committee of Vice-Chancellors and Principals, now Universities UK, http://www.universitiesuk.ac.uk/; Bristol: Higher Education Funding Council for England, http://www.hefce.ac.uk

de Miranda, A. and Kristiansen, M. (2000) 'Technological determinism and ideology: the European Union and the Information Society', paper at POSTI 3 conference, http://www.esst.uio.no/posti/workshops/miranda.html

Demeritt, D. (2000) 'The new social contract for science: accountability, relevance, and value in US and UK science and research policy', *Antipode*, 32(3): 308–29.

Dutton, W. (ed.) (1996) *Information and Communication Technologies: Visions and Realities.* Oxford: Oxford University Press.

ERT (1989) *Education and Competence in Europe.* Brussels: European Round Table of Industrialists, <http://www.ert.be>

——(1995) *Education for Europeans: Towards the Learning Society.* Brussels: European Round Table of Industrialists, <http://www.ert.be>

——(1997) *Investing in Knowledge: The Integration of Technology in European Education.* Brussels: European Round Table of Industrialists, <http://www.ert.be>

——(1998) *Job Creation and Competitiveness through Innovation.* Brussels: European Round Table of Industrialists, <http://www.ert.be>

EU Presidency (1997) Presidency Conclusions from the Amsterdam Summit, SN 150/97, Annex, pp. 10–13.

Evans, G. R. (2001) 'The integrity of UK academic research under commercial threat', *Science as Culture*, 10(1): 97–111.

Federici, S., Caffentzis, G., and Alidou, O. (eds) (2000) *A Thousand Flowers: Social Struggles Against Structural Adjustment in African Universities.* Trenton, NJ/Asmara: Africa World Press.

Fine, B. (2000) *Social Theory and Social Capital*. London: Routledge.

FGS (2000) *Prague 2000: Why We Need to Decommission the IMF and the World Bank*. Bangkok: Focus on the Global South, <www.focusweb.org>

Garnham, N. (2000) ' "Information Society" as theory or ideology', *Information, Communication & Society*, 3(2): 139–52.

Gottschalk, P. (1998) 'Cross-national differences in the rise of earnings inequality: market and institutional factors', *Review of Economics and Statistics*, 80: 489–503.

Harris, M. (2000) 'HE of the future', *AUTLOOK*, 215: 10–11. London: Assn of University Teachers, <http://www.aut.org.uk>

Harvey, D. (1998) 'University, Inc.', *Atlantic Monthly*, October, http://www.theatlantic.com/issues/98oct/ruins.htm

Harvie, D. (2000) 'Alienation, class and enclosure in UK universities', *Capital & Class*, 71: 103–32.

Hatcher, R. and Hirtt, N. (1999) 'The business agenda behind Labour's education policy', in *Business Business Business: New Labour's Education Policy*, pp. 12–23, London: Tufnell Press, <http://www.tpress.free-online.co.uk/hillpubs.html>, see also <http://users.skynet.be/aped>

HEFCE (2001) E-university press releases, www.hefce.ac.uk/partners/euniv/

Hill, D. (1999) *New Labour and Education: Policy, Ideology and the Third Way*. London: Tufnell Press, <www.tpress.free-online.co.uk/index.html>

Hills, Sir Graham (1999) 'The university of the future', in M.Thorne (ed.) *Universities of the Future*. London: (Cabinet) Office of Science and Technology.

Hirtt, N. (2000) 'The "Millennium Round" and the liberalisation of the education market', *Education and Social Justice*, 2(2): 12–18.

IMF (2000) *Globalisation: Threat or Opportunity?* Washington, DC: International Monetary Fund.

Johnston, R. (1999) 'Beyond flexibility: issues and implications for higher education', *Higher Education Review*, 32: 55–67.

Johnstone, D. Bruce, Arora, A., and Experton, W. (1998) *The Financing and Management of Higher Education: A Status Report on Worldwide Reforms*. Washington, DC: World Bank, Departmental Working Paper, http://www-wds.worldbank.org

Joint WB/UNESCO Task Force on Higher Education and Society (2000) *Higher Education in Developing Countries: Peril and Promise*, Washington, DC/Paris: World Bank, <http://www.worldbank.org/html/extpb/abshtml/14630.htm>

Klausenitzer, J. (2000) 'The World Bank and education', *Education and Social Justice*, 2(3): 37–8, 59.

Lucas, C. (1999) *Watchful in Seattle*, http://www.greenparty.org.uk/globalisation

Marcuse, H. (1978) 'Industrialization and capitalism in the work of Max Weber', in *Negations: Essays in Critical Theory*, pp. 201–26. Boston: Beacon Press; reprinted in London: Free Association Books, 1988.

McLaren, P. (2000) *Che Guevara, Paulo Freire, and the Pedagogy of Revolution*. Lanham, Maryland: Rowman & Littlefield.

McLeod, D. (2000) 'Clever business', *The Guardian* Education section, 28 November.

Marx, K. (1976) *Capital*. Vol. 1. London: Penguin (especially 'The fetishism of the commodity and its secret', pp. 163–77).

Monbiot, G. (2000) *Captive State: The Corporate Takeover of Britain*. London: Macmillan.

Moore, M. (1999) 'The future of international trade in services', <http://www.wto.org/wto/speeches/mm6.htm>

Newby, H. (1999) 'Some possible futures for higher education', http://www.universitiesuk.ac.uk

—— (2001) 'Home and away—national and international perspectives on university collaborations', speech at conference on 'Co-operation and collaboration: promoting strategic alliances in higher education', 23 January.

Newman, R. and Johnson, F. (1999) 'Sites for power and knowledge? Towards a critique of the virtual university', *British Journal of Sociology of Education*, 20(1): 79–88.

Noble, D. (1998) 'Digital diploma mills: the automation of higher education', *Monthly Review*, 49(9): 38–52; also in *Science as Culture*, 7(3): 355–68; other material available at <http://thecity.sfsu.edu/~eisman/digital.diplomas.html>, <www.communication.ucsd.edu\dl\ddm2.html>

Nunn, A. (2002) 'GATS, higher education and "knowledge-based restructuring" in the UK', *Education and Social Justice*, 4(1): 32–43.

Oosterlynck, S. (2001) 'The Bologna Declaration: towards the construction of an European Higher Education Market?', *Education and Social Justice*, 3(2): 24, email stijn_oost@yahoo.com

Ovetz, R. (1996) 'Turning resistance into rebellion: student struggles and the global entrepreneurialization of the universities', *Capital & Class*, 58: 113–52.

Passerini, K. and Granger, M. (2000) 'A developmental model for distance learning using the Internet', *Computers & Education*, 34: 1–15.

Rikowski, G. (2001) *The Battle in Seattle: Its Significance for Education*. London: Tufnell Press, <http://www.tpress.free-online.co.uk/seattle.html>

Robins, K. and Webster, F. (1985) 'New technology and the critique of political economy', in L. Levidow and R.M. Young (eds) *Science, Technology and the Labour Process: Marxist Studies*. Vol. 2. pp. 9–48, London: Free Association Books.

—— —— (1999) *Times of the Technoculture: From the Information Society to the Virtual Life*. London: Routledge.

Rose, N. (1999) *Powers of Freedom: Reframing Political Thought*. London: CUP.

Rosenfeld, A. (2000) 'The internet learning dream', *LSE Magazine*, Winter: 4–5.

Slaughter, S. and Leslie, L.L (1997) *Academic Capitalism: Politics, Policies and the Entrepreneurial University*. Baltimore, MD: Johns Hopkins University Press.

Smith, A. and Webster, F. (eds) (1997) *The Postmodern University? Contested Visions of Higher Education in Society*. Buckingham: Open University Press.

Veblen, T. (1918) *Higher Learning in America: A Memorandum on the Conduct of Universities by Business Men*. New York: Hill and Wang.

Willmott, H. (1995) 'Managing the academics: commodification and control in the development of university education in the UK', *Human Relations*, 48(9): 993–1027.

Winner, L. (1998) 'Report from the Digital Diploma Mills Conference', *Science as Culture*, 7(3): 369–77, text available at http://www.oreilly.com/~stevet/netfuture/, conference details available at <http://thecity.sfsu.edu/~eisman/digital.diplomas.html>

WDM (1999) <http://www.wdm.org.uk/cambriefs/WTO/GATS.htm>

12

Digital Discourses, OnLine Classes, Electronic Documents: Developing New University Technocultures*

Timothy W. Luke

PROLOGUE: CYBERSPACE AS ENVIRONMENT

To the extent that individuals and groups now choose, or are coerced, to communicate, keep accounts, publish, buy products, work, access documents, or learn online in computer networks, the digital domain inescapably is becoming a vital new venue for the conduct of everyday life. At the same time, however, cyberspace today is also evolving into a heteronomous global anarchy. In each one of its many proliferating layers of functionality, new would-be authorities are competing to control its uses in what is still essentially a self-help system of platform wars, chip races, and operating system alliances.

Dizard characterizes the Internet's networks of networks as the 'Meganet', or,

... a powerful but enigmatic engine of change, the biggest and most complex machine in human history. Its effects are paradoxically universal and parochial, uniting and dividing, constructive and destructive. It will create a new communications culture, overlaid on old ethnic, economic, religious, and national patterns and attitudes. An electronic environment is evolving in which old guideposts are submerged in a stream of bits and bytes exchanging a bewildering variety of messages among billions of individuals (Dizard 1997: 14).

Unlike many overwrought celebrations of cyberspace, his analysis at least highlights how the machinic infrastructure of boxes and wires, cables and satellites, servers and relays, that underpin the computer networks are, in turn, generating a new technoculture.

* This paper was originally presented at Learning On Line '98: Building the Virtual University, Hotel Roanoke, Roanoke, VA, 18–21 June 1998.

The expansive telemetries of the digital domain are displacing, subsuming, and reshaping the material markets of closed territorialities in the real world (Deibert 1997). While the name is anachronistic, this 'wired world' plainly is, as one enthusiast asserts, much more than just its boxes and wires:

It is an entirely new product space. It is an entirely new market space. The Internet product space, combined with the World Wide Web market space, establishes one of the most powerful platforms ever contrived for doing business. The Wired World is to the friction-free economy what the interstate highway system, air cargo system, and telephone/fax system were to the old economy   (Lewis 1997: 115).

Even though such enthusiasts continue to effuse over 'a near-infinite supply of products, services, and ideas' that this friction-free economy apparently produces at 'a near-zero cost' (Lewis 1997: 115), its modularization, specialization, and acceleration of many goods and services online actually is not generating an economy free of friction. Indeed, it is scorching many who feel its first effects.

Cyberspace cannot be dismissed as an ephemeral playground of electronic fantasies. Transnational businesses instead are turning it into a temporal environment in which important daily events are set and at which new social discourses are addressed (Cairncross 1997). Digital networks are becoming a basis for reimagining community (Anderson 1991), because they now materially surround individuals and groups as environments. They mediate economic forces, articulate political directives, and circulate social constraints as informational effects. Work is accomplished through cyberspace, culture is refashioned out of cyberspace, and power is transmitted within cyberspace. In these ways, as the digerati (Brockman 1996) assert, digital domains now operate as a primary scene of society and essential setting for the economy. So it is not at all surprising that many are seeking to put the Net to educational purposes to serve society as well as to find profit in the economy.

THE VIRGINIA TECH CYBERSCHOOL: BASIC FOUNDATIONS

To understand the significance of using computers to teach college and university courses, however, one should not fixate upon either the Net or the machines themselves. Shopworn humanist laments about chips and cables tripping up autonomous personal development in telematic tangles of electronic alienation utterly miss what is really happening: fundamental changes in the workings of human culture and communication technology. The acts and artifacts used to reproduce cultural understandings among specific social groups are changing profoundly: print discourses, face-to-face classes, paper documents are being displaced by digital discourses, online classes, electronic documents. The former will not entirely disappear, but so too can they not be counted upon to continue reigning unquestioned. The latter will never fully be perfected, but one cannot expect them to remain oddities.

Many misconstrue this change as a confrontation of humans with machines, but it is, in fact, the conflict between two different technocultures—one older and tied to mechanism, print, and corporal embodiment, another newer and wired into electronics, codes, and hyperreal telepresences. Building the virtual university is one piece of this new technoculture, just as the first founding of medieval universities articulated yet another technoculture tied to the scriptorium, lecture hall, and auditor. Even though they can throw much light upon each other, the struggle between these university technocultures also do not exhaust the entire range of profound structural change occurring within tertiary education with informationalization in the global economy and society.

This chapter seeks to place the virtual university with its many perils and prospects amidst the social conflicts being caused by these larger transformations. First, it aims to reveal why existing university practices are so difficult to change, and, second, it tries to suggest how some emergent technocultural values can lead more easily towards rapid change. Yet, it also worries about what sort of changes, and defined by whom in the larger society? Most importantly, however, it supports building a type of the virtual university as a supplement to existing tertiary institutions. Today's colleges and universities can leverage network technologies to create truly new learning communities and develop new learned discourses, rather than turning online learning into a substitute for present-day universities. Those projects of substitution represent a misguided effort to commodify what universities have always done, but what also should never be sold.

The Cyberschool faculty in the College of Arts and Sciences at Virginia Tech have worked as a loosely organized, bottom-up network of individual scholars (Luke 2000). While operating with new technology, their activities illustrate, once again, how technology is not, as many believe, 'just technology'. It also is culture, economics, and politics; and, when technology is combined with education, it can become even more culturally unstable, economically demanding, and politically threatening. On one side, many exponents of technologically-enhanced teaching envision it as leading to new discursive formations, intellectual conventions, and scientific practices. On the other side, many opponents regard any effort taken towards effecting such change as malformations, unconventionalities, and malpractices. Along with their individual attempts, then, to transform their own courses, the Cyberschool faculty also have operated as an on-campus advocacy organization, or interdepartmental social movement to further publicize and popularize the use of computer-mediated communication in university instruction. This is very important because, despite what many futurists claim, technology does nothing on its own. Technically-driven change is neither automatic nor easy; and, every apparent technological innovation usually is hobbled by significant anti-technological resistance. Yet, the myths that most people share about machines make it quite difficult to think outside of the box when it comes to technology. If nothing else, the experiences of the Cyberschool faculty at Virginia Tech have exposed the emptiness of these myths as these scholars have set about constructing the basic foundations for one virtual university.

Virginia Tech began building its virtual campus in 1993 with the launch of the Faculty Development Initiative (Luke 2000). An experiment in the implementation of distributed computing, the FDI put a new Apple desktop computer, a suite of applications, and nearly a week's worth of hands-on training into the hands of ordinary faculty with the hope that they, first, would quit using the old, expensive mainframe system and, second, might start playing around with the new personal computer in their teaching, research, and service. Without this first piece of almost accidental history, much less would have occurred on this one campus because it got computers out of the control of those who everyone once knew *should* have them—engineers, computer scientists, chemists—and into the possession of those who many thought, and maybe still think, do not need them—philosophers, political scientists, poets. Yet, once those who did not need or could not use personal computers got a hold of them, many things began to change rapidly, fundamentally, and unpredictably.

A small group of faculty in the College of Arts and Sciences was charged by a new Dean in 1993–94 to propose new strategies to break the credit-for-contact paradigm with digital technologies. This committee advanced a proposal to construct a 'virtual college' in November 1994 (Luke 1994) around a series of online courses, which became known as the work of the Virginia Tech Cyberschool. Because of the Blacksburg Electronic Village, students and faculty had the Internet access and technical skills to make this vision a reality in summer 1995, with the first Cyberschool classes. The university self-study of 1996–98 aimed at reimagining Virginia Tech to play upon its high technology strengths, including the enhancement of its online teaching capabilities. Totally online and complete MA degree programmes in physical education and political science went up on the WWW in 1996–97, and Virginia Tech OnLine—a full service virtual campus site—was activated in 1997–98. All graduate theses and dissertations were required to be archived as digital documents in 1997, and all entering students were required to own a personal computer in 1998.

Eight years after the first FDI cohort, Virginia Tech had scores of fully online classes up and running, hundreds of faculty participating in this grand rethinking of the university's affairs, and thousands of students trained and equipped to deal after graduation with the digital cultures of work, leisure, and public life that started burgeoning off-campus. Almost all of this change came from within the faculty ranks, but it was assisted significantly at every turn by a small cadre of dedicated technical specialists in the Office of Educational Technologies. Given the scope and depth of these moves toward a virtual university, the original pioneers at Virginia Tech broke out of the skunkworks box they occupied in 1993 or 1994 (Luke 2000). Indeed, the notion of a 'virtual university' continuously challenges, questions, or even threatens the daily operations of the 'material university' at Virginia Tech in many fundamental ways. And, this collision of values and practices continues to be one of contradictory technocultures. As Lucinda Roy observes, these cultural conflicts require us 'to assess what we've learned and start anew with some new approaches' (Young 1998c: A24). Consequently, this analysis is based upon nearly ten years of experience with administrators and faculty who supported the Virginia Tech Cyberschool. These remarks outline, first, what we have learned at Virginia Tech, and, second, some thoughts about these new approaches in a broader national context.

POWER/KNOWLEDGE AND DIGITALIZATION

As Foucault suggests, the modernization project lies at the heart of all present-day disciplinary systems of authority and control, but this project is also always contested, incomplete, and ongoing rather than accepted, complete, and over with. He also indicates how the economic take-off of Western industrial growth saw 'the traditional, ritual, costly, violent forms of power' exercised by traditional sovereign authorities in corporal forms of command supplanted by 'a subtle, calculated technology of subjection' (Foucault 1979: 221) managed by modern professional-technical experts through many more non-corporal forms of control. To understand the workings of modern economies and societies, 'the two processes—the accumulation of men and the accumulation of capital—cannot be separated; it would not have been possible to solve the problem of the accumulation of men without the growth of an apparatus of production capable of both sustaining them and using them; conversely, the techniques that made the cumulative multiciplity of men useful accelerated the accumulation of capital' (Foucault 1979: 221).

These relations cannot be ignored today in the much more reflexive modernization projects of informational enterprises, transnational capital, and neoliberal regimes. As Bowles and Gintis (1976: 11–17) assert, a 'correspondence principle' typically fuses many practices in the workplace and schooling for the political economy of contemporary society. Yet, a contradictory dynamic also plays itself out here. On the one hand, schools typically stabilize and protect modes of cultural instruction better suited to past systems of economy as they sustain cultural reproduction, while businesses, on the other hand, often innovate and undercut fixed modes of instruction in developing new systems of economy as they revolutionize economic production. The mode of instruction packs many ancient traditions in its extensive baggage, but it also is forced to carry all of this on quicker, more frequent trips to destinations where they are not needed, not wanted, and not appreciated.

The Corporal Basis of Teaching

On one level, as Ed Neal (1998: B4) claims, many university faculty do have 'a healthy skepticism' about the efficacy of electronic technology in teaching. On another level, however, most educators also cannot break with traditional modes of authority as they cling to their everyday procedures of professorial labour.

Foucault's (1979: 3–69) sense of the coercive juridical power wielded by traditional sovereigns survives in the status and role of university level 'professing'. And, it is very clear that a lot of resistance to the virtual campus, which also faced the Virginia Tech Cyberschool, comes from those among the professorate who are anxious about losing this power. In many ways, there still is a considerable measure of petty personal sovereignty attached to the professorial role, which still conveys legitimacy to the learning derived from the old medieval lector/auditor relationships of the lecture hall. When and where the professor, and his/her disciplinary colleagues in each department, decide to supply their knowledge, this is the time and location at which students are called to appear. Like a prince or princess in his or her feudal court, the professor stands in front of and over the students working with a clear spatial display of superiority. These relations repeat themselves in the convening of examinations, arrangement of office hours, giving of grades, and provision of written recommendations for students in any given class. This much derided 'sage on the stage' model of education is a stable recapitulation within a modern institution of older feudal practices drawn from these ancient systems of personal sovereignty. Its legitimacy and authenticity is tied to command, control, communication, and intelligence over bodies: it is a regime of/or corporal instruction. When asked, professors inevitably will refer to embodied interactions as the benchmark of authentic learning. Professors will say that they must see the students, have them appear physically in seminar rooms and offices, observe them directly doing seat time in lecture halls, make them sit for examinations, and watch them perform in labs in order to attest to their learning. Attendance in class sitting below the lectern, like appearance in court kneeling before the throne, is tacitly the corporal sign of submission to professorial authority as well as the physical validation of whatever student learning is taking place in the presence of professorial power/knowledge. Successful corporal instruction inculcates real knowledge for these authorities, because it develops, if nothing else, *Sitzfleisch*.

As petty as this seems, many educators cannot forsake these small shreds of personal sovereignty. For them, it is a remarkable source of individual empowerment, professional identity, and vocational legitimacy that in their eyes ought not to be abridged in any way, particularly those that interpose computer-mediated communications between teachers and learners. Becoming, as the standard tag line suggests, 'a guide on the side' represents to them an inauthentic form of education. Why? Mostly because it can be a profound loss of personal sovereignty as well as a loss of corporal control over the student body. The legitimation question is paramount: if we do not see them, if they do not come to class, to labs, to our offices, may be even to campus, then how do we know that they are learning, studying, or even doing the work?

The innate suspicion of professors about student dishonesty and indolence typically runs wild before the screens of online education. While these concerns are real, these same professors also almost totally ignore how students find clever means to evade their personal sovereignty in systems of corporal instruction. The most distance-creating form of distance education is the megalecture section of introductory courses in which hundreds or thousands of students sit through the tedium of old science, humanities, or business classes in stadium-style seating. Physical presence in the same room really guarantees, in and of itself, nothing unless and until this spectacle of professorial authority engages students in active learning. At times it has, but mostly it does not. Yet, it seems quite clear now that online education actually can require more student activity in learning, but this may jar the professor inasmuch it relies upon mostly non-corporeal and post-sovereign forms of educational practice. Professorial anxieties about online learning should instead centre more correctly upon the rapid intrusion of other more disciplinary forms of control being exerted over faculty in many ways rather than worrying about the diminution of their already compromised remnants of personal sovereignty (Foucault 1979: 195–288).

The corporeal quality of conventional higher education also is expressed in its assumptions about providing instruction through deeply-emplaced, on-supply, synchronous forms of practice. Online education's more disemplaced, on-demand, asynchronous practices do not require the same social interactions between bodies occupying the same real estate. This is always implied by contact institutions, and efforts to change this often proves highly disconcerting to both professors and students. Many believe that their professorial powers will not work unless and until the student body materializes on campus, in accord with the venerable agrarian calendar that once freed students from the fields to study through the fallow months following the harvest. And, many traditional students believe that they are not getting full value for their time and effort unless they submit to these time-honoured practices. The university is heavily embedded at special geographical sites in bricks-and-mortar buildings devoted to unique educational purposes, its faculties decide when and where they will supply their learned teachings to students physically assembled on campus, and material imparted directly to learners presumes their constant attendance in a physical presence. Higher education, like many other essentially carceral institutions, has relied upon this system of corporal instruction, and it follows closely on behind other even more corporal forms of teaching at the primary and secondary levels of education. To push purposely beyond corporal modes of engagement through telematics is a fundamental shock to this highly routinized pedagogical tradition.

F2F versus Online: A Platform War?

This confrontation of online courses with face-to-face (F2F) classes has sparked a great conflict in the academic world; yet, this controversy also enables one to see how much of struggle might be reinterpreted as a battle between different 'operating systems'. The presumption by anti-technological proponents of F2F traditional teaching is that their styles of professional operation are rooted in unmediated human contact, free from any technical contaminants, while online courses represent totally alienating submission to the cold calculi of computers without any meaningful human contact whatsoever. Unfortunately, these human(ist) (mis)readings of computer-mediated communication, on the one hand, fruitlessly collide, on the other hand, with technified celebrations of human/computer interactions as just another technology, which really is believed to be nothing new, even though it is thought to be qualitatively better.

Here new recognitions must be made. Traditional teaching in F2F classes is not pure unmediated human contact; these courses also unfold within, and because of, a complex collective of technologies. In fact, many commonplace criticisms of traditional university teaching implicitly target the drawbacks built into most of these technologies. First, a built environment of special purpose buildings shackles the F2F platform for education, channelling the conduct of teaching to single purpose spaces where students must sit and listen while professors mostly stand and talk. Corporal attendance and mental attentiveness are hard-wired expectations in the lecture/examination hall as a central processing technology of F2F classes, but this apparatus is also further supported by the associated technologies of dormitories, dining halls, stadia, and playing fields to sustain the student body as well as libraries, research labs, studios, and arts centres to develop the student mind. Second, technocultures of print discourse, oral argument, bureaucratic record keeping, literary interpretation, written examination, and degree granting mediate faculty–student interactions in a fashion that many have excoriated over the decades for cultivating passivity, sophistry, indifference, pedantry, irrelevance, and futility. Time-serving and rote-recapitulation of empty orthodoxies often are performed in F2F instruction, according to many, in exchange for degrees, but few effectively question these cycles of self-perpetuating delusions because they too want the union cards or lunch tickets represented by doing 'seat time' to take their degrees.

F2F teaching, however, persists, because it is a simple, resilient, and ubiquitous operating system. It is accepted almost universally as *the* technology of teaching, despite its many intrinsic flaws. Moreover, its qualities as an operating system also are now almost completely naturalized and virtually unquestioned, even though a particular technic with very certain quiddity constitute its fundamental functionality. If technology is 'know how', then many types of very stable know-hows make such F2F teaching at universities possible. It permeates everything that faculty and students both know and do. Yet, to assert that F2F teaching is uncontaminated by technology simply is too clever by half. Such claims, whether conscious or not, only mistake the contingent artifices of one operating system as being 'technology', while ignoring the comparable fixed verities in another now more-naturalized system of operations.

Online teaching is obviously an operating system, if only because it is mediated continuously through computer-operating systems. Even so, the tacit assumptions of its operations do not necessarily conform to the allegations laid against it by traditionalists. First, any built environment can promote alienating experiences, but so too can it possibly enhance communicative outcomes for human interaction. The emotional intensity and psychosocial diversity experienced in having online persona suggests that computer-mediated communications are not merely forms of distant dehumanized social disengagement. Second, the rhetorics of representation used in online communication can rival, if not surpass, those used to advance cultural, intellectual, and social messages in the built environments of contact institutions. In addition to text and graphics, online instruction can interweave audio, video, film, voice, and data through a single site to appeal to many different types of learning styles in ways that ordinary lectures, seminars, or labs conducted in a F2F style cannot. A much higher degree of active student participation is needed simply to navigate through online instructional sites, and the possibilities for team-based, collectively organized, and jointly created documents for/of learning are possible from many different points in ways that F2F contact teaching cannot easily approximate.

Given these practices, online education has not been warmly welcomed on many university campuses. Some resist it because it obviously will require massive new investments in rapidly changing expensive infrastructure. Others resist it because it forces them out of comfortable fixed routines as they adapt to demands from another medium grounded in less academic and more postliterate styles of interaction. Still others resist it because it interposes a complex machinic apparatus between teachers and learners. And, a few resist it because it demands a reallocation of their time and energies away from research to the troubling and taxing pursuits of instruction. Ultimately, however, it is opposed, because its practices undercut the personal sovereignty of professors.

Informationalization and Individualization

Online education often seems more *au courant*, because it articulates technologically and institutionally deeper structural changes in advanced industrial societies that are associated with greater individualization, increased personal choice, and lesser social solidarity. Still, it also cannot be disassociated from the changes that telematics have promoted in the workings of universities, the operations of many workplaces, the provisions of state-supported public goods, or the conventions of learned discourse. No discussion of online education should ignore its second and third order consequences in the economy and society by focusing solely on its first order of business in the academy. As Bowles and Gintis assert, there always is a powerful correspondence principle at play in the organization of instruction whose modes of delivery on campus are expected to prefigure practices off campus in the organization of production and its mode of labour. To discuss learning online, then, implies a broader investigation of the lessons those offline want such educational activities to anticipate, if not actually convey, in the mission of teaching.

The operational practices of online education mesh quite closely with today's de-concentration of collective solidarities and reorientation toward highly individualized life situations. What were the essentially fixed necessities of collective existence for economic class, political inequality, and social status in earlier forms of industrial society are being displaced by increasingly flexible options of personal choice in the contemporary development of informational society. As Beck asserts,

Individualization in this sense means that each person's biography is removed from given determinations and placed in his or her own hands, open and dependent on decisions. The proportion of life opportunities which are fundamentally closed to decision-making is decreasing and the proportion of the biography which is open and must be constructed personally is increasing. . . . In the individualized society the individual must therefore learn, on pain of permanent disadvantage, to conceive of himself or herself as the center of action, as the planning office with respect to his/her own biography, abilities, orientations, relationships and so on   (Beck 1992: 135).

Under these conditions of social reproduction, class distinctions persist; but, at the same time, they often lose significance as signs of social mobility. Instead, they are redefined as socially-aggregated outcomes of individual choices, they lead to flexible ever changing political coalitions, and they frequently resurface in sets of conflicts defined by ascribed traits like race, gender, and ethnicity.

Online education essentially is the organization of instruction around delivery systems and discursive modules that can be accessed by individuals from their laptop or desktop computers on demand. While small groups of students can collaborate in many different kinds of educational experiences, the basic target of most educational activities for online teaching is the individual. Indeed, highly individuated options are expected out of online instruction by individuals to fit seamlessly into and around the other clusters of choice their life histories gel within, as they develop socially and culturally over time. Inasmuch as their technical designers can foresee these new realities, many course sites presume entrance and exit into their lessons by individuals—discretely, asynchronously, flexibly, and unrestrictedly—in order to function. Narratives of national unity, stories of scholarly worth, and discussions of civilizational purpose can be entirely extraneous at such sites because individuals are seeking personal goals, vocational benefits, and individual ends that usually stand separate and apart from any traditional collective entity.

In complete conformity with global markets, online education can both isolate and standardize individuals in their life experience. The private sphere is not a realm of liberty apart from all environmental connections; it is instead a zone where 'the outside turned inside and made private, of conditions and decisions made elsewhere, in the television networks, the educational system, in firms, or the labor market . . . with general disregard of their private, biographical consequences' (Beck 1992: 133). Individual strings of choice are often threaded into and around loose collective institutions that foster joint dependency rather than real independence. Normality, however, is less and less institutionally planned, socially validated, and politically enforced.

Instead, the marketplace and labour assignments become the central organizing force of identity for many individuals, who are left assembling their lives out of a bevy of options in the sphere of school and work. 'The key to a livelihood,' as Beck asserts, 'lies in the labour market. Suitability for the labour market demands education. Anyone who is denied access to either of these faces social and material oblivion. Without the proper training, the situation is every bit as devastating as with training but without corresponding jobs' (Beck 1992: 133). Online education captures these currents in its mechanics. For the most part, it can be a quick, cheap, and effective way to turn inside deliberation into outside instruction, while bringing those with jobs (businesses) and those with training for jobs (would-be employees known as students) into a mutually satisfying equilibrium out in the market. The larger needs of corporate employers demanding a labour force can be matched with the smaller wants of individuals exercising their individual options without preparing everyone *en masse* with skills that private enterprise might not need *en bloc*.

A VIRTUAL UNIVERSITY OR VIRTUALLY A UNIVERSITY?

The Virginia Tech Cyberschool has had an interesting history, and its development enables one to see the close interconnections between digitalization and power/knowledge in technocultural clashes between F2F and online teaching. At the same time, Virginia Tech's Cyberschool is only one among the nearly one thousand online universities that *Forbes* has counted out on the WWW, and it is only one of the 999 other virtual university experiments that have been eclipsed by the hoop-la over the Western Governors University. Here the possibilities for online learning at the university level acquire some of their most interesting and insidious implications, which deserve further and much closer consideration.

A consortium of seventeen Western states under the auspices of the Western Governors Association (WGA) resolved in February 1996 to collaborate together in the creation of a 'virtual university'. This new entity, or the Western Governors University (WGU), aims to push beyond the liberal education of traditional degree programmes to 'enhance the marketplace for demonstrated competence through certification that is widely accepted by employers and traditional institutions of higher learning' by prototyping 'expected competencies' from any WGU course of study (Western Governors Association 1997). Most importantly, the WGU has intended to operate as a broker for 'multiple-source instructional inputs', whose acceptance for vending through the WGU will require 'an explicit statement of the competencies that should be achieved upon completion, as well as an indication of the assessment methods that will be employed to certify these competencies' (Western Governors Association 1997). Because the WGU must function in 'the telecommunications age', the WGA directs that 'flexibility and adaptability' be regarded as survival skills for individuals and institutions: 'This premise,' the WGA believes, 'is no less applicable to legal form, governance, organization, and structure than it is to technology and content' (Western Governors Association 1997).

Oddly enough, the Western Governors University was launched as the nation's most preeminent 'virtual university' at a Western Governors Association meeting during 1996 in Las Vegas, Nevada, the nation's foremost 'virtual city'. Pushed by Governor Michael O. Leavitt of Utah and Governor Roy Romer of Colorado, the WGU operates as a multistate combine, with its chief academic offices in Denver, its chief administrative offices in Salt Lake City, its main library support services in Albuquerque, and its basic registration and billing units in Pullman, Washington. Thus, the WGU was imagined to be a 'virtual corporation' created by an inter-state government consortium. Like most virtual corporations, the WGU headquarters are small, low-overhead offices that have been charged with the task of only setting quality control standards, fixing policy expectations, and developing governance rules. Real academic services, however, are outsourced from independent commercial vendors or provided locally by public institutions at many distributed sites as WGU 'franchises'. By undercutting the average annual student costs of $9,000 at a typical state university, the WGU serves non-traditional older students, traditional college students needing extra courses, employees seeking various sorts of retraining, and lifelong learners in the personal enrichment market. Competency-assessment, and not degrees, is the main measure of student success, but the WGU now offers a multi-track Associate of Arts degree (Western Governors University 1998).

The WGU, then, has few traditional collegiate forms. Its internal structures essentially are those of a shell. This is 'a matter of operational convenience and efficiency' to implement its 'degree-granting, licensed and accredited' missions without 'the creation of a substantial overhead component' (Western Governor Association 1997). By combining 'technologically-delivered educational programming' with a certainty of 'certification through competency-assessment', the design criteria of the WGU are those shared by mobile, transnational capital formations, only now put into an academic setting: market-oriented, independent, client-centred, degree-granting, accredited, competency-based, non-teaching, high-quality, cost-effective, quickly-initiated, and regional in form and substance. Rather than trying to do everything, like a comprehensive state institution or a culturally enriching private school, the WGU aims to be a flexible, reflexive, hollowed-out telematic junction for packaging/promoting/providing 'outsourced content' through a regionalized network of knowledge networks already operating on the local, state, national, or international level. Thus, as Governors Leavitt and Romer advocate, its greatest value-adding potential is to be centred on four discrete tasks in today's fast capitalist economy:

1. Creating broader markets for existing educational and assessment services rather than by creating an independent capacity to provide those services.

2. Fostering the development of new products and/or providers where unmet needs are identified and where sharing the costs of materials development and promotion is possible.

3. Utilizing incentive (market) rather than regulatory mechanisms to ensure the effective functioning of the WGU.

4. Working to remove barriers to interstate flows of educational activities and competency-based assessments (Western Governors Association 1997).

The bottomline here is 'the bottomline' as the market reckons it, or the neoliberal faith that 'the WGU can provide significant benefits to all of its constituent groups at a lower cost than current approaches' (Western Governors Association 1997).

The whole point of innovation for the WGU since its launch in 1996 has not been technological: it has instead been institutional, using technology and competition 'to break down the barriers of regulations, bureaucracies, tradition, and turf' (Western Governors Association 1997). And, this approach has attracted considerable corporate interests, including a large grant in February 1997 from the AT&T Foundation. As Rick Bailey, AT&T's law and government public affairs vice president and WGU Board of Trustee's member asserts, 'AT&T is committed to supporting projects that benefit education and serve the needs of the public . . . The Western Governors University is clearly such a project. It's a bold, "break the mold" approach to higher education in the western states' (Western Governors Association 1997). While the WGU features a few schools with established academic reputations, like the University of Hawaii, Washington State University, and Northern Arizona University, many of its members are much less distinguished, like Eastern New Mexico University, Colorado Electronic Community College, and Chadron State College (Nebraska), as sites of scholarly research or university-level teaching. Despite this obvious lack of solid, high-quality academic foundations, the WGU's development plans for the virtual university, even though the school has not yet served even 1,000 students, have acquired awesome mythic dimensions. Indeed, the WGU has exploited this bizarre fame in a canned Power Point demonstration on its websites, which begins with this screen: 'Western Governors University . . . at times, reputation precedes reality' (Western Governors Association 1997).

Critics of how higher education occurs on traditional campuses, like Governors Leavitt and Romer, fall prey to the fallacy of generalization, believing the resistance to change that they see in one state or at one institution is true of all other states and institutions. In fact, much of the innovation, as the Virginia Tech Cyberschool indicates, behind the deployment of computers in higher education begins first, and voluntarily so, on many different university campuses. Something else, then, is at work in criticisms like those from Governor Leavitt of Utah, namely, the cost-cutting agendas of neoliberalism in the political economy of post-Cold War welfare states.

If we can associate Indiana University, Colorado University, or North Carolina State University with the states that have taxed their citizens and businesses to support them, then the 'virtual university' being built by the WGU must be recognized as a very fitting artifact of the current neoliberal era. Instead of standing for a political community's vision of its self and society as a special site for civic *Bildung*, like the traditional university has always tried to do, the WGU is a creature of states that are virtually repudiating their sovereign mission in favour of franchising out their public authority to the private sector by facilitating the business ventures of big corporations. WGU, in turn, puts outside corporate and commercial providers as well as other sovereign state providers of educational services on a par with public universities from inside its home base states by submitting all these 'providers' to its competency regime of degree accreditation.

Even though it is a non-profit, private corporation, the WGU hopes to make money by brokering knowledge sources to learning clients—private individuals, corporate concerns, and other public entities. By 2006, or ten years after its inception, the WGU hopes to enroll 8,000 students in its competency-based degree programmes, or that market where states have traditionally supported public education, but it also wants to see 15,000 students in its job-skills-oriented certificate programmes, 30,000 students in corporate training programmes, and 42,000 students taking classes from other institutions—public and private, state and corporate, intro-WGU state and non-WGU state—to meet its business plan objectives (Blumenstyk 1998*a*: 21). The virtualization of state is readily apparent in these goals, which centre upon not the ultimate socialization of 18–23-year-olds but rather upon the job training of students over age 25.

The capability for online learning at Western Governors University is intriguing, but many critics mistake these technological bells-and-whistles as the real innovations of WGU. In fact, online learning already has been available at many other schools, including Virginia Tech, for nearly ten years. The bigger changes at Western Governors University are embedded in the institutional assumptions behind its operations and structures. Utah Governor Michael O. Leavitt, one of WGU's main architects, attacks the symbolic economy of 'academic credits' that underpins higher education, arguing these systems of valourization are antiquated, monopolistic, and irrational. Because the value of such education is tied to institutional prestige, its transportability is limited due to incommensurate transferability standards, and its worth is weighed only in the aggregate as pieces of completed degrees, Leavitt's analysis of higher education is simple—it is a 'kind of feudal system'—and his solutions for its modernization is direct—competition from 'the Internet, new institutions like the for-profit University of Phoenix.... A plethora of corporate-sponsored training programmes are creating vast opportunities for the kind of lifelong learning that many Americans now are seeking.... The market is driving it. People are demanding it' (Blumenstyk 1998*b*: A23). In turn, the WGU will create its own new system of academic knowledge units of value for easy exchange, common measurement, and permanent storage in a new 'kind of "currency"—the tests of competencies that will show whether the students have mastered the course material. . . . so that employers and other institutions can at least be assured of what the student knows' (Blumenstyk 1998*b*: A23).

Western Governors University has been about constructing a new type of educational centre, which essentially serves as a broker of knowledge between outsourced content providers and individual client learners whose joint copro-duction of learning is then vetted by a common new regime of accreditation grounded upon competency examinations. As Governor Leavitt suggests, the WGU will operate as

'a kind of New York Stock Exchange of technology-delivered courses.' He envisions a cata-logue with listings from hundreds of institutions, corporations, and publishers, giving students ready access to thousands of educational opportunities.   (Blumenstyk 1998*a*: A23)

While the WGU has pushed other regions toward this model, including the Southern Regional Electronic Campus, the R21 Alliance, Fathom, and the essen-tially dead California Virtual University, the dreams of the WGU's founders have not been fully realized.

Nonetheless, this model of higher education still has many devotees. Beneath it, the state could elect to end its financial support for public university sys-tems, seeing them as bastions of 'a feudal system' for outmoded guild privileges, and then shift its financial backing to systems of individual choice, giving stu-dents vouchers to spend where the marketplace and competency regime show the best education can be had. Beside it, the market could balloon for savvy public-supported or clever for-profit privately-backed institutes of higher learn-ing, building off of popular frustrations with high taxes, elitist universities, and declining degree values. And, behind it, business supposedly would find many more skilled workers faster, cheaper, and easier than it does now, and at a lower cost, as WGU-styled educational consortia reduce the need to pay for expensive public university systems. The real innovation of the WGU is this effort to create a new symbolic economy of academic achievement, moral economy of personal choice, and public economy of lower costs.

The WGU model of building a virtual university is unfortunate, because it pur-posely seems devoted to developing substitutes for traditional public and private universities by undercutting their missions of liberal education, civic socializa-tion, and universal enlightenment with narrowly-focused labour force training agendas. Instead of inviting traditional universities to reform themselves from within, the public sentiment behind the WGU pushes competitive marketplace pressures onto the university campus to compel academics to make change. This model may work, but it also might destroy many qualities of university life that have made it so innovative for the economy and society at large. Fortunately for now, the WGU lacks a great deal of credibility: it comes from the weakest, newest, and most powerless part of the US, or the Mountain West. Not one of its member institutions is considered a top-tier school in teaching or research, and only two small, regional state universities—Northern Arizona and Washington

State—have representatives on its governing board. In many ways, then, it remains more of a 'virtual junior college' than a virtual university.

Other states and traditional universities, which do not want to forsake their sovereign mission or historical roles, can, nonetheless at the same time, learn something from the WGU virtual university, and begin to adapt similar policies and programmes as a supplement to, instead of a substitute for, traditional modes of F2F education. These moves might add something new to existing styles of teaching, serve new constituencies of place-bound over-twenty-five students, and provide higher quality academic credits, degrees, or lessons to a changing marketplace before commercial providers make more inroads into this vitally important dimension of our collective life.

MORE MARKETS, MORE QUESTIONS

Most dimensions of life connected to economic production, as the WGU indicates, have been colonized and captured long ago by instrumental rationality and the logic of commodification. The world of work and circuits of consumption see competitive markets setting their exchange value, and defining, in turn, the practical standards for their business operations. Even so, there are spheres of existence still relatively untransformed by such forces, and most of them lie in the dimensions of cultural reproduction. While there are obvious exceptions to these rules, many people still believe that family life, religious faith, artistic work, national identity, and general education should not be subject to the same naked relations of modern buying and selling out in the marketplace. And, when such relations do occur, they often are associated with poor quality, bad taste or even fundamental immorality.

Strangely enough, however, distance education has been one area where these negative associations are often made, but not always and usually for the wrong reasons. Online teaching is a fast-growing distance education mode, but, as the WGU's plans show, it usually is pitched at 'mature' students beyond the typical 18–23-year-old market. Online teaching arguably is best suited for the lifelong-learning student, and the acceptance of it has increased as the proportion of these members of the student body has grown. In 1972, 28 per cent of college and university students were over twenty-five, a figure that rose to 34 per cent in 1980, and 41 per cent in 1994 (Gubernick and Ebeling 1997). Consequently, there was an explosion of distance learning in the 1990s. During 1993, *Peterson's College Guide* listed ninety-three schools with online courses available for enrollment. The 1997's edition tallied up 762 such institutions, and nearly a million college and university students were taking online courses as opposed to 13 million in traditional contact institutions (Gubernick and Ebeling 1997). By 2000, one in three American colleges and universities were offering an accredited degree online, while online enrollments were well over a million (Huffstutter and Fields 2000: 1).

Merely meeting these rising demands, however, is not what distance learning is about.

Distance Education as Market Thinking

As *Forbes* confidently asserts, 'Modern technology brings education to the students rather than forcing students to subsidize fancy campuses and feather bedding faculties' (Gubernick and Ebeling 1997: 3). Once liberated from such expensive sites of study, in turn, *Forbes* also believes students 'will willingly dispense with the beer drinking, dating, and fellowship' of on campus life, because 'the aim is to deliver a basic product at a reasonable price' (Gubernick and Ebeling 1997: 4). Here education as labour force training is being substituted for personal liberation and social cultivation in the assumption of delivering 'a basic product at a reasonable price.' Business wants it both ways. First, it knows higher education, as even the Education Commission of the States found, is one of the top two or three priorities of most political jurisdictions (Schmidt 1998: A38). Still, it does not want to pay to cover these social overhead costs, because tax avoidance serves the interest of its profits. And, second, it still needs a skilled workforce equipped with basic, reasonably priced education to run its firms and factories. Hence, it agrees with Milton Friedman that universities could dispense with athletics, research, and student services and provide cyberstudents a degree 'at a fraction of the cost of attending a traditional Ivy League college' (Gubernick and Ebeling 1997: 4). In turn, the upper crust can then send their offspring to expensive, contact institutions, like Princeton, Yale, or Harvard, to get the best education that F2F interaction can buy without interference from the working classes.

The capitulation of many higher education outlets to the marketplace leaves the original mission of modern universities hanging in limbo as state governors, university governing boards, and sometimes even the public, increasingly expect very different outcomes from a college education. The purposes of civic *Bildung* required by Alexander von Humboldt or the freedoms of liberal learning hoped for by Cardinal Newman are being trampled in the quest to retrain 'the labour force' to suit the corporate sector. As Governor Paul E. Patton of Kentucky, chair-elect of the Education Commission of the States, asserts with regard to college graduates, 'we have businesses demanding a product that, in many cases, they are not finding. ...It's not that we're doing a bad job. We're just not doing enough' (Schmidt 1998: A38). A recent survey of thirty-five governors by the Education Commission discovered that these chief executives believe most colleges and universities are unresponsive to state needs, faculty tenure should not be protected, and research that offers no clear benefit to the economy ought to be halted. Speaking about these issues with some apparent omniscience, Kay M. McClenny, the vice-president of the Education Commission, said the governors were drawing distinctions between academic research 'that is fundamentally important to society versus the stuff that is generated to promote tenure' (Schmidt 1998: A38).

In this zone of active antagonism to liberal education and academic freedom, the allegedly inefficient aspects of collegiate education are being redlined for sacrifice to create savings and improve services. Under the banner of accountability, higher education is being pushed into the service of the corporate sector. Economic productivity, consumer satisfaction, and growth promotion are now the *sine qua non* of effective university policies. And, to accelerate these market-building changes, greater marketization is being pushed upon university administrations and faculties. Indeed, 37 per cent of state governors agreed in the 1990s that Microsoft or Disney ought to compete with colleges and universities (Schmidt 1998: A38). All of the governors polled by the Education Commission of the States believed 'colleges should be held more accountable for meeting state, local, and regional needs, and nearly all thought it was important for states to link spending on colleges with institutional performance, put more emphasis on faculty productivity, give students incentives to pursue careers in certain fields, and reorganize sectors of education into a seamless system covering kindergarten through the first two years of college,' while, at the same time, helping to stimulate 'competition among higher-education institutions and between the field's private and public sectors, have colleges collaborate with businesses in developing their curricula, and integrate applied or on-the-job experiences into academic programs' (Schmidt 1998: A38).

This structural shift toward building the virtual university, however, releases some momentum at existing colleges and universities, pushing digital discursive tools and electronic documents into the everyday practices of teaching, departmental administration, and professional academic research. At Virginia Tech, all faculty are given new personal computers every few years in exchange for sitting with educational technologists in a series of two-, three-, or four-day workshops; at UCLA, the Instructional Enhancement Initiative is building web pages for every course at the university; and at the University of Florida all 42,000 of its students are required to have personal computers (McCollum 1998: A27–9; Young 1998: A29). These specific initiatives are illustrations of how shifts in university technocultures are being backed by institutional programmes to transfer new techniques and tools to those who need them to thrive in the emergent technoculture.

Yet, few realize how these are neither one-time expenditures nor finished projects. Instead, these strategic decisions are structural reorientations in the manner of professional work, the mode of communicating knowledge/information/wisdom, and the matriculation of students at American universities. Not all of the critics' charges are unwarranted, but the substantive managerial prejudices tipped in favour of business, the willingness to let private sector solutions rule simply because they are privately exercised, and the dangerous acceptance of businesses designing curricula are all marks of a simplistic ideology at work. In fact, there is little sign of any reasoned analysis of the facts.

The globalization of business over the past fifty years is not a story in which private entrepreneurs worried much about the civic life or moral autonomy of those they were selling to, buying from, or leaving behind in search of profit. Allowing business to set the standards for intellectual activity will quickly lead to liberal learning, individual autonomy, and cultural *Bildung* being written off as inefficient, unproductive, and wasteful. And, while graduates might be less ill-prepared for the labour force, they will be essentially unprepared for the rigours of their civic life or personal development during their days in the working class.

Naive Instrumentalism versus Paranoid Anti-commercialism

Worries about employment levels and job control at the virtual university are very valid concerns for professors, especially given all of this raw market rhetoric; but, it is not clear that technology *per se* is causing employment to be lost or personal autonomy in the workplace to be abridged. On the one hand, it is evident that tenure-track employment levels have been declining as university administrators hire more part-time and non-tenure-track professionals out of the swelling contingent labour force of PhD-holding workers. AAUP figures from 1995 indicate that the proportion of the professorate working on non-tenurable contracts rose from 19 per cent in 1975 to 28 per cent in 1995, while tenure-track contracts fell from 29 to 20 per cent in the same period (Wilson 1998: A12). Overall proportion of tenured professors held constant at 52 per cent in 1975 and 1995, but the number of non-tenure-track professors working full time nearly doubled from 1975 to 1995 as the number of full-time tenure-track professors fell 12 per cent (Wilson 1998: A12). Part-timers and non-tenure-track talent is estimated to be 42 per cent of all instructors nationwide in 1998, while this figure stood at only 22 per cent in 1970 (Wilson 1998: A12). On the other hand, these figures show that tenure-track employment has been eroding dangerously for nearly three decades. At this point, technological innovations cannot be blamed for causing this tendency. Still, the willingness to use part-time and tenure-track employees to save money also comes with a will to pressure them into utilizing these new technologies in their work. David L. Potter, provost at George Mason University, notes 'we get a lot of energy out of non-tenure track people', and 'these people come cheaper than a tenure-track hire' (Wilson 1998: A14). Because they work for less, have no job security, and are entitled to no academic freedom, these kinds of workers can be expected to adapt themselves to technology-intensive teaching in which they might merely tend software structures, contribute nothing creatively to the teaching mission, and conform to someone else's standardized curriculum.

The job control issue is one that cuts both ways with technologically enhanced teaching. At this juncture, before an extensive lock-in has had a chance to solidify, the first waves of innovators have tremendous opportunities to exercise extraordinary autonomy in a context of great ferment as they experiment with many radical changes in the academy. Prospects of big money to be made here still are mobilizing hardware, and software manufacturers. As Cisco Systems CEO, John Chambers, claims, 'the next big killer application for the Internet is going to be education. Education over the Internet is going to be so big it is going to make e-mail usage look like a rounding error' (Chambers 1999: A19). Once their development contracts and production cycles lock many universities into using their goods and services, there will be much less personal control by professors over their workplaces. Even now, existing forms of online teaching are constrained by strict licensing agreements, intellectual property rights, rigid copyright rules, incompatible machine platforms, spotty ISP services, and bloated equipment interfaces, all of which lessen individual creativity and freedom in teaching.

This question is particularly significant in the 1990s and 2000s because of the very hierarchical, top-down fashion in which most American universities are being managed. Quite often, the higher central administration at any university is staffed by people who do not teach, and may indeed have never taught. Consequently, virtually none of them have used digital teaching technologies, which have emerged for the most part only in the last five years, and only a few really understand what is involved in using them. Yet, these same administrators increasingly treat higher education as a business in which, as Mary Burgan, AAUP general secretary, says, 'you hire and fire at will' (Wilson 1998: A12). The stage, then, is set for people, like Wallace Loh, former dean of the College of Law at the University of Washington and now higher-education adviser to Washington's Governor, Gary Locke, to tout the 'brave new world of digital education' (Monaghan 1998a: 1). On this new terrain, Loh believes higher education should undergo, and rightly so in his mind, 'the same kind of rigorous reorganization that has taken place in health care-style in recent years' (Monaghan 1998b: A23). With new technologies, and amidst a managed care style *perestroika*, Loh believes faculty at Washington's public colleges and universities could accommodate another 20,000–80,000 students by the year 2020 without a massive new infusion of resources, because they would essentially lose their job control and professional autonomy: some could design course software, while others could teach or serve in traditional faculty roles' (Monaghan 1998b: A23). Faculty at the University of Washington, who do teach and many times use this technology, are, of course resisting Loh's vision, arguing it strives to 'carelessly echo corporate fads without taking into account the already downsized nature of the state's universities and colleges' (Monaghan 1998b: A26).

Loh's celebration of cybernetic flexibility leads him down the road of 'naive instrumentalism' as he touts the omnipotence of networks, claiming before the people of Washington state that 'where you live—even if you live in Forks or Zillah—won't be a barrier to learning, because technology will make both teachers and knowledge available worldwide. So you might take a course from a university in Japan or China or Belgium' (Monaghan 1998a: 3). Even without remembering how disastrous 'managed care' is proving for America's health-care industries, Loh's naivete here is considerable. He quite innocently equates more technology with more personal choice, additional market variety or greater instrumental control. The fact that technological availability itself can be a bar-rier, where you live often is purposely organized to be a barrier to many things, and worldwide access for a few is going to be another barrier for the many. All of this escapes Loh's awareness because it would make his 'brave new world of digital education' seem to much like the cowering old world of F2F learn-ing. Other academics, like former banker and now Michigan State University president, Peter McPherson, actually welcome these tendencies as unavoidable natural events because of market pressures: 'every sector of business that has gone through this struggle has always said "we can't do it". That's what health care said, that's what the automobile companies said. But the markets do work, and change does come' (*Forbes*, 19 June 1997: 3). Even though he does not teach this way himself, Peter Drucker also signs off on market momentum as necessary and inevitable. 'Universities won't survive,' Drucker asserts, 'the future is outside the traditional campus, outside the traditional classroom. Distance learning is coming on fast' (*Forbes*, 19 June 1997: 1).

All of this may be true, but it also reveals a high level of naive instrumentalism with regard to teaching, learning, technology, and tradition. Because computers are being used, as with health care, automobile manufacturing, or business at large, higher education is assumed to be just another business, when it is clear that it is not. Even so, voices like Loh's, McPherson's or Drucker's naively claim that the instrumentalities of computers can be used to only create greater effi-ciency, flexibility or productivity. Once this occurs, everything will otherwise more or less remain equal. In other words, instruments only do what we believe they will and/or what we direct them toward doing. Yet, all indications are that these expectations are false.

Loh's utopian vision of transnational education, for example, is technically feasible, but also socially and culturally subversive. Education is about social reproduction: being a Belgian, Chinese, or Japanese might immediately become problematic if Belgians were to teach Chinese, Chinese to instruct Americans, and Americans to profess before Japanese. For some, it might seem like the pedagogical foundations of Kant's perpetual peace, but the WWW home pages of most right wing extremist groups fervently argue that this development is the mark of the beast: the advent of the New World Order. Business might want all of them buying the basic products of workforce preparedness, but Belgians, Chinese, and Americans have wanted to teach and learn something extra: Belgian culture, Chinese civilization, American democracy. The fetishiza-tion of technology and the marketplace can scrap this all in favour of more employable skills.

Drucker's ideological attachment to markets and technology ratifies this change: the future is outside, beyond, ahead of the 'traditional' campus and classroom. Perhaps, but then again those places are technologies, too, and what has been going on there is civic cultivation, personal liberation, cultural development. For some, athletics is a form of individual subjectivity to cultivate a type of moral agent, political actor, and team player, and for others research has been an effort to constantly redynamicize human cultural development. So Friedman's naive instrumentalism verges upon the tacitly totalitarian vision shared by many economists, who arrogantly presume, once again, to know what is always the best choice for others or what all other humans need, want or desire. Distance learning is coming on fast, but these anti-intellectual dismissals of the university are quite distant from what has been understood as real learning. Indeed, like McPherson, these analyses turn degrees into basic commodities, like station wagons, hamburgers, or full hospital beds, and then pontificate about how their provision must follow the same modes of production as GM, McDonalds, and HCA.

The reality of the commodification mindset suffusing American higher education cannot be denied, especially in the face of declining public support and government funding. A quick pass through recent issues of *The Chronicle of Higher Education* reveals this national forum for some collective consideration of the university touting 'boom times' for the for-profit higher education industry (Strosnider 1998: A36–8), the grip of Microsoft on college and university information technologies (*The Chronicle*, 24 April 1998: A27–34), visions of profit with digital presses from university libraries (Guernsey 1998: A27–8), and the struggle over property rights as well as profit potentials in the development of online courses (Guernsey and Young 1998: A21–3). We live in a capitalist society after the end of the Cold War, and it seems unlikely that the marketplace as a general background condition will collapse in the near future. Nevertheless, this does not mean that everything is now, or should be in the future, a commodity.

Just as one ought not to be seduced by these visions of neutral utopian necessity in the naive instrumentalist reading of computer-mediated communication, so too should one not fall victim, like David Noble, to a position of 'paranoid anti-commercialism' in which anything digital is superefficient capitalism at work. Computers, in fact, can change everything; and, if you do not believe that it will, then simply listen attentively to what often quoted enthusiasts like Loh, Drucker or McPherson claim. Once brought online, education online will burst on the academic scene in a big way, but not necessarily at a profit. Many universities in the USA have economic development officers, corporate research parks, sponsored research administrators, intellectual property attorneys, and patent procurement personnel already hard at work transforming faculty into producers of product. So Noble's plaintive call to resist commodification now, because it might erode the 'independence and job security of the faculty' (Young 1998*a*: A29) clearly is many days late and a few dollars short.

Again, in not apparently having taught this way himself, Noble fails to see how non-commodifiable much of human knowledge actually is. In practice, most universities are finding *Forbes'* ideological incantations about intrinsic efficiencies in computer based technologies to be utterly wrong-headed. Digitalization costs more, not less. It really takes more people, not fewer. Optimal class size online often falls, not increases. Computer technology is a rapidly obsolescing permanent cost, not a long paying investment. Students must work more, and far actively, not less and much more passively. Hence, most distance learning is heavily subsidized, like Third World country airlines or old-time Soviet military units, by other activities, and it often cannot face successfully a rigorous audit. Yet, at the same time, naive instrumentalism from above and the right ought not to be met only by paranoid anti-commercialism from below and the left. Just as Jeremy Rifkin has emerged as the *bête noire* of the biotechnology industry, David Noble, a noted historian of technology from York University in Toronto/Ontario, is being pumped up into a knee-jerk critic of all online teaching *per se* after attacking UCLA's recent efforts to institute a 'one course, one web page' programme of computerization (Young 1998*b*: A31).

In a WWW essay, Noble (1997) attacks all digitalization efforts as nothing but a purposive exercises in commodification by university administrators to sell online materials on the open market. At a conference convened in May 1998 at Harvey Mudd College in Claremont, California, Noble declared 'it's high noon for higher education', because digital technologies boil down to a 'transformation of faculty into producers of product' (Young 1998*a*: A29). The World War/Cold War grant getting games of the 1914–89 era long ago transformed universities and their faculties into producers of product. This process was far advanced in 1994 when the WWW was insignificant; it did not suddenly begin only then in strictly marketplace terms. Consequently, Noble's paranoid anticommercialism is misplaced. Digitalization is another sign of deeper changes already afoot before Netscape's advent, and it represents a bigger shift in contemporary learning cultures than the commodification agendas that have poisoned university life since at least the stagflation days of the 1970s.

Of course, digitalization will further advance new waves of commodification in knowledge production, ranging from massive digital library technologies to tiny desktop courseware packages. Even though it is unclear who will buy such goods, and while there are thousands of competing providers with the same product, 'the growth of distance education and the widespread use of multimedia course materials have convinced some administrators and faculty members that they're sitting on gold mines' (Guernsey and Young 1998: A21). The future that Noble fears is possible, but the present is one in which development costs, legal confusion, bandwidth constraints, cultural inertia, and uncertain profits all stand in the way of much rampant economic success. Markets are markets, as Noble and Drucker both note in their own ways, but markets for art, gold, stocks, currency or weapons all behave very differently in the abstract, much less concretely in Norway, Iran, Thailand, or Brazil. Digitalization will lead professors to produce product, administrators to claim ownership, students to purchase use rights, companies to distribute access, but it is not at all clear that this commodification will revalouraize contingent investments sufficiently to recover any overhead, much less turn back serious points on margin. And, if it does, it will happen very differently at various schools in many different places. Moreover, the implosion of many 'dot coms' in 2000 and 2001 does not suggest that success here is assured.

Critiques like Noble's run afoul of an assumption of 'Disneyification'. That is, once Disney gets involved, it means the demise of higher education as we know it. On the one hand, there is an alliance of hardware, software and connectivity providers who want to transform education into product through expensive multimedia production. This can occur, and there are efforts afoot to work wonders for learning, particularly for the K-12 market. In the future, there might be enough basic bandwidth and installed equipment to make this workable everywhere, but this is not true now. On the other hand, online learning already has been developing at universities for five years using much more basic and inexpensive techniques to generate a new mix of active telepresence, asynchronous interactivity, and online community through demanding forms of digital discourse. These approaches must adapt to the limited bandwidth, often antiquated equipment, and basic user skills actually existing now. So, most online learning is commodified neither thoroughly nor effectively, because it assumes a level of user co-production that evades Disneyfied commodification. Even Disney has discovered this reality out in the education market at its new Celebration centres in Florida where it once aspired to teach lifelong education courses in quite substantive areas of study. Almost no one took them, so Disney went back to teaching French cooking, music appreciation, and watercolor painting.

THE VIRTUAL UNIVERSITY AND PERFORMATIVITY

Having said all this, new university technocultures of online learning still are the markers of major cultural, economic, and political change. The development of digital domains online erodes the sovereign authority and exclusive territoriality of nation states by reconfiguring the entire globe into a vast internal market for mobile, flexible networks of transnational capital. While it is not 'friction-free', Lyotard suggests, 'economic powers have reached the point of imperiling the stability of the State through new forms of the circulation of capital that go by the generic name of *multinational corporations*,' and these new modes of circulation 'imply that investment decisions have, at least in part, passed beyond the control of the nation-states' (1984: 5). These capital formations, in turn, allow private interests to contest public authorities in a continual contest within cyberspace over 'who will know' as telematic technologies 'make the information used in decision making (and therefore, the means of control) even more mobile and subject to piracy' (Lyotard 1984: 6).

Such online resources are growing so pervasive that bits are becoming measures of value, power, and knowledge. In the telemetries of cyberspace, knowledge begins 'circulating along the same lines as money, instead of for its "educational" value or political (administrative, diplomatic, military) importance; the pertinent distinction would no longer be between knowledge and ignorance, but rather, as is the case with money, between "payment knowledge" and "investment knowledge"—in other words, between units of knowledge exchange in a daily maintenance framework (the reconstitution of the work force, "survival") versus funds of knowledge dedicated to optimizing the performance of a project' (Lyotard 1984: 6).

Fabricating these digital domains, and then continuously struggling to master their telemetrical terrain, fulfills Lyotard's prophecies about the 'postmodern condition'. That is, 'knowledge in the form of an informational commodity indispensable to productive power is already, and will continue to be, a major—perhaps *the* major—stake in the worldwide competition for power,' in fact, the struggle over cyberspace intranationally and transnationally illustrates how fully the residents of nation-states must fight for 'control of information, just as they battled in the past for control over territory, and afterwards for control of access to and exploitation of raw materials and cheap labor' (Lyotard 1984: 5). Today, data/information/knowledge in telematic forms, online and off-line, 'is and will be produced in order to be sold, it is and will be consumed in order to be valorized in a new production: in both cases, the goal is exchange' (Lyotard 1984: 4). In another register, Negroponte continuously puffs up the potentialities of this change as 'being digital' (1995: 11–20), which leads to a celebration of digitalization as the latest grand moment of modernization. The shift from a society organized around making and moving matter, or 'atoms', to one focused upon inventing and integrating information, or 'bits' is well underway.

In this fast capitalist economy, everything in society, the marketplace, and culture,

is made conditional on performativity. The redefinition of the norms of life consists in enhancing the system's competence for power. That this is the case is particularly evident in the introduction of telematic technology: the technocrats see in telematics a promise of liberalization and enrichment in the interactions between interlocuters; but what makes this process attractive for them is that it will result in new tensions in the system, and these will lead to an improvement in its performativity.   (Lyotard 1984: 64)

The social pragmatics of performative capital slowly supplant a deeply embedded metanarrative of grounded social contracts once set-in-place with the loosely defined just-in-time protocols of fluid temporary arrangements. The impermanent understanding of personal and social identity in such transnational markets is now favoured 'due to its greater flexibility, lower cost, and the creative turmoil of its accompanying motivations—all of these factors contribute to increased operativity' (Lyotard 1984: 66).

These observations from Lyotard provide a much needed frame of reference to place around the project of computer-mediated distance education. For better or worse, the mode of information as well as the mode of production are reshaping rapidly and rawly the mode of instruction. The acts and artifacts that anchored traditional technocultures of teaching are being supplemented by those developing in new technocultures—both on campus and off, during work hours and after, in disciplines and outside of them. Too many enthusiasts for the use of computers in teaching get stuck on their machines at home when, in fact, no one stands alone and apart from these larger changes in companies, markets, states, and societies all over the world.

The eclipse of national territoriality by transnational telemetry follows from the 'omnipolitanization' of the planet Earth over the past two or three decades of global capitalist development. Omnipolitanization flows from the hyper-concentration of urbanized values and practices in a '*world-city*, the city to end all cities', and 'in these basically eccentric or, if you like, *omnipolitan* conditions, the various social and cultural realities that still constitute a nation's wealth' give way to unsettled impermanent forms of community in which many social forms of exchange 'will no longer look any different from the—automatic—interconnection of financial markets today' (Virilio 1997: 75). In keeping with Jameson's explorations of postmodernity, omnipolitanization 'is what you have when the modernization process is complete and nature is gone for good' (1991: ix). Economy and society, culture and politics, science and technology assume the qualities of an artificial second nature with their own time within/over/beyond the now lost rhythms of first nature's geophysical time and space, which are now long gone in the dust of multiple modernizing projects. Economics and politics here, as the creation of such telemetrical cyberspaces indicates, are increasingly unhinged from fixed social formations (Rifkin 1995).

After learning online, and then working online, those who collaborate culturally, economically, and politically in the collective construction of actual transnational communities in telematic telemetries may, in turn, not necessarily hold as dear their nominal nationality within traditional territorial space (Reich 1991). Instead, they increasingly could slip into other organizational registers. Once there, in many online applications, where telematic time and space let them work and live virtually, they often become co-accelerant, commotive, or con-chronous agents of fast capitalist firms, digital design alliances or performative professional groups. Moving from the spatio-temporal perspectives of territoriality to the acceleration effects of instant communication, all of Earth's inhabitants may well wind up thinking of themselves more as *contemporaries* than as *citizens*; they may in the process slip out of the contiguous space, distributed by quota, of the old Nation-State (or City-State), which harboured the *demos*, and into the atopic community of a 'Planet-State' that unfolds as 'a sort of *omnipolitan* periphery whose *centre will be nowhere and circumference everywhere*' (Virilio 1995: 36). Individuals, in turn, may judge their personal success in these omnipolitan spaces more often by the goods and services shared by the other 'successful fifth' of global co-accelerants than by the condition of the 'failed four-fifths', who might still be their co-inhabitants at some fixed place, they will be no longer commotive contemporaries riding along with them on the fast capitalist tracks in polyglot global flows (Reich 1991).

This more 'borderless' world of digital exchange also constitutes a standing invitation for all to become even more 'orderless' as such technoeconomic flows displace once heavily emplaced social formations and individual activities. As one of the key architects of these changes asserts, the most rational form of global order will be one of completely un-stated (b)orderlessness. Echoing Governors Leavitt's and Romer's hopes for the WGU, the state apparatus, either online or off-line, should do nothing to retard global flows. It should instead serve as another accelerant for change, shifting its services from a civic national to a private nodal focus 'so as to: allow individual's access to the best and cheapest goods and services from anywhere in the world; help corporations provide stable and rewarding jobs anywhere in the world regardless of the corporation's national identity; coordinate activities with other governments to minimize conflicts arising from narrow interest; avoid abrupt changes in economic and social fundamentals' (Ohmae 1990: appx.).

EPILOGUE: DIGITAL TECHNOCULTURE

Universities, like all social institutions, embed their practices in very specific technologies and cultures in order to produce the goods and services of teaching, research, and service. Thousands of people must master a particular technical know-how and share certain cultural meanings made manifest in many different acts and artifacts for any university to function effectively. Digitalization represents a profound change in the technologies that many people use to perform their work at universities, and the cultural assumptions used to operate in pre-digital environments will not necessarily mesh well with digital systems of operation. Online education represents a major cultural transformation in university technocultures, but, as this analysis suggests, it is only one part of many larger social shifts toward digital discourses, documents, and disciplines as print is supplanted by code in the generation, circulation, and utilization of information.

Discussions of technology and education all too often become bogged down in purely technical analysis of means-ends calculations involved in getting more academic content out to students faster, cheaper, and better. While such debates have merit, they miss the bigger questions of power and knowledge implied by the mobilization of new technologies in the educational process. Know-how about know-how is one of today's most important forms of power, and education about education is a key form of knowledge. A sophisticated awareness of these linkages soon discloses a great deal about variations in any given group of individuals' overall life changes, relative wealth, and power potential. Likewise, a decision to use this technology here rather than there or that technology later instead of now in educational settings expresses cultural preferences, economic realities, and political expectations about individual values and collective goals in quite suggestive ways. Consequently, these decisions are central rather than peripheral to the workings of contemporary economies and societies, and they need to be considered very seriously.

Disembedding education from its traditional sites and styles of provision, of course, immediately raises the problem of commodification. Yet, one already confronts the commodified qualities of higher education at the start of every academic year in evergreen newspaper stories about rising tuition costs or on personal finance TV segments about monthly savings programs to finance a college degree for new babies. A college education has been neither mandatory nor free in the United States for ever; and, as a discretionary purchase, it has had commodified qualities for a very long while. Nonetheless, a college degree has also been a fairly immobile bundle of interconnected, place-dependent goods whose benefits were derived from an extended stay with a specific faculty to be exposed to their unique curricular programmes of study, which culminated in a completed educational experience in which the student took a degree. Money was paid and work was performed to convey education services, but these services are difficult to quantify or classify apart from a degree. The degree, as a commonly accepted credential, is what represents, guarantees, and denotes education attained, making its commodification a very unwieldy, often non-fungible, and basically complicated process.

Online education, however, as the WGU illustrates, can work on entirely different planes with many more discrete instructional units in a register of valourization tied to individual competencies rather than university degrees. Here, some regime of competency testing and certification can define knowledge bits, skill sets, and functional abilities in ways that specific short courses of study could capture and then transmit to learners. Then, a standard certification system would validate their competency rather than a university faculty and administration attesting to some vague ideal of education with a degree that has been conveyed to the student after two, four, six, or eight years of study.

At the WGU, what was an imperfectly commodified product now can circulate more freely and widely, and the political economy of each of its learning packages changes significantly. Who owns it, who produces it, who uses it, what valourizes it, what certifies it, what sells it, why fund it, why continue it, and why protect it? These are all questions raised by the new practices of online teaching. The continuing drift toward greater individualization and broader globalization, as Beck argues, does provide a new impetus for competency regimes and personal certification in discrete skills. Still, the enduring interest in grounded collective identities with deeper cultural localization supports the disciplines of degree winning in more universal traditions of learning. Nonetheless, the proliferating possibilities for choice from so many online menus of learning will challenge any institutional solution to this problem as students mix-and-match courses of study from many different places, and then either ask to include them in programmes of study for degrees or appear before competency boards for skill certification.

Without being as apocalyptic about it as Birkerts is, the process of digitalization itself, apart from commodification, does bring a fundamental transformation in many fixed forms of being. With the advent of computer-mediated communication, 'the primary human relations—to space, time, nature, and to other people—have been subjected to a warping pressure that is something new under the sun. . . . We have created the technology that now only enables us to change our basic nature, but that is making such change all but inevitable' (Birkerts 1994: 15). This change is caused by the move from printed matter to digital bits to accumulate, circulate, and manipulate stores of knowledge. There are, as Turkle (1996: 17) claims, different 'interface values' embedded in each particular medium, and those embodied in print inculcate a special measured, linear, introspective type of consciousness that have anchored our understandings of higher education for several centuries.

Inasmuch as digital libraries with their own digital discourses, documents, and disciplines supplant libraries of print, a remarkable erasure of experience can indeed occur. Again, Birkerts asserts:

our entire collective subjective history—the soul of our societal body—is encoded in print. . . . If a person turns from print—finding it too slow, too hard, irrelevant to the excitements of the present—then what happens to that person's sense of culture and continuity? (Birkerts 1994: 20).

Shrewdly enough, Birkerts recognizes his worries and warnings are overdetermined questions, leaving no one an effective path for taking one strand of the question out at a time for easy analysis. Instead we are left with a sense of profound loss and immeasurable gain as the popularity of digital modes of communication builds and spreads. Without succumbing to Birkert's fears that everything changes unalterably, when it is run through electronic circuitries, and mostly for the worse, we should realize in the same moment that everything will not remain the same only now in silicon instead of on paper. Along the fractures of this faultline, what is new and different in digitalization must be found so that we might address what impact it will have upon the technoculture of universities.

No technology exists simply as such with its own immanent dynamics separate and apart from the declared and implied uses for it. Some of these might be unintended and unanticipated, but they too derive from human use. Online learning today represents a cluster of technical applications that has been invested with special importance and power. One does not need to visit EDUCAUSE's websites to witness computer-mediated communication talked up as being truly representative of 'the coming change', 'high tech alternatives', or, most starkly, 'an inevitable future'. All of this may be true, but only if people, singly and in groups, do many things to turn this shared anticipation into lived actuality. Quite often, other forces in government, big business or the professions will steer the realization of 'the future' in particular directions, and the current futurist mythos of computerization connects the technologies of online learning to high paid jobs, the world of work, and national competitiveness. This collective of causal forces cannot be ignored in online learning; a quick glance at the agendas of EDU-CAUSE immediately confirms this observation. Nonetheless, these technologies clearly can support cultural pursuits beyond the world of work and apart from the conduits of commerce, particularly if people consciously organize them to serve these ends. But, here again, which people, where, and for what purposes are questions that are still open.

While all of these possibilities for cultural enhancements do exist, there are no assurances that every course in an online format will feature any or all of them. Moreover, as Neal (1998: B4–5) suggests there is no systematic appraisal of how, why or when multimedia techniques actually improve learning beyond the 'gee whiz' satisfactions of high technology in operation. Here, doing it at all usually is taken as a qualitative improvement, because no one else is doing much of it, and it therefore looks, feels, and sounds so different. Being astounded, however, is not the same thing as actually making improvements, and being different may also not work out well. Consequently, a truly radical rethinking of educational discourse in a digital register, which relies upon online classes and electronic documents, is needed in order to develop guidelines for a new university technoculture. Until and unless we understand how digital discourses do what they have done in learning or improve what has been done in teaching, two unsavory outcomes will continue: neo-conservative questioners of virtual universities like Birkerts will continue to be heeded, and neoliberal reformers like Governor Leavitt of Utah will persist in pushing his vision of the virtual university against traditional learning. Both developments are an invitation to learn more about everything that we do so that we might teach more effectively in defense of what is worth defending.

To say this, however, is not enough. In a context that militates against anticipating the nature, direction, and impact of change, we must try to think through the implications of digitalization upon the economy and society, culture and government, individual and group. The containment fields, information banks, and energy sources constructed around print since the fifteenth century are being put into question by digital discourses, online communities, and electronic documents, despite the fact that many proponents believe they are only playing around with computers. Very few voices are raising issues of this sort, but those questions need to be coped with before their unintended consequences derail or disable the positive changes that might arise out of these transformations. The virtual university is a perfect place for academics to enter these discussions. Who builds it, how is it built, why it will be built, and where it is built are all questions whose answers will reshape academic life and the larger societies served by virtual universities in the years to come for better and for worse.

To conclude, there are many ironies and inconsistencies at work in learning online. At one level, getting more computers into the classroom is only about that, and advancing or retarding that change will affect students in today's economy once they graduate. Yet, at the same time, making these changes must reconfigure settled patterns of behaviour and thought—both on and off campus—about what a university education ought to be about, and how it should be attained. Once these reconfigurations slip into or out of place, depending upon one's expectations, everything else from the marketplace out beyond the classroom abruptly intrudes into view.

So, at a second level, building the virtual university, either as a supplement to or substitute for traditional universities, plays with the issues of modernization and markets as one reshapes, or refuses to reshape, teaching around new computing technologies. To resist computers, one might, at the same time, try to stop the growth of campus computing and also resist, if only for a moment, the advance of an immense informational economy. This will validate the claim that universities are only bastions of feudalism opposed to any change. Ironically, to advance computerization, one will, at the same time, assist the informationalization of economy and aid, if only in some small way, the proliferation of marketized behaviours where it may be inappropriate and unwanted.

Likewise, for institutions like the university that value enduring collective traditions, computerization ironically is a mechanism for accentuating greater individualization through relations tied to one student, one computer, or, one learner, one node. Still, for an institution that also promotes individual achievement, digitalization can be a tool for accessing many other collective traditions through new relations grounded in many different cultures, networks or identities. In the final analysis, modernization is neither a unimodal nor a unidirectional event, and learning online should be able to develop along several different paths in responding to its pressures, which can preserve its traditional missions of personal liberation and civic cultivation without submitting its audiences entirely to the dictates of excessive commercialization.

REFERENCES

Anderson, B. (1991) *Imagined Communities*, revised edn. London: Verso.

Beck, U. (1992) *The Risk Society*. London: Sage.

Birkerts, S. (1994) *The Gutenberg Elegies: The Fate of Reading in an Electronic Age*. New York: Fawcett.

Blumenstyk, G. (1998a) 'Western Governors U. takes shape as new model for higher education', *The Chronicle of Higher Education*, XLIV(22), February 6: A21–4.

—— (1998b) 'Utah's governor enjoys role as a leading proponent of distance Learning', *The Chronicle of Higher Education*, XLIV(22), February 6: A21–4.

Bowles, S. and Gintis, H. (1976) *Schooling in Capitalist America: Educational Reform and the Contradictions of Economic Life*. New York: Harper Colophon.

Brockman, J. (1996) *Digerati: Encounters with the Cyber Elite*. San Francisco: Hardwired.

Cairncross, F. (1997) *The Death of Distance: How the Communications Revolution Will Change Our Lives*. Boston, MA: Harvard Business School Press.

Chambers, J. (1999) 'Next, it's e-ducation', *The New York Times* (November 17): A19.

The Chronicle of Higher Education (1998) 'Microsoft's reach in higher education: a special report', *The Chronicle of Higher Education*, XLIV(33), April 24: A25–4.

Deibert, R. J. (1997) *Parchment, Printing, and Hypermedia: Communication in World Order Transformation*. New York: Columbia University Press.

Dizard, W. Jr. (1997) *MegaNet: How the Global Communications Network will Connect Everyone on Earth*. Boulder, CO: Westview Press.

Foucault, M. (1979) *Discipline & Punish: The Birth of the Prison*. New York: Vintage.

Gubernick, L. and Ebeling, A. (1997) 'I got my degree through e-mail', *Forbes* (June 19).

Guernsey, L. (1998) 'Digital presses transform librarians into entrepreneurs', *The Chronicle of Higher Education*, XLIV(37), May 22: A27–9.

—— and Young, J. R. (1998) 'Who owns online courses?', *The Chronicle of Higher Education*, XLIV(39), June 5: A21–3.

Huffstutter, P. J. and Fields, R. (2000) 'A virtual revolution in teaching', *The Los Angeles Times* (March 3), 1, 23.

Jameson, F. (1991) *Postmodernism, or the Cultural Logic of Late Capitalism*. Durham: Duke University Press.

Lewis, T. G. (1997) *The Friction-Free Economy: Marketing Strategies for a Wired World*. New York: Harper Collins.

Luke, T. W. (1994) 'Going beyond the conventions of credit-for-contact', http://www.cyber.vt.edu/docs/papers.html

—— (2000) 'Building a virtual university: working realities from the Virginia Tech Cyberschool', in C. Werry and M. Mowbray (eds) *Online Communities: Commerce, Community Action, and the Virtual University*. Upper Saddle River, NJ: Prentice Hall PJR.

Lyotard, J.-F. (1984) *The Postmodern Condition: A Report on Knowledge*. Minneapolis: University of Minnesota Press.

McCollum, K. (1998) ' "Ramping up" to support 42,000 student computers on a single campus', *The Chronicle of Higher Education*, XLIV(28), March 20: A27–9.

Monaghan, P. (1998a) 'University of Washington professors denounce governor's embrace of online education', *The Chronicle of Higher Education* [online version] (June 9).

—— (1998b) 'University of Washington professors decry governor's vision for technology', *The Chronicle of Higher Education*, XLIV(41), June 19: A23–6.

Neal, E. (1998). 'Using technology in teaching: we need to exercise healthy skepticism', *The Chronicle of Higher Education*, XLIV(41), June 19: B4–5.

Negroponte, N. (1995) *Being Digital*. New York: Knopf.

Noble, D. (1997) 'Digital diploma mills', http://firstmonday.dk/issues/issue3.1/noble/

Ohmae, K. (1990) *The Borderless World: Power and Strategy in the Interlinked Economy*. New York: Harper & Row.

Reich, R. (1991) *The Work of Nations: Preparing Ourselves for 21st Century Capitalism*. New York: Knopf.

Rifkin, J. (1995) *The End of Work*. New York: Putnam.

Schmidt, P. (1998) 'Governors want colleges to change to respond to economic needs, survey finds', *The Chronicle of Higher Education*, XLIV(41), June 11: A38.

Strosnider, K. (1998) 'For-profit education sees booming enrollments and revenues', *The Chronicle of Higher Education*, XLIV(20), January 23: A36–8.

Turkle, S. (1997) *Life on the Screen: Identity in the Age of the Internet*. New York: Touchstone.

Virilio, P. (1997) *Open Sky*. London: Verso.

Western Governors Association (1997) 'Smart states: virtual university', http://www.westgov.org/smart/vu/vu.html

Wilson, R. (1998) 'Contracts replace the tenure track for a growing number of professors', *The Chronicle of Higher Education*, XLIV(40), June 12: A12–14.

Young, J. (1998a) 'Skeptical academics see perils in information technology', *The Chronicle of Higher Education*, XLIV(35), May 8: A29–30.

—— (1998b) 'A year of web pages for every class', *The Chronicle of Higher Education*, XLIV(36), May 15: A29–31.

—— (1998c) 'An artist unexpectedly finds herself transformed into a technology advocate', *The Chronicle of Higher Education*, XLIV(40), June 12: A23–4.

13

Rehearsal for the Revolution

David F. Noble

> Those who cannot remember the past are condemned to repeat it.
>
> George Santayana

All discussion of distance education these days invariably turns into a discussion of technology, an endless meditation on the wonders of computer-mediated instruction. Identified with a revolution in technology, distance education has thereby assumed the aura of innovation and the appearance of a revolution itself, a bold departure from tradition, a signal step toward a preordained and radically transformed higher educational future. In the face of such a seemingly inexorable technology-driven destiny and the seductive enchantment of technological transcendence, sceptics are silenced and all questions are begged. But we pay a price for this technological fetishism, which so dominates and delimits discussion. For it prevents us from perceiving the more fundamental significance of today's drive for distance education, which, at bottom, is not really about technology, nor is it anything new. We have been here before.

In essence, the current mania for distance education is about the commodi-fication of higher education, of which computer technology is merely the latest medium, and it is, in reality, more a rerun than a revolution, bearing striking resemblance to a past today's enthusiasts barely know about or care to acknow-ledge, an earlier episode in the commodification of higher education known as correspondence instruction or, more quaintly, home study. Then as now, distance education has always been not so much technology-driven as profit-driven, whatever the mode of delivery. The common denominator linking the two episodes is not technology but the pursuit of profit in the guise and name of higher education. A careful examination of the earlier, pre-computer, episode in distance education enables us to place the current mania not only in historical perspective but also in its proper political-economic context. The chief aim here

This chapter appears in David F. Noble, *Digital Diploma Mills: The Automation of Higher Education*, Monthly Review Press, 2002, and is reproduced with the author's permission.

is to try to shift our attention from technology to political economy, and from fantasies about the future to the far more sobering lessons of the past.

Before proceeding with the historical analysis, it is important to spell out what is meant by both education and commodification, since these terms are often used with little precision. To begin with, education must be distinguished from training (which is arguably more suitable for distance delivery), because the two are so often conflated. In essence, training involves the honing of a person's mind so that that mind can be used for the purposes of someone other than that person. Training thus typically entails a radical divorce between knowledge and the self. Here knowledge is usually defined as a set of skills or a body of information designed to be put to use, to become operational, only in a context determined by someone other than the trained person; in this context the assertion of self is not only counter-productive, it is subversive to the enterprise. Education is the exact opposite of training in that it entails not the disassociation but the utter integration of knowledge and the self, in a word, self-knowledge. Here knowledge is defined by and, in turn, helps to define, the self. Knowledge and the knowledgeable person are basically inseparable.

Education is a process that necessarily entails an interpersonal (not merely interactive) relationship between people—student and teacher (and student and student)—that aims at individual and collective self-knowledge. (Whenever people recall their educational experiences they tend to remember above all not courses or subjects or the information imparted but people, people who changed their minds or their lives, people who made a difference in their developing sense of themselves. It is a sign of our current confusion about education that we must be reminded of this obvious fact: that the relationship between people is central to the educational experience). Education is a process of becoming for all parties, based upon mutual recognition and validation and centring upon the formation and evolution of identity. The actual content of the educational experience is defined by this relationship between people and the chief determinant of quality education is the establishment and enrichment of this relationship.

Like education, the word commodification (or commoditization) is used rather loosely with regard to education and some precision might help the discussion. A commodity is something created, grown, produced, or manufactured for exchange on the market. There are, of course, some things which are bought and sold on the market which were not created for that purpose, such as 'labour' and land—what the political economist Karl Polanyi referred to as 'fictitious commodities'. Most educational offerings, although divided into units of credit and exchanged for tuition, are fictitious commodities in that they are not created by the educator strictly with this purpose in mind. Here we will be using the term commodity, not in this fictitious, more expansive, sense but rather in its classical, restricted sense, to mean something expressly created for market exchange. The commoditization of higher education, then, refers to the deliberate transformation of the educational process into commodity form, for the purpose of commercial transaction.

The commodification of education requires the interruption of this fundamental educational process and the disintegration and distillation of the educational experience into discrete, reified, and ultimately saleable things or packages of things. In the first step towards commodification, attention is shifted from the experience of the people involved in the educational process to the production and inventorying of an assortment of fragmented 'course materials': syllabi, lectures, lessons, exams (now referred to in the aggregate as 'content'). As anyone familiar with higher education knows, these common instruments of instruction barely reflect what actually takes place in the educational experience, and lend an illusion of order and predictability to what is, at its best, an essentially unscripted and undetermined process. Second, these fragments are removed or 'alienated' from their original context, the actual educational process itself, and from their producers, the teachers, and are assembled as 'courses', which take on an existence independent of and apart from those who created and gave flesh to them. This is perhaps the most critical step in commodity formation. The alienation of ownership of, and control over, course material (through surrender of copyright) is crucial to this step. Finally, the assembled 'courses' are exchanged for a profit on the market, which determines their value, by their 'owners', who may or may not have any relationship to the original creators and participants in the educational process. At the expense of the original integrity of the educational process, instruction has here been transformed into a set of deliverable commodities, and the end of education has become not self-knowledge but the making of money. In the wake of this transformation, teachers become commodity producers and deliverers, subject to the familiar regime of commodity production in any other industry, and students become consumers of yet more commodities. The relationship between teacher and student is thus re-established, in an alienated mode, through the medium of the market, and the buying and selling of commodities takes on the appearance of education. But it is, in reality, only a shadow of education, an assemblage of pieces without the whole.

Again, under this new regime, painfully familiar to skilled workers in every industry since the dawn of industrial capitalism, educators confront the harsh realities of commodity production: speed-up, routinization of work, greater work discipline and managerial supervision, reduced autonomy, job insecurity, employer appropriation of the fruits of their labour, and, above all, the insistent managerial pressures to reduce labour costs in order to turn a profit. Thus, the commoditization of instruction leads invariably to the 'proletarianisation' or, more politely, the 'de-professionalization' of the professoriate. (As investors shift their focus from health care to education, the de-professionalization experienced by physicians is being extended to professors, who now face what some Wall Street spokesmen are already calling EMOs, the education counterpart to HMOs.)

But there is a paradox at the core of this transformation: Quality education is labour-intensive, it depends upon a low teacher–student ratio, and significant interaction between the two parties—the one utterly unambiguous result of a century of educational research. Any effort to offer quality in education must, therefore, presuppose a substantial and sustained investment in educational labour, whatever the medium of instruction. The requirements of commodity production, however, undermine the labour-intensive foundation of quality education (and with it, quality products people will willingly pay for). Pedagogical promise and economic efficiency are thus in contradiction. Here is the Achilles heel of distance education. In the past as well as the present, distance educators have always insisted that they offer a kind of intimate and individualized instruction not possible in the crowded, competitive environment of the campus. Theirs is an improved, enhanced education. To make their enterprise profitable, however, they have been compelled to reduce their instructional costs to a minimum, thereby undermining their pedagogical promise. The invariable result has been not only a degraded labour force but a degraded product as well. The history of correspondence education provides a cautionary tale in this regard, a lesson of a debacle hardly heeded by those today so frantically engaged in repeating it.

The rhetoric of the correspondence education movement a century ago was almost identical to that of the current distance education movement. Anytime, anywhere education (they didn't yet use the word 'asynchronous') accessible to anyone from home or workplace, advance at your own pace, profit from personalized, one-on-one contact with your instructor, avoid the crowded classroom and boring lecture hall. In brief, correspondence instruction emerged in the last decade of the nineteenth century along two parallel paths, as a commercial, for-profit enterprise, and as an extension of university-based higher education. At the heart of both was the production and distribution of pre-packaged courses of instruction, educational commodities bought, sold, and serviced through the mail.

The commercial effort arose in the expectation of profiting from the growing demand for vocational and professional training, generated by increasingly mechanized and science-based industrial activity, and rapidly devolved into what became known as diploma mills. The university effort arose in response to the same demand for vocational training, as an attempt to protect traditional academic turf from commercial competition, to tap into a potent new source of revenues, and as a result of a genuinely progressive movement for democratic access to education, particularly adult education. While the universities tried initially to distinguish themselves in both form and content from their increasingly disreputable commercial rivals, in the end, having embarked down the same path of commodity production, they tended invariably to resemble them, becoming diploma mills in their own right.

The parallels with the present situation are striking. For-profit commercial firms are once again emerging to provide vocational training to working people via computer-based distance instruction. Universities are once again striving to meet the challenge of these commercial enterprises, generate new revenue streams, and extend the range and reach of their offerings. And although trying somehow to distinguish themselves from their commercial rivals—while collaborating ever more closely with them—they are once again coming to resemble them, this time as digital diploma mills. In the following pages we will examine in some detail the history of the correspondence education movement in the US, looking first at the commercial ventures and then at the parallel efforts of the universities. The account of the university experience is based upon heretofore unexamined archival records of four of the leading institutions engaged in correspondence instruction: the University of Chicago, Columbia University, the University of Wisconsin, and the University of California, Berkeley. Following this historical review of the first episode in the commodification of higher education, we will return to the present to indicate some similarities with the current episode.

* * *

Thomas J. Foster established one of the earliest private, for-profit correspondence schools in Pennsylvania in the late 1880s to provide vocational training in mining, mine safety, drafting, and metalworking. Spurred by the success of these efforts, he founded in 1892 the International Correspondence Schools, which became one of the largest and most enduring enterprises in this burgeoning new education industry. By 1926 there were over three hundred such schools in the US, with an annual income of over $70 million (one and a half times the income of all colleges and universities combined), with fifty new schools being started each year. In 1924 these commercial enterprises, which catered primarily to people who sought qualifications for job advancement in business and industry, boasted of an enrolment four times that of all colleges, universities, and professional schools combined. Copyrighted courses were developed for the firms in-house by their own staff or under contract with outside 'experts', and were administered through the mail by in-house or contract instructors. Students were recruited through advertisements and myriad promotional schemes, peddled by a field salesforce employed on a commission basis.

In their promotional activities and material, targeted to credulous and inexperienced youth, the commercial firms claimed that their courses would guarantee students careers, security, wealth, status, and self-respect. 'If you want to be independent,' one firm pitched, 'if you want to make good in the world; if you want to get off somebody's payroll and head one of your own; if you want the many pleasures and luxuries that are in the world for you and your family; if you want to banish forever the fear of losing your job—then—sign the pay-raising enrolment blank! Get it to me! Right now!' The chief selling point of education by means of correspondence, the firms maintained, was personalized instruction for busy people. 'The student has the individual attention of the teacher while he is reciting, though it is in writing,' another firm explained. The student 'works at his own tempo set by himself and not fixed by the average capacities of a large number of students studying simultaneously. He can begin when he likes, study at any hours convenient to him, and finish as soon as he is able'.

In all of the firms a priority was placed upon securing enrolment and the lion's share of effort and revenues was expended in promotion and sales rather than in instruction. Typically between 50 and 80 per cent of tuition fees went into direct mail campaigns, magazine and newspaper advertisements, and the training and support of a sales staff responsible for 'cold canvassing', soliciting 'prospects' and intensive follow-ups and paid by the number of enrolments they obtained. 'The most intensive work of all the schools is, in fact, devoted to developing the sales force,' John Noffsinger observed in his 1926 Carnegie Corporation-sponsored study of correspondence schools written when the correspondence movement was at its peak. 'This is by far the most highly organised and carefully worked out department of the school'. 'The whole emphasis on salesmanship is the most serious criticism to be made against the system of correspondence education as it now exists,' Noffsinger noted. 'Perhaps it cannot be avoided when schools are organised for profit,' he added. Indeed, the pursuit of profit tended inescapably to subvert the noble intentions, or pretensions, of the enterprises, especially in what had become a highly competitive (and totally unregulated) field in which many firms came and went and some made handsome fortunes. In a burgeoning industry increasingly dominated by hucksters and swindlers who had little genuine knowledge of or interest in education *per se*, promotional claims were easily exaggerated to the point of fraud and the salesforces were encouraged to sign up any and all prospects, however ill-prepared for the coursework, in order to fulfil their quotas and reap their commissions (which often amounted to as much as a third of the tuition). Enrolees were typically required to pay the full tuition or a substantial part of it upfront and most of the firms had a no-refund policy for the 90–95 per cent of the students who failed to complete their course of study. (In Noffsinger's survey of seventy-five correspondence schools only 2.6 per cent of the enrolled students completed the courses they had begun.)

The remarkably high dropout rate was not an accident. It reflected not only the shameless methods of recruitment but also the shoddy quality of what was being offered—the inevitable result of the profit-driven commodification of education. If the lion's share of revenues were expended on promotion—to recruit students and secure the upfront tuition payments—a mere pittance was expended on instruction. In the commercial firms the promotional staff was four to six times—and oftentimes twenty to thirty times—the size of the instructional staff and compensation of the former was typically many times that of the latter. In some firms, less than one cent of every tuition dollar went into instruction. For the actual 'delivery' of courses—the correction of lessons and grading of exams— most firms relied upon a casualized workforce of 'readers' who worked part-time and were paid on a piecework basis per lesson or exam (roughly twenty cents per lesson in the 1920s). Many firms preferred 'sub-professional' personnel, particularly untrained older women, for routine grading. These people often worked under sweatshop conditions, having to deliver a high volume of lessons in order to make a living, and were unable therefore to manage more than a perfunctory pedagogical performance. Such conditions were of course not conducive to the kind of careful, individualized instruction promised in the company's promotional materials. (As Noffsinger pointed out in his Carnegie study, 'the lack of personal contact between teacher and student' was the 'chief weakness' of the instruction.) The central 'pedagogical' concern of the firms was clearly to keep instructional costs to a bare minimum, a fact caricatured in vaudeville sketches of correspondence education in which all work was done by a lone mail-clerk and the instructors dropped out of sight altogether.

All of this made perfect economic sense, however, and was summed up in correspondence industry jargon in the phrase 'dropout money'. Since students were required to pay their tuition upfront without the possibility of a refund, and instructors were paid on a piecework basis, once students dropped out there was no further instructional expense and what remained of the upfront payment was pure profit: 'dropout money'. Given the economics of this cynical education system, there was no incentive whatsoever to try to retain students by upgrading the conditions of instruction and thereby improving the quality of course offerings. The economics in fact dictated the opposite, to concentrate all efforts upon recruitment and next to nothing on instruction. Already by the mid-1920s—when the correspondence movement was at its peak—increasing criticism of the commercial correspondence firms had largely discredited the industry, which was coming to be seen as a haven for disreputable hustlers and diploma mills. In 1924, the New York Board of Regents condemned the schools for their false claims and for their no-refund policies. 'There is nothing inherent in correspondence as a method of instruction to disqualify it as a way to education,' wrote Noffsinger, an avid supporter of adult distance education (and later official of the National Home Study Council, established to try to regulate the industry). 'Unfortunately,' however, he lamented, 'the majority of correspondence schools are not well equipped and still less conscientiously conducted. They are commercial enterprises designed to make quick and easy profits. Many of them are in the shady zone bordering on the criminal. A large proportion of those who enrol in correspondence courses are wasting time, money, and energy or even are being swindled'. Noffsinger condemned 'the victimisation of hundreds of thousands who now are virtually robbed of savings and whose enthusiasm for education is crushed'. In the commercial schools, Noffsinger warned, 'the making of profit is their first consideration, a dangerous situation at best in education'.

The evolution of university-based correspondence instruction closely paralleled that of the commercial schools. Following some early stillborn experiments in academic correspondence instruction in the 1880s, the university-based movement began in earnest in the 1890s; by the teens and twenties of this century it had become a craze comparable to today's mania for online distance education. The first entrant into the field was the newly founded University of Chicago whose first president William Rainey Harper was an early enthusiast for distance education. By the time he moved to Chicago from Yale, Harper had already had considerable experience in teaching via correspondence through the Chautauqua organization in New York state, and he made the Home Study Department one of the founding pillars of the new university. Following the lead of Chicago, other institutions soon joined the ranks of the movement, notably the state universities of Wisconsin, Nebraska, Minnesota, Kansas, Oregon, Texas, Missouri, Colorado, Pennsylvania, Indiana, and California. By 1919, when Columbia University launched its home study programme, there were already seventy-three colleges and universities offering instruction by correspondence. Emphasizing the democratization of education and hoping to tap into the lucrative market exploited by their commercial rivals, the universities echoed the sales pitch of the private schools.

Hervey F. Mallory, head of the University of Chicago Home Study Department proclaimed the virtues of individualized instruction, insisting that education by correspondence was akin to a 'tutorial relationship' which 'may prove to be superior to the usual method of teaching'. 'The student acts independently and for himself but at the same time, being in contact with the teacher, he is also enabled to secure special help for every difficulty'. Correspondence study, the department advertized, offered three 'unique advantages': 'you receive individual personal attention; you work as rapidly as you can, or as slowly as necessary, unhampered by others as in a regular class'; and your studies 'may begin at any time and may be carried on according to any personal schedule and in any place where postal service is available'. Mallory insisted that correspondence study offered an education better than anything possible in 'the crowded classroom of the ordinary American University'. 'It is impossible in such a context to treat students as individuals, overcome peer pressure for conformity, encourage students who are shy, slow, intimidated by a class setting'. Home study, by contrast, 'takes into account individual differences in learning', and the students 'may do course work at any time and any place, and at their own personal pace'. From the evangelical perspective of its proponents, then, correspondence education was more than just an extension of traditional education; it was an improvement, a means of instruction at once less costly and of higher quality, an advance, in short, which signalled a revolution in higher education. 'What warrant is there for believing that the virility of the more ancient type of cloistered college and university could be maintained, except here and there, in our business civilisation?' Mallory asked rhetorically. 'The day is coming', President Harper prophesied, heralding that revolution, 'when the work done by correspondence will be greater in amount than that done in the classroom of our academies and colleges, when the students who shall recite by correspondence will far outnumber those who make oral presentations'.

As was the case with the commercial schools here too the promises and expectations of enthusiasts were thwarted by the realities of commodity production. Although they were not for-profit organizations *per se*, the correspondence programmes of the universities were nevertheless largely self-supporting and hence, *de facto*, profit-oriented; a correspondence programme's expenses had to be covered 'by profits from its own operations,' as Carl Huth of the University of Chicago's Home Study Department put it. And while it was initially assumed that this new form of instruction would be more economically efficient than traditional classroom-based instruction, the pioneers quickly discovered that correspondence instruction was far more costly to operate than they had imagined, owing primarily to the overhead entailed in administration. Almost from the outset, therefore, they found themselves caught up in much the same game as their commercial rivals: devising promotional schemes to boost enrolment in order to offset growing administrative costs, reducing their course preparation and revision expenses by standardizing their inventory and relying on 'canned courses', and, above all, keeping instructional compensation to a minimum through the use of casual employment and payment by piece rate. Before too long, with a degraded product and drop-out rates almost comparable to that of the commercial firms, they too had come to depend for their survival upon 'dropout money'.

From the outset, the leaders of the university programmes pointedly distinguished their work from that of their disreputable commercial counterparts. It was unfortunate that the universities had 'stepped aside to leave large part of the field of adult education to commercial schools or even to confidence men and swindlers,' Mallory noted, but the new university programmes would correct for that failure. 'The most important fact about the university system of correspondence instruction in contrast to that of the commercial schools,' he argued, 'is the fact of institutional background, and that background is a great public-service institution—a modern university . . . an organic whole whose spiritual or immaterial aspects are far more important than the concrete parts'. The Home Study Department of the University of Chicago, he insisted, was 'interwoven with the university' and thus reflected its exalted traditions and mission—what would today be called 'brandworthiness'. Accordingly, the Home Study Department initially emphasized that its courses would be taught by the same professors who taught courses on campus and, indeed, at the outset even President Harper himself offered a course by correspondence. But within a few years, most of the course delivery was being handled by an assortment of instructors, readers, associate readers, fellows, lecturers, associate lecturers, and assistants, their pay meagre and their status low. They were paid on a piece rate basis—roughly thirty cents per lesson and, under university statutes, received no benefits. Representatives from the regular faculty ranks were largely those at the lower rungs who took on correspondence work in order to supplement their own quite modest salaries. In order to make out, the Home Study instructors were compelled to take on a large volume of work which quickly devolved into uninspired drudgery, and it was understood that there was no future in it.

Initially, the Home Study Program was selective in its recruitment, requiring evidence of a prospective student's ability as a prerequisite for enrolling. Students had to have sufficient reason for not enrolling as a resident student and had to 'give satisfactory evidence, by examination or otherwise, that he is able to do the work required'. (The University of Chicago required at least partial resident matriculation for those seeking degrees and required examinations for credit given by correspondence.) Eventually, however, such entrance requirements were dropped in order to increase enrolments. According to the Home Study brochure some years later, 'You need not take an entrance examination, nor present a transcript of work done elsewhere. Your desire to enrol in a particular course will be taken as evidence that you are prepared to do the work of that course'. Although there were some early efforts at advertising and salesmanship, these were kept within what were considered proper bounds for a respectable institution of higher education—a university policy lamented by the Home Study Department, especially in the face of competition from other, more aggressive, institutions such as Columbia.

As in the case of the commercial schools, here too the reduced quality of the courses combined with the lack of preparation of those enrolled produced a very high drop-out rate. And like the commercial schools, the University of Chicago adopted a no-refund policy; tuition was to be paid in full at the time of registration and, once registration was completed, fees were not refundable. As late as 1939, and despite the criticism of commercial schools on just this count, the University's president Robert Hutchins, the renowned champion of classical education, reaffirmed this policy. 'The registration and tuition fee will not be refunded to a student whose application has been accepted and who has been duly enrolled in a course,' Hutchins wrote to a correspondence student. 'This statement reflects standard practice in correspondence schools everywhere'.

Columbia University did not join the correspondence movement until 1919, but quickly became a leader in the field with revenues matched only by the University of Chicago. It owed its success to an unusually ambitious programme aimed at a national and international market and an aggressive promotional effort that rivalled that of the commercial schools. A Home Study programme was first proposed in 1915 by James Egbert, Columbia's head of extension, and the idea was enthusiastically endorsed by Columbia's president Nicholas Murray Butler, an avid supporter of adult education who had earlier in his career been the founding director of Columbia's summer session for part-time students. In full flower by the mid-twenties, the Columbia correspondence programme was providing instruction to students in every state and fifty foreign countries.

Although Columbia never gave academic credit for its correspondence courses aside from a certificate of completion, the university nevertheless strove to distinguish its offerings from those of the commercial schools, emphasising 'personal contact and supervision', concentrating on recognized academic subjects, limiting the number of students in each course, and keeping standards high through regular review of material by the appropriate academic faculty. The twofold aim of Home Study, according to Egbert, was to extend the enlightening reach of the university while at the same time generating additional revenue. He and his colleagues soon discovered, however, that the preparation of course materials and the administration of the programme were more demanding, labour-intensive, and expensive than had been anticipated. To offset these costs, they moved to broaden the correspondence curriculum into more lucrative vocational areas of every sort and to expand their promotional activities in an effort to enlarge the enrolment. In 1920 Home Study had 156 students; by 1926 there were nearly five thousand and that number was doubled by 1929. As Egbert undertook 'to apply business methods' to his expanding operation, the programme employed a national salesforce of sixty 'field representatives' (as compared to one hundred instructors) who were paid a commission according to the number of students they enrolled. In addition, Columbia mounted a full-scale national advertising campaign in the manner of the commercial firms, with such themes as 'Profit By Your Capacity to Learn', 'Will you Increase Your Fixed Assets?', 'Turning Leisure to Profit', 'Who Controls Your Future?', 'Who is Too Old to Learn?', and 'Of What Can You Be Certain?' In 1929, Egbert proudly unveiled plans for a vastly expanded enterprise that would be housed in a new twelve-story building. Compared to the lavish expenditure on promotion, the Home Study programme kept its instructional expenses to a minimum. Here too all payment for instruction was on a piece rate, per lesson basis. As at Chicago, while some faculty engaged in Home Study in order to supplement their salaries, they were likely to be 'academic lame ducks', as one Home Study official described them, and the bulk of instruction was performed by a casualized low-status workforce of instructors, lecturers, and assistants. Overworked and undervalued, they were not quite able or inclined to provide the 'personal contact' that was promised. While the Home Study Department continued to boast that all of their courses were 'prepared so as to enable the instructor to adjust all study to the individual needs of each student', that 'direct contact is maintained between the student and the instructor *personally* (emphasis in original) throughout the course,' and that correspondence students 'can attain the many advantages of instruction of University grade, under the constant guidance, suggestion, and help of regular members of the University teaching staff,' the reality was otherwise. Together with fraudulent advertising and an indiscriminate enrolment policy, inescapably perfunctory instruction produced a dropout rate of 80 per cent, a rate comparable to that of the for-profit commercial schools.

The experience of two of the largest state university correspondence programmes, Wisconsin and California (Berkeley) was similar to that of the private Chicago and Columbia, even though their institutions could draw upon public funds, because here too the departments were required to be largely self-supporting (public subsidy might be available for overhead but not instruction, which had to be borne by student fees). The Regents authorized correspondence courses at Wisconsin as early as 1891, a year before the University of Chicago, but it was not until 1906 that an actual correspondence department was established as part of Wisconsin's famous Extension programme. From the very beginning, it was made explicit that correspondence courses 'shall not involve the university in any expense'. Originally correspondence instruction was conducted under the auspices of the regular faculty although the actual instructional duties were performed by 'fellows' and 'advanced students'. Because of the onerous workload, faculty participation was minimal and enrolment remained small. The effort was revived under President Charles R. van Hise and his new director of extension Louis E. Reber, two engineers attuned especially to the training needs of industry.

Van Hise had recognized the economic potential of correspondence instruction, judging from the experience of the commercial schools, and he commissioned a study of the for-profit firms. 'The enormous success of the commercial correspondence schools suggested that here was an educational opportunity which had been neglected by the Universities', van Hise wrote in 1906. 'There are tens of thousands of students in the State of Wisconsin who are already taking correspondence work in private correspondence schools, probably more than thirty thousand, and they are paying for this work outside of the State more than three-quarters of a million dollars per annum'.

Up to this point, Wisconsin's correspondence courses had offered primarily academic and cultural fare under the auspices of the academic departments, but van Hise, at the behest of businessmen who offered to make donations to the University if it reactivated correspondence study, pushed the enterprise in a decidedly vocational and industrial direction. Reber, formerly the Dean of Engineering at Pennsylvania State University, had the same industrial orientation, viewing correspondence study primarily as a way of providing a trained workforce for industry. 'It would be difficult under present conditions to provide a better means for meeting the persistent and growing demand for industrial training than the methods of correspondence study adopted by the University', he observed. 'This fact has been cordially recognised and the work encouraged and aided by employers of men wherever it has been established'. Before coming to Wisconsin, Reber visited the International Correspondence Schools in Scranton and undertook to refashion the Wisconsin correspondence programme along the same lines as that leading commercial enterprise. Reber succeeded in having the correspondence department established independent of the regular faculty, with its own non-academic staff of instructors and with its courses removed from faculty control. Under Reber's direction the Wisconsin correspondence programme grew enormously, drawing one of the largest enrolments in the country. The dropout rate was roughly 55 per cent and 'dropout money' was the name of the game.

Berkeley's programme was modelled on Wisconsin's. Initially Berkeley's correspondence courses were meant to be the academic equivalent of resident courses, taught by university faculty and supervised by academic departments, and the university pledged to 'place each student in direct personal contact with his instructor'. But here too, the programme administrators discovered that, as director Baldwin Woods later explained, 'correspondence instruction is expensive'. Thus, for economic reasons, the programme moved to expand enrolment by catering to the greatest demand, which was for vocational courses for people in business and industry, by engaging in 'continuous promotion', employing 'field representatives', and relaxing admissions standards ('there is no requirement for admission to a class save the ability to pursue the work with profit'). Enrolment increased fourfold and fees were later increased to whatever the market would bear. Most of the instructional work was done by low-status, part-time 'readers' described by one director as 'overworked' who were paid on a piece rate basis of twenty-five to thirty-five cents per lesson. Not surprisingly, the drop-out rate averaged 70–80 per cent. Students were required to pay full tuition upfront and a partial refund was allowed only if no more than two lessons had been completed. In 1926, the President's Report declared that 'the fee for a course must be set to bring in income. Expansion must be largely profitable'.

At the end of the 1920s, after nearly four decades in the business of correspondence instruction, the university-based programmes began to come under the kind of scrutiny and scathing criticism heretofore reserved for the commercial schools. The first and most damning salvo came from Abraham Flexner, one of the nation's most distinguished and influential observers of higher education. Best known for his earlier indictment of medical education on behalf of the Carnegie Foundation, Flexner had served for fifteen years as general secretary of the Rockefeller-funded General Education Board and later became the founding director of the Institute for Advanced Study at Princeton. After his retirement from the General Education Board in 1928, Flexner delivered his Rhodes Lectures on the state of higher education in England, Germany, and the United States, which were published in 1930 under the simple title *Universities*. In his lectures on the situation in the United States, Flexner excoriated the American universities for their commercial preoccupations, for having compromised their defining independence and integrity, and for having thereby abandoned their unique and essential social function of disinterested critical and creative inquiry. At the heart of his indictment was a scornful assessment of university-based correspondence education, focusing in detail upon the academically unseemly activities of the University of Chicago and Columbia University. Flexner acknowledged the social importance of correspondence and vocational education but questioned whether they belonged in a university, where they distracted the institution from its special intellectual mission, compromised its core values, and reoriented its priorities in a distinctly commercial direction. The rush to cash in on marketable courses and the enthusiasm for correspondence instruction, Flexner argued, 'show the confusion in our colleges of education with training'. The universities, he insisted, 'have thoughtlessly and excessively catered to fleeting, transient, and immediate demands', and have 'needlessly cheapened, vulgarised, and mechanised themselves', reducing themselves to 'the level of the vendors of patent medicines'.

He lampooned the intellectually trivial kinds of courses offered by the correspondence programmes of Columbia, the University of Chicago, and the University of Wisconsin, and wondered about what would make 'a great university descend to such humbug'. What sort of contribution is Columbia making towards a 'clearer apprehension of what education really is?', Flexner asked. He particularly decried Columbia's indiscriminate enrolment practices and especially its elaborate and deceptive promotional effort which, he argued, 'befuddles the public' and generates a 'spurious demand'. If Columbia's correspondence courses were genuinely of 'college grade' and taught by 'regular members of the staff', as Columbia advertised, then why was no academic credit given for them?

If correspondence instruction was superior to that of the traditional classroom, then why did not Columbia sell off its expensive campus and teach all of its courses by mail? 'The whole thing is business, not education', Flexner concluded. 'Columbia, untaxed because it is an educational institution, is in business: it has education to sell [and] plays the purely commercial game of the merchant whose sole concern is profit.' Likewise, he bemoaned as 'scandalous' the fact that 'the prestige of the University of Chicago should be used to bamboozle well-meaning but untrained persons... by means of extravagant and misleading advertisements'. Finally, pointing out that regular faculty in most institutions remained justifiably sceptical of correspondence and vocational instruction, he assailed the 'administrative usurpation of professorial functions' and the casualization of the professoriate. 'The American professoriate', Flexner declared, 'is a proletariat'.

Flexner's critique of correspondence education, which gained widespread media attention, sent shockwaves through academia, prompting internal efforts to raise standards and curtail excessive and misleading advertising. At Columbia, the blow was eventually fatal to the correspondence programme. A year after the publication of Flexner's book—and the unveiling of Columbia's ambitious plans for a vastly expanded programme with its own grand headquarters—President Butler wrote to his Extension director Egbert that 'a good many people are impressed unfavorably with our Home Study advertising and continually call my attention to it. I should like to have you oversee this advertising very carefully from the viewpoint of those who criticize it as "salesmanship", etc'. The result of this belated concern was a severe restriction of advertising (which lasted at Columbia until the late 1960s). The continued unwillingness of Columbia's Administrative Board to grant academic credit for correspondence courses—largely because of the low regard in which these courses were held by the regular faculty—coupled with the restrictions on general advertising which the Board had now come to deem 'inappropriate and unwise' effectively undermined the effort to maintain enrolments sufficient to sustain the Department (especially in the midst of the Depression) and it was finally officially discontinued in 1937. A year after Flexner's critique, and partly in response to it, the American Association for Adult Education launched a Carnegie Corporation-funded survey of university-based correspondence courses under the direction of Hervey Mallory, longtime head of the Home Study Department at the University of Chicago. Published in 1933 as *University Teaching By Mail*, the study, which generally endorsed and called for the improvement of the correspondence method, acknowledged the validity of much of criticism.

Referring explicitly to Flexner, the study noted that 'many believe that correspondence instruction is not a function of college or university' and wondered 'how does it come that literature and art have fallen to the absurd estate of commodities requiring advertisement and postal shipment?' The study argued, however, that while 'there is something fine and entirely right in the demand for independence, integrity, and disinterestedness', on the part of universities, the 'ideals of practical service, of experiment in educational method, and of participation in the life of the community' are not incompatible with it, and insisted that many, especially mature, students had benefited from correspondence instruction. The study conceded, on the other hand, that 'it may be that schoolmen and businessmen have created the demand by a false propaganda of success through education, of promise of additions to the pay envelopes proportional to the number of courses, certificates, credits, and degrees, and other rewards displayed in correspondence study advertising'.

In surveying the weaknesses of the method, the study acknowledged the narrowly utilitarian motive and also the 'very real isolation' of most correspondence students, owing not only to the intrinsic limitations of the correspondence method of instruction but also to the pressures on instructors which further undermined its promise. 'One of the charges against the correspondence study system is that it tends to exploit the student by inducing him to enrol and pay fees, and then fails to give adequate service in return', the study observed; students routinely complained about 'insufficient corrections and comments by the instructor' and the 'lack of "personal" contacts with instructors' which contributed to the excessively high drop-out rates. In the light of such apparently inescapable weaknesses of correspondence instruction, the authors of the study abandoned altogether earlier evangelical expectations about this new method some day supplanting traditional education and insisted instead, much more modestly, that correspondence instruction should be employed only as a supplement to, rather than a substitute for, classroom instruction. 'No reputable proponent of home study seriously suggests that correspondence teaching should replace classroom instruction,' the authors declared.

Correspondence study is not advocated as a substitute for campus study, but is established as a supplement with peculiar merits and demerits. Correspondence courses are of the most value to the individual when taken in conjunction with a residence program. They are not a substitute for education. They should not be taken merely in conjunction with one's job or avocation, nor are they to be used simply as a hobby or as an exercise of will power by itself. They serve individual purposes best when they fit into a long-time, socialized program of education.

Earlier claims about the alleged superiority of correspondence over classroom instruction were likewise abandoned and various attempts to 'experimentally' compare the two were dismissed as scientifically spurious and inconclusive.

The study devoted considerable attention to the unsatisfactory working conditions of instructors—notably that they were overworked and underpaid—in accounting for the failings of the method, which depended ultimately upon 'the willingness of the instructor to give a generous amount of attention to the student'. 'When that fails', the authors noted, 'the special merit of the correspondence method, individual instruction, remains individual chiefly on the students' side alone—this is the chief weakness in method—perfunctory reading of reports, lack of helpful suggestions, and delay and neglect by overburdened' instructors. Instructors excused their perfunctory performance on the grounds that the pay was too small to merit the effort and the authors of the survey confirmed that the workload of instructors was typically excessive and that 'the compensation in nearly all the institutions is very small'. 'The excuse of instructors that pay is too little has some merit. The merit of the excuse lies in the fact that in most cases in the present system the pay is small by the piece, and piecework may be irksome to the teachers both when it is light and when it is heavy, in the first place perhaps because the tangible reward is slight, in the second because the work piles up beyond one's schedule'. Most instructors, the study also found, worked on a part-time, fee-for-service basis, with little supervision which meant both that they suffered from job insecurity and that there was a noticeable 'difficulty of maintaining standards'. 'The employment of readers or graders or fee instructors, as they are variously called, has been severely criticized on the assumption that such readers are not qualified teachers or are doing a merely perfunctory job of paper criticism'. 'Nearly all university correspondence teachers might be designated as fee instructors', the study found, 'since few are on a salary basis'.

While the authors of the Carnegie study criticized such pedagogically counterproductive employment practices—and also the 'usual policy of the universities not to refund fees' to students who drop out—they placed the blame not so much on the university correspondence programmes *per se* but rather on the commercial pressures with which they were unfairly burdened. 'Most university correspondence courses are underfunded and understaffed', they noted, 'and each is forced to be self-supporting, leaving them no choice but to adopt the unseemly commercial practices of their for-profit cousins'. 'Correspondence instruction in the university should not be required to "pay its way" in a business sense any more than classroom instruction', the authors insisted. 'The business methods should not be those of a commercial concern whose prime motive is to dispose of commodities or services for a money profit'. Yet the survey showed that such was clearly the case. Although the authors warned that 'university correspondence administration should not lay itself open even remotely to objection on grounds of dubious commercial practices, such as "charging what the traffic will bear", exacting from students fees that will yield a profit, or giving instructors poor compensation in order to keep costs low', they knew that, given the circumstances in which they were compelled to operate, the circumstances of commodity production, they had no other option.

The belatedly modest and critical tone of the Carnegie survey signalled that the heyday of correspondence education was over. The great expectations of this first foray into the commodification of higher education had been exploded and the movement was spent. Strong criticism of the private, for-profit correspondence schools was ritually repeated over the years, with little noticeable effect, particularly in a series of studies sponsored by the American Council on Education. Likewise, subsequent examinations of university-based correspondence education continued to confirm the findings of the 1933 survey. Thirty years later the General Accounting Office was warning veterans on the GI Bill not to waste their federal funds on correspondence courses. In 1968 the Carnegie-funded Correspondence Education Research Project, which had been commissioned by the National Home Study Council (later renamed the Distance Education and Training Council) and the National University Extension Association, found that correspondence courses suffered from poor quality, perfunctory instructor performance, and a very high drop-out rate; that instructors endured low pay (on a piece rate basis) and low status; that programmes continued to rely upon 'drop-out money' to survive; and that there was little prospect for improvement 'as long as correspondence instruction is held in such low esteem'.

All such investigations and attendant efforts at reform and regulation invariably failed to change the picture, even as correspondence programmes adopted the latest media of delivery, including film, telephone, radio, audio-tapes, and television. Universities continued to offer correspondence instruction, of course, but the efforts were much more modest in their claims and ambitions. Poor cousins of classroom instruction, they were for the most part confined to institutionally separate and self-supporting extension divisions and carefully cordoned off from the campus proper, presumably to spare the core institution the expense, the commercial contamination, and the criticism.

* * *

Like their now forgotten forebears, today's proponents of distance education believe they are leading a revolution that will transform the educational landscape. Fixated on technology and the future, they are unencumbered by the sober lessons of this cautionary tale or by any understanding of the history they are so busy repeating. If anything, the commercial element in distance education is this time even stronger, heralded anew as a bold departure from tradition. For, now, instead of trying to distinguish themselves from their commercial rivals, the universities are eagerly joining forces with them, lending their brand names to profit-making enterprise in exchange for a piece of the action.

The four institutions examined here as prominent players in the first episode of distance learning are, of course, at it again. The University of Wisconsin has a deal with Lotus/IBM and other private contractors to develop and deliver online distance education, especially under the auspices of its Learning Innovations Center, while University of California has contracts with America Online and Onlinelearning.net for the same purposes. And the University of Chicago and Columbia are among the most enterprising participants in the new distance education gold rush. The University of Chicago signed a controversial deal with a start-up online education company called UNEXT.com, which is headed by Chicago trustee Andrew Rosenfield and bankrolled in part by junk bond felon Michael Milken. Principal investors in the company include the dean of the law school and two of Chicago's Nobel-prize-winning economists. The new game is less about generating revenues from student fees than about reaping a harvest from financial speculation in the education industry through stock options and initial public offerings.

The first university to sign up with UNEXT was Columbia, which has licensed UNEXT to use the school's logo in return for a share in the business. 'I was less interested in the income stream than in the capitalization. The huge upside essentially is the value of the equity in the IPO', Columbia's business school dean Meyer Feldberg, a friend of Milken's, told the *Wall Street Journal.* 'I don't see a downside', he added, betraying an innocence of Columbia's history that would make Flexner roll over in his grave. 'I guess our exposure would be if in some way our brand name is devalued by some problem with this experimental venture.' Columbia has also set up its own for-profit online distance education company, Morningside Ventures, headed by an executive formerly with the National Football League, satellite, and cable TV companies. Columbia's Executive Vice President Michael Crow explained the need for the company with hyperbole reminiscent of that of his prophesying predecessors in the correspondence movement. 'After a thousand years, university-based education is undergoing a fundamental transformation', he declared; 'multi-media learning initiatives' are taking us beyond the classroom and the textbook. And he acknowledged the essentially commercial nature of this transformation. 'Because of the technologies required and the non-traditional revenue streams involved', he noted, 'corporations will play a major role in these new forms of education. We felt the need for a for-profit company to compete effectively and productively'.

Last but not least, Columbia has now become party to an agreement with yet another company which intends to peddle its core arts and science courses. Columbia will develop courses and lend its brand name to the company's product line in return for royalties and stock options. According to one source, the company has already been busy recruiting faculty to the enterprise as course developers and has suggested the possibility of using professional actors to deliver them.

For the time being, however, until the actors arrive, the bulk of university-based online distance education courses are being delivered in the same manner as correspondence courses of old, by poorly paid and overworked low status instructors, working on a per-course basis without benefits or job security and under coercion to assign their rights to their course materials to their employer as a condition of employment. The imperatives of commodity production, in short, are again in full force, shaping the working conditions of instructors until they are replaced once and for all by machines, scriptwriters, and actors.

Just as the promoters of correspondence instruction learned the hard way that the costs of their new method were much higher than anticipated and that they had to lower their labour costs to turn a profit, so the promoters of online instruction have belatedly discovered that the costs of this latest new method are prohibitive unless they likewise reduce their labour costs. As Gregory Farrington, president of Lehigh University, observed recently, 'unless the new technologies can be used to increase the average teaching productivity of faculty, there is virtually no chance that those technologies will improve the economics of traditional higher education'. But increasing the 'teaching productivity of faculty'—whether through job intensification, outsourcing, or the substitution of computers for people—essentially means increasing the number of students per teacher and this invariably results in an undermining of the pedagogical promise of the method, as the experience of correspondence instruction clearly demonstrates. And the degradation of the quality of the education invariably destroys the incentive and motivation of students. Already the drop-out rates of online distance education are much higher than those of classroom-based instruction.

So here we go again. We have indeed been here before. But there are differences between the current rage for online distance education and the earlier debacle of correspondence distance education. First, the firewalls separating distance education programmes from the core campus are breaking down; although they first took hold on the beachheads of extension divisions, commercial online initiatives have already begun to penetrate deeply into the heart of the university. Second, while the overhead for correspondence courses was expensive, the infrastructural expense for online courses exceeds it by an order of magnitude—a technological tapeworm in the guts of higher education. Finally, while correspondence programmes were often aimed at a broad market, most efforts remained merely regional. The ambitious reach of today's distance educators, on the other hand, is determinedly global in scale, which is why the World Trade Organization is currently at work trying to remove any and all barriers to international trade in educational commodities. In short, then, the dire implications of this second distance education craze far outstrip those of the first. Even if it fails to deliver on its economic or pedagogical promise, as it surely will, its promoters will push it forward nevertheless, given the investment entailed, leaving a legacy of corruption and ruin in its wake. In comparing Napoleon III with Napoleon I, Karl Marx formulated his famous dictum 'first time tragedy, second time farce'. A comparison of the past and present episodes of distance education suggests perhaps a different lesson, namely, that sometimes the tragedy follows the farce.

14

Some Consequences of the New Information and Communication Technologies for Higher Education

Martin Trow

The role of the new information and communication technologies in higher education is so very large, and growing so rapidly that it can hardly be sketched in a brief chapter. We might recall that only five years ago very few people could have anticipated or even imagined the enormous explosion of communications worldwide over the internet, and the profound effects that has had and is having on our universities—both as research and as teaching institutions. What can we say that might be relevant to this information revolution in five years—that, it seems to me, is the minimum we might ask of ourselves if we are to be of any use to policy makers in this area.

Rather than summarize what is currently happening—an inventory of events and developments that would be obsolete before the words were on paper[1]— I will try instead to conceptualize part of what is happening, searching for a language for discussing it that is close to empirical reality and that will be useful longer than the latest short-lived bits of software and applications.

My thanks to Diane Harley for her reading of an early draft.

[1] The literature on ICTs is already enormous, and growing rapidly. But for the most part this writing centres on current developments and those anticipated in the immediate future of interest to policy-makers. This paper is forward-looking. Instead of citations to this current literature, the alternative is to cite websites that are continually revised and in touch with contemporary developments in the future. See, for example, Higher Education in the Digital Age: A Citation Database, at http://media2.bmrc.berkeley.edu/projects/edtech/index_js.html. That website has links to other sites bearing on ICTS in higher education, many of them also maintained. For a paper about ICTs with a shorter time horizon from a comparative perspective, See M. Trow (2000) 'From Mass Higher Education to Universal Access: The American Advantage', *Minerva*, **37**(Spring): 1–26.

DEFINING CHARACTERISTICS OF THE INFORMATION AND COMMUNICATION TECHNOLOGIES

Let me start by suggesting that the new information and communication technologies (ICTs) have some general and defining characteristics that are likely to survive changes in the technology itself.

I see five such defining characteristics—characteristics which shape how the new technologies affect and will increasingly change the forms and processes of the institutions of higher education in every advanced society. They are:

(1) the *speed of change* of these new technologies;
(2) the tendency of ICTs to *weaken and blur institutional and intellectual boundaries* of all kinds;
(3) the *democratizing effect* of these technologies on higher and post-secondary studies of all kinds, both through the expansion of access and the levelling of the status of institutions;
(4) the widely *varying impact* of ICTs on different academic subjects and kinds of education;
(5) the quite *different ways in which students of different talents and motivation use* the new technologies.

A word on each of these defining characteristics.

Speed of Change

As for *the speed of change*, I need not give examples—they are all around us, in dizzying array. But the consequences of this speed of change have not been adequately identified and assessed. And that is because the speed of change of the information and communication technologies centring around the computer and internet is unique in history—we hardly know how to discuss its implications. There is, I suggest, no precedent for our situation with respect to ICTs. For one thing, the speed of change defeats broad comprehensive planning. Planning on any scale needs a reasonable time horizon—at least three to five years—in which the outcomes of plans can be anticipated, and some rational links can be made between a policy and its intended outcomes. But the ICTs do not give us that time horizon. For example, an American college I know well cannot even decide whether to invest in the installation of glass fibre wiring in new student residence halls to connect them with the fast servers on the central campus, or to delay to see whether wireless connections to a central server on campus will do as well. The pressures from students and parents not to delay are very great; the costs of installation of a technology which may be obsolete in three years even greater.

Business firms and individuals are faced with these kinds of decisions constantly, without being able to make them flow from rational planning based on broad forward looking research. The meteoric rise and fall of the dotcoms remind us of the costs of having to make decisions about the new technologies and their use and applications without being able to predict very far ahead. In higher education one outcome is that many big American universities are not doing much, if any, institution-wide planning for the adoption of the ICTs, but are giving these decisions over to departments and research units—a form of decision by trial and error which, if properly monitored, can at least be treated as small scale experiments. It is what an institution does when it doesn't know what to do—and in its own way, it is a highly rational decision.

While American universities have adapted to the difficulties of broad institution or system-wide planning for the new technologies by not doing it, it is even more troubling to reflect that the speed of technological change affects our ability to do *research* about the new technologies and their effects. One of the important questions about the new forms of teaching online is the need to discover more about the social psychology of learning under those conditions—how effective it is, in different subjects, and with different kinds of students, in different settings: younger and more mature students, more or less highly motivated, studying at home or on the job, and so forth. Currently, we know very little about any of that, yet the answers obviously bear on the wisdom of making learning online a major part of our provision of advanced study. The trouble is that what we might learn today about the effectiveness of current forms of instruction over current technologies may just not apply tomorrow when band width is essentially free, software more sophisticated, and when teaching over interactive video connections will be guided more by what has been learned through trial and error from previous experience than by systematic research. Essentially our research in this area today—and there is little enough of it—is about current experiments with primitive technologies establishing base-lines for comparison with later experiments with better technologies employing better and maybe quite different forms of instruction. But that is a modest kind of research, and not a base on which we can confidently advise decision-makers, either in government or in our own institutions.

Everywhere we turn, we see major commitments by big institutions coming to naught, foundering on unforeseen shoals in uncharted waters. California created a Virtual University a few years ago, and gave it up a few months later. The Western Governors University, begun with much high level support, has scaled down its ambitions sharply. And even the consortia of great research universities which are entering the competition for what they believe to be potentially large sums for training people for work online are redesigning themselves and taking on private business firms as partners—both as sources of start-up funds and of needed experience.

If we consider many of the other major technological transformations around us, we are struck by how many of them are nineteenth-century inventions: the telegraph and telephone; the railroad and automobile, electric lights and grids, with the airplane coming early in the twentieth century, radio in the 1920s and television in the 1930s and 1940s. In each case, private institutions and public agencies had time to reflect and consider and make general policies for the new technologies, policies which, whether wise or not, were at least relevant to the technologies to which they were addressed. With respect to the ICTs, I suggest that the speed of change does not give policy making bodies the time horizons that they need for those policies to be rationally related to the situations to which they are addressed even a few years down the road.

One example: during 2000, the US Congress became concerned about the impact of the new technologies on the ownership of intellectual property that was being distributed through it in ways that made it available to many users without payment or even acknowledgement of the authors and creators of the new knowledge. The Congress asked the National Academy of Science/National Research Council to do an expert study which would advise the Congress on what legislation it should pass to deal with the conflicting claims of users and creators of knowledge, and that would bear on art of all kinds—writing, music etc., as well as information and knowledge. The highly qualified committee, including engineers, lawyers, and other specialists, wrote a long report in which essentially they advised the Congress to do nothing—do not write any legislation in an area so little understood, legislation which was likely to do more harm than good given our ignorance about what best to do.[2] The subsequent total confusion in our courts and legislatures about what to do about Napster is a case in point.

The Tendency of ICTs to Blur and Weaken Institutional and Intellectual Boundaries of All Kinds

To take an example familiar to us all, ICTs blur or destroy the distinction between pure and applied research, as the private sector finds use quickly for many discoveries, including those thought to be the products of pure research in maths, science, and engineering, and even in economics and the social and behavioural sciences.[3] In their fierce search for competitive advantage, private businesses reach directly into university laboratories, and pay well for even modest advantages in their access to new findings and technologies. The easy movement of people, information, and ideas between universities and the private sector, and in both directions, is a characteristic of the new economy and its relation to universities.

The new technologies also undermine the distinction between non-profit and for-profit institutions, as their employees and scientists mingle in the same

---

[2] 'The Digital Dilemma: Intellectual property in the Information Age', The National Academy of Science Press, Washington, DC 2000.

[3] M. Gibbons, C. Limoges, H. Nowotny, S. Schwartzman, P. Scott and M. Trow (1994) *The New Production of Knowledge: The dynamics of science and research in contemporary societies.* Sage Publications, London. The recent sequencing of the human genome is an example of what we were discussing in that book.

laboratories, work on common research problems, and profit from discoveries in similar ways, stimulated by similar or identical motives.

ICTs blur the distinction between teaching and research, as more and more research perspectives are introduced into the classroom, and even into the undergraduate curriculum, where the net makes genuine research possible for the first time to undergraduates without easy access to big libraries or other good sources of information. The computer and web have an inherent bias towards research rather than scholarship, towards analysis and the testing of ideas against evidence, rather than the search for meaning in a text. We are already seeing the effects of that in our classrooms, as teachers take their abler undergraduate students into their labs and to the frontiers of research. Where that happens, it really does change the climate of undergraduate education, often for the better. But again, it links undergraduate education even more closely to the discovery of new knowledge, rather than to a renewed appreciation of the art, literature, and wisdom of the old, as in earlier conceptions of liberal education.

ICTs undermine the boundaries of disciplines, and make all study inherently interdisciplinary. We see this dramatically in the biological sciences, where in the 1990s the boundaries between the historical subdisciplines of biology broke down under the impact of new discoveries in molecular and genetic biology. In this decade the boundaries of biology are yielding to common interests with engineers, with chemists, with physicists, and with physical anthropologists, among others. In my own university, these penetrations across old disciplinary lines have already resulted in new kinds of physical arrangements, with people establishing offices and joining research groups and labs as governed by their scientific interests rather than their departmental appointments.[4] We are seeing clearly that academic departments may still be useful for administrative purposes, but that they are increasingly irrelevant, and even a hindrance, to the creation of new knowledge. That is all in part a function of the increasing division and recombination of scientific specialities—but the work across specialist lines is in large part made possible by the new ICTs.

The new technologies weaken the boundaries of the university and college itself. Students now may be living anywhere, and lecturers also may be online from Australia or America or Denmark. Many academics are also working part-time for private industry which can be anywhere—and the efforts of governments and universities to limit those connections run the risk of their losing their best scientists to the private sector altogether, or to other countries more tolerant of those dual loyalties.

ICTs have also clearly weakened the role of the library as a major centripetal force. Information comes online from everywhere, and liberates scholars from

---

[4] M. Trow (2002) 'Leadership and Academic Reform: Biology at Berkeley', in Rogers Hollingsworth (ed.) *Organizations and Innovation: Performance in Biomedical Science.* Cambridge: Cambridge University Press.

dependence on their own libraries. In addition we have competing forms of online publication:

(1) e-books, with whole libraries in their massive storage capacities;
(2) books on demand—printed out and bound as you drink your coffee, and sold to you for less than the price of a book in a book store;
(3) on-line publishing—where articles and whole journals now arrive via the net, and at much lower cost than the published journals, whose publishers raise their prices as their subscriptions decline. There are now some thousands of scientific journals published exclusively online—with cheaper and faster access to knowledge. Moreover, many are peer reviewed and continue to serve that important function for the academic career.
(4) The American firm Questia is preparing a world-class online research library, initially with 'More than 250,000 books and journals ... available online for university students within three years ....'[5]

All these forms of online publishing and others compete with one another, but all together they undermine the old functions of the university library—and with it the historical core of the traditional research university. University libraries are seeking new functions, and may find some, but whatever they may be it is likely they will be less in integrating the university than in adapting to the centrifugal tendencies of the new technologies.

ICTs are also tending to blur the distinction between research universities and other kinds of post-secondary institutions. On the one hand, research becomes easier in many fields through access to the net—even to people in what were formerly colleges offering chiefly professional and semi-professional training. On the other hand, the research universities are also doing more teaching in applied fields as the distinction between what is pure and what is applied breaks down. Commercial firms are indifferent to the status of the university or college where research of interest to them can be done. And with broader access to all institutions, the students in different kinds of institutions begin to look more alike. Students even in research universities are working more during term time and are more varied than formerly in age and social origins. The class links between different forms of higher education are still present, but breaking down.

The Democratization of Higher Education

The blurring of distinctions between elite, mass, and universal access forms of higher education—the institutions as well as their students—is a joint product of the development of ICTs and also of the democratization of all forms of higher education. This pattern of democratization presses towards an equality of status and funding between different kinds of institutions. Of course these trends are

---

[5] *The Times Higher Education Supplement*, 6 November 2000.

still in their early stages, but the direction of change is clear enough, and unlikely to be reversed. If we look to the UK, we can see that in 1992 a Government decision was made to transform all the then polytechnics into universities. It is clear a decade later that what happened was much closer to the transformation of the universities into polytechnics—most clearly in their loss of autonomy to increasing control and micromanagement by government agencies, and the decline of the prestige that formerly attached to those elite institutions and their members that accompanied that autonomy. All institutions are pressed to justify themselves by their contributions to national economies—and look more alike in trying to meet that common expectation.

   The democratization of higher education, the growth of access, and the efforts of governments to control costs has led in many countries to a marked growth in the numbers of temporary and part-time teachers—some happy to be working part-time, others unhappily chasing from one lecture room to another in two or even three different universities. But democratization has much more powerful and direct effects on higher education than through the growth of part-time teachers. The new technologies have a democratizing effect by transforming knowledge into a commodity to be bought from scientists and scholars and sold over the internet worldwide—the teaching itself, and not just the books that are instruments of teaching. Democracy in the realm of culture and ideas always has a dual character. On the one hand, it becomes increasingly possible through the new technologies to give access to more and more people to information and ideas, especially to the idea that they can gain and use new information and knowledge all their lives. Distance learning simply makes possible as never before the expansion of mass higher education to universal access, to people in their homes and workplaces and not just in seminar and lecture rooms. We educators cannot but applaud the extension to more and more people of the chance to gain knowledge, skills, and learning, and of the application of that knowledge and those skills to the problems of living.

   On the other hand, the transformation of knowledge into a commodity reduces the authority of knowledge, of the great books and the wisdom in them, and of the academic profession itself under the steady pressure, from states and consumers alike, to justify ourselves always against the pragmatic test: of what use are you and what you teach. Here the old concerns are not irrelevant: a superabundance of information may be the enemy of knowledge, and a superabundance of knowledge the enemy of understanding and wisdom. This is too large a subject for a short chapter, but I cannot visit this important subject without acknowledging, even so elliptically, the danger to humanistic studies inherent in technological advances which have led so directly to the commercialization of research, and now to the commercialization of teaching.

   The deep penetration of market forces into the institutions of higher education implicates them ever more deeply in the life of other institutions. And that makes it more difficult for universities to retain their own unique identity, their institutional autonomy. A basic conception of institutional autonomy is the answer to the question: to what extent does the institution define its own ends, as compared with the extent to which it is a means to the ends of other institutions and answers to their needs. Universities have always balanced these two conceptions; ICTs and the commercialization of research and teaching that they accelerate shift the balance away from university autonomy toward their being a means—a very important means, but a means nonetheless—to the achievement of ends and policies defined by the market and by the government.

I made reference to five defining characteristics of the new ICTs. I have spoken about three of them: the speed of change, the weakening of academic boundaries and distinctions, both institutional and intellectual, and the role of the new technologies in accelerating the democratization of knowledge, and its ambiguous outcomes. Two other fundamental characteristics of ICTs are that they have enormously different significance and utility for different kinds of subjects, and for different kinds of students.

Differences Among Subjects

With respect to academic subjects and disciplines, it is pretty clear that the new technologies have a less ambiguous role to play in the straightforward transmission of skills and knowledge than in the search for meaning. So the earliest online courses have been in basic pre-research level mathematics, in the teaching of foreign languages, and in introductory courses in business, engineering, and the sciences. They are less immediately useful for courses which involve the search for insight and understanding in art and ideas, where a teacher wants to be in the company of one or a few students, each with a copy of a book in his or her hand, exploring the significance and meaning of a passage or character or event or poem or philosophical idea. But what we are experiencing now, in the childhood of ICTs, may not carry into their adolescence or maturity—where interactive video connections among the members of a small widely dispersed seminar may prove the technology to be as fruitful for humanistic studies as in the transmission of technical information at a distance.[6] I have seen such a seminar made up of advanced students of medieval history studying an illuminated manuscript more closely and effectively through an interactive video connection than would have been possible without the magnification of the manuscript, together with the discusssion among the scholars made possible by an electronic link between Berkeley and Columbia University, each of which owns half of that manuscript. Still, at the moment and for a while ahead, humanistic studies of the kind currently organized in small seminars will be lagging in their applications of the new technologies. And of course that is partly because the teachers of those

---

[6] A new application throws its shadow far ahead. It is called 'the access grid'; it is a 'a low cost interactive apparatus through which one network site can interact (in both audio and video) with up to 50 other sites . . . This has the potential to change the nature of remote education and the ultimate function of a school or university.' *The Times Higher*, 9 February 2001, pp. 22–3.

subjects tend to be less enthusiastic about the new technologies, and also on average less skillful in their use.

Differences Among Students

Of great significance for the impact of ICTs on higher studies are the characteristics of students, and among these are their motivations—essentially how seriously they are engaged in their studies. We already see, and hear from other teachers, that when students are serious students, they can use the web to enrich their lectures and reading, and develop their insights and understanding of a subject. But when students are rather passive—and the number of such students grows with the expansion of access, students wanting mainly to gain the certificates needed to get a better job after they leave the university—they are less likely to use the resources of the net to deepen or broaden their knowledge. Rather, they use it to find ways to make their written work look more sophisticated and professional, borrowing from sources all over the world, and often crossing the line to plagiarism, innocently or knowingly. The new technologies currently make it easier to fake getting an education for those less interested in actually getting one, one of the many ironies associated with these new forms of communication and information.

DISAGGREGATION AND DIVERSE EFFECTS OF ICTs

What these defining characteristics of the new information and communication technologies suggest is that we cannot speak very usefully, or at least cannot go very far in our analysis of ICTs, as a single phenomenon, but must specify very soon how and where they are being used. We must disaggregate the world in which ICTs are used to get any sense of their diverse effects and consequences.

Two examples of diverse effects, from opposite points on an extended continuum of effects, make clear the necessity when speaking of ICTs in connection with higher education to specify who and where and when and what for. The first analysis of the decoded sequence of the three billion chemical bases making up the roughly 30,000 genes in the human genome is a triumph of computer science, without which these tremendous discoveries could not have been made in our lifetime.[7] But equally important, all this information is now online, available for further work by thousands of university-based scientists all over the world,

---

[7] See the issue on 'The Human Genome', *Science*, 10 February 2001, **291**(5507). One of the two organizations which together sequenced the human genome is a commercial biology company, Celera, the other a consortium of publicly-supported laboratories, including the American NIH and the Department of Energy's Joint Genome Institute, the British Sanger Center supported by the Wellcome Trust, the Whitehead Institute, and two American university laboratories— Washington University and Baylor.

for all the kinds of things they may be interested in exploring. The achievement by the scientists aided by their computers is just the first achievement; the net now empowers other scientists beyond their wildest dreams. One of the research team leaders said that he had spent ten years of his life searching for and studying the structure of one gene; now another scientist can find that information on the net in 15 seconds, but more than that, can see that gene in relation to all its neighbours and others with whom it interacts. The coming explosion of discovery in all branches of biology, not least in the health sciences, must transform the practice of medicine over the next few decades—a matter of personal as well as professional interest to all of us.

At a far distance from that happy story of the central role of ICTs in contemporary scientific research is the rather more ambiguous impact of the same technologies on the academic profession. We are currently seeing widespread efforts to project teaching beyond the classroom, both to students in one's own institution in their homes and halls of residence, and beyond that to students outside the boundaries of the university, near and far, in other universities and in their homes or workplaces. Indeed, the energy and resources currently being poured into these efforts can hardly be chronicled. Almost every day we hear of consortia of great universities combining their resources to create possibilities for distance learning of various kinds. Alongside and in sharp competition with them—so far rather more successfully—we see for-profit bodies, like the University of Phoenix in the US or the quasi-universities being created by multinational corporations. The burgeoning universe of distance learning providers—still far more a potentiality than an achievement—nevertheless raises serious questions about the nature and survival of the universities that we know and love.

I mention in this connection only one facet of that development: if some kinds of teaching can be highly rationalized, employing brilliant lecturers at world renowned institutions equipped with all the resources of the net at their finger tips, there is at least a reasonable possibility that more modest institutions will choose to use those world-class resources, hitherto confined to a small number of leading research universities. They might be forced to use them by their competition for students looking for star teachers expounding the latest or deepest understanding of their subjects. But each of those institutions currently has its own instructors teaching most if not all of the subjects that are also taught online by star lecturers from institutions with famous brand names. The transformation of college and university teachers—most of whom have earned a doctorate or other higher degrees themselves, many of them active researchers—into what amounts to teaching assistants in other people's courses, cannot be welcome to them. That must affect not only their autonomy, but also their tenure, pay, and academic freedom. That fear, already alive in academia, is not unfounded, only a little premature.

But even more serious than the slow loss of the cherished freedom and autonomy of the academic in his/her own subject is the inevitable loss of the status and rewards that accompany that professional freedom and autonomy.

We already see signs of the deprofessionalization of the academic work force in some countries in the form of central governmental control over institutions through their external assessments and evaluations, and its intervention into the curriculum by the setting of minimal national standards of achievement, subject by subject. Here we see the blurring of the traditional distinction between secondary and higher education. But the rationalization of teaching through the new technologies must tend to reduce even further the professional status of the academic. That in turn will affect recruitment to the academic labour force, and not for the better.

A crucial question for academic life is whether higher education can recruit in each generation a fair share of its most able, creative and talented people, in competition with the interesting, challenging and materially rewarding work generated by the high tech and multinational industries outside the academy. Undermining the status and rewards of teaching must have negative effects on that ability to recreate the academic profession. But the quality of the teaching and learning in our colleges and universities depends far more on the quality of the academics in them than on any reviews or assessments generated by external reviewing bodies. And a decline in the quality of the recruits to academic life in the face of competition from interesting and well-paid work in the private sector would be a pattern very hard to reverse. It would be a classic vicious cycle. We have seen it happen in secondary school systems around the world, and not least in the United States, as our ablest teachers were drawn off over the past half century by the new and more rewarding opportunities created by the expansion of higher education. The irony here is that intrusive efforts by governments to make universities more responsive and rewarding to students may make the academic profession less rewarding to the ablest potential recruits to it.

SOURCES OF FUTURE DEMAND FOR CONTINUING GROWTH OF HIGHER EDUCATION

Discussions of ICTs assume that there will be a growing demand for education that cannot be met through traditional forms and structures. Americans take growing demand for higher education so much for granted that we scarcely analyse its sources in history, cultural attitudes, changes in the economy and demographic change. Certainly growth is not taken as given in most other countries. Nevertheless, while growth is perhaps clearer in the US than elsewhere, some of the same forces are present in all advanced societies, in some of them even more strongly than in the US. Growth in demand for higher education rests on three fundamental developments in society—economic, cultural, and demographic.

1. One such development is the growing gap in income between those who have had some experience of higher education, and those who have gone

no further than secondary school. The difference in income is found to be related to every year of additional higher education.

2. This differential in income and wealth in turn is related to changes in the economy. It is a commonplace that wealth is increasingly based on information, on a rapidly changing technology, and almost equally rapid changes in the organization of economic activities. Part of the driving force behind the expansion of higher education lies in the globalization of our economies. In this world of rapid change rooted in knowledge and information the rewards for gaining education, and for continuing education, are increasingly visible as providing better life chances, not just at the beginning of a career but all through life.

3. Rapid changes in the global market provide a long-range reward for more education, both liberal and vocational. But the impact is equally great in the short- term, by radically increasing the demand for training in the new technologies and organizational arrangements. Not so long ago workers at every level could count on functioning in jobs effectively for decades with little more than the skills with which they entered the job. That is no longer true, and the market for training of employees on the job has grown rapidly in recent decades. There is no reason to believe that this growth of demand for continuing training to keep up with the rapid changes of doing business will not continue.

4. In addition, it is well documented that the more education that people have had, the more they want. The demand for continuing education arises first among those who have had considerable education. We are now seeing the effects of the growth of access over the past few decades; looked at another way, we are seeing that mass higher education is providing the demand base for the movement to universal access.[8]

5. Rarely noticed in this connection, is the remarkable increase in life expectancy in advanced societies in the past half-century. Better health and longer life lead to more time and energy for education. We have scarcely begun to see the use of the net for education of various kinds by retired people. In all advanced nations the numbers of retired people is growing, in some countries very rapidly. Moreover, those coming to retirement age in the future will be computer literate, in the way that current retirees are not.

6. While population growth has slowed or halted in the countries of the European Union, and dramatically reversed in Japan, there are still many countries experiencing high population growth. Even the richest societies, among them California in the US, cannot provide higher education for the projected numbers at the same cost levels as at present. California will almost certainly need to provide access to every kind of post-secondary institution, from community colleges to the University of California,

---

[8] On the movement from mass to universal access, see M. Trow, fn. 1.

through a mix of traditional and distance learning, and is already planning to do so.

7. Finally, we need to address the force of the youth culture. The world young people are growing up in is tied to the electronic revolution in ways that those who grew up in a pre-net world can hardly imagine. Those young people, and those yet to be born, will be using the electronic media, for post-secondary education as for many other uses, casually and constantly, formally or informally.

Of course the rate of growth of demand for higher education, some of it online, will depend on many other factors besides those mentioned above. For example, use of the net for any purpose is affected by the idiosyncratic policies of national telephone systems. The United States and Finland are among the few countries whose citizens are charged a fixed monthly fee for local phone service, which means that there is no additional charge for connecting to the net through a local provider. And it is perhaps not an accident that those two countries lead in the proportions of their population who are connected to the net. Moreover, the use of the net for the education of a labour force at work will be affected, among other things, by state subsides for those activities where they are provided. Subsidies to students for the costs of part-time distance learning will vary between countries, as they do currently. And there are other factors, not discussed, which will affect whether demand grows or not, and if so how fast. But my guess is that on balance, the factors in favour of growth, coupled with the development of the technologies and their decline in relative cost, will make for a growth in demand over time, an increasing proportion of which will be met at a distance online.

THE MIX OF TRADITIONAL AND DISTANCE LEARNING

An important issue in the emergence of web-based higher education is the physical locus of learning: where is it experienced, and in what combinations of propinquity and synchronicity with traditional forms of instruction. We can locate existing and future forms of education involving ICTs along a continuum, from (a) all of it provided in existing ways and situations, to (b) traditional venues interspersed with distance learning, to (c) distance learning interspersed with direct contacts between students and teachers, to (d) higher education provided all or nearly all at a distance.

Moreover, the middle of that continuum—types (b) and (c)—is in some ways the most interesting, as most clearly involving traditional institutions of higher learning rather than the marginal institutions which have long relied on distance learning with little or no direct meeting of teachers and students. In what we will call 'mixed provision', we increasingly see such combinations of traditional and distance learning as these:

(1) traditional courses on campus using ICTs in ways that allow students to take all or part of a specific course physically and temporally removed from the class or lecture room;
(2) arrangements that allow students to take some courses on campus and some online off campus within the same term or year;
(3) arrangements that break the normal years to allow students to enrol in some fraction of their course in residence on campus and some part off campus online—the issue there being what fraction of each. The nature of the experience will clearly be different if the student is asked or required to take one semester of eight online off campus, as compared with taking half or three quarters of their course work off campus.

Each of these arrangements, of requiring students to take a portion of their traditional college or university education off campus, is already being discussed, not primarily for the learning or curricular advantages of these arrangements, but as potential responses to large and rapid increases in enrolments in higher education that challenge institutions and governments to find the money and physical facilities for on campus education in traditional forms. As is often the case, radical innovations in traditional forms of instruction will be driven less by intellectual than by financial and political forces—in this case, the overwhelming costs associated with the growth of enrolments inherent in the demographics of twenty-first century America. While these demographic pressures are not present or as strong in Western Europe or in Japan, the growth of demand for higher education is not wholly dependent on demographics, as I suggest above. The need for a broadly educated society, and for continuing education both on the job and in the home, will tend to increase the demand for post-secondary and continuing education. And it is that growth of demand, especially for non-traditional forms of higher education, that will provide the stimulus for the expansion of the use of ICTs in higher education. Where, for whatever reasons, as, for example, the steep demographic decline in Japan, growth of demand is weak, both pressures and incentives to expand access through ICTs at a distance will also be weaker as traditional institutions are hard pressed to maintain their existing enrolments.

FUNCTIONS OF HIGHER EDUCATION, AND THE DIFFERENTIAL IMPACT OF ICTs

In the past century and a half, in addition to the creation of knowledge through research and scholarship, the two dominant purposeful functions of colleges and universities have been to shape the mind and character of students—the elite function—and to provide skills and knowledge as preparation for a variety of jobs and careers—the vocational function. Of course the line between these is not absolute: in a sense, the qualities of mind that mark the liberally educated person are high recommendations themselves for a range of leadership roles in the society, and thus have a latent vocational function, while some vocational training and education does in fact shape the mind and character beyond the narrow requirements of competence in the world of work. But still, the distinction between the two is visible in an institution's catalogue, in the curriculum leading to a degree, and in the syllabus of a course.

But the functions of higher educational institutions are not confined to the expressed purposes of these institutions. Like all institutions, colleges and universities have functions and consequences that are not necessarily intended, and some of them undesired. Thus, another perspective on the impact of ICTs can be gained by reflecting on their potential effects on both the traditional and on the new and emerging functions of colleges and universities. Among these are the following:[9]

- the liberal education of youth: the shaping of mind and character
- the acquisition of useful skills and knowledge
- professional education and socialization
- research and scholarship: the creation of knowledge
- the provision of apprentice training for research: research assistants
- the education of adults for personal pleasure
- entertainment, for example, college sports
- status acquisition, both through gaining a degree and borrowing the status of the awarding institution
- friendship and mate search
- networking
- stockpiling of youth; keeping them out of the job market
- offloading late adolescents/young adults out of the home into a protected environment
- the preparation of low cost teachers: short-contract, not on tenure track, and teaching assistants

Some of these functions will be heavily affected by the expansion of distance learning made possible by the ICTs, those that exist at this writing and those still to be created. The chief of these functions of universities responsive to the ICTs is research. On the one hand, research in every academic subject is now heavily dependent on communications across the web. On the other, the recent decoding of the human genome is dramatic evidence, if any more is needed, of the capacity of public and private research labs outside of universities to do research

---

[9] Some functions are unique to particular countries. For example, in the United States, colleges and universities serve a central function in the acculturation of immigrants to American society. In addition, American colleges and universities, collectively, legitimate the social and political system by providing channels of mobility which are seen as guarantors of the American Dream. In other countries, university systems historically have played comparable roles in nation-building.

at the highest levels.[10] But other functions will be less vulnerable to the new technologies, and provide continuing support and justification for traditional forms of higher education for the foreseeable future. Elite forms of undergraduate education, involving the shaping of mind and character and not just the transfer of skill and knowledge, will survive as an important though diminishing fraction of post-secondary education as a whole. Traditional forms of liberal education require conditions and relationships between students and teachers similar to those associated with the socialization of research scientists and scholars in graduate study. While research is increasingly independent of its traditional venues, research training is not. As far ahead as we can see, the physically close and extended relationship of student and mentor will be necessary for a student to become a scientist or scholar through a socialization into the norms and perspectives of science and its subdisciplines.

The acquisition of status—by gaining credentials and degrees, and borrowing the status of the awarding institution—can also be done at a distance, though not so successfully at this moment as through residency. But that may well change in the near future. What is not likely to change is the appeal of the traditional university to parents who are glad to hand their late adolescents/young adults off to another institution for help in transforming them into successful adults. Nor are we likely to see a loss of the parallel appeal to the youthful students themselves of the traditional university or college as a place to make friends of all kinds and degrees, some of whom become life partners and others business connections through forms of networking.

The point here is that the survival of the traditional university does not depend on its maintaining a near monopoly of advanced teaching and research—a monopoly which it has already lost. The traditional university performs a variety of other functions, some having little to do with education *per se*. And these, alongside the elite functions of character formation and socialization to science, scholarship, and the professions will ensure the survival of the traditional institutions, though they will look different too.

CONCLUSION

It is a clouded crystal ball into which we peer to see the future of our universities and colleges, cloudy because of the uncertainties of the development of the new technologies of information and communication. The only thing we can be sure about is that these developments will have large and cumulative effects on our universities and colleges. I have tried to make my own crystal ball a little less cloudy by identifying some defining characteristics of these technologies and their effects. In addition, I have explored some of the sources of a continuing growth of demand for higher education in many if not all advanced societies

---

[10] See also Gibbons *et al.*, fn. 3.

that will accelerate the introduction of ICTs. The future will see a combination of traditional and distance learning rather than the replacement of traditional forms. This perspective is supported by the differential effects of ICTs on the varied functions of higher education. But the short history of the computer and the net has provided us with many surprises, some of them even welcome. I suspect it will continue to do so.

Afterword: What will be the Global Identity of the University?

Kevin Robins and Frank Webster

In the introduction to this book, we suggested that, if the university is some-how 'in crisis', then this crisis is primarily a crisis of the national-liberal model of the university. As Bill Readings (1996: 15) put it, the modern university has been 'the institution charged with watching over the spiritual life of the rational state, reconciling ethnic tradition and statist rationality. The university, in other words, is identified as the institution that will give reason to the common life of the people, while preserving their traditions...' What Readings maintains, along with other commentators, is that this national frame of reference no longer 'works' as it once did—the university is no longer called upon to per-form this act of reconciliation. The processes of globalization are increasingly challenging both the centrality and the coherence of the national imaginary. And what we are presently experiencing are the consequences of globalization in the sphere of higher education, too. As Gerard Delanty (1998: 15) observes, 'know-ledge is increasingly being globalised—detached from its traditional reliance on the nation-state and its custodians, the intellectuals and university professors...' And what we are being told, by a great many interested parties, is that the future of higher education now lies with the future of the global-virtual university.

One reaction to the perceived crisis of the academy has been to defend the liberal model and ideal of the university in the face of what is perceived as the corporate and/or technocratic takeover of higher education. Another—we should probably say *the* other—response has been to embrace the promise and potential of the new global-corporate-technological university, celebrating the new developments in terms of rationalization and real modernization in higher education. And so we have the terms of the contemporary 'debate' on higher education: a debate between those who continue to advocate the principles of liberal education and those who claim to stand for progress and the future. It is, we think, a false debate. What it constructs is an unproductive divide between those who take the position of conservatives and pessimists, on the one hand, and those others who regard themselves as progressivists and optimists, on the other. We suggest that it is a debate between what are, in fact, two equally problematical and undesirable alternatives. And a debate, moreover, that fails to put before us the real issues, as well as some of the real options that we may now have.

Given the nature of the changes that have been occurring in recent years, both in society in general and in higher education in particular, there can surely be no question of sustaining the liberal-national model of the university in the longer term. And we would say that this is no bad thing. Indeed, we might use the present moment to reflect on what has been problematical in the historical nationalization of culture and knowledge. In the university context, why would we want to hang on to national institutions, traditions, and ideals at a time when counter-national, or even post-national, possibilities seem to be on offer? Is this not a time when we might try to re-energize the cosmopolitan values that are also part of our intellectual legacy? So let us, by all means, look to the future. But let us do so with a sober and critical spirit. Which is to say that we have to be sceptical about the hype now surrounding the idea of the virtual university. We must be careful about the combination of neoliberal ideology and technological mythology that is at the heart of this vision for the future of higher education (Robins and Webster 1999: ch. 9). If the virtual university now seems to be promising to take us beyond the national-liberal era of higher education, then we need to reflect on just what kind of global or transnational academic order it promises to bring into existence. We cannot make the assumption that a globalized academic culture will automatically translate into a cosmopolitan academic culture. We should remind ourselves, rather, that the globalization of knowledge could take quite different forms and directions, with both repressive and emancipatory possibilities.

In some form or other, it seems to us, globalization is what the future will be about. But what we have to recognize is the contested nature of the globalization agenda (Mongin 1996). The version of globalization that we are most exposed to is what we might call the corporate ideology of globalization (the version that is systematically elaborated in the pages of *Harvard Business Review*, for example). This is principally an economic agenda, concerned above all with the creation of global business organizations, networks, and markets. We may also say that it is, at the same time, very much a *Western* economic agenda. As David Slater (1995: 367) says, these 'influential and well-diffused visions of the global' in fact 'conceal a limiting, enclosed and particularly centred position that is characterised by historical and geopolitical amnesia'. Globalization in this version may be seen as representing an extension and 'modernization' of the imperial project. Slater (1995: 368) suggests that the key questions, with respect to contemporary 'global imaginations', are 'Whose globe? Whose imagination?' These important questions look to other ways of thinking about globalization, and suggest that there can be other perspectives on, and possibilities in, global change. Alternative perspectives on globalization (to be found in the pages of *Le Monde Diplomatique*, for example) are less deterministic, and put greater emphasis on new, and often oppositional, cultural and political dynamics. Here the concern is much more with 'globalization from below', with the new cultural configurations that have been created through global migrations and flows, and with the new possibilities that may consequently exist for a more cosmopolitan world order. If the first version of globalization is about adaptation and accommodation to the expansionist logic of global capital accumulation, this latter version stands for challenging the logic of the market, and for creating a more accommodating—and cosmopolitan—cultural-political order from out of the mobilities and encounters associated with global change.

It is in this context—with respect to the corporate versus cosmopolitan possibilities of global change—that we should consider the future of higher education. Prevailing strategies for a future higher education system—strategies centred on the virtual university paradigm—generally reflect the corporate globalization agenda. The expectation is that universities will re-invent themselves on the model of the transnational or global corporation. Universities have consequently tended to adopt a more managerial and market-oriented approach to (what has become) the business of higher education. The 'traditional' ideals of liberal education have been replaced by a new discourse of rationality, efficiency, flexibility, competitiveness, and so on. The keyword is now 'excellence', where, as Bill Readings (1996: 117) argues, 'excellence brackets the question of value in favour of measurement, [and] replaces questions of accountability or responsibility with accounting solutions'. Universities have to adopt a new managerial ethos because they are now involved in a new competitive game, both amongst themselves and with new kinds of 'for-profit' educational enterprises. The virtual university agenda points to the significance of new distance-learning technologies for promoting intense competition in a global-scale knowledge and learning market. One informed observer presents us with the following scenario:

Internet-mediated distance learning will bring a new and potentially explosive kind of competitive pressure to bear on traditional higher education. Through distance-learning (DL), the traditional institutions will compete with each other in a manner in which many previous size and geographic limitations will disappear . . . Access to DL courses is no longer restricted to a location, as are traditional university classes, or to a time, as are traditional classes or televised DL courses. Instead, it becomes global and asynchronous to provide maximum flexibility and opportunity for the student.   (Armstrong 2001: 491)

We should, of course, be cautious about how much this corresponds to the reality of higher education now. But the key point, it seems to us, is that it is this kind of rhetoric that is now motivating change in higher education across the world.

What the new corporate, or corporate-style, rhetoric of the virtual university claims to be putting on offer is some kind of global knowledge and information utopia. As one advocate enthusiastically puts it, in his conception of the 'academy in a wired world':

> For individuals and institutions, globally, one now sees that the movement of information is essentially unbounded.... And knowledge, which was once captured in the cloistered halls and libraries of academia, in a wired world, is instantly made available. Similarly students who once travelled great distances to listen to lectures of scholars, can now access this knowledge via the world of the internet.   (Abeles 1998: 606)

What we need to recognize, however, is what has to happen to knowledge for this scenario of ubiquitous and instantaneous availability of information to be conceivable—attending lectures of scholars involved something quite different from 'accessing' knowledge through the Internet. The information which becomes globally available is possible only in consequence of its abstraction and standardization. 'Where economies and governments function on a global scale', argues Theodore Porter (1994: 228–9), 'local knowledge deriving from face-to-face interactions will almost inevitably be inadequate. Knowledge detached from the skills and close acquaintanceships that flourish in local sites, becomes information'. A world of information is, then, a world of knowledge detached from local contexts, 'a world of standardised objects and neutralised subjects'. (Porter 1994: 221)

What appears to be crucial in the global information domain is performative or instrumental knowledge. Readings (1996) refers to it as 'dereferentialised' knowledge. For Delanty (1998: 5), what is at issue is the 'end of knowledge', whereby knowledge is 'no longer a transcendent narrative but has entered the production process'; and what we are now seeing is 'the end of the concept of knowledge associated with the Enlightenment and which harks back to Plato' (see also Delanty 2001). In the 'academy of the wired world', we may say that knowledge is no longer autonomous, nor is it any longer associated with the project of human emancipation.

The question, then, is whether it is possible to resist this corporate agenda for the globalization of higher education—whether it possible to reinvent the university now on the basis of an alternative, more cosmopolitan, strategy for higher education. This would involve a struggle over the nature and significance of knowledge in these global times. It would mean contesting the would-be hegemony of instrumental and performative knowledge. Rather than thinking in terms of a progressivist narrative of transition from liberal to instrumental knowledge—or, as Gibbons *et al.* (1994) express it, from Mode 1 to Mode 2 knowledge—we might consider the modern era in terms of an accumulation of different knowledges. Ronald Barnett (1997: 3) rightly points to 'the multiplication of our ways of knowing in the modern world', and argues that contemporary societies are in fact characterized by the possession of 'multiple knowledges'. What we have to acknowledge, then, is the diversity of knowledges that have now become available to us—knowledges from different parts of the world, based on different experiences, different perspectives, and different values.

It is useful here to distinguish two models of cosmopolitanism. On the one hand, there is the cosmopolitan vision that comes from the corporate logic of globalization (globalization 'from above'). This is about the possession of the skills and character traits that make a person mobile in the global corporate space—the skills and character traits of Reich's 'symbolic analysts'. This version of cosmopolitan is about being able to fit into the global enterprise culture at any of its (metropolitan) locations around the world—about the possession of dereferentialized and abstract skill (travelling skills). We might call it the American Express model of cosmopolitanism. On the other hand, and in opposition to the corporate vision, we can identify another version of cosmopolitanism—a cosmopolitanism, or let us say a cosmopolitan potential, that derives from globalization 'from below'. This form of cosmopolitanism derives from new global forms of the migrations of peoples, ideas, and institutions. It is a more complex vision, and raises more difficult, but also more significant and interesting, questions. It is concerned with how people might live together with differences—how peoples who have different histories and cultures might construct new kinds of relationships with each other. It is a cosmopolitanism that is concerned with the new forms of encounter that globalization brings about.

We would argue that it is this latter form of cosmopolitanism that is now crucial for rethinking the role of the university. It seems to us that universities now have the possibility of reinventing themselves as places of encounter for cultures and knowledges from across the world. In this context, we are highly sympathetic to Fred Halliday's plea for an expansion of 'area studies', and to his argument that 'provision for, and insistence on, foreign language competence is more important than all the hype about information technology' (Halliday 1999: 108). There may seem to be little apparent 'profit' in urging further study of Estonia or Uzbekistan, or of recommending a place inside the university for Urdu or Arabic, but we would argue that there are good reasons for this kind of cultural investment. As Immanuel Wallerstein's Gulbenkian Commission team (1996: 89) puts it, foreign language competence is more than a matter of translation, because 'knowledge of languages opens the mind of the scholar to other ways of organising knowledge'. But it is not just a question of distant area studies. We would also note that this expression of cosmopolitan values would also involve universities in reaching out to the diverse and multicultural communities that now exist in their locality. In connecting with its immediate neighbours, in engaging with its local area, the university could also engage with issues (and possibilities) of encounter—of knowledges, cultures, histories, ways of life. Our point is that there is now a pressing need to engage with the complexities of a globalized world (surely September 11 brought home this truth?). As their national moorings are loosened, shouldn't universities be reinstituting themselves on a global-cosmopolitan basis?

As well as making accommodation for cognitive complexity and diversity, universities might also be resisting the growing abstraction and instrumentalization of knowledge. In his book, *On the Internet* (2001), Hubert Dreyfus has developed a critique of the abstract model of knowledge and communication that is privileged in the virtual university agenda. His immediate critique is directed towards new virtual technologies that 'diminish one's involvement in the physical and social world' (Dreyfus 2001: 102). But his fundamental objection is to an underpinning epistemology that is predicated on the ideal of a disembodied and disembedded subject of knowledge—Dreyfus regards it as the technological fulfilment of the Platonic/Christian epistemological model. And what he proposes is an alternative epistemology, predicated on an alternative relation to the world. The crucial question to be posed in the context of contemporary technological developments, he says, 'is whether our relation to the world is that of a disembodied detached subject or an involved embodied agent' (Dreyfus 2001: 54). In his view, it must be the latter—what must be maintained is 'a sense of being in direct touch with reality'. Dreyfus is defending an alternative (pragmatist) model of knowledge, involving an engaged sense of relation to both the physical and the social world.

And this epistemological defence seems to us to have resonance in the context of contemporary debates on the future of higher education. For if the virtual university deals in decontextualized or dereferentialized knowledge, might we not suggest that an alternative agenda should provide a space for embedded and situated knowledge? The cosmopolitan university would be one that addressed the decline of the national context of knowledge and culture, and was capable of reflecting on the emergence of new global and local frames (Taylor 1996). It would be an institution committed to understanding the new global realities, and at the same time grounded in, and producing awareness out of, its own local space. That is, it would aspire to produce a 'contingent universalism' (Wallerstein 1996: 59) which takes seriously 'a plurality of world views without losing the sense that there exists the possibility of knowing and realizing sets of values that may in fact be common, or become common, to all humanity' (p. 87).

What will be the global nature of the university? This question should provoke a debate that extends beyond educational and technological specialists to the wider public. In the context of global change, it has now become an issue of the most profound significance and urgency.

REFERENCES

Abeles, T. (1998) 'The academy in a wired world', *Futures*, 30(7): 603–13.

Armstrong, L. (2001) 'A new game in town: competitive higher education', *Information, Communication and Society*, 4(4): 479–506.

Barnett, R. (1997) *Realizing the University*. London: Institute of Education.

Delanty, G. (1998) 'The idea of the university in the global era: from knowledge as an end to the end of knowledge?', *Social Epistemology*, 12(1): 3–25.

Delanty, G. (2001) *Challenging Knowledge: The University in the Knowledge Society.* Buckingham: SRHE and Open University Press.

Dreyfus, H. L. (2001) *On the Internet.* London: Routledge.

Gibbons, M., Limoges, C., Nowotny, H., Schwartzmann, S., Scott, P., and Trow, M. (1994) *The New Production of Knowledge.* London: Sage.

Halliday, F. (1999) 'The chimera of the "international university"', *International Affairs,* 75(1): 99–120.

Mongin, O. (1996) 'Les tournants de la mondialisation: la bataille des interprétations', *Esprit,* November: 155–71.

Porter, T. M. (1994) 'Information, power and the view from nowhere', pp. 217–230 in L. Bud-Frierman (ed.) *Information Acumen: The Understanding and Use of Knowledge in Modern Business.* London: Routledge.

Readings, B. (1996) *The University in Ruins.* Cambridge, Mass.: Harvard University Press.

Robins, K. and Webster, F. (1999) *Times of the Technoculture: from the Information Society to the Virtual Life.* London: Routledge.

Slater, D. (1995) 'Challenging Western visions of the global: the geopolitics of theory and North-South relations', *European Journal of Development Research,* 7(2): 366–88.

Taylor, P.J. (1996) 'On the nation-state, the global, and social science', *Environment and Planning A,* 28(11): 1917–28.

Wallerstein, I. (chair) (1996) *Open the Social Sciences: Report of the Gulbenkian Commission on the Restructuring of the Social Sciences.* Stanford, CA.: Stanford University Press.

Index